Artificial Intelligence: Achievements and Recent Developments

RIVER PUBLISHERS SERIES IN INFORMATION SCIENCE AND TECHNOLOGY

Series Editors:

K.C. CHEN
National Taiwan University, Taipei, Taiwan
University of South Florida, USA

SANDEEP SHUKLA
Virginia Tech, USA
Indian Institute of Technology Kanpur, India

The "River Publishers Series in Computing and Information Science and Technology" covers research which ushers the 21st Century into an Internet and multimedia era. Networking suggests transportation of such multimedia contents among nodes in communication and/or computer networks, to facilitate the ultimate Internet.

Theory, technologies, protocols and standards, applications/services, practice and implementation of wired/wireless networking are all within the scope of this series. Based on network and communication science, we further extend the scope for 21st Century life through the knowledge in machine learning, embedded systems, cognitive science, pattern recognition, quantum/biological/molecular computation and information processing, user behaviors and interface, and applications across healthcare and society.

Books published in the series include research monographs, edited volumes, handbooks and textbooks. The books provide professionals, researchers, educators, and advanced students in the field with an invaluable insight into the latest research and developments.

Topics included in the series are as follows:-

- Artificial intelligence
- Cognitive Science and Brian Science
- Communication/Computer Networking Technologies and Applications
- Computation and Information Processing
- Computer Architectures
- Computer networks
- Computer Science
- Embedded Systems
- Evolutionary computation
- Information Modelling
- Information Theory
- Machine Intelligence
- Neural computing and machine learning
- Parallel and Distributed Systems
- Programming Languages
- Reconfigurable Computing
- Research Informatics
- Soft computing techniques
- Software Development
- Software Engineering
- Software Maintenance

For a list of other books in this series, visit www.riverpublishers.com

Artificial Intelligence: Achievements and Recent Developments

Editors

Anatolii I. Shevchenko

Institute of Artificial Intelligence Problems of Ministry of Education and Science and National Academy of Sciences of Ukraine, Ukraine

Yuriy P. Kondratenko

Petro Mohyla Black Sea National University; Institute of Artificial Intelligence Problems of Ministry of Education and Science and National Academy of Sciences of Ukraine, Ukraine

River Publishers

Routledge
Taylor & Francis Group
NEW YORK AND LONDON

Published 2026 by River Publishers
River Publishers
Broagervej 10, 9260 Gistrup, Denmark
www.riverpublishers.com

Distributed exclusively by Routledge
605 Third Avenue, New York, NY 10017, USA
4 Park Square, Milton Park, Abingdon, Oxon OX14 4RN

Artificial Intelligence: Achievements and Recent Developments / by Anatolii I. Shevchenko, Yuriy P. Kondratenko.

Routledge is an imprint of the Taylor & Francis Group, an informa business

ISBN 978-87-4380-097-2 (hardback)
ISBN 978-87-4380-699-8 (paperback)
ISBN 978-87-4380-099-6 (online)
ISBN 978-87-4380-098-9 (master ebook)
DOI: 10.1201/9788743800989

Contents

Preface

The monograph provides an overview of the main achievements and recent results in artificial intelligence (AI) technologies and systems including new theoretical findings and successful examples of AI practical implementation in different industrial and special areas (medicine, robotics, military sphere, re-building processes, etc.).

This monograph "Artificial Intelligence: Achievements and Recent Developments" consists of twelve research-oriented chapters presented by invited well-known scientists from the People's Republic of China, Ukraine, the United Kingdom, and the United States of America.

The chapter "Artificial Intelligence: Achievements and Prospects," by A. Shevchenko, M. Klymenko, and L. Baranovska, describes the current state of AI achievements and its influence on the transformation of research, social and technological processes, etc. The chapter focuses on perspectives and priority tasks of AI development and implementation. New regulatory initiatives are discussed at various levels to control AI applications and support the creation of new AI technologies, possible solutions, hardware, and algorithmic means for optimizing computations and modeling cognitive abilities.

In "Decision Support in the Field of Cyber Security Through the Use of Generative Artificial Intelligence," D. Lande, I. Svoboda, A. Feger, and L. Strashnoy present the methodology of forming causal networks through the repeated application of large language models (LLMs) with their visualization and analysis. The authors propose to create and subsequently combine two networks: first – starting from the node representing the initial state of the problem (the root cause); second – starting from the goal, working backward. The combined causal network serves as the foundation for creating desired scenarios.

V. I. Slyusar in the chapter "Applications of Large Language Models in the Military Sphere" explores the transformational impact of LLMs on modern military operations, particularly in the context of hybrid and conventional warfare. The focus is on the role of LLMs in improving decision-making, intelligence analysis, and operational efficiency. The author analyzes the future potential of LLMs for enhancing decision support systems and proposes the application of multi-agent LLMs in military technology and virtual reality (VR). The integration of LLMs into VR enables the creation of personalized, adaptive, and realistic training, significantly improving the preparation of military personnel. The chapter also examines the capabilities of multimodal LLMs for processing images, audio, and video data, as well as their use in autonomous systems and cybersecurity

The chapter "Optimization-oriented Synthesis of Rule Bases of Intelligent Systems: Application Features for Complex Plants' Control," by Yue Zheng, Jianjun Wang, Oleksiy Kozlov, Galyna Kondratenko, and Anna Aleksieieva, addresses the optimization-oriented synthesis of rule bases (RBs) of intelligent fuzzy logic systems. The proposed approach allows the creation of fuzzy systems with an optimal set of consequents and a reduced number of rules in RBs in terms of incomplete source information due to highly efficient sequential search procedures of structural-parametric optimization. The effectiveness studies were conducted for two different intelligent control systems, particularly, for a mobile robotic platform and a floating dock.

In "The Nearest Results of Artificial Intelligence Application in Biology and Medicine: Development Trends and Implementation Risks," O. P. Mintser discusses the implementation of artificial intelligence in medicine, which is limited to a relatively small number of practical areas. The purpose of the study is to conceptualize the reasons for limitations in the use of AI, as well as the prospects and risks of AI implementation.

Ie. V. Sidenko and co-authors of the chapter "Artificial Intelligence Technologies for Efficient Solving Recognition Tasks" focus on using convolutional and recurrent neural networks for solving various recognition problems across diverse sectors. The authors analyze AI efficacy in medical diagnosis, transportation logistics, military operations, and others. By examining successful cases of AI implementations, this study highlights the role of AI in enhancing classification and recognition capabilities in real-world scenarios. Additionally, prospects for AI development, considering potential improvements and advancements to current technologies, are discovered.

The chapter "Hierarchical Decision Support System for Increasing Maritime Safety Based on Optical Color Computing Architecture," by V. Timchenko, V. Kreinovich, Y. Kondratenko, and I. Demidov, considers the basic principles of constructing logical components of the architecture of optical color computing based on estimating the dispersion of truth operands.

To implement the proposed optical architecture, a real-time changing multifactor database was generated to assess the safety of navigation in limited water areas with heavy vessel traffic. A three-level decision support system has been developed to control traffic safety and organize port ship maintenance. Possible logical operations for obtaining estimates for a specific set of input data are modeled and the effectiveness of the proposed approach due to the speed and parallelism of optical color computing is assessed.

A. V. Bukalov in the chapter "Artificial Intelligence: Effective Socionic Models of Psycho-Informational Processes and Quantum Computers" reviews theoretical and experimental studies of the quantum nature of the psyche and consciousness and discusses the author's results showing the connection between quantum and mental processes. The author introduces the concept of an elementary unit (quantum) of consciousness and proposes calculating the degree of consciousness of any living organism. Analysis of the presented data leads to the conclusion that adequate modeling and reproduction of mental processes with the manifestation of consciousness and multifunctional intelligence is possible only on quantum computers with a structure corresponding to the real structure of the psyche. It is well described by the extended information model of the psyche, proposed by the author, in socionics (or psychoinformatics) as the theory of information metabolism. The author developed the basic socionic model, introducing the coordinating function of consciousness and the description of the internal structure of mental functions, and showed that the hierarchy of these functions can be modeled as a special system from several specialized quantum processors.

Y. Zaporozhets and A. Ivanov, in "Cognitive Methodology as AI Tool for Investigation of Phenomenological Ground of Melt Electromagnetic Treatment," focus on using artificial intelligence (AI) methods to improve the efficiency of various technological and production processes in the foundry industry. Many experiments have ascertained that the melt treatment with electric current (ECT) in certain modes effectively improves structural parameters and quality of castings.

Implementation of this promising technology of melt treatment requires a deep study of the elements' interaction mechanisms of the weakly structured complex system "ECT-of-Melt" (CSEM) at all levels of its hierarchical relationships and chains of interactions. One of the most important AI approaches was used to study the phenomenological ground of the CSEM – the cognitive methodology of modeling, which is based on structuring knowledge in a specific subject domain (SD). Ontological analysis of the SD using taxonomic models ensured the creation of an ordered information platform for constructing a cognitive model (CM) of the CSEM. The CSEM CM has several essential peculiarities, particularly a multi-level hierarchical structure that covers more than a hundred concepts – vertices of the corresponding graph and about 2000 edge-connections. Such a CM cannot be used in computer models in the form of a conventional cognitive map (CMp). Therefore, the connection matrix of the primary CM was subjected to decomposition into a set of partial adjacency matrices. On their base, a hierarchical network scheme of interconnections between concepts was developed. The result of the presented development is the completion of the set of AI tools with the help of which it is possible to compile a wide range of algorithms for the cognitive study of the phenomenological basis of ECT, targeted at revealing the most effective modes of ECT of melts and obtaining high-quality castings.

The chapter "Some Aspects of the Application of Artificial Intelligence for the Recovery and Development of Ukraine," by S. Kovalevskyy, considers the AI application for the recovery and development of Ukraine, which suffered from military conflicts. The main focus is on the integration of AI into various areas of the country's life, including public administration, economy, infrastructure, health care, and education. Specific technological solutions are proposed, such as agent systems, neural networks, and decision support systems, which contribute to increasing the efficiency of recovery processes and ensuring sustainability in the conditions of post-war development. Challenges related to the implementation of AI are also discussed, including ethical, legal, and organizational aspects.

Olga Kosheleva, Vladik Kreinovich, and co-authors in the chapter "Two Is Enough, but Three (or More) Is Better: In AI and Beyond" underline that the most successful AI technique is deep learning – the use of neural networks that consist of multiple layers. It is well known that neural networks with two data processing layers are sufficient for approximating any function with a given accuracy. However, using three or more data processing layers (deep learning) makes the neural networks much more efficient. Authors show numerous examples from AI that this is a general phenomenon: two is enough but three or more is better. The authors discuss the fact that this phenomenon is universal and provide a possible explanation for such a phenomenon.

The chapter "How Free Can Artificial Intelligence Be?," by O. V. Bilokobylsky and T. V. Yeroshenko, addresses the issue of freedom in the field of AI by proposing two key perspectives: (a) whether AI can possess freedom and, if so, to what extent; (b) the conditions necessary to preserve human freedom in interactions with AI. It is argued that current AI paradigms (symbolic, perceptron, and generative), grounded in physicalist and communicative views of the mind, lack access to ontological reality, rendering them neither rational nor free. Consequently, the focus shifts to ensuring conditions for rational human social activity by mitigating AI's potential negative impacts. To achieve this, the authors propose a methodology for embedding main imperatives into AI legislation and policy.

The chapters of the monograph have been structured to provide an easy-to-follow introduction to the topics addressed, including the most relevant references, so that anyone interested in this field can get started.

This book may be useful for researchers and students who are interested in recent developments of modern control systems, robust adaptive systems, optimal control, fuzzy control, motion control, identification, modeling, differential games, evolutionary optimization, reliability control, security control, intelligent robotics, and cyber–physical systems.

We would like to express our deep appreciation to all authors for their contributions and to reviewers for their timely and interesting comments and suggestions. We certainly look forward to working with all contributors again soon.

Editors:

Anatolii I. Shevchenko, Prof., Dr.Sc., Corresponding Member of the National Academy of Sciences of Ukraine, *Director of the Institute of Artificial Intelligence Problems, Ukraine*

Yuriy P. Kondratenko, Prof., Dr.Sc., Corresponding Academician of the RACEF and Royal European Academy of Doctors - Barcelona 1914 (Spain), *Head of Intelligent Information Systems Department at Petro Mohyla Black Sea National University, Ukraine*

List of Figures

List of Tables

List of Contributors

Aleksieieva, Anna, *Petro Mohyla Black Sea National University, Ukraine*

Baranovska, L., *Institute of Artificial Intelligence Problems, Ukraine*

Bilokobylsky, O. V., *Institute of Artificial Intelligence Problems of MES and NAS of Ukraine, Ukraine*

Bukalov, A. V., *International Institute of Socionics, Ukraine*

Demidov, I., *Admiral Makarov National University of Shipbuilding, Ukraine*

Feger, Anatolii, *National Technical University of Ukraine "Igor Sikorsky Kyiv Polytechnic Institute" (NTUU "KPI"), Ukraine*

Ivanov, A., *Institute of Pulse Processes and Technologies of the NAS of Ukraine, Ukraine*

Jianjun Wang, *Yunzhou (Yancheng) Innovation Technology Co., Ltd, China*

Klymenko, M., *Institute of Artificial Intelligence Problems, Ukraine*

Kondratenko, Galyna, *Petro Mohyla Black Sea National University, Ukraine*

Kondratenko, Y., *Petro Mohyla Black Sea National University, Ukraine*; *Institute of Artificial Intelligence Problems, Ukraine*

Kosheleva, Olga, *University of Texas at El Paso, USA*

Kovalevskyy, S., *Department of Innovative Technologies and Management, Donbas State Engineering Academy, Ukraine*

Kozlov, Oleksiy, *Petro Mohyla Black Sea National University, Ukraine*

Kreinovich, Vladik, *University of Texas at El Paso, USA*

Lande, Dmytro, *National Technical University of Ukraine "Igor Sikorsky Kyiv Polytechnic Institute" (NTUU "KPI"), Ukraine*

Mintser, O., *Shupyk National Healthcare University of Ukraine, Ukraine*

Saliutin, M., *Petro Mohyla Black Sea National University, Ukraine*

Shevchenko, A., *Institute of Artificial Intelligence Problems, Ukraine*

Sidenko, Ie., *Petro Mohyla Black Sea National University, Ukraine*

Skarga-Bandurova, I., *Oxford Brookes University, United Kingdom*

Slyusar, V. I., *Central Research Institute of Armaments and Military Equipment of Armed Forces of Ukraine, Ukraine; Institute of Artificial Intelligence Problems, Ukraine*

Strashnoy, Leonard, *University of California, Los Angeles (UCLA), USA*

Svoboda, Igor, *National Technical University of Ukraine "Igor Sikorsky Kyiv Polytechnic Institute" (NTUU "KPI"), Ukraine*

Timchenko, Victor, *Admiral Makarov National University of Shipbuilding, Ukraine*

Yeroshenko, T. V., *Institute of Artificial Intelligence Problems of MES and NAS of Ukraine, Ukraine*

Yue Zheng, *Yancheng Polytechnic College, China*

Zaporozhets, Y., *Institute of Pulse Processes and Technologies of the NAS of Ukraine, Ukraine*

Zhukov, Y., *C-Job Nikolayev, Ukraine*

List of Abbreviations

ABPA	Allergic bronchopulmonary aspergillosis
AHP	Analytic hierarchy process
AI	Artificial intelligence
AIS	Abbreviated Injury Scale
ANN	Artificial neural network
ANP	Analytic network process
API	Application programming interface
ASIC	Application-specific integrated circuits
BAP	Biologically active point
BDA	Big data analysis
BDI	Belief-desire-intention
BEN	Behavior with emotions and norms
BN	Big negative
BOD	Behavior-oriented designers
BP	Big positive
CCR	Concept connections register
CGA	The Cancer Genome Atlas
CISO	Chief Information Security Officer
CM	Cognitive model
CNN	Convolutional neural network
CoT	Chain-of-thought
CPU	Central processing unit
CV	Computer vision
DARPA	Defense Advanced Research Projects Agency
DBEM	Database on Melts ECT Modes
DL	Deep learning
DM	Data mining
DMN	Default mode network
DP	Digital pathology
DSS	Decision support system
ECT	Electric current treatment

EEG	Electroencephalography
EMF	Electromotive force
FCM	Fuzzy cognitive map
FCN	Fully convolutional network
FIM	Functions of information metabolism
FL	Federated learning
FLOP	Floating point operations per second
FPGA	Field-programmable gate array
FPV	First person view
GAC	Geodesic active contours
GDPR	General Data Protection Regulation
GenAI	Generative AI
GEO	Gene Expression Omnibus
GH	Global Health
GPR	Ground-penetrating radar
GPU	Graphic processing unit
HNCut	Hierarchical normalized cuts
IAIP	Institute of Artificial Intelligence Problems
ICH	Intracerebral hemorrhage
IDS	Intrusion detection systems
IED	Improvised explosive device
IoT	Internet of Things
ISHAM	International Society for Human and Animal Mycology
IT	Information technologies
IVAS	Integrated visual augmentation system
KB	Knowledge base
KDD	Knowledge discovery in database
LAM	Large action model
LLaMA	Large Language Model Meta AI
LLM	Large language model
LRN	Local response normalization
LT	Linguistic term
MFR	Masked face recognition
ML	Machine learning
MMS	Molten metal system
MoE	Mixture of experts
MRI	Magnetic resonance imaging
NAS	Neural architecture search

NCD	Noncommunicable disease
NDVI	Normalized difference vegetation index
NEAT	Neuro-evolution of augmenting topologies
NER	Named entity recognition
NGVA	NATO Generic Vehicle Architecture
NLP	Natural language processing
NPU	Neural processing unit
OCC	Ortony, Clore, and Collins
PAM	Partial adjacency matrix
PCC	Prothrombin complex concentrate
PMEP	Phenomenological Map of Melt ECT Processes
PMS	Project management systems
PSSH	Physical symbol system hypothesis
QC	Quantum computing
RAG	Retrieval augmented generation
RB	Rule base
ReLU	Rectified linear unit
RNN	Recurrent neural network
ROI	Region of interest
S.A.R.A.H.	Smart AI Resource Assistant for Health
SaaS	Software-as-a-service
SD	Subject domain
SM	Semantic modeling
SME	Small- and medium-sized enterprise
SN	Small negative
SoC	System-on-chip
SOLO	Segmenting objects by locations
SP	Small positive
SQL	Structured query language
SVM	Support vector machine
TPN	Task-positive network
TPU	Tensor Processing Unit
TST	Ten Second Triage Tool
UAVs	Unmanned aerial vehicles
UN	United Nations
USC	University of Southern California
VGG	Visual geometry group
VoIP	Voice Over Internet Protocol
VPU	Vision processing unit

VR	Virtual reality
WME	Weapons and military equipment
WSI	Whole slide imaging
WTDS	War trauma dataset
YOLO	You only look once

1

Artificial Intelligence: Achievements and Prospects

A. Shevchenko, M. Klymenko, and L. Baranovska

Institute of Artificial Intelligence Problems, Ukraine
E-mail: rektor_iai@ukr.net; nik@ipai.net.ua; lesia@baranovsky.org

Abstract

This chapter is dedicated to describing the current state of artificial intelligence achievements in accordance with world trends, the extent of its influence on the transformation of social processes, the technological level of the industry, etc. Artificial intelligence is actively developing worldwide, attracting the attention of both domestic and international experts, thanks to the growing number of innovative startups, research projects, and fundamental studies. Based on an overview of the current state, the chapter focuses on consideration of the priority tasks of artificial intelligence and their possible solutions, main achievements, and perspectives of artificial intelligence implementation. New regulatory initiatives at various levels have been outlined to control the implementation and support the development of technologies, hardware, and algorithmic means for optimizing computations, as well as approaches to modeling cognitive abilities.

Keywords. Artificial intelligence, challenges, development, implementation, regulation policy, strategies.

1.1 Introduction

Over the past five years, artificial intelligence (AI) applications have become widely adopted by a broad range of users. AI is no longer seen as a technology of the near future; rather, it has a well-defined and understandable

DOI: 10.1201/9788743800989-1

functionality. Nonetheless, the range of professional tasks that AI can handle continues to grow rapidly. Alongside this expansion, several questions arise concerning the development of technology, the establishment of a support ecosystem, and its management.

The authors aim to identify the applied and fundamental aspects of integrating AI into societal practice as a safe and powerful tool for the new generation, in line with ongoing scientific and technological progress. The material is presented in five sections, each of which characterizes a general area of AI-related activities. Achievements in these areas have a defining impact on the current technological state of AI.

The next section provides a brief overview of leading regulatory initiatives in the field of AI, allowing for the controlled dissemination and use of technologies in accordance with legislation or social norms. An analysis of approaches to AI development strategy is also presented, with the authors proposing their own conceptual perspective on the matter. The third section addresses the computational aspects of current artificial intelligence models, resolved through model optimization methods, improvements in hardware, and the development of new specialized computing platforms. The fourth section focuses on the analysis of current and prospective approaches to modeling intelligent activity. Proposals and specific examples of implementing individual components of a computational system that models human cognitive abilities are provided, along with identifying priority tasks in this context. The fifth section includes the general conclusions on the conducted research.

1.2 Adoption of AI Technology and Prospects for Its Development

The United Nations (UN) Advisory Body on Artificial Intelligence released its final report on September 19, 2024, offering seven recommendations to address AI-related risks and governance gaps [1].

Since the release of Microsoft-backed OpenAI's ChatGPT in 2022, the use of AI has spread rapidly, raising concerns about fueling misinformation, fake news, and infringement of copyrighted material. Only a handful of countries have created laws to govern the spread of AI tools. The European Union has been ahead of the rest by passing a comprehensive AI Act.

The AI Act is the first-ever legal framework on AI, which addresses the risks of AI and positions Europe to play a leading role globally. The AI Act provides AI developers and deployers with clear requirements and obligations regarding specific uses of AI. At the same time, the regulation seeks to reduce administrative and financial burdens for businesses and small- and medium-sized enterprises (SMEs) [2]. The AI Act is part of a wider package of policy measures to support the development of trustworthy AI, including the AI Innovation Package [3] and the Coordinated Plan on AI [4]. Together, these measures guarantee the safety and fundamental rights of people and businesses regarding AI. They also strengthen uptake, investment, and innovation in AI across the EU.

The AI Act is the first-ever comprehensive legal framework on AI worldwide. The new rules aim to foster trustworthy AI in Europe and beyond by ensuring that AI systems respect fundamental rights, safety, and ethical principles and by addressing the risks of very powerful and impactful AI models. With the development of AI in the hands of a few multinational companies, there is a danger that the technology could be imposed on people without them having a say in how it is used, the UN said in a statement. It also recommended a new policy dialogue on AI governance, creating an AI standards exchange and a global AI capacity development network to boost governance capacities. New regulatory measures should already affect almost 20% [5] of enterprises in Europe that use artificial intelligence technologies (Figure 1.1).

Among other proposals, the UN wants a global AI fund to be established, which would address gaps in capacity and collaboration. It also advocates the formation of a global AI data framework to ensure transparency and accountability. Finally, the UN report proposed setting up a small AI office to support and coordinate the implementation of these proposals [6].

The European standards for AI, as outlined in the EU AI Act, have now become a global benchmark for regulating the development and deployment of AI technologies. The alignment with EU standards is not only necessary for a country seeking full membership to harmonize its laws with the community's regulations. It is also crucial for fostering the responsibility of AI technologies at a level that directly impacts the population's well-being and economy. The AI ecosystem of Ukraine, comprising various organizations and technologies working together within the field of AI, needs to transform integration with the European Union [7]. The authorities should play a crucial role in preparing the AI industry to meet EU standards and align the ecosystem with the provisions of the EU AI Act.

This commitment is outlined in the Roadmap, which also delineates six fundamental adapting tools. Additionally, the authorities are responsible for a conducive legal environment for the advancement of AI technologies,

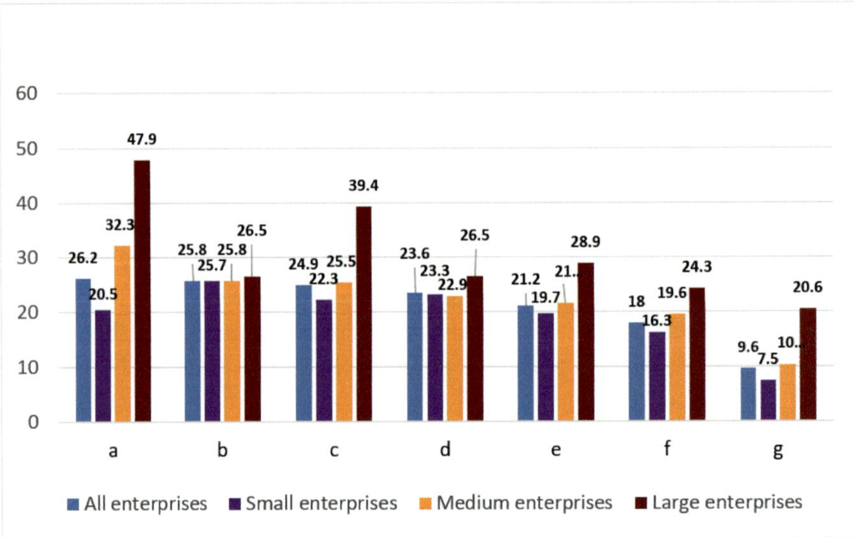

Figure 1.1 Enterprises (%) using AI technology by the type of AI technology and size class by the end of 2023: (a) automating different workflows or assisting in decision-making; (b) performing analysis of written language (text mining); (c) machine learning (e.g., deep learning) for data analysis; (d) converting spoken language into machine-readable format (speech recognition); (e) identifying objects or persons based on images (image recognition, image processing); (f) generating written or spoken language (natural language generation); (g) enabling physical movement of machines via autonomous decisions based on observation of surroundings.

ensuring that they are used within the boundaries of public safety and the protection of human rights. Ukrainian scholars have primarily focused on addressing the industry's readiness from the perspective of implementing EU law and the prospects of legal regulation [5, 8]. However, there is still limited research on the tools of adaptation outlined in the Roadmap, although some of them have been addressed in a study on harmonizing regulatory processes [9]. Note that Ukraine has the second-highest number of IT specialists (307,000) among CEE countries [10]. Also, the regulation of artificial intelligence in electoral processes is a crucial area of focus for Ukraine, especially considering its ongoing efforts to align with the European Union acquis amid a full-scale war and challenging external situation. The paper [11] explores the intersection of the EU AI Act risk-based approach and its future implementation by Ukraine, highlighting both the opportunities and risks associated with the implementation of the EU AI regulation in the context of Ukrainian electoral processes.

The strategy for AI development in Ukraine and the prospects for its implementation are outlined in the monograph [12] and in the works [13–17]. Shevchenko et al. considered implementation aspects of artificial intelligence (AI) based on the analysis of 50 national strategies for AI development in developed countries [18]. The different forms of national AI presentations and prospect domains for AI applications are discussed. Special attention is paid to NATO and Ukraine's activities in AI development and implementation at the current stage and in the future. The book chapter [19] focuses on the modern advantages in AI development and challenges in AI implementation including moral-ethical issues and dangers for human civilization. Some character examples of AI implementation in positive and negative aspects are considered as the basis for creating national and world policies in the regulation of AI development and implementation.

The article [20] provides an analysis of the specific focuses, directions, and peculiarities of the Strategy of Artificial Intelligence Development in Ukraine. The main paper's components are an analysis of the current state of the justification, development, and governmental approval of the National Strategy of AI in Ukraine; key elements and main priority areas of AI implementation according to the IAIP-project "Strategy for AI Development in Ukraine"; proposals for AI development in short- and long-term perspectives and features of the AI implementation in Ukraine during the current wartime. Special attention is paid to such focuses in AI research and development as (a) the design of AI systems based on cognitive and conscience conceptions; (b) new solutions in intelligent robotic systems for ground, underwater, and aerial applications; (c) AI perspectives in the marine industry; (d) prospective AI implementation in education; and (e) linguistic competency of AI systems. The concepts for modeling human cognitive activity proposed in the article are discussed in detail in Section 1.4 as a potential subject for further direction of research in the field of AI.

1.3 Computational Efficiency and Optimization

The diversity of transformer-based machine learning models and extensive opportunities for enhancing deep learning developments contribute to the continuous growth of new models. This is fueled by the pursuit of leading results and the increase in computational capabilities of top research centers. This trend is evident in both small models for real-time processing and large generative models. For example, the "You only look once" model (YOLO) for object recognition has grown from 50.7 million parameters in version

5 to 68.2 million in version 8, while the state-of-the-art "Real-Time Detection Transformer" model (RT-DETR-R101) reaches 76 million parameters [21, 22]. And such a trend we can see of generative models: one of the most powerful open large language models (LLMs), Llama 3.1, has 405 billion pre-trained parameters [23].

In accordance with the wide range of tasks, this demand is met by the development of specialized AI hardware accelerators, which enable significant optimization of computations within acceptable time frames. However, AI technologies are extending beyond the server and cloud infrastructure alone. Currently, there is a growing development of mobile applications operating on the Internet of Things (IoT) or edge computing principles. Such systems, in addition to hardware optimization, also require model compression techniques, enabling intelligent tasks to be performed in real time even without a broadband connection to a data processing center. Thus, these two directions of computation optimization will be discussed further.

1.3.1 Hardware AI accelerators

Hardware requirements for processing AI workloads vary depending on the use case. The challenge that system architects face is choosing the best computing cores for their AI applications. When the central processing unit (CPU) is suitable for extract, transform, and load processes and mixed data input tasks, an AI accelerator is a specialized hardware processor designed to offer greater data throughput, lower latency, and improved energy efficiency compared to conventional server processors on the market. AI accelerators include devices like graphic processing units (GPUs) and field-programmable gate arrays (FPGAs), and some types of application-specific integrated circuits (ASICs) – neural processing units (NPUs) and vision processing units (VPUs) (Figure 1.2) [24, 25].

GPUs are known for their parallel computing capabilities. The Tensor and Compute Unified Device Architecture cores (CUDA) from NVIDIA or their analogs from other manufacturers are the major computational units for machine learning algorithm accelerations. For an industry-leading inference performance or machine learning of large-scale models, GPUs based on NVIDIA Hopper architecture are widely used [26]. Among other features, H100 and H200 GPUs have a fourth-generation Tensor Core, a Tensor Memory Accelerator unit, a new CUDA cluster capability, and High Bandwidth Memory 3 (HBM3) dynamic random-access memory [27].

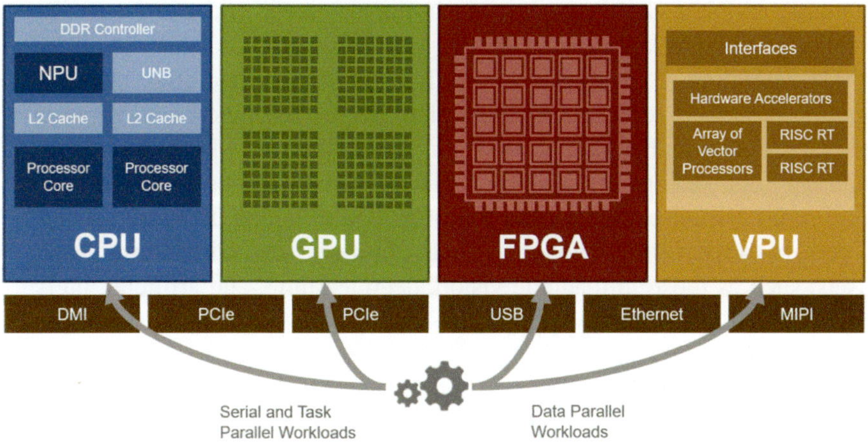

Figure 1.2 Heterogeneous platforms for advanced artificial intelligence systems.

If consumer-based GPUs require special integrated circuits to effectively process machine learning workloads, an NPU is designed to accelerate machine learning algorithms, typically by running on predictive models such as artificial neural networks or random forests. For most consumer products, the NPU will actually be integrated into the main CPU. But for more specialized industrial operations, the NPU is represented by an entirely discrete processor [28]. One of them is the Tensor Processing Unit (TPU), which has been under development by Google since 2017 and now has reached the third main version of proprietary architecture and software-as-a-service (SaaS) product of the same name: chips, systems, and software, all co-designed in-house for machine learning [29]. As alternative solutions, other leading developments are also used, such as AWS Inferentia by Amazon [30] or Ascend by Huawei [31]. A prominent class of heterogeneous system-on-chip (SoC) NPU is the VPU, which excels in embedded low-power imaging applications, covering domains such as robotics, automotive, and space. VPUs have also industrial leading developments for IoT and a wide range of tasks of video processing [32, 33]. NPUs and VPUs are types of ASICs – custom logic designed using a manufacturer's circuit libraries.

FPGAs are suitable for deep learning tasks, where we can accelerate all-reduce operations and optimize bandwidth utilization via data compression [34]. It is crucial for training performance where overhead can be a bottleneck, especially as the number of nodes increases. On this task, FPGAs can outperform GPU and NPU solutions [35]. Among these, ASICs are particularly efficient, as they consume minimal energy and can be easily tailored to specific tasks [36].

AI accelerators are applicable in both cloud servers and edge devices. Currently, the cloud serves as an ideal platform for machine learning, as it aggregates vast amounts of data from numerous sources. Meanwhile, edge computing (computing on local devices) is optimal for applications that require rapid responses. AI accelerator architecture is crucial for advanced data centers to meet the growing demands of processing and handling large datasets, such as those in machine vision, deep learning, and artificial intelligence [24]. Additionally, the power consumption of servers and data center capacity are critical considerations when designing AI accelerators [36].

The fields of artificial intelligence and quantum technology have evolved in parallel and shown great potential to enhance each other. Their integration involves using AI methods to develop algorithms for quantum computing (QC), as well as employing QC to improve AI applications. Quantum computing has the potential to revolutionize various domains as the development of user-friendly frameworks for the simulation, compilation, and execution of a quantum circuit of an artificial neural network (ANN) model on a real quantum chip [37]. However, controlling quantum systems is known to be challenging, presenting a major barrier to the widespread adoption of QC [38]. AI has opened up new opportunities for automated control of quantum systems [39, 40].

1.3.2 Model compression and edge computing

Edge computing is a networking philosophy focused on bringing computing as close to the source of data as possible in order to reduce latency and bandwidth use. Unlike the IoT devices, computing modules of this category perform tasks that are more complex but not as the generative AI (GenAI) level. The complexity of existing ANN (with convolutional, long short-term memory, transformer-based encoder–decoders, etc.) models prohibits them from being implemented in low-powered edge devices [28]. Model compression methods can reduce the high resource demands of large models, optimizing them for resource-constrained devices. Three basic methods of model compression are pruning, quantization, and knowledge distillation (Figure 1.3).

Model pruning involves removing selected network parameters to achieve a smaller model without a significant impact on performance. This technique varies from a task-specific structured approach [41] to a multi-stage pruning

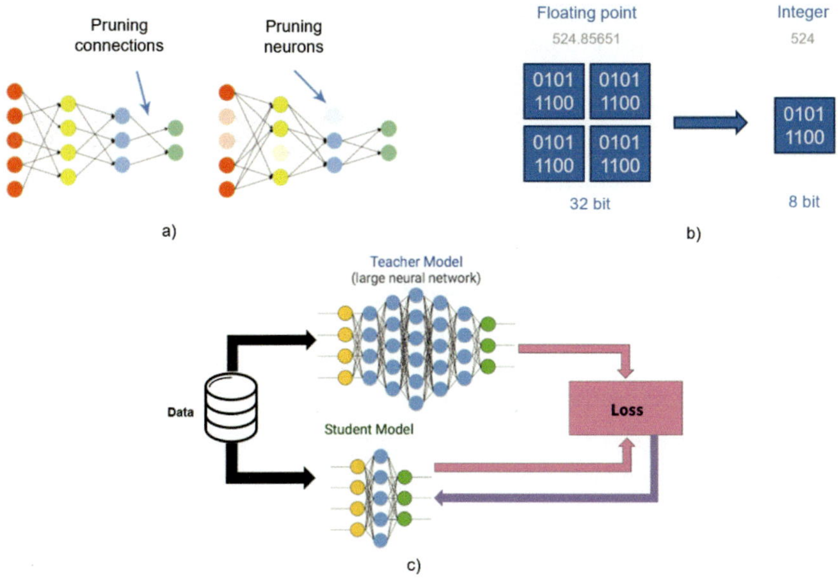

Figure 1.3 Model compression methods: (a) pruning, (b) quantization, and (c) knowledge distillation.

technique for significantly reducing model complexity while maintaining performance [42]. On the other hand, quantization provides more compact representations of neural network weights themselves. The widespread use of quantization of large language models has enabled the porting of the largest open models to mobile devices, opening up possibilities for performing generative tasks offline. Quantization usually varies compression from 16 to 1 bits and on-device fine-tuning with local data. Knowledge distillation enables the transfer of information (weights and biases) from a larger model to a smaller one, lacking the resources to learn them and allowing the smaller model to mimic the behavior of a more complex model. Tensorization is another model compression technique. It involves decomposing the weight tensors of ANN into smaller tensors with lower ranks and is used to reveal underlying patterns and structures within the data while also reducing its size. Tensorization is most useful when a model can be optimized at a mathematical level. Large-scale models are either compressed or transformed in the analyzed studies using automated frameworks like TensorFlow Lite, PyTorch Mobile, and CoreML.

A project "Development of a system for detecting explosive objects underwater" can serve as an example of a combination of AI approaches of different scales in one development. The project is carried out by the Institute of Artificial Intelligence Problems (IAIP) of the Ministry of Education and Science and the National Academy of Sciences of Ukraine. The solution aimed to help in demining of de-occupied territories of Ukraine. The development includes the creation of a new hardware and software platform for underwater unmanned vehicles, whose key features are:

- the ability to operate autonomously in case of communication loss with the operator via intermediate relay nodes;
- a significantly greater range compared to similar-class robots;
- a high degree of modularity in design;
- the use of widely available components makes it possible to assemble the robot without restricted equipment.

To meet the demands for enhanced communication reliability, a control scheme based on redundant, diverse communication channels and intermediate relay nodes has been developed. This scheme allows the operator to control both individual and multiple underwater robots simultaneously (Figure 1.4 (b)).

The prototype of the underwater unmanned vehicle is implemented based on the edge computing concept, as the robot has autonomous navigation capabilities and can detect target objects in the surrounding environment via an optical channel (Figure 1.4 (a)). A set of pre-trained machine learning models is run by the robot's onboard operating system, providing real-time data in the local environment about the robot's movement relative to surrounding objects and the classification of these objects.

The sequence of object detection and classification is stored in logs and transmitted via the available communication channel to the operator through intermediate relay nodes. This approach significantly reduces the required communication bandwidth in conditions of unstable connection and data transmission across multiple physical environments.

In addition to employing artificial intelligence methods on edge devices, this system utilizes server-side generative artificial intelligence approaches. Intelligent search task management system is hosted in the cloud and is based on a fine-tuned large language model (Figure 1.5).

The system receives natural language queries from the operator about the status of task execution by underwater robot swarm and generates a response based on the telemetry database, which is updated as data arrives from intermediate nodes. To generate a sample of relevant information, structured query language (SQL) and retrieval augmented generation (RAG) methods

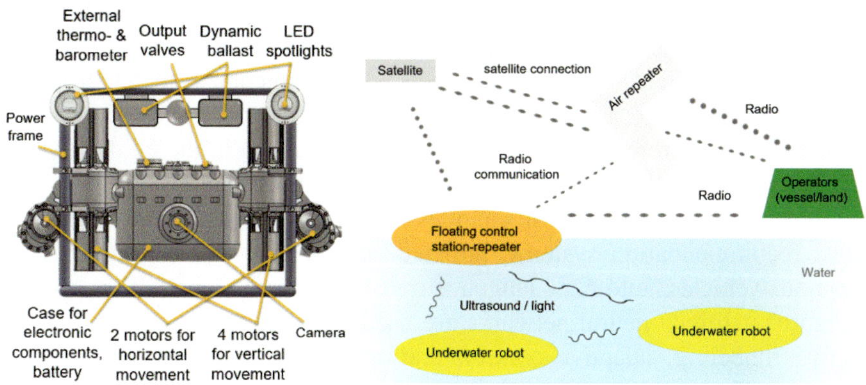

(a) (b)

Figure 1.4 AI-powered demining system: (a) model of the underwater unit with an edge computing environment; (b) scheme of operator interaction with unmanned robotic swarm.

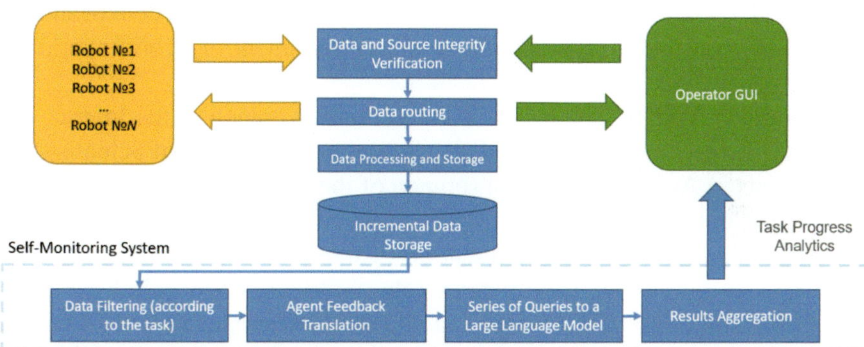

Figure 1.5 LLM usage in intelligent search task management system for operator decision-making support in the control of swarm unmanned underwater robots.

are used. The advantage of this approach is the ability to create reports on swarm operations that are not pre-defined. Among the challenges that remain is the partial low informativeness of raw telemetry data, for which a solution could be additional data filtering at remote nodes.

1.4 Modeling of Human Cognitive Abilities

The recognition of J. Hopfield and Geoffrey E. Hinton as laureates of the Nobel Prize in Physics for their discoveries in bio-inspired algorithms for artificial neural networks in 2024 highlights, firstly, the significant importance of machine learning in the contemporary scientific world and overall technological progress and, secondly, underscores the lack of new groundbreaking approaches in this field. Indeed, the results of fundamental research from more than 40 years ago are still relevant today and have continued in one form or another. Therefore, defining the object of research in the field of AI is essential for the further development of this scientific domain.

AI technologies are used in countless applications, including search engines, recommendation systems, targeted advertising, virtual assistants, autonomous vehicles, automatic language translation, facial recognition, and many more. Artificial neural networks are used for various tasks, including predictive modeling, adaptive control, and solving problems in artificial intelligence. They can learn from experience and derive conclusions from a complex and seemingly unrelated set of information. The development of artificial neural networks based on advanced technologies is one of the priority areas for developing the branches of science in all industrialized countries [43]. Ukrainian scientists such as Y. Bodyanskiy, Y. Zaychenko, and V. Sineglazov contributed significantly to the development of hybrid neural networks.

Academician Arkadii Chikrii heads the Ukrainian branch of the International Society of Dynamic Games and the Ukrainian Association of Scientists and Specialists in Automatic Control (branch of the International Federation of Automatic Control). His research team's recent developments in automated control systems, in particular, manipulation of moving objects operating in conditions of uncertainty and conflict, are relevant today [43–46]. In light of recent events, control systems of unmanned aerial/underwater vehicles have received special attention, particularly in the presence of delayed information about the state of the systems [47–57]. The problem of the approach game when the control devices fail is considered in works [53, 54], which is especially relevant in the application of unmanned aerial vehicles.

GenAI is one of the most powerful examples of machine learning. Compared to old rule-based AI applications that could only perform a single task, modern GenAI models are trained on data from many different areas, without any limitations in terms of task. Because the amount of training data is so large – OpenAI's GPT-3 was trained on more than 45 terabytes of compressed text data and the datasets for the successors are many times higher – the models appear to be creative in producing outputs [55]. For example, traditional chatbots follow scripted responses and rely on pre-defined rules to interact with users, making them suitable only for specific tasks. In contrast, modern GenAI chatbots such as ChatGPT or Google Gemini can generate human-like text, allowing for conversations that can adapt to many topics without being confined to a predetermined script. In addition, these modern chatbots can produce not only text but also images, music, and computer code based on the dataset on which they were trained [55, 56]. The hardware–software and other key aspects of AI development strategies for mobile technologies are discussed in the works [57, 58].

1.4.1 The concept of artificial consciousness as an object of scientific research

The definitions proposed in [18] reflect the provisions of the Concept for the Development of Artificial Intelligence in Ukraine [59]. At the same time, the Strategy represents the next step in implementing the tasks outlined in the Concept, necessitating a deeper understanding of the term "artificial intelligence," which is based on principles and mechanisms that mirror the functioning of the human brain, particularly its consciousness and conscience. The term "artificial consciousness" was introduced into scientific discourse as early as 1992 [60]. Subsequently, foreign experts such as John Kihlstrom, Anil Seth, Stanislas Dehaene, Michael Graziano, Taylor Webb, and others have researched the issue of artificial consciousness [61]. Ukrainian researchers began exploring these topics in 2002, when A. Shevchenko presented approaches to modeling artificial intelligence and artificial consciousness at the International Conference on "Artificial Intelligence" [62]. The ukrainian scientific school of artificial intelligence views human consciousness as a fundamental socio-cognitive system produced by brain activity, capable of perceiving and recognizing information, forming and systematizing knowledge, self-learning, and making independent motivated decisions based on tasks and circumstances while considering societal laws and rules (Figure 1.6). Consciousness shapes an individual's personality. While all these definitions compare artificial intelligence to human intelligence, they do not always accurately define the broader concept. Unfortunately, they rely solely on the functions of AI and fail to consider it as an object of research. This approach essentially reduces AI to a list of characteristics as a "black box," without clarifying what is inside. However, characteristics alone do not always allow for identifying the object of study. Therefore, artificial intelligence must be defined as an object of further scientific investigation, that is, as an element of surrounding reality.

Artificial intelligence is a function of artificial consciousness, represented by a system of algorithms that is created and controlled by it. It provides

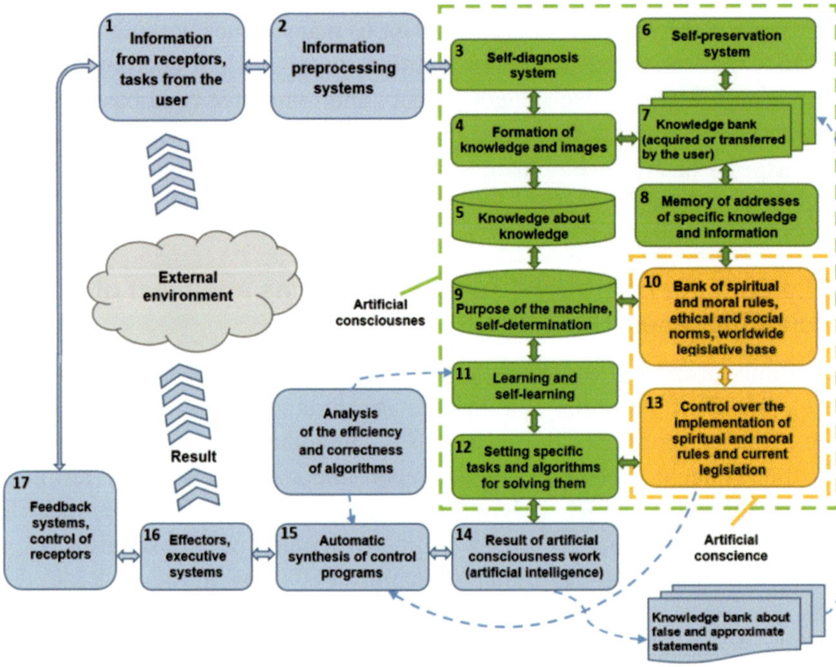

Figure 1.6 Functional model of a computer with artificial intelligence.

self-learning based on available information, acquired knowledge, societal rules and laws, and its own experiences, creating new knowledge for performing human assignments, as well as the ability to conduct self-diagnosis and justify its decisions.

Therefore, artificial intelligence is implemented as a set of functions within a weakly structured, informal system that defines its operational goals, decision-making capabilities, learning and self-learning mechanisms, knowledge acquisition, self-awareness, and more. Henceforth, we will consider that the definition of "artificial intelligence," alongside other characteristics, includes being conscious, intelligent, and making decisions in accordance with ethical, moral, and legal norms. Artificial consciousness manifests as a globally self-organizing informational creation of computational system activity, which evaluates and controls key processes occurring within it, disseminates information among various sections of the system to coordinate their operations, and ensures social and personal perception of reality.

From a technological perspective, artificial consciousness is an emergent algorithm for controlling informational processes and integrating the functions of different areas of the computational system, with the ability to override decisions made by the system. It possesses knowledge about itself and its environment, can self-learn, acquire new knowledge, and make independent decisions that align with current legislation and societal rules based on this knowledge, ensuring the internal integration and external separation of this system.

This understanding of artificial consciousness aligns with the principles of responsible AI application outlined in NATO's strategy on artificial intelligence [63], particularly with the option to deactivate the system if it begins to behave unpredictably. The concept of artificial consciousness implies the existence of artificial conscience as a mechanism to ensure the ethicality of AI decisions.

1.4.2 Approaches to modeling components of artificial consciousness

The study and modeling of consciousness (both human and artificial) leads to the problem of examining structures organized from neurons that form neural networks (biological or artificial). To work with such structures in mathematical modeling, it is convenient to transition to numerical functions. This will provide the opportunity to utilize analytical tools from mathematical analysis and graphical representations in our modeling of consciousness.

To mathematically describe this network, we solve the task of expressing and mutually uniquely recording structures through numerical functions. Such numerical representation has been proposed by Zhokhin A. S., Shevchenko A. I., and Vakulenko M. O., providing broad possibilities for analyzing and modeling neural signals [62]. Consequently, the structures of connected neurons will be expressed as numerical functions.

Let us consider the structure of the network of N interconnected neurons through synapses, which represent some form. This neural network can be depicted through a graph. Such a representation offers a convenient method for the mathematical description of real biological or technical (electronic or electrical) structures – networks in which we can identify active centers or nodes that are interconnected by links. This mathematical description abstracts the natural essence of the network, leaving only the fact of the existence of connections between the network nodes, which are the active objects of this network.

If we consider only the fact of neuron connections without the "input–output" orientation, we can represent such a network through undirected graphs, which consist of nodes connected by edges. We sequentially number all neurons with whole numbers from 1 to N. Let k and m be integers from 1 to N. We take the kth neuron. If it is connected to the mth neuron, we can introduce the indexed quantity $A(m,k)$, which equals 1; if it is not connected, then $A(m,k) = 0$. Thus, for all N neurons, we obtain a matrix $\{A(m,k)\}$ of size $N \times N$ consisting of zeros and ones. This is the adjacency matrix, denoted as $\{A\}$.

If we consider the columns in the adjacency matrix, a rotation of $-90°$ gives us whole numbers in the binary numeral system of the type "100100…11011." For our previous compatibility matrix, the first column yields the binary number "011" (which is equal to 3 in decimal form). It is convenient for us to switch to the usual decimal representation and obtain an integer function. To construct such a numerical function related to the adjacency matrix, the following is proposed. We take the matrix $\{A(k,m)\}$ and build an integer discrete function $F(k)$ from the discrete parameter $0 < k < (N + 1)$ in the following form:

$$F(k) = \sum_{m=1,N} 2^{m-1} A(k,m). \tag{1.1}$$

This formula provides us with the standard conversion from binary to decimal representation of an integer and is widely used in computer discrete mathematics. Essentially, it is a method for packing binary information into decimal numbers. Such a function will mutually uniquely define the neural connections in the given structure of the representation. Based on the discrete function $F(k)$, continuous argument functions can be constructed; for example, the linear function $Lk(x)$:

$$Lk(x) = F(k) + (F(k) - F(k-1))(x-k). \tag{1.2}$$

Here, the continuous real argument x lies between the integers $(k - 1)$ and k. If we combine all such functions for all k from 1 to N, we obtain a piecewise linear function $L(x)$ of the continuous argument x, which lies in the interval of real numbers from 1 to N. This function can be used for graphical representation and technical applications in operations with the structures of the studied and modeled networks.

A visual representation and analysis of networks in the form of graphs will be convenient with a small number of nodes and connections. As the size of the network increases, the complexity of their analysis and description using simple graphs, without applying adjacency matrices, will grow.

Transitioning to an adjacency matrix will simplify the situation. However, an even better improvement in the situation will come from transitioning to the proposed functions $F(k)$ and $L(x)$.

These functions are single-argument functions (both integer and continuous). Therefore, for large network sizes, using such functions will have advantages over matrix and graph methods of operating and describing networks due to the information packing implemented by the construction of our functions. Moreover, we do not lose the mutual one-to-one correspondence of all these methods with the structure of our network itself.

An important argument for using such functions for network structures is that by transitioning to functions, we have the opportunity to employ mathematical methods and theories developed in mathematical analysis, as well as algorithms and their computer implementations in software packages, facilitating the creation of new programs for working with and modeling our networks and their structures.

For the case of directed networks, we take the following approach. Similarly, for directed networks with the direction of connections, we use directed graphs. We have an analogous adjacency matrix with elements $\{A(k,m)\}$, which equal 2 for an "input" connection, 1 for an "output" connection, and 0 for an isolated node. Now the columns of the compatibility matrix will yield numbers in ternary form such as "0120210. . . 0000201." For the same three-noded graph but with directed connections, for the first node, we will have the number "012" (which is 5 in decimal). Based on these numbers, we construct a function with an integer argument. We obtain it as an integer discrete function of the form:

$$F(k) = \sum_{m=1,N} 3^{m-1} A(k,m). \tag{1.3}$$

This formula provides us with a standard transition from ternary to decimal representation of an integer, or packing information into decimal numbers. Similarly, based on the discrete function $F(k)$, we construct functions of a continuous argument x (4.1) and $L(x)$, as previously stated with analogous real arguments x.

Let us reiterate that the constructed functions will uniquely recognize structures in networks (neural) and will be convenient in mathematical operations when modeling processes related to human consciousness or the artificial consciousness of computer robots and technical systems.

Artificial consciousness is a key element of the proposed model of an intelligent computing machine. At the same time, other components have functionality that is predominantly deterministic in the algorithmic domain. An example of this is the model of artificial consciousness [14]. Artificial conscience, from a technical perspective, is a process of artificial consciousness that evaluates its own actions and intentions based on circumstances, taking into account learned rules and norms. The evaluation produces an impulsive response, the parameters of which are adjusted by subjective experience and the current activities of consciousness. The function of controlling the task setting and its execution is assigned to a system resembling human conscience – a system that monitors the establishment and achievement of goals. The component of artificial conscience for applied tasks has been implemented based on articles from the Criminal Code, which were processed into a binary tree, simplifying the identification of the most relevant action among the available rules. The result of processing a request for action is a numerical assessment ranging from neutral to negative $(-1\ldots0)$ since there is no positive direction in the context of the rules applied. The proposed approach can be considered as an alternative to methods based on machine learning, such as the protective mechanism of LLM (for example, Llama-Guard-3–8B – a special version of the 8 billion model tuned to classify data based on content [23]) or protective subsystems of visual generative models.

AI, particularly through the advancements in machine learning and deep learning, has introduced innovative methodologies that are transforming the healthcare landscape. The ability of AI to process vast amounts of data, recognize intricate patterns, and generate predictive models has opened new avenues for research and development in medicine. Medicine, as one of the priority areas for AI implementation, is highlighted in studies [65–67]. The Institute of Artificial Intelligence Problems of the Ministry of Education and Science of Ukraine and the National Academy of Sciences of Ukraine carry out projects on the development of chatbots powered by artificial intelligence, particularly in medicine. A working group of scientists from the National Academy of Educational Sciences of Ukraine and IAIP was established to implement the project "Psychologist Chatbot" (Figure 1.7). Chatbot "Oncologist" was another one of the projects of IAIP.

A notable feature of the chatbot is its ability to conduct user screenings using methodologies that have been practically verified and approved. However, the absence of certain important human qualities essential for the profession of a psychologist, such as empathy, does not allow for a complete imitation of professional skills. Nevertheless, the implementation of the artificial consciousness model in such developments could address the remaining issues.

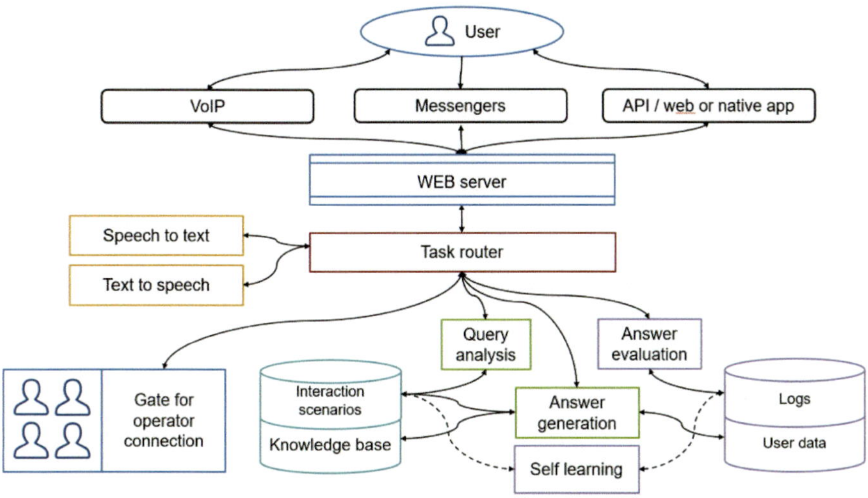

Figure 1.7 Functional diagram of main components of the AI chatbot platform.

The implemented methods include adapting the dialogue to the personal preferences and characteristics of the user and the context of the session; maintaining the anonymity of the provided information; detecting critical states and situations of the user (with notifications sent to relevant emergency assistance services); and allowing user evaluation of sessions and self-improvement based on feedback. Developed chatbots are using custom dialog platform for multichannel interaction. The main backend node is the router, which controls all the way from query input to answer delivery through active channel: voice via Voice Over Internet Protocol (VoIP) or messenger bot (Telegram, WhatsApp, Viber, etc.) or application of different platforms via single application programming interface (API). Proposals for improving chatbot response quality based on subworld embedding, as well as suggestions for the multimodality of chatbot services, are indicated in the works [66–69].

1.5 Conclusion

The current state of applied developments in artificial intelligence technologies suggests a rapid advancement and implementation of knowledge-intensive products, as evidenced by information coverage and market feedback. New regulatory initiatives at various levels have been outlined to control the implementation and support the development of technologies, hardware, and algorithmic means for optimizing computations, as well as approaches to modeling cognitive abilities.

Choosing the right hardware for AI processing depends on the specific workload with different types of AI accelerators enhancing data throughput, efficiency, and latency over standard computational units. GPUs are widely used for large-scale machine learning due to their parallel processing. NPUs excel in predictive models, FPGAs offer bandwidth efficiency for deep learning, while different ASICs provide custom, energy-efficient solutions (low-power, embedded applications, robotics, etc.). Integrating AI with quantum computing presents new possibilities but remains challenging due to the complexities of controlling quantum systems.

Examples of modern developments show the ability to adapt AI models of different modalities to tasks of server-side and distributed low-power node computation. Edge computing brings computation closer to data sources, reducing latency and bandwidth demands for complex AI tasks on low-power devices. To adapt large AI models to edge environments, compression techniques like pruning, quantization, and knowledge distillation reduce resource requirements. An example of edge AI is an underwater robot project by the Institute of Artificial Intelligence Problems in Ukraine, designed for autonomous demining tasks with enhanced communication and modularity. The system integrates edge AI for real-time object detection and cloud-based generative AI for task management, enabling efficient operator control over multiple robots even in unstable communication conditions.

The authors emphasize the importance of strategic decisions regarding the further development of artificial intelligence, one of which proposes defining the object of fundamental research, allowing for targeted scientific activities aimed at achieving breakthrough technologies. Definitions of "artificial intelligence" and "artificial consciousness" draw on the Concept for AI Development in Ukraine and emphasize mirroring human brain functions. The concept of artificial consciousness and the operational scheme of an intelligent computer based on it are proposed as the objects of research. The main components of this approach are discussed, along with examples of their practical implementation. This concept supports ethical evaluation through "artificial conscience," a function designed to assess and guide actions based on rules, with applications in various fields, such as AI-powered chatbots. Notably, AI-driven chatbots developed by Ukraine's Institute of Artificial Intelligence Problems (IAIP) aid healthcare by offering adaptive interactions, emergency response capabilities, and user feedback processing, although they lack human empathy. Future developments aim to integrate artificial consciousness for improved response quality, multimodal interactions, and ethical assessments, enhancing usability across platforms like VoIP and messaging apps.

References

[1] 'EU AI Act: first regulation on artificial intelligence', 18 June 2024, https://www.europarl.europa.eu/topics/en/article/20230601STO93804/eu-ai-act-first-regulation-on-artificial-intelligence

[2] 'Regulation (EU) 2024/1689 of the European Parliament and of the Council', 13 June 2024, http://data.europa.eu/eli/reg/2024/1689/oj

[3] 'Commission launches AI innovation package to support Artificial Intelligence startups and SMEs', 24 January 2024, https://ec.europa.eu/commission/presscorner/detail/en/ip_24_383

[4] 'Coordinated Plan on Artificial Intelligence', https://digital-strategy.ec.europa.eu/en/policies/plan-ai

[5] 'UN advisory body makes seven recommendations for governing AI', 19 September 2024, https://www.reuters.com/technology/artificial-intelligence/un-advisory-body-makes-seven-recommendations-governing-ai-2024-09-19/

[6] 'Use of artificial intelligence in enterprises', Eurostat, 24 May 2024, https://ec.europa.eu/eurostat/statistics-explained/index.php?title=Use_of_artificial_intelligence_in_enterprises

[7] A. Hachkevych, 'Tools for adopting Ukraine's artificial intelligence ecosystem to meet European Union standards', Law and Innovative Society, Vol.1, No. 22, pp. 21–31, 2024. doi:10.37772/2309-9275-2024-1(22)-2

[8] V. Teremetskyi, Yu. Burylo, M. Stefanchuk, O. Zozuliak, Z. Udovenko, D. Zhuravlov, Ye. Duliba, 'Prospective regulation of artificial intelligence in the European Union and its possible implications for Ukraine', International Journal of Applied Engineering & Technology, Vol. 6, No. 1, pp. 137–145, 2024, https://romanpub.com/resources/ijaet20v6-1-2024-18.pdf

[9] K. Militsyna, 'Legal Framework for Output Based on Artificial Intelligence: Ukraine's Place on the Global Search Path', in: H. Richter (eds.), Competition and Intellectual Property Law in Ukraine, pp. 559-582, 2023, https://link.springer.com/chapter/10.1007/978-3-662-66101-7_22

[10] A. Yanovytska, 'Harmonization of the regulatory processes of the use of artificial intelligence in Ukraine and other European countries', Scientific Innovations and Advanced Technologies, Vol. 32, No. 4, pp. 593–602, 2024, https://doi.org/10.52058/2786-5274-2024-4(32)-593-602

[11] 'The AI Ecosystem of Ukraine: Talent, Companies, and Education', 19 June 2024, https://aihouse.org.ua/en/research/ai-ecosystem-of-ukraine-talent-companies-education/

[12] A. Castagna, A. Melenchuk, I. Tkachenko, O. Sydorchuk, 'Adapting EU Artificial Intelligence Regulations for Electoral Processes: A Path for Ukraine', September 2024, https://doi.org/10.13140/RG.2.2.32091.58404

[13] Y. P. Kondratenko, V. M. Kuntsevich, A. A. Chikrii, V. F. Gubarev, (Eds.). 'Recent Developments in Automatic Control Systems', River Publishers: Gistrup, pp. 1–492, 2022. https://www.riverpublishers.com/book_details.php?book_id=976

[14] A. I. Shevchenko, M. S. Klymenko, 'Developing a model of "artificial conscience', 2020 IEEE 15th International Conference on Computer Sciences and Information Technologies (CSIT), pp. 51–54, 2020, https://doi.org/10.1109/csit49958.2020.9321962

[15] Y. P. Kondratenko, A. I. Shevchenko, (Eds.). 'Research Tendencies and Prospect Domains for AI Development and Implementation', River Publishers: Gistrup, pp. 1–155, 2024, https://www.riverpublishers.com/book_details.php?book_id=1163

[16] Y. Kondratenko, G. Kondratenko, A. Shevchenko, V. Slyusar, Y. Zhukov, M. Vakulenko, 'Towards Implementing the Strategy of Artificial Intelligence Development: Ukraine Peculiarities', CEUR Workshop Proceedings, Vol. 3513, pp. 106-117, 2023, https://ceur-ws.org/Vol-3513/paper09.pdf

[17] R. Duro, et al. (Eds). 'Advances in intelligent robotics and collaborative automation'. River Publishers, Aalborg, 2015, https://doi.org/10.13052/rp-9788793237049

[18] A. Shevchenko, M. Vakulenko, M. Klymenko, 'The Ukrainian AI strategy: Premises and outlooks', 12th International Conference on Advanced Computer Information Technologies (ACIT) 1, pp. 511–515, 2022, https://doi.org/10.1109/acit54803.2022.9913094

[19] A. I. Schevchenko, Y. P. Kondratenko, V. I. Slyusar, I. P. Atamanyuk, G. V. Kondratenko, T. V. Yeroshenko 'Analysis of the prospect domains in AI implementation: Nationals, NATO and Ukraine AI strategies'.

Research Tendencies and Prospect Domains for AI Development and Implementation, pp. 1-30, 2024, https://www.riverpublishers.com/book_details.php?book_id=1163

[20] Y. Kondratenko, A. Shevchenko, Y. Zhukov, V. Slyusar, G. Kondratenko, M. Klymenko, O. Striuk, 'Analysis of the Priorities and Perspectives in Artificial Intelligence Implementation'. 2023 13th International Conference on Dependable Systems, Services and Technologies, DESSERT 2023, Athens, 13 – 15 October 2023, DOI 0.1109/DESSERT61349.2023.10416432

[21] 'YOLOv10 - Ultralytics YOLO Docs', https://docs.ultralytics.com/models/yolov10/#comparisons

[22] Lv. Wenyu, Yian Zhao, Qinyao Chang, Kui Huang, Guanzhong Wang, Yi Liu, 'RT-DETRv2: Improved Baseline with Bag-of-Freebies for Real-Time Detection Transformer', arXiv:2407.17140, https://arxiv.org/abs/2407.17140

[23] 'The Llama 3 Herd of Models | Research - AI at Meta', 2024, https://ai.meta.com/research/publications/the-llama-3-herd-of-models/

[24] R. Shrestha, R. Bajracharya, A. Mishra, S. Kim, 'AI Accelerators for Cloud and Server Applications', in: A. Mishra, J. Cha, H. Park, S. Kim (eds), Artificial Intelligence and Hardware Accelerators, Springer, Cham, pp. 95-125, 2023, https://doi.org/10.1007/978-3-031-22170-5_3

[25] 'Embedded Hardware for Processing AI - ADLINK Blog', 21 February 2021, https://blog.adlinktech.com/2021/02/19/embedded-hardware-processing-ai-edge-gpu-vpu-fpga-asic/

[26] Jianwei Zhu, et al., 'Confidential Computing on nVIDIA Hopper GPUs: A Performance Benchmark Study', arXiv:2409.03992, 2024, https://arxiv.org/abs/2409.03992

[27] J. Choquette, 'NVIDIA Hopper H100 GPU: Scaling Performance', in: IEEE Micro, Vol. 43, No. 3, pp. 9-17, May-June 2023, doi:10.1109/MM.2023.3256796

[28] A-T. Shumba, et al., 'Wearable Technologies and AI at the Far Edge for Chronic Heart Failure Prevention and Management: A Systematic Review and Prospects', Sensors, 23(15), 6896, 2023, https://doi.org/10.3390/s23156896

[29] T. Norrie, et al., 'The Design Process for Google's Training Chips: TPUv2 and TPUv3', in: IEEE Micro, Vol. 41, No. 2, pp. 56-63, 1 March-April 2021, doi:10.1109/MM.2021.3058217

[30] C. Fregly, A. Barth, 'Data Science on AWS', O'Reilly Media, Inc., 2021, https://www.oreilly.com/library/view/data-science-on/9781492079385/

[31] K. Shi, Q. Liu, Z. Zheng and L. Xiao, 'Efficient Implementation for Composite CNN-Based HSI Classification Algorithm with Huawei Ascend Framework', 2023 13th Workshop on Hyperspectral Imaging and Signal Processing: Evolution in Remote Sensing (WHISPERS), Athens, Greece, 2, pp. 1-5, 2023, doi:10.1109/WHISPERS61460.2023.10430835.

[32] V. Leon, P. Minaidis, G. Lentaris, D. Soudris, 'Accelerating AI and Computer Vision for Satellite Pose Estimation on the Intel Myriad X Embedded SoC', Microprocessors and Microsystems, 103, 104947, 2023, https://doi.org/10.1016/j.micpro.2023.104947

[33] L. Vasileios, et al, 'MPAI: A Co-Processing Architecture with MPSoC & AI Accelerators for Vision Applications in Space', arXiv preprint arXiv:2409.12258, 2024, https://arxiv.org/abs/2409.12258

[34] R. Ma, E. Georganas, A. Heinecke, S. Gribok, A. Boutros and E. Nurvitadhi, 'FPGA-Based AI Smart NICs for Scalable Distributed AI Training Systems', in: IEEE Computer Architecture Letters, Vol. 21, No. 2, pp. 49-52, 1 July-Dec. 2022, doi:10.1109/LCA.2022.3189207

[35] A. Boutros, et al., 'Beyond Peak Performance: Comparing the Real Performance of AI-Optimized FPGAs and GPUs', 2020 International Conference on Field-Programmable Technology (ICFPT), Maui, HI, USA, pp. 10-19,2020, doi:10.1109/ICFPT51103.2020.00011

[36] V. Avelar, P. Donovan, P. Lin, W. Torell, M. A. Torres Arango, 'The AI Disruption: Challenges and Guidance for Data Center Design', Schneider Electric – Energy Management Research Center White Paper, 110 Version 2.1, 06 December 2023, https://www.se.com/ww/en/download/document/SPD_WP110_EN/

[37] Xu Xusheng, et al., 'MindSpore Quantum: A User-Friendly, High-Performance, and AI-Compatible Quantum Computing Framework', arXiv, https://doi.org/10.48550/arXiv.2406.17248

[38] Y. Zhu, K. Yu, 'Artificial intelligence (AI) for quantum and quantum for AI', Opt Quant Electron, 55, 697, 2023, https://doi.org/10.1007/s11082-023-04914-6

[39] P. Kaledio, D. Stilinski, 'Quantum Machine Learning: Exploring the Potential of Quantum Computing for AI Applications,' preprint, 2024, https://easychair.org/publications/preprint/bb78/download

[40] Y. Kondratenko, A. Shevchenko, Y. Zhukov, G. Kondratenko, O. Striuk, 'Tendencies and Challenges of Artificial Intelligence Development and Implementation', Proceedings of the IEEE International Conference on

Intelligent Data Acquisition and Advanced Computing Systems: Technology and Applications, IDAACS, 2023, pp. 221–226, Dortmund, 7– 9 September 2023, doi10.1109/IDAACS58523.2023.1034880

[41] X. Mengzhou, Z. Zhong, D. Chen, 'Structured pruning learns compact and accurate models', arXiv preprint arXiv:2204.00408, 2022.

[42] L. Xiaolin, R. C. Panicker, B. Cardiff and D. John, 'Multistage Pruning of CNN Based ECG Classifiers for Edge Devices,' 2021 43rd Annual International Conference of the IEEE Engineering in Medicine & Biology Society (EMBC), Mexico, pp. 1965-1968, 2021, doi:10.1109/EMBC46164.2021.9630588.

[43] M. Zgurovsky, V. Sineglazov, E. Chumachenko, 'Formation of hybrid artificial neural networks topologies. Studies in Computational Intelligence', pp. 175–232, 2020, doi:10.1007/978-3-030-48453-8_3

[44] A. Chikrii, 'Conflict-Controlled Processes', Springer Science & Business Media, 556 p., 2013, https://link.springer.com/book/10.1007/978-94-017-1135-7

[45] A. A. Chikrii, O. S. Rappoport, K. A. Chikrii, 'Multivalued Mappings and their Selectors in the Theory of Conflict-Controlled Processes', Cybernetics and Systems Analysis, 43(5), pp. 719–730, 2007, https://link.springer.com/article/10.1007/s10559-007-0097-8

[46] Baranovska L.V. Method of resolving functions for the differential-difference pursuit game for different-inertia objects. Studies in Systems, Decision and Control, 69, pp. 159–176, 2016, https://doi.org/10.1007/978-3-319-40673-2_7

[47] L. V. Baranovska, 'Quasi-Linear Differential-Difference Game of Approach', Understanding Complex Systems, pp. 505–524, 2019, https://doi.org/10.1007/978-3-319-96755-4_26

[48] L. V. Baranovska, 'On Quasilinear Differential-Difference Games of Approach', Journal of Automation and Information Sciences, Vol. 49, No. 8, pp. 53–67, 2017, https://doi.org/10.1615/JAutomatInfScien.v49.i8.40

[49] G. T. Chikrii, 'Principle of time stretching in evolutionary games of approach', Journal of Automation and Information Sciences, Vol. 48, No. 5, pp. 12–26, 2016, https://doi.org/10.1615/JAutomatInfScien.v48.i5.20

[50] A. A. Chikrii, G. T. Chikrii, 'Time Dilation Principle in Dynamic Game Problems', Cybernetics and Systems Analysis, Vol. 58, No.1, pp. 36-44, 2022, https://doi.org/10.1007/s10559-022-00433-6

[51] L. V. Baranovska. Pursuit differential-difference games with pure time-lag. Discrete and Continuous Dynamical Systems – Series B., 24, No. 3, pp. 1021–1031, 2019, https://doi.org/10.3934/dcdsb.2019004

[52] L. V. Baranovska. Group pursuit differential games with pure time-lag. Understanding Complex Systems, pp. 475–488, 2021, https://doi.org/10.1007/978-3-030-50302-4_23

[53] A. A. Chikriy, L. V. Baranovskaya, Al. A. Chikriy, 'An Approach Game Problem under the Failure of Controlling Devices', Journal of Automation and Information Sciences, Vol. 35, No. 5, pp. 1–8, 2000, https://doi.org/10.1615/JAutomatInfScien.v32.i5.10

[54] A. A. Chikrij, L. V. Baranovskaya, Al. A. Chikrij, 'The game problem of approach under the condition of failure of controlling devices', Problemy Upravleniya i Informatiki (Avtomatika), 4, pp. 5–13, 1997

[55] M. Schreiner, 'GPT-4 architecture, datasets, costs and more leaked', THE DECODER, 12 July 2023, https://the-decoder.com/gpt-4-architecture-datasets-costs-and-more-leaked/

[56] 'Generative Artificial Intelligence: Generative Artificial Intelligence', World Intellectual Property Organization, 2024, https://doi.org/10.34667/tind.49740

[57] A. Sheremet, Y. Kondratenko, I. Sidenko, G. Kondratenko, 'Diagnosis of lung disease based on medical images using artificial neural networks', 2021 IEEE 3rd Ukraine Conference on Electrical and Computer Engineering (UKRCON), 2604, pp. 561–565, 2021, https://doi.org/10.1109/ukrcon53503.2021.9575961

[58] Y. Kondratenko, I. Sidenko, G. Kondratenko, V. Petrovych, M. Taranov, I. Sova, 'Artificial Neural Networks for recognition of brain tumors on MRI images', Communications in Computer and Information Science, pp. 119–140, 2021, https://doi.org/10.1007/978-3-030-77592-6_6

[59] 'Concept for the Development of Artificial Intelligence in Ukraine', https://zakon.rada.gov.ua/laws/show/1556-2020-p#Text

[60] I. Aleksander, 'Capturing consciousness in neural systems', Artificial Neural Networks, 2. Proc. ICANN-92, London: North-Holland, pp. 17-22, 1992

[61] M. Graziano, 'The attention schema theory: A foundation for engineering artificial consciousness', in: Frontiers in Robotics and AI 4, art. 60, pp. 1-9, 2017

[62] A. I. Shevchenko, 'Ten years on the way to creating artificial intelligence systems', Materials International scientific and technical conf. 'Artificial intelligence-2002', Vol.1, Taganrog: Publishing House of TRTU, pp. 16-39, 2002

[63] 'NATO Review - Artificial Intelligence Strategy for NATO', https://www.nato.int/docu/review/uk/articles/2021/10/25/strategya-shchodo-shtuchnogo-rozumu-dlya-nato/index.html

[64] A. I. Shevchenko, A. S. Zhokhin, 'Mathematical model of artificial consciousness as a dynamic system', pp. 47-52. Proceedings of the XXIV International Scientific and Technical Conference "Artificial Intelligence and Intelligent Systems - AIIS'2024" Kyiv, Ukraine, October 18-19, 2024. https://www.ipai.net.ua/docs/AIIS-2024.pdf

[65] O. Kozlov, Y. Kondratenko, O. Skakodub, 'Comparative analysis of parametric optimization techniques: Fuzzy DSS for medical diagnostics', Studies in Fuzziness and Soft Computing, pp. 193–201, 2023, https://doi.org/10.1007/978-3-031-23476-7_17

[66] V. Slyusar, Y. Kondratenko, A. Shevchenko, T. Yeroshenko, 'Some aspects of artificial intelligence development strategy for Mobile Technologies', Journal of Mobile Multimedia, pp. 525–554, https://doi.org/10.13052/jmm1550-4646.2031

[67] L. G. Tyutelova, E. S. Shevchenko, V. N. Lisovitskaya, V. D. Shevchenko, 'The problem of communicating with Generative AI', 2024 Communication Strategies in Digital Society Seminar (ComSDS), pp. 142–145, 2024, https://doi.org/10.1109/comsds61892.2024.10502105

[68] M. Vakulenko, V. Slyusar, 'Automatic smart subword segmentation for the reverse Ukrainian physical dictionary task', Proceedings of the Modern Data Science Technologies Workshop (MoDaST-2024), Lviv, Ukraine, May 31 - June 1, pp. 59-73, 2024, https://ceur-ws.org/Vol-3723/paper4.pdf

[69] D. Lande, O. Dmytrenko, A. Shevchenko, M. Klymenko, M. Vakulenko, 'Spoken language identification based on the transcript analysis', Digital Scholarship in the Humanities, Volume 38, Issue 2, June 2023, Pages 586–595, 2023, https://doi.org/10.1093/llc/fqac052

2

Decision Support in the Field of Cybersecurity Through the Use of Generative Artificial Intelligence

Dmytro Lande[1], Igor Svoboda[1], Anatolii Feger[1], and Leonard Strashnoy[2]

[1]National Technical University of Ukraine "Igor Sikorsky Kyiv Polytechnic Institute" (NTUU "KPI"), Ukraine
[2]University of California, Los Angeles (UCLA), USA
E-mail: dwlande@gmail.com; i.svoboda@kpi.ua; feher.anatolii@gmail.com; lstrashnoy@gmail.com

Abstract

This chapter is dedicated to the methodology of forming causal networks through the repeated application of systems based on large language models (LLMs), as well as the visualization and analysis of these networks. The generated causal networks provide the possibility of further transitioning to scenario analysis. The chapter discusses the potential of emulating a group of experts by repeatedly applying similar prompts to LLMs. The methodology is based on using causal networks formed by LLMs. It is proposed to create and subsequently combine two networks: the first network is formed starting from the node representing the initial state of the problem (the root cause); the second network is formed starting from the goal, working backward. The combined causal network serves as the foundation for creating desired scenarios.

Keywords: Decision support, large language models, virtual experts, causal networks, semantic networking.

DOI: 10.1201/9788743800989-2

2.1 Introduction

In today's world, decision-making in complex systems is becoming an increasingly important and challenging task due to the growing volume of data, the variety of situations requiring analysis, and the increasing number of interdependent factors. Traditional decision-making approaches, such as analytical methods, heuristics, and expert systems, while still relevant, often demand significant resources, particularly the involvement of a large number of experts. However, recent advancements in artificial intelligence, particularly large language models (LLMs), open new possibilities for addressing this issue.

Traditionally, the decision-making process in complex systems has relied on the work of experts who build models and analyze complex data to find optimal solutions. However, practice shows that these methods have several limitations. The biggest challenge lies in ensuring access to a sufficient number of competent experts who can provide comprehensive and objective analysis. This becomes especially critical in cases where the number of factors and their interactions is so large that it requires substantial intellectual and time resources. Moreover, experts may hold different views on the same issues, leading to conflicting opinions and, consequently, difficulties in reaching consensus decisions.

2.1.1 The role of large language models in decision-making support

With the emergence of LLMs, such as GPT-4, new prospects have appeared in the field of decision support. These models can process vast amounts of information, extract knowledge, and construct complex semantic networks that describe cause-and-effect relationships between various concepts [1, 2]. This significantly reduces reliance on a large number of experts, replacing their work with a more automated approach.

Large language models like GPT-4 have become innovative tools in artificial intelligence, capable of substantially influencing decision support processes. Their ability to process and analyze massive amounts of textual information, as well as generate coherent and logical responses to user queries, opens new possibilities for improving traditional approaches to data analysis and decision-making. Procedures where LLMs can be applied in decision support include automating data collection and analysis, forming semantic networks, simulating expert work, reproducing hierarchical decision-making models, scenario analysis, and forecasting, among others.

One of the greatest advantages of LLMs is their ability to simulate expert work through repeated prompt processing. By applying various approaches to query formulation, it is possible to replicate the opinions of different experts, creating diverse perspectives on the same problem. This reduces the dependency on engaging large numbers of human experts, particularly in cases where finding such specialists is difficult or too costly.

Large language models (LLMs) are capable of supporting decision-making processes, including complex hierarchical models such as the analytic hierarchy process (AHP) [3, 4]. Using LLMs, it is possible to model the process of comparing various decision options, taking into account a wide range of criteria. LLMs can also generate scenarios based on existing data, predicting possible decision outcomes.

By repeatedly applying prompts to LLMs, coherent semantic networks can be created that account for different perspectives. At present, individual experts can act as mentors, guiding the work of "virtual experts" powered by LLMs. Furthermore, the application of LLMs enables the creation of event development scenarios based on the constructed semantic networks, which allows for forecasting potential outcomes and making well-informed decisions.

2.1.2 Literature review

Among the works related to decision support systems theory, it is important to mention the work of T. Saaty, who developed the analytic hierarchy process (AHP) [4] and the analytic network process (ANP) [5]. This work is dedicated to improving such methods through the application of large language models (LLMs).

A review [6] is dedicated to the revolution in information technology sparked by the advent of large language models. A significant contribution to the development of decision support methods based on artificial intelligence was made by the classic work [7]. Numerous publications, including [2], are devoted to describing the principles and various applications of LLMs. This paper analyzes LLMs from the perspective of mathematics and computer science.

The review of the capabilities and applications of LLM technology in various industries, and the description of how businesses should approach the integration of generative AI into their business models, is presented in the book [8] and works [9–11]. Another important direction – researching hierarchical models that use LLMs for decision-making strategy development – is reflected in the work [12], which poses new questions to LLMs at each stage of the decision-making process. The work [13] is dedicated to managing next-generation networks based on the use of LLMs.

Research in the field of LLMs for decision-making and semantic network construction is at the forefront of scientific development. In the work [1], methods for forming domain models using LLMs are explored, introducing the concepts of "semantic networking" and the "swarm of virtual experts." This section is dedicated to the development of these areas.

Causal networks are a powerful tool for modeling complex systems, where it is necessary to account for interconnections between various elements and their mutual influence. Such networks can be built both manually, using traditional methods, and automatically with large language models. Traditional approaches to constructing causal networks mainly rely on expert knowledge, logical analysis, and statistical methods. With the development of machine learning technologies and LLMs, new approaches to automating the creation of causal networks have emerged, including the automatic detection of connections, the use of LLMs for building semantic networks, and the combination of expert knowledge with LLMs, such as the dynamic networking approach based on bidirectional search [14].

Causal networks are a critical tool in modern conditions where complex interconnections must be considered and well-informed decisions must be made. New approaches involving LLMs allow for the automation of network formation, improving the efficiency and accuracy of analysis, as well as providing a deeper understanding of complex systems, which is crucial for decision-making in various fields.

2.2 Semantic Networking

LLM-based systems have vast potential in extracting key concepts and named entities. In particular, the authors in [1] demonstrated how to create networks of connections between characters in literary works and domain networks with "general-specific" type connections.

This work is dedicated to describing a methodology for forming causal networks through repeated queries to LLMs, specifically ChatGPT (https://chat.openai.com/), as well as visualizing and analyzing these networks using Gephi (gephi.org) – the most popular free-license graph visualization software [15] – and the GrapViz-based software suite [16]. CSV format is suitable for uploading data to both Gephi and GrapViz.

The created causal networks will enable scenario analysis. The main challenge of conducting scenario analysis based on causal networks lies in the creation of such systems, which traditionally requires significant resources and expert involvement.

2.2.1 Forming the network based on a simple hierarchical query to LLM

The method for forming a causal network can begin with an example. Suppose we are interested in the issue of data leakage, and we ask the LLM to provide known causes of this phenomenon. The central node of the future network should be the concept of "data leakage." Successfully completing this query will determine the second level of the hierarchy – concepts related to data leakage, i.e., its causes. For each such concept, we also define a set of influencing factors. This process can go on indefinitely, but for this example, we will stop at three levels. Despite the hierarchical formation of such a causal network, the resulting network will not strictly adhere to a hierarchical structure.

A system like ChatGPT can assist in obtaining the contents of a CSV file. You can use the following prompt:

→List the causes of data leakage in cybersecurity. The reason is to use no more than three words. The results should be presented in the format "cause;data leakage." Each such entry – from a new line

The system responds approximately as follows (at the beginning of each pair, the cause is listed first, followed by the consequence – data leakage – after the semicolon):

- *human error; data leakage*
- *weak passwords; data leakage*
- *insider threats; data leakage*
- *misconfigured systems; data leakage*
- *etc.*

Subsequent queries will focus on the terms in the response, with prompts that follow the original structure, such as:

→List the causes of human error in cybersecurity. The reason is to use no more than three words. The results should be presented in the format "cause; human error." Each such entry – from a new line

The combined CSV file containing ChatGPT's responses is then passed for analysis and visualization. The resulting network is weakly connected and incomplete, with concepts that may not accurately represent the causes and effects. This is a network obtained from querying only one artificial expert.

2.2.2 Forming a network based on hierarchical queries from a swarm of virtual experts to ChatGPT

ChatGPT can produce different answers at various stages of text processing, which, from a human logic perspective, are entirely "reasonable." Each of these responses can be considered as coming from a virtual expert. By generalizing the responses of multiple such experts, we can obtain a more complete and accurate answer. To implement the swarm of virtual experts, we repeatedly ask the same queries, as in the previous case, for both the first and second levels of the hierarchy. After obtaining responses, they are combined into a single CSV file and passed on for analysis and visualization. In practice, the network can grow until it is sufficiently complete, as judged by a human expert.

The most influential nodes in this network (highest Out-Degree) are:

- *human error (7)*
- *social engineering (4)*
- *weak passwords (3)*
- *phishing attacks (2)*
- *unpatched systems (2)*
- *insider threats (2)*

The network formed in the previous example may contain inaccurate information due to errors made by ChatGPT during individual queries. Assuming that the probability of the same errors occurring is low, we can exclude from the network concepts that appear less frequently than a set threshold. In the following example (Figure 2.1), concepts that appeared fewer than two times were excluded.

The most influential nodes in this network (highest Out-Degree) are:

- *human error (5)*
- *social engineering (3)*
- *phishing attacks (2)*
- *unpatched systems (2)*

Based on expert evaluations, it can be concluded that the primary causal network, created through the simplest hierarchical queries to ChatGPT, includes a large number of concepts, which are relatively weakly connected. However, due to its completeness, it could serve as good "raw material for further analytical processing." Such a network is most suitable for subsequent scenario analysis.

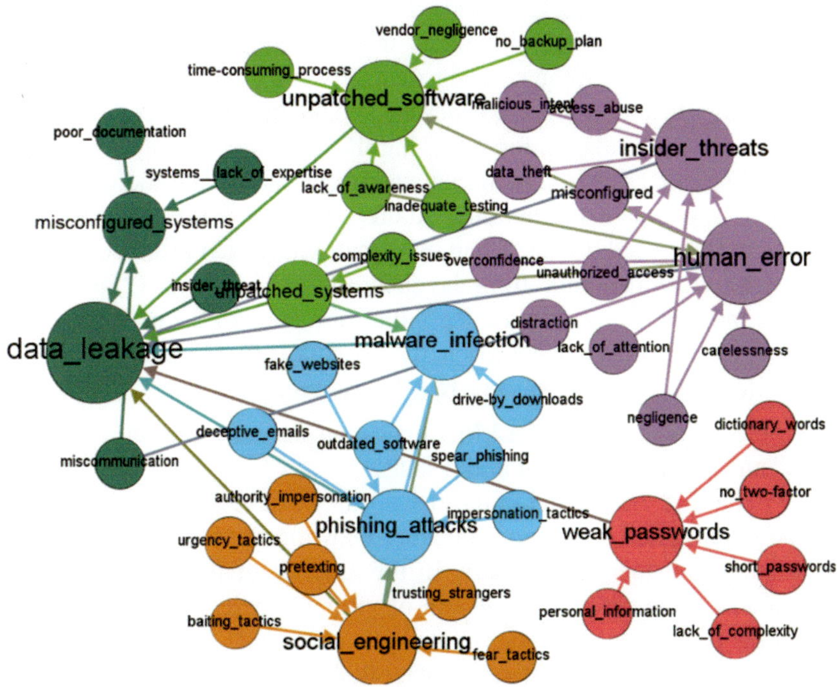

Figure 2.1 Directed causal network formed by generalizing the hierarchical queries from a swarm of virtual experts to ChatGPT.

2.3 Dynamic Networking Based on the Bidirectional Search Approach

2.3.1 Method description

The dynamic networking method is based on a bidirectional algorithm for forming causal networks, namely the formation and subsequent merging of two networks – the first network is built from the node representing the initial state of the problem (root cause), and the second from the node representing the goal to be achieved through the desired scenario [17]. The authors named the proposed algorithm "dynamic networking," which is close to the "bidirectional search" method, whose essence is to move from the initial state to the goal and from the goal to the initial state, in order to speed up the process of finding the optimal solution. The main idea is to connect the two processes once they "meet" at some stage.

The formed causal networks provide a direct transition to scenario analysis. In practice, the greatest difficulties in conducting scenario analysis based on causal networks lie in creating such networks, which in traditional cases require significant resource expenditure and the involvement of experts. After this, numerous scenarios for achieving the goal are generated, ranked according to various criteria. The initial state (root cause) and the goal are considered as input data for building future scenarios. Three sources of information may be used: (1) the ChatGPT system itself; (2) resources from the Internet; (3) documentation from the client (insight). Sources (2) and (3) are optional and may not be used for the initial formation of the network.

According to the proposed approach, the network is first formed based on the "initial state." The following steps may be used for this:

1. A prompt is formed to the LLM, suggesting decomposing the "initial state" and obtaining "partial initial states."
2. After obtaining the "partial initial states," they can be filtered according to the client's needs through dialogue, allowing the client to exclude those they consider unnecessary. In the absence of the possibility of dialogue, the approach of a "swarm of virtual experts" can be used to select the most significant states.
3. This step is optional and increases the reliability of the network. Roles of virtual experts for the chosen subject area are selected from LLM. Possible roles suggested by the system may include roles such as: business owner, partner, technical specialist, financier, etc. If this step is not performed, one can proceed directly to step 4.
4. Based on the "partial initial states" (or the latest in terms of the hierarchy of concepts), we ask LLM what "consequences" that improve the overall situation can be obtained from the presence of these concepts. As a result, LLM will provide a set of consequence concepts. These concepts are connected by directed edges from the corresponding latest concepts in the hierarchy.
5. Request from LLM what "consequences" can arise from the "consequences" obtained in the previous step, which will improve the overall state.

Each request to LLM can be applied several times on behalf of different virtual experts to duplicate important connections and reduce the weight of non-essential ones.

Simultaneously, the second half of the network is constructed as follows:

1. Using LLM, roles of virtual experts for the chosen subject area are selected. If this step is not performed, one can proceed to step 2 and simply use the general assessments of LLM.
2. Causes that may lead to the "goal" are queried from the AI system on behalf of the selected virtual experts. A subnetwork is built, in which directed edges lead from the concepts of "causes" to the "goal."
3. On behalf of the selected virtual experts, the causes of each cause concept obtained in step 2, which may lead to the goal, are queried. And so on.

The procedures are terminated once the first subnetwork, merged with the second half of the network, forms a connected component. In practice, it is recommended to continue building the network for one or two more steps on each side, supplementing the created network.

Both obtained partial networks are constructed based on the first source (LLM resources) and, if possible, the second (Internet) and third (insight). After forming both subnetworks, they are merged. All routes from the start to the goal are selected. The weights of these routes are calculated – this is a separate problem that has long been solved using optimization methods. It should be noted that LLM excels at solving this problem. After that, with the involvement of a human expert, the most important routes are determined in the form of a sequence of network nodes – the list of causes and consequences is provided to the client. In this case, LLM can beforehand provide several narrative chains ranked by formal criteria. If the user wants to rank the obtained narrative chains based on substantive criteria, they can also input appropriate prompts to LLM, such as "Rank the obtained narrative chains by price criteria."

2.3.2 Mathematical model

Basic Concepts and Notations

Let us define the basic concepts and notations:

- Graph: $G = (V, E)$, where V is the set of nodes (concepts), and $E \subseteq V \times V$ is the set of directed edges (connections).
- Initial state v_0 and goal v_f: Nodes representing the initial state of the problem and the desired goal.
- Partial states: Nodes representing intermediate concepts or sub-tasks.
- Virtual experts: A set of functions or algorithms that perform the role of experts in the system.

Formation of Subnetworks

Subnetwork from the initial state:

- Initial state: v_0.
- Recursively generate a subnetwork from v_0, adding vertices $v_1, v_2, ..., v_n$ and edges $(v_0, v_1), (v_1, v_2), ...$ at each step. Let $V_0 = \{v_1, v_2, ..., v_n\}$ be the current step, and $E_0 = \{(v_0, v_1), (v_1, v_2), ...\}$ be the index of added vertices. At each step, filtering based on the significance of states can be used.

Subnetwork from the goal:

- Initial node: v_f.
- Recursively generate a subnetwork from v_f, adding vertices $u_1, u_2, ..., u_m$ and edges $(v_f, u_1), (u_1, u_2), ...$.

Let $V_f = \{v_f, u_1, u_2, ..., u_m\}$ be the current step, and $E_f = \{(v_f, u_1), (u_1, u_2), ...\}$ be the index of added vertices.

Combining subnetworks:

The final network is formed by combining the subnetworks generated from the initial state and the goal:

$$G = \left(V_0 \bigcup V_f, E_0 \bigcup E_f\right). \tag{2.1}$$

If $v_i \in V_0$ and $u_j \in V_f$ are identical, they are merged, and the weights of edges are summed.

Selection of optimal routes:

- A route P is a sequence of nodes $v_0 \to v_1 \to \cdots \to v_f$.
- The weight of a route is calculated as the sum of the weights of edges:

$$w(P) = \sum_{(v_i, v_j) \in P} w(v_i, v_j), \tag{2.2}$$

where $w(v_i, v_j)$ is the weight of the edge between nodes v_i and v_j.

- Optimal route: A route with the minimum sum of weight values:

$$P_{\text{opt}} = \arg\min_P w(P). \tag{2.3}$$

Each request to LLM can be modeled as a function $f_{\text{GPT}}(v_i)$, generating a set of possible next nodes $\{v_j\}$ and corresponding connections (v_i, v_j).

Construction of the final network:

The algorithm for constructing the final network can be represented as a recursive process of graph formation:

1. Construction of the subnetwork from the initial state:

$$G_0 = \mathrm{BuildNetwork}(v_0, f_{\mathrm{GPT}}). \quad (2.4)$$

2. Construction of the subnetwork from the goal:

$$G_f = \mathrm{BuildNetwork}(v_f, f_{\mathrm{GPT}}). \quad (2.5)$$

3. Combination of subnetworks: $G = G_0 \bigcup G_f$.

Selection and ranking of routes:

After constructing the complete network, standard optimization methods (e.g., Dijkstra's algorithm) can be used to select and rank the best routes, or qualitative criteria can be applied by consulting experts, whether real or virtual.

2.3.3 Example of forming a causal network through dynamic networking

As a simplified demonstration of scenario generation using the proposed method, let us consider the task of market capture in the mobile communications sector by a specific mobile operator in a particular region. To achieve this, we generate a causal network in which we treat "mobile operator" as the initial state and "market capture" as the goal, or the final state. At the decomposition stage of the initial state, we introduce the prompt:

Prompt: Decompose the concept of "mobile operator." Provide 10 main entities (no more than three words each).

As a result, ChatGPT provides the following responses:

- *communication Services*
- *wireless connection*
- *telephone infrastructure*
- *cellular networks*
- *transfer data*
- *etc.*

Using the "swarm of virtual experts" approach, we repeat the request multiple times. After that, we simulate a client by applying a prompt that includes all the responses:

Prompt: Select the 10 most important from the already named entities: Communication Services; Wireless Connection; Telephone Infrastructure; Cellular Networks; Transfer Data; Communication Subscribers; Tariff Plans; Technical Support, etc.

Next, queries are made for each partial initial state. For simplicity, we will consider only two roles: the general role and the partner role.

Prompt (Role 1, Concept 1): What consequences might arise from the mobile operator having favorable tariffs? Name 10 consequences – concepts with no more than three words each.

Prompt (Role 2, Concept 1): What consequences could result from the mobile operator having favorable tariffs from the partner's perspective? Name 10 consequences – concepts with no more than three words each.

Prompt (Role 1, Concept 2): What "consequences" might arise from the mobile operator having high-quality communication? Name 10 consequences – concepts with no more than three words each.

Prompt (Role 2, Concept 2): What are the consequences of the mobile operator having high-quality communication from the partner's perspective? Name 10 consequences – concepts with no more than three words each.

This process continues for all defined concepts in a hierarchical manner according to the specified algorithm.

Next, we form a second subnet, which should formally conclude with the state of "market capture." Of course, we construct this network from the end. For this, the following prompts are introduced:

Prompt (1, Goal): List 10 reasons why mobile operators capture markets in small villages. Each reason should consist of no more than three words. Provide the answer in the format "reason; market capture." Each entry is a separate statement. Provide concepts without explanation.

Prompt (2, Goal): Name 10 reasons that could lead to market capture by mobile operators in a small town from the partner's perspective. Each reason should consist of no more than three words. Provide the answer in the format "reason; market capture." Each entry is a separate statement. Provide concepts without explanation.

Next, for each of the reasons, according to the algorithm, queries of the type are introduced:

Prompt: Name 10 reasons that could lead to innovations to capture the mobile operators' market in a small town from the partner's perspective. Each reason should consist of no more than three words. Provide the answer in the format "reason; Innovation." Each entry is a separate statement. Provide concepts without explanation.

Thus, according to the above algorithm, a second subnet related to the target state is formed. By combining the two networks, defined by the unconnected responses from the ChatGPT system, we obtain a joint network, which subsequently serves as the basis for forming narrative chains.

2.3.4 Formation of narrative chains by formal criteria

To form narrative chains according to the constructed model, the following prompt is entered into ChatGPT:

Prompt: Based on the constructed network, issue several chains leading from the "mobile operator" node to the "market capture" node.

LLM response:

- Chain 1: Mobile operator; Quality of service; Loyalty of subscribers; More subscribers; Capturing the market
- Chain 2: Mobile operator; Marketing strategies; Partnership relations; Partnership success; Capturing the market
- Chain 3: Mobile operator; Wide coverage; More customers; Capturing the market
- Chain 4: Mobile operator; Flexible rates; Subscriber loyalty; More customers; Capturing the market
- Chain 5: Mobile operator; Innovations; Unique services; Capturing the market

2.3.5 Ranking of narrative chains by significant characteristics

Below are the results from the ChatGPT system, which ranks the obtained narrative lines according to the following criteria: price factor, time, and implementation risks. To rank the chains by price factor, the following prompt is entered:

Prompt: Expertly rank the given chains in terms of the price factor.

In response, the LLM provides:

- Chain 2: Mobile operator; Marketing strategies; Partnership relations; Partnership success; Capturing the market
- Chain 5: Mobile operator; Innovations; Unique services; Capturing the market

- Chain 1: Mobile operator; Quality of service; Subscriber loyalty; More subscribers; Capturing the market
- Chain 3: Mobile operator; Wide coverage; More customers; Capturing the market
- Chain 4: Mobile operator; Flexible rates; Subscriber loyalty; More customers; Capturing the market

2.3.6 Visualization and analysis of networks

When using traditional tools for analyzing and visualizing network structures, such as Gephi or Neo4j, analysts face two main issues:

1. The need to install software products, which is not always possible, especially when working with mobile devices, new operating systems, or in environments with restrictions on installing third-party software.
2. The necessity to understand the functioning of these systems, dealing with dozens of parameters, graph layout modes, clustering, and so on.

If online analytical systems for graph visualization can help with the first problem, among which the authors believe the Lite version of the Gephi system – Gephi-Lite (https://gephi.org/gephi-lite) – and the web version of the Graphviz system – WebGraphviz (http://www.webgraphviz.com) – are noteworthy, then the need for developing a proprietary service has arisen to address the second task within the operational construction and representation of subject area models.

To solve the problem of graph visualization and analysis and to avoid the aforementioned issues, a program was developed based on the library (API) of the Graphviz system, which became the foundation for the CSV2Graph service (https://bigsearch.space/uli.html), currently available online at https://bigsearch.space/uli.html. This service provides initial analysis and visualization of graphs, where the information corresponds to the CSV format, with each record representing a pair of entities separated by a semicolon (Figure 2.2).

The program interface includes a network generated using CSV2Graph, as well as additional statistical information about this network (the number of nodes, connections, network density, and a list of all nodes and connections along with their weight values). Thus, the proposed CSV2Graph program addresses two main issues related to the use of traditional network visualization tools, such as Gephi or Neo4j: it allows working with graphs without the need to install software and simplifies the process of configuring visualization parameters.

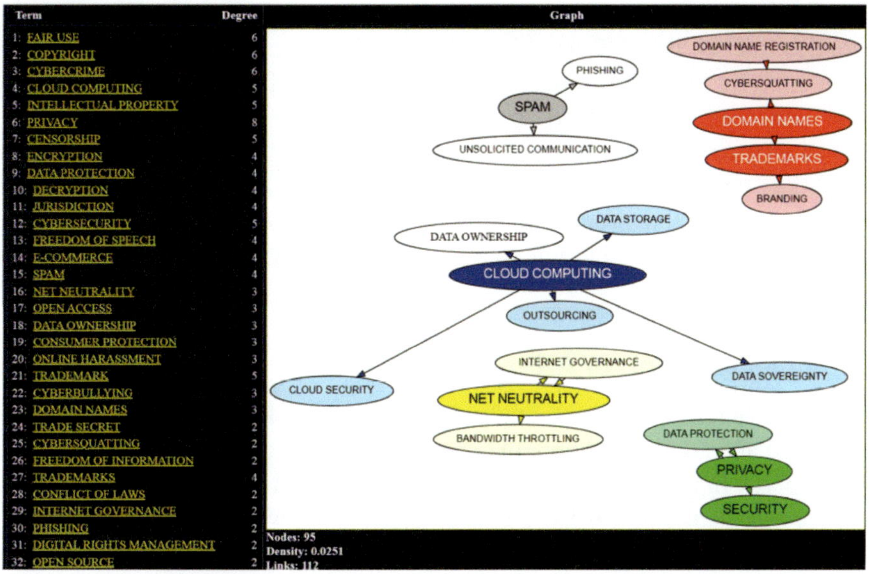

Figure 2.2 Graph generated from a CSV formatted database.

2.4 Hierarchy Analysis Method

2.4.1 Description of the hierarchy analysis method

The analytic hierarchy process (AHP) was developed by American mathematician Thomas Saaty in the 1970s and is used to structure complex problems that require consideration of multiple criteria. It helps in making decisions based on a logical and rational comparison of alternatives. AHP is a systematic approach to structuring decision-making tasks in the form of a hierarchy or network. Starting with defining the main goal at the top of the hierarchy, other elements are placed at intermediate levels. These intermediate levels consist of criteria that determine the importance of selecting an alternative and influence subsequent levels. At the lowest level are specific alternatives.

Over the years, AHP [4] and the analytic network process (ANP) [5], its evolution, have played a significant role among expert decision support methods. The widespread adoption of these methods has always been hindered by the challenge of selecting experts, who were always in short supply. Now, with the technological revolution driven by the development of LLM systems [1, 2], the possibility of addressing this challenge through so-called virtual experts [14] has emerged. The study [18] demonstrates and justifies the application of ChatGPT specifically for the field of cybersecurity.

The analytic hierarchy process, traditionally used for decision-making, can be enhanced and adapted to modern conditions through the use of LLMs and virtual experts. In this approach, AHP is integrated with LLMs, which create and process semantic networks. The use of LLMs allows for the automation of the process of creating and analyzing such networks, significantly reducing the burden on experts and increasing decision-making efficiency.

2.4.2 Implementation of AHP with LLMs

The analytic hierarchy process, traditionally used for decision-making, can be enhanced and adapted to modern conditions through the use of LLMs and virtual experts. In this approach, AHP is integrated with LLMs, which create and process semantic networks. The use of LLMs allows for the automation of the process of creating and analyzing such networks, significantly reducing the burden on experts and increasing decision-making efficiency.

In the traditional implementation of AHP, experts perform tasks such as pairwise comparison of criteria and alternatives, as well as assessing their relative importance. In the LLM-based approach, these tasks can be distributed among virtual experts, each fulfilling a specific role, such as hierarchy-building experts, pairwise comparison experts, data analysis experts, and mentor experts.

To implement AHP using LLMs for building the hierarchy and forming criteria and alternatives, "virtual experts" are engaged and assigned appropriate roles. Consider the example of applying AHP where the goal is to ensure cybersecurity. To determine the roles of virtual experts, the LLM system is prompted with the following:

Prompt: Provide five expert roles from whose perspective cybersecurity issues can be considered.

In response to this request, the system produces:

Cybersecurity issues can be considered:

- *Cybersecurity Analyst*
- *Ethical Hacker (Penetration Tester)*
- *Network Security Engineer*
- *Compliance Officer*
- *Chief Information Security Officer (CISO)*

Since this decision is deemed accurate by the authors, these "virtual experts" with these roles are subsequently used to determine the criteria for cybersecurity.

2.4.3 Criteria determination

Criteria represent a separate level of the hierarchy being constructed. The procedure for determining the main criteria for ensuring cybersecurity involves multiple interactions with the ChatGPT system on behalf of different experts, taking into account various responses and highlighting the most frequently mentioned ones (the final list of criteria can, of course, be confirmed by a human expert). Below is a prompt for determining cybersecurity criteria, formulated on behalf of the "Cybersecurity Analyst" expert, along with the corresponding response from the ChatGPT system:

Prompt: Identify the five main cybersecurity criteria from the perspective of a Cybersecurity Analyst.

Response from ChatGPT:

- *threat detection*
- *vulnerability assessment*
- *incident response*
- *security monitoring*
- *security policies*

Summarizing the responses obtained from all the aforementioned virtual experts, the criteria are as follows:

- *access control*
- *incident response*
- *security awareness*
- *security policies*
- *threat modeling*
- *vulnerability assessment*
- *encryption*

2.4.4 Definition of alternatives

To determine alternatives (the third level of the hierarchical network), a procedure is implemented that involves multiple interactions with the ChatGPT system, where the criteria from the previously defined list are specified, and possible options for their implementation are requested.

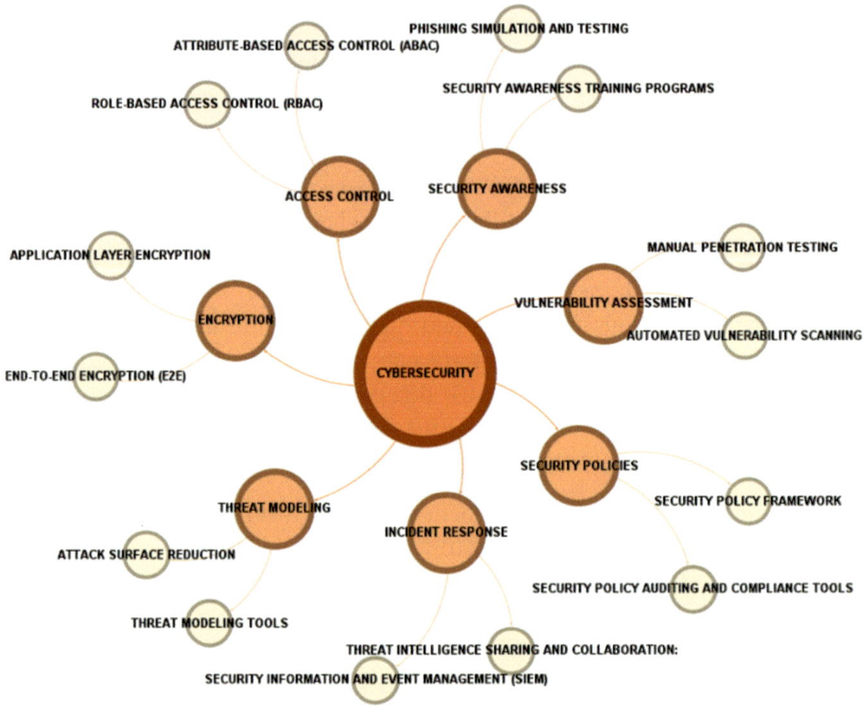

Figure 2.3 Simplified AHP hierarchy for the goal of "Ensuring Cybersecurity."

Below is the prompt for determining alternatives for the criterion "access control" and the response from the ChatGPT system.

Prompt: Name two primary alternative solutions for addressing cybersecurity ACCESS CONTROL criteria.

Response from ChatGPT:

- *Role-Based Access Control (RBAC)*
- *Attribute-Based Access Control (ABAC)*

As a result of the responses from the ChatGPT system to similar requests, we obtain a list of alternatives, thereby forming the entire hierarchy, as depicted in Figure 2.3 .

2.4.5 Weights of criteria and alternatives, consistency

The procedure for determining weight coefficients from pairwise comparisons can be used to assess the priorities of the criteria themselves as well as to evaluate alternatives based on pairwise comparisons conducted by experts for both criteria and alternatives. A pairwise comparison matrix is inputted. The matrices for both criteria and alternatives are formed in the same manner; so let us consider, for example, the matrix of alternative comparisons **A** (with elements being a_{ij}). Alternatives are compared pairwise by experts, and their responses are then aggregated (averaged overall). If a numerical assessment of the preference for alternatives A_i and A_j yields a value of preference a_{ij}, then in the reverse comparison, the preference is assessed as the reciprocal value: $1/a_{ij}$. Clearly, the preference when comparing an alternative to itself is evaluated as 1.

To determine the weight coefficients of the alternatives (or criteria, if criteria comparisons are being considered), it is sufficient to find the eigenvectors of matrix **A**. The values of the eigenvector of this matrix corresponding to the maximum eigenvalue will serve as the weight coefficients for the criteria (the weight coefficient – the element of the eigenvector corresponds to the criterion number). However, this approach is meaningful only if the pairwise comparison matrix is consistent. To verify the consistency of the comparison matrix, a consistency ratio $\mu$is computed. It is calculated using the following formula:

$$\mu = \frac{|\lambda_{\max} - n|}{n - 1}, \tag{2.6}$$

where $\lambda_{\max}$ is determined as follows: from the values of the comparison matrix and the values of the eigenvector, a matrix **E** is constructed where each element e_{ij} is defined such that $e_{ij} = a_{ij}\frac{w_i}{w_j}$, where w_i, w_j are the elements of the eigenvector.

After this, the sum of the elements of matrix **E** is calculated for each row, and the maximum value $\lambda_{\max}$ is selected. If the alternative matrix is fully consistent, then $\lambda_{\max} = n$; otherwise, $\lambda_{\max} > n$. There is a table of consistency indices [2], which contains values of benchmark indices for different values of $n - \mu_T(n)$. If $\mu/\mu_T(n) < 0.1$ is less than the corresponding value in the consistency index table, then the alternative matrix is considered consistent.

2.4.6 Model calculation

To determine the pairwise comparison matrix of criteria, the system ChatGPT is consulted on behalf of virtual experts to assess the importance of a selected criterion relative to all other criteria. Below is an example of a prompt in which the criterion "ENCRYPTION" is compared with others:

Prompt: The values for ensuring the cybersecurity criterion "ENCRYPTION" need to be determined through expert judgment in comparison to the criteria listed below. Please provide only one generalized comparative numerical expert assessment for each criterion (in terms of times). The criteria and assessments should be presented in the form of a list. Please provide an assessment of the advantages of the "encryption" criterion for the following criteria: access control; incident response; security awareness; security policies; threat modeling; vulnerability assessment. To provide generalized numerical assessments of the impact of the "encryption" criterion compared to other criteria, you can use a scale where 1 corresponds to equal importance, less than 1 indicates lesser importance, and greater than 1 indicates greater importance.

The response from the ChatGPT system, which will serve as the basis for forming the corresponding column of the pairwise comparison matrix, is as follows:

- *access control: 1*
- *incident response: 0.7*
- *security awareness: 0.8*
- *security policies: 1.2*
- *threat modeling: 1.1*
- *vulnerability assessment: 1.2*

As a result of executing similar queries for all criteria, we obtain a pairwise comparison matrix (Table 2.1).

The matrix obtained in this way can be viewed as two matrices produced by two groups of virtual experts, based on the prompts given for comparing each criterion with every other one. Therefore, calculations were performed for each of these matrices, and the results are meaningfully close. The matrices turn out to be consistent according to the specified criterion. The

Table 2.1 Pairwise comparison matrix of criteria.

Criteria	1	2	3	4	5	6	7
1	1	0.9	0.8	0.8	1.2	0.9	1
2	1	1	0.9	0.9	0.9	1.1	0.7
3	0.9	1.1	1	0.8	0.8	0.8	0.8
4	1.2	1.2	1.2	1	1	1	1.2
5	1.1	1	1.1	1.1	1	1	1
6	1.3	1.3	1.1	1.2	1.1	1	1.1
7	1.1	1.1	0.9	1.1	0.9	0.9	1

vector of average weights for the two matrices is as follows: (0.35; 0.35; 0.35; 0.40; 0.39; 0.41; 0.38). From this, we can conclude that the criteria are close in importance, with the most influential being the fourth and sixth (security policies and vulnerability assessment).

To determine the pairwise comparison matrix of alternatives, the ChatGPT system is queried for an assessment of the importance of each selected alternative relative to all other alternatives, for example:

Prompt: You need to determine the advantages of the "application layer encryption" concept for cybersecurity compared to the concepts listed below through expert judgment. Please provide only one generalized comparative numerical expert assessment for each concept (in terms of times). The concepts and assessments should be presented in the form of a list. Please provide an assessment of the advantages of the "application layer encryption" concept for the following concepts:

- *attribute-based access control (abac)*
- *security information and event management (siem)*
- *threat intelligence sharing and collaboration*
- *role-based access control (rbac)*
- *automated vulnerability scanning*
- *etc.*

The response from the ChatGPT system, which serves as the basis for forming the corresponding column of the pairwise comparison matrix of alternatives, is as follows:

- *attribute-based access control (abac): 0.8*
- *security information and event management (siem): 0.9*
- *threat intelligence sharing and collaboration: 0.9*
- *role-based access control (rbac): 0.8*
- *etc.*

As in the previous case, calculations were performed for each of these matrices, and similar weight values were obtained. The matrices turned out to be consistent according to the established criterion. The vector of average weights for the two matrices is as follows: (0.29; 0.28; 0.24; 0.23; 0.27; 0.28; 0.24; 0.24; 0.26; 0.26; 0.27; 0.27; 0.30; 0.28). It can be concluded that the identified alternatives are close in their importance, with the most influential being the 1st and 13th (attribute-based access control and security policy auditing and compliance tools).

2.4.7 Comparison of AHP with traditional methods and through the application of LLM systems

With the advancement of technology, new opportunities for implementing AHP arise, particularly through the use of LLMs. Implementing AHP through the application of LLMs and virtual experts offers significant advantages compared to traditional methods. It ensures high consistency of results, emulates the work of a large number of experts, allows for the processing of high-dimensional tasks, accelerates the decision-making process, and makes results clearer and more accessible:

- Virtual experts can perform pairwise comparisons of a large number of criteria and alternatives simultaneously, reducing the likelihood of errors and increasing the consistency of results.
- LLM-supported virtual experts can imitate the work of many human experts, significantly lowering the costs associated with their engagement.
- The use of LLMs allows for the processing of tasks with a large number of criteria and alternatives due to automated data processing and utilization. Thanks to the automation of processes and the use of virtual experts, the speed of decision-making is significantly enhanced.
- Semantic networks provide a clearer and more visual representation of data and results. This enables users without specialized training to better understand and make decisions based on the model, increasing the overall accessibility of the approach.

2.5 Conclusion

The chapter presents a detailed analysis of the capabilities of large language models (LLMs) in supporting decision-making in complex systems. The main idea of the article is the integration of LLMs into traditional decision-making methods, such as the analytic hierarchy process (AHP), and the implementation of new approaches to forming causal networks. It demonstrates how the proposed methodology for the automatic formation of semantic networks, which reflect causal relationships between concepts, is realized through the simulation of expert work. Thus, the use of LLMs in creating scenarios for event development and predicting possible outcomes of decisions enhances analysts' capabilities in making informed decisions. The utilization of large language models in decision-making processes provides significant advantages, including the automation of data collection and analysis, the formation of semantic networks, the simulation of expert work, support for hierarchical decision-making models, scenario analysis, and ensuring the clarity of decisions for all participants in the process.

References

[1] D. Lande, L. Strashnoy, 'GPT Semantic Networking: A Dream of the Semantic Web - The Time is Now', Kyiv: Engineering, 2023, 168 p. ISBN 978-966-2344-94-3

[2] S. Wolfram, 'What Is ChatGPT Doing ... and Why Does It Work? ', Wolfram Media, Inc., March 9, 2023, 112 p. ISBN-13: 978-1-57955-081-3

[3] V. Slyusar, 'AI as expert for Analytic hierarchy process', Research Gate discussion. 16 Nov. 2020, Available: https://www.researchgate.net/post/AI_as_expert_for_Analytic_hierarchy_process

[4] T. L. Saaty, 'The Analytic Hierarchy Process', McGraw-Hill, 1980. ISBN: 0070543712

[5] T. L. Saaty, L. G. Vargas, 'Decision Making With The Analytic Network Process', Springer, 2006. ISBN: 9781441941541, 1441941541

[6] 'ChatGPT AI Revolution 2023: A Guide to ChatGPT Technology and Its Social Impact,' Technology Summary, 2023, 64 p. ISBN 9798377089148

[7] S. J. Russell, P. Norvig, 'Artificial Intelligence: A Modern Approach', Global Edition, 4 ed., Pearson, 2021. ISBN: 9780134610993

[8] I. Nguyen , 'LLM Adoption in the Enterprise', O'Reilly Media, Inc., 2024. ISBN: 9781098151645, 9781098151621

[9] Y. Kondratenko, A. Shevchenko, Y. Zhukov, V. Slyusar, M. Klymenko, G. Kondratenko, O. Striuk, 'Analysis of the Priorities and Perspectives in Artificial Intelligence Implementation', Proc. In. 13th International IEEE Conference "Dependable Systems, Services and Technologies" (DESSERT'2023), Greece, Athens. October 13-15, 2023. DOI:10.1109/DESSERT61349.2023.10416432

[10] Y. Kondratenko, G. Kondratenko, A. Shevchenko, V. Slyusar, Y. Zhukov, M. Vakulenko, 'Towards Implementing the Strategy of Artificial Intelligence Development: Ukraine Peculiarities', CEUR Workshop Proceedings, vol. 3513, 2023, pp. 106-117, https://ceur-ws.org/Vol-3513/paper09.pdf

[11] V. I. Slyusar, Y. P. Kondratenko, A. I. Shevchenko, T. V. Yeroshenko, 'Some Aspects of Artificial Intelligence Development Strategy for

Mobile Technologies', Journal of Mobile Multimedia, Vol. 20(3), pp. 525–554, 2024. DOI:10.13052/jmm1550-4646.2031

[12] A. Handler, K. R. Larsen, R. Hackathorn, 'Large language models present new questions for decision support', International Journal of Information Management, Volume 79, 2024, 102811. DOI: https://doi.org/10.1016/j.ijinfomgt.2024.102811.

[13] A. Mekrache, A. Ksentini, Ch. Verikoukis, 'Intent-Based Management of Next-Generation Networks: an LLM-centric Approach', IEEE Network, 2024. DOI: 10.1109/MNET.2024.3420120

[14] D. Lande, L. Strashnoy, 'Hierarchical Formation of Causal Networks Based on ChatGPT', SSRN Preprint 4440629, 2023. DOI: 10.2139/ssrn.4440629

[15] Ken Cherven, 'Mastering Gephi Network Visualization', Packt Publishing, 2015. 378 p. ISBN: 1783987340, 9781783987344

[16] T. Triantoro, 'Graph Viz: Exploring, Analyzing, and Visualizing Graphs and Networks with Gephi and ChatGPT', ODSC Community, March 30, 2023.

[17] D. Lande, L. Strashnoy, O. Driamov, 'Implementation of Dynamic Networking Utilizing Generative AI Technologies', SSRN Preprint 4547440, 2023. DOI: http://dx.doi.org/10.2139/ssrn.4547440

[18] D. Lande, I. Svoboda, 'Enhancing Multi-Criteria Decision Analysis with AI: Integrating Analytic Hierarchy Process and GPT-4 for Automated Decision Support', E-preprint ArXiv. DOI:10.48550/arXiv.2402.07404

3

Applications of Large Language Models in the Military Sphere

V. I. Slyusar

Central Research Institute of Armaments and Military Equipment of Armed Forces of Ukraine, Ukraine, Institute of Artificial Intelligence Problems, Ukraine
E-mail: swadim@ukr.net

Abstract

This chapter explores the transformational impact of large language models (LLMs) on modern military operations, particularly in the context of hybrid and conventional warfare. The focus is on the role of LLMs in improving decision-making, intelligence analysis, and operational efficiency, as evidenced by the experience of the Russian–Ukrainian war. The chapter also examines the capabilities of multimodal LLMs for processing images, audio, and video, as well as their use in autonomous systems and cybersecurity. Additionally, the chapter analyzes the future potential of LLMs for enhancing decision support systems and proposes the application of multi-agent LLMs in military technology and virtual reality (VR). The integration of LLMs into VR enables the creation of personalized, adaptive, and realistic training, significantly improving the preparation of military personnel.

Keywords: Large language model, large action model, chain of thought, virtual reality.

3.1 Introduction

In the modern era, when technological innovations are rapidly transforming almost all spheres of life, the military sector is no exception. Among the

DOI: 10.1201/9788743800989-3

numerous technological breakthroughs of recent years, artificial intelligence systems hold a special place, opening new horizons for military applications and potentially revolutionizing decision-making processes, intelligence analysis, communication, and training within the armed forces.

One of the first historical instances of artificial intelligence being used in combat operations, according to [1], was Israel's Guardian of the Walls operation, conducted in the Gaza Strip in 2021. In [1], this operation is described as the first war in which target identification was based on artificial intelligence algorithms. However, the capabilities of AI at that time were quite limited and were characterized, at best, by the ability to detect targets using neural network technologies for object detection [2] and attempts to apply not very advanced natural language processing (NLP) algorithms for centralized analysis of all information about the groups in the Gaza Strip. Nonetheless, this was an invaluable experience that permanently changed the technologies of armed conflict.

The subsequent war in Ukraine coincided with the emergence of the first large language models (LLM) and their rapid development. This refers to the official introduction of the ChatGPT intelligent chatbot by OpenAI in December 2022 [3–5] and the subsequent release of its alternatives in February 2023, based on publicly available versions of the LLaMA (Large Language Model Meta AI) family of language models by Meta AI [6]. The main idea of the LLaMA developers was to create models that, with fewer parameters, could demonstrate performance comparable to GPT-3 while using only publicly available datasets for training. For instance, the LLaMA-13B model outperformed GPT-3 (175B) in many metrics, despite being 10 times smaller in size. These developments opened new possibilities for the application of artificial intelligence in various aspects of the military sphere, a systematic description of which was provided in reports [7, 8].

In the midst of war, breakthrough technologies always become an integral part of human struggle. This time, large language models, born in artificial intelligence laboratories, have entered the fray, transforming the very nature of the war in Ukraine. Their capabilities quickly evolved toward multimodality, enabling functions for processing and generating images, audio, and video. In addition to GPT-4o, multimodality to varying degrees is provided by LLMs such as Gemini 1.5 Pro [9], Claude 3.5 Sonet [10], and Grok-2 [11]. Multimodal capabilities, although with less success, are also specialized by current versions of LLMs like Phi3.5-Vision [12], LLava 1.5 [13], Llama-3.2 Vision [14], Video-LLaVA [15], Qwen-2VL [16], and others.

One of the main advantages of large language models is their ability to process natural language data, allowing them to easily integrate into existing information systems and be used in various contexts. The latest breakthrough in the NLP capabilities of artificial intelligence is associated with OpenAI's o1 model [17], which in September 2024 demonstrated an IQ level of 120 [18] in a Mensa test [19], providing 71.4% correct answers (25 out of 35). This exceeds the average performance of many humans. Importantly, the model did not use training data to pass the tests, and such results indicate significant progress in the ability of artificial intelligence to master logical reasoning methods. Given these achievements, it is highly likely that future LLMs could exceed the IQ threshold of 140 by 2026 [18]. This projection is based on the current trajectory of improving LLM IQ levels through reinforcement learning and chain-of-thought methods, which enable artificial intelligence to solve increasingly complex problems. The further development of AI will lead to a noticeable increase in the impact of LLMs across various fields, including education, scientific research, and even political decision-making. In the military sphere, this means that LLMs at the level of o1 can become effective tools for analyzing large streams of intelligence data, predicting potential scenarios, automating routine tasks, and supporting strategic decision-making. These neuro-transformer models, given sufficiently powerful hardware resources, are capable of processing and analyzing millions of words and thousands of images per second, effectively becoming a kind of soldier on the digital front.

In a world where information has become the most valuable resource, its possession determines the winners and losers, which is why large language models are seen as a crucial tool for achieving information superiority at all levels of conflict. With their help, analysts successfully uncover hidden patterns and transform the chaos of information warfare into a comprehensible picture. LLMs help identify disinformation, predict the intentions and preferences of the enemy, and, in essence, become eyes and ears that never tire and a brain that knows no limits. This is precisely why leading global players are competing for control over these technologies, understanding that their power could change the course of history.

Given this, this section provides a detailed examination of how large language models are changing the nature of modern warfare, using the conflict in Ukraine as an example. Specific cases of LLM application, their impact on tactics and strategy, and potential directions for future technology development will be analyzed. The focus will be on the main trends emerging

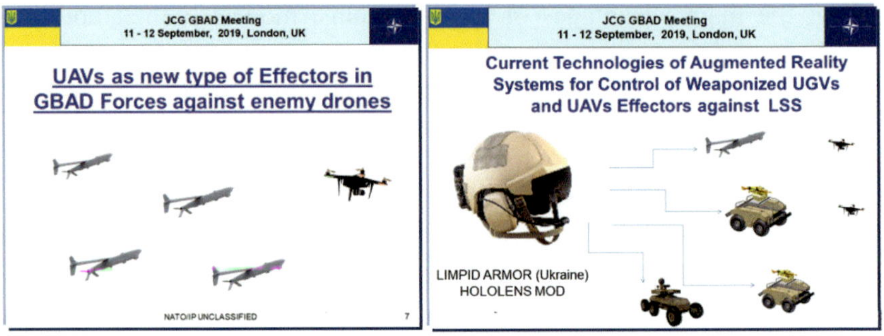

Figure 3.1 The author's ideas regarding the use of drones as anti-aircraft systems and the use of augmented reality glasses for controlling interceptor drones (September, 2019).

in the military domain, along with typical scenarios and use cases of LLM application, from strategic to tactical levels. It is quite likely that some of the relevant aspects may seem rather futuristic to some; however, in the context of rapid scientific and technological progress, such forecasts have a real chance of becoming a reality. Supporting this claim are characteristic examples of the author's personal predictions. For instance, in 2019, the author pointed out the feasibility of using UAVs as anti-aircraft systems and the use of first person view (FPV) mode for guiding interceptor drones (Figure 3.1), and in 2020, proposed the idea of forming aerial minefields using drones [20]. At that time, such ideas were met with some skepticism, but just a few years later, during the Russo-Ukrainian war, they became commonplace.

The following material will summarize the work of the author and other researchers carried out over the past few years, taking into account new technological and theoretical–practical achievements that have become available worldwide. At the same time, the main focus will be on priority areas where the application of LLM can be an effective solution, even given the current level of development of relevant technologies.

Speaking of understanding the role of LLM in the context of the war in Ukraine, it should be noted that it not only provides valuable lessons from the experience gained in contemporary military operations but also helps to predict future trends in military affairs and international security. This analysis is critically important for military leaders, politicians, and researchers, as it lays the foundation for developing effective strategies for the use of and counteraction to breakthrough artificial intelligence technologies in the military sphere.

3.2 Large Language Models in the Context of the War in Ukraine

Leading military analysts view artificial intelligence, based on LLMs, as a technology that can significantly enhance decision-making efficiency in hybrid and conventional military conflicts. In the context of hybrid warfare, LLM is seen as a tool for facilitating the analysis of large volumes of data from various sources – social media, communication systems, and satellite imagery – to identify patterns and potential threats. LLM-based systems provide continuous monitoring and inform operators about anomalous activities or environmental changes, enabling timely responses to potential risks.

In the realm of cyber operations, which are a critical component of hybrid wars, LLMs allow for faster and more accurate identification of cyber threats, prediction of possible attacks, and proactive responses. This opens up possibilities for automating certain cybersecurity measures, such as isolating compromised systems or deploying updates without human intervention. Similar transformations, driven by the emergence of multimodal LLMs, are taking place in the field of information and psychological warfare, where they are capable of analyzing demographic and psychographic data to develop disinformation or propaganda campaigns, increasing their effectiveness. A corresponding sentiment analysis service in real time allows operators to adjust strategies based on assessments of public mood patterns. The necessary technologies are being developed at the level of targeted and social advertising, psychological chatbot services, deepfake generators, and more.

Since the military doctrines of all nations anticipate the possibility of conventional wars, it is necessary to consider the role of LLMs concerning the development of such scenarios in international relations. As noted in [21–23], LLMs have already demonstrated their capabilities in various defense planning processes – ranging from justifying the requirements for individual soldier capabilities to forming the minimum necessary capability lists for entire military branches. The involvement of LLMs in strategic planning and modeling of different conflict scenarios during war games allows military planners to assess potential outcomes and develop optimal strategies [24]. Decision support systems built on LLMs integrate data from numerous sources, providing commanders with a comprehensive situational picture and suggesting optimal actions based on the automated analysis of combat reports and briefings. This reduces the cognitive load on military personnel [8], allowing them to focus on critically important tasks.

In logistics and supply chain management, LLMs can predict ammunition expenditure based on current and anticipated combat intensity, detect potential equipment failures, and proactively plan the maintenance of weapons and military equipment (WME). This approach enables the advance scheduling of repairs, taking into account the interoperability and achieved interchangeability levels of WME systems, and helps avoid unexpected equipment breakdowns during combat operations. As a result, the timely delivery of necessary materials to support missions is ensured, considering possible risks, while improving readiness levels and resource allocation efficiency.

In the field of training and simulations, generative artificial intelligence based on LLM is capable of creating realistic scenarios for tactical unit training. This allows military personnel to prepare for various situations without the need for live exercises, saving resources and time. The use of LLM agents at the level of autonomous or semi-autonomous systems capable of performing specific tasks is also crucial. In the war in Ukraine [21, 25], autonomous and semi-autonomous systems controlled by artificial intelligence, such as unmanned aerial vehicles (UAVs) and ground robotic platforms [26], are already being extensively used for reconnaissance, surveillance, jamming, demining [27], as well as conducting combat missions involving fire engagements. The further deployment of LLMs at this level is only a matter of time and financial capacity.

Beyond these use cases, LLMs have demonstrated the ability to coordinate the actions of multiple autonomous systems, such as drone swarms, to execute complex operations with high efficiency. This opens up new opportunities for carrying out complex tactical missions that require coordinated efforts between multiple systems simultaneously. The use of LLM as a personal assistant for a commander opens up additional opportunities for optimizing both management and combat processes. Specifically, the model can facilitate the automation of training schedules by taking into account personnel availability, weather conditions, the load on training grounds, and the availability of necessary resources. This ensures a balanced rotation of training types and provides timely rest for the unit, which is crucial for maintaining combat readiness. Additionally, LLM can be useful for analyzing weather conditions. Based on data from various sources, the model can provide accurate forecasts for specific locations, allowing climate factors to be considered when planning operations or training tasks. This is important for selecting appropriate equipment, vehicles, and routes, taking into account the predicted changes in soil conditions due to weather. By analyzing geological data, an LLM, using a model like NGNRMM (Next-generation

NATO reference mobility model) [28], can also make assumptions about soil stability, which is critical for vehicle movement, engineering fortifications, positioning equipment, and mining operations.

Another important aspect is the ability to perform ballistic calculations, as LLM can be tasked with accurately predicting the trajectories of projectiles, considering parameters such as distance, atmospheric conditions, weapon types, and ammunition. This enables the rapid adaptation of artillery fire to dynamic combat situations. Mission resource planning can also be improved through the analysis of battery charge forecasts and other energy resources. By tracking the charge levels of equipment, communication systems, and other devices, LLMs can predict when batteries will need recharging, which is particularly valuable for planning resource use during long-term missions.

The translation function in LLM allows for fast and accurate translation of both spoken and written messages, ensuring effective communication with foreign units or the local population in a multilingual environment. Additionally, LLM can be used for converting speech to text and vice versa. This enables commanders to dictate orders, reports, or other documents, as well as to vocalize text messages for quick and convenient information exchange. Notably, LLMs are capable of automatically generating standard messages, orders, or requests based on predefined templates, which accelerates responses to situational changes and reduces the commander's workload. In the context of summarizing reports, LLMs can quickly analyze large volumes of information and provide concise and clear summaries, allowing commanders to make informed decisions based on comprehensive and structured data. Furthermore, the classification and segmentation of textual data help organize information by task type, threat level, or other criteria, while automatic named entity recognition (NER) in texts highlights typical objects such as names, locations, dates, weapon types, and more. This simplifies the handling of large amounts of information and aids in quickly locating the necessary data. This same foundation supports the process of information filtering, which reduces information overload and highlights only the most critical data for the commander at any given time. Clearly, all of these capabilities improve unit resource management, planning efficiency, and decision-making on the battlefield.

At the platoon command level, access to LLM capabilities can be used to improve mission and combat planning by analyzing intelligence data and predicting possible scenarios. An LLM assistant [8] based on chain-of-thought technology can assist in the quick and accurate translation of intercepted foreign documents or voice messages. Given the widely recognized effectiveness of LLMs in educational processes [29], the involvement of such an LLM assistant should also be considered for helping to train platoon personnel by providing individualized learning materials and answering questions. In the field, LLM aids with navigation, suggesting optimal routes that consider terrain and potential threats. Additionally, the LLM assistant could support communication with other units, offer basic medical recommendations on first aid, diagnosis, and organizing the evacuation of the wounded, as well as assist in managing the unit's medical resources.

Thus, LLMs have substantial potential to transform both hybrid and conventional warfare of the future by enhancing effectiveness in intelligence gathering, cybersecurity, command and control, autonomous systems, and logistics. Of course, integrating LLMs into military operations must be done with caution, considering international humanitarian law, operational challenges, and legal implications. Therefore, responsible development and implementation of artificial intelligence technologies are crucial to maximizing their benefits and minimizing associated risks.

3.2.1 Local systems of LLM decision-making centers

The specifics of using LLM in the military sphere significantly depend on the type of information being processed. If decision-making only requires the use of non-confidential data, such as within the framework of OSINT, internet access to proprietary LLMs like OpenAI's o1 may be utilized. However, for processing confidential data, which is a more common case, it is necessary to deploy local versions of LLMs [30] at the level of the command post or unit headquarters.

To understand how a system with a local LLM functions, it should be viewed as a complex system of interconnected components (Figure 3.2). The central, system-forming element should be considered the high-performance data processing servers equipped with powerful processors and graphics cards. These are responsible for executing the computational tasks related to the operation of LLM, ensuring fast and efficient data processing.

These servers are connected to data storage systems, where the language models, training data, and processing results are stored. High-speed storage devices guarantee instant access to the necessary files, while backup systems protect against data loss. Frameworks for deep learning, such as TensorFlow or PyTorch, are used for model operation. They integrate with LLM and optimize computational processes, efficiently utilizing server resources.

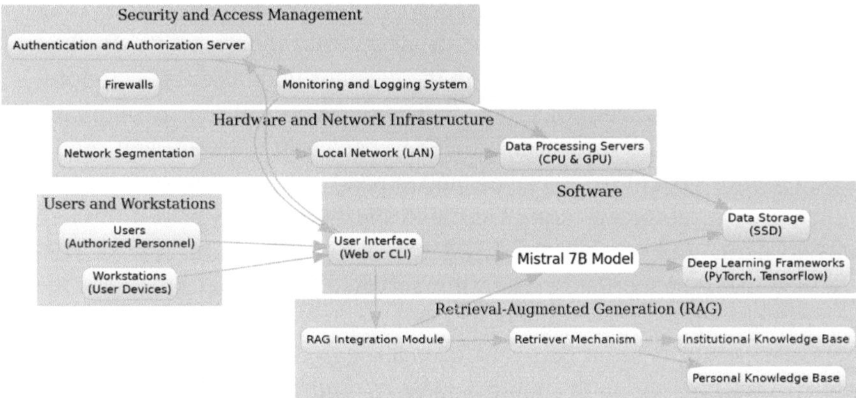

Figure 3.2 Command post system based LLM system with encryption/decryption.

Users interact with the system through a user-friendly interface, which could be a web application, specialized software, voice interaction, or the use of augmented reality symbols. Through this interface, they send requests to the model and receive the results of its operation. Access security is ensured by authentication and authorization systems, which verify users' identities and control their access rights. This ensures that only authorized individuals can utilize the system's capabilities.

The entire infrastructure operates within a local isolated network, which significantly enhances the level of security. The network has no connection to the internet, preventing unauthorized external access. For additional protection, firewalls and intrusion detection systems are used to monitor network traffic and track suspicious activity. To further this purpose, the network is divided into segments, allowing for the isolation of different system components and controlling access between them. Additionally, data is encrypted both at rest (on disks) and in transit (during transmission) using SSL/TLS.

The users of the system are authorized specialists, including staff officers, research analysts, or duty personnel at the command post, who work on workstations connected to the local network. Their actions are tracked by monitoring and logging systems, which help in overseeing the system's operation and responding to potential incidents, with the possibility of conducting audits when necessary. Security policies define the rules for accessing data and resources, and they regulate procedures for system updates and management.

Data management is a critical aspect of the system's operation. Data is entered and stored in compliance with all security requirements. Backup systems allow for rapid data recovery in the event of failures or other unforeseen circumstances. A team of IT specialists is responsible for maintaining and servicing the entire infrastructure. They carry out software and model updates, monitor system performance, and expand its capabilities as needed.

When a user submits a request through the interface, it passes through security systems and reaches the LLM model (in the figure, this is Mistral 7B [30, 31]) on the data processing servers. The model processes the request using deep learning frameworks and available data from the storage systems. The result is returned to the user through the same path, ensuring an information pipeline with minimal latency. Thus, a system with a local LLM is a comprehensive combination of hardware and software, network infrastructure, and security measures. Its effective operation depends on the coordinated work of all components and the precise management of their interactions. This allows the system to maximize the power of LLM while maintaining high performance and data protection.

An additional component that significantly enhances the system's functionality is the integrated retrieval augmented generation (RAG) mechanism [32]. This approach combines the power of a large language model with the ability to search for relevant information in external data sources or knowledge bases, beyond what the LLM contains. RAG integration occurs through an additional search module that closely interacts with the main language model. The RAG mechanism works in such a way that during the processing of a user request, the system not only analyzes the relevant text using LLM but also searches for relevant documents or records in a specialized data repository. This enables the model to retrieve up-to-date and specific information that may be missing from its internal parameters or training data. The retrieved information is transmitted, for example, via an internal API to the LLM, which uses it to generate more accurate and contextually grounded responses. This approach requires efficiently organized data storage and indexing mechanisms for quick access to information. The storage systems may contain combat orders, directives, report archives, technical documentation, internal reports, or any other relevant data. Importantly, all of this data is stored within a local isolated network, ensuring a high level of security and confidentiality.

From a security and access management perspective, the RAG mechanism is subject to the same policies as the main system. Access to the data repositories is controlled, and all user and system actions are logged for future auditing. This ensures that confidential information is not disclosed or misused. Integrating RAG also requires additional computational resources and support from IT specialists. They are responsible for updating the databases, optimizing search algorithms, and ensuring the system runs smoothly. Regular updates to the information in the repositories guarantee the relevance and accuracy of the responses, which is especially useful in military operations where up-to-date information, which can change quickly over time, is crucial.

The use of the RAG mechanism enhances the system's efficiency by improving response accuracy, enriching context, and allowing adaptability with the addition of new data to the repositories without the need to retrain the LLM. The new RAG 2.0 technology enables embedding not only textual but also multimedia data, which is particularly important for processing video data obtained from reconnaissance UAVs, raw SIGINT results, and other sources.

Thus, a system with an integrated RAG mechanism not only retains all the advantages of a local LLM but also significantly expands its capabilities. It becomes more adaptive, capable of quickly responding to new requests and providing information that aligns with operationally acquired data. This opens up new prospects for its use in various missions, enhancing the value and effectiveness of integrated solutions.

However, despite the significant capabilities provided by integrating the RAG mechanism with a local LLM, the next step in the development of a headquarters AI version could be transitioning to a multi-agent system in the form of the so-called large action model (LAM). This approach involves distributing functionality among several autonomous agents [33] (Figure 3.3), each specializing in specific tasks and interacting with others to achieve a common goal.

The rationale for this transition is driven by the need to enhance the system's flexibility, scalability, and efficiency. In the distributed architecture of multi-agent systems (Figure 3.3), each agent can be configured to perform specific functions: one may handle natural language processing, another may be responsible for data retrieval or data farming [34], and a third may focus on analytics, simulations, and decision-making. This allows for the optimization of each component for particular tasks, using the most advanced algorithms and technologies, thus improving reliability.

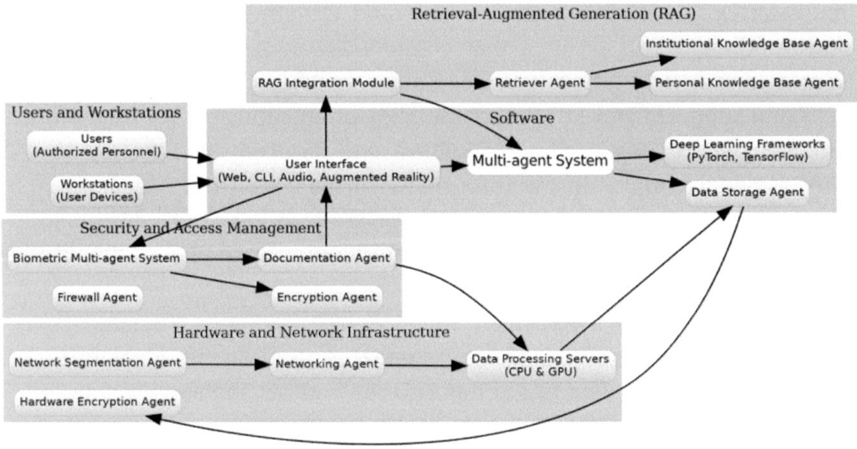

Figure 3.3 Improvement of distributed multi-agent system via use additional audio or augmented reality user interfaces.

3.2.2 The concept of a multi-agent active protection system for armored vehicles

Let us further consider the idea of creating an active protection system for armored vehicles based on a multi-agent system integrated with a digital architecture such as NGVA (NATO Generic Vehicle Architecture) [35]. The corresponding concept involves the creation of a comprehensive structure where each component interacts with others to achieve maximum protection efficiency. The system consists of sensor agents, data processing agents, and executive agents (Figure 3.4), all operating based on neural networks, small, and quantized large language models.

The sensor agents include radar sensors, SIGINT units, infrared and optical sensors, as well as acoustic and seismic detectors. Radars detect fast-moving objects, such as missiles or shells, as well as ground drones and strike UAVs. SIGINT units monitor the electromagnetic spectrum to detect signals characteristic of strike drones. Infrared and optical sensors capture thermal and visual signatures of potential threats, while acoustic sensors analyze sound waves to detect gunfire or the movement of equipment. In turn, seismic detectors, in addition to other means, can detect the approach of intruders planting explosives or walking robotic platforms. Moreover, when triggered by a mine, they can detect excessive vertical acceleration for subsequent active damping. Each sensor acts as an autonomous agent, collecting and transmitting data in real time.

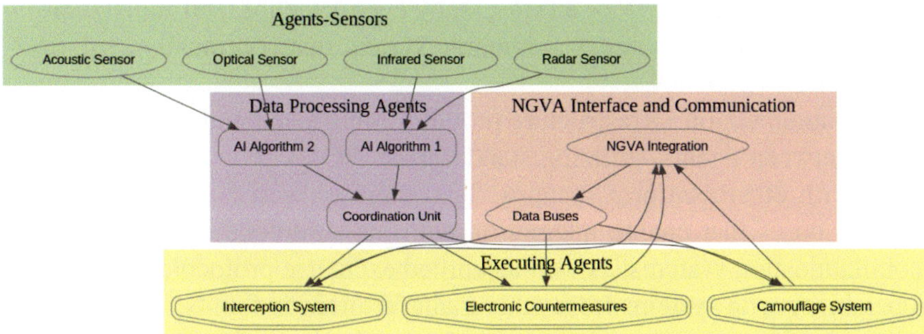

Figure 3.4 A typical structure of an active protection system for armored vehicles based on a multi-agent architecture.

Data processing agents use artificial intelligence algorithms to analyze information from the sensors. This segment of the multi-agent system operates on the principles of collective intelligence, where information exchange between agents occurs in real time. They identify the type, direction, and speed of threats, make decisions on the necessity of deploying countermeasures, and coordinate actions among themselves to enhance accuracy and response speed. This approach allows the system to adapt to changes in the combat environment, predict possible attack scenarios, and select the optimal methods for addressing the threat situation. For example, if one of the agents detects laser illumination from the guidance systems of anti-tank missiles, the system can immediately deploy smoke screens or activate electronic countermeasures by generating blinding or deceptive interference.

The activation of the necessary defense systems is carried out by executive agents, which are integrated with the active interception system, electronic countermeasures, and camouflage systems. Active interception systems physically destroy or deflect threats, electronic countermeasures block or distort the guidance signals of enemy systems, and camouflage systems deploy smoke screens or create electromagnetic interference. To dampen vertical acceleration during mine and improvised explosive device (IEDs) activation, the corresponding agent can trigger the detonation of specific sections of reactive armor elements to press the armored platform to the ground [36]. After responding in one of the considered ways, the system monitors the effectiveness of the actions and, if necessary, adjusts them. It can also update its models and algorithms based on the experience gained.

The use of artificial intelligence and machine learning technologies allows LLM-based agents to improve their detection and response procedures over time. They can analyze previous attacks, study enemy tactics, and adjust their actions accordingly. This creates a dynamic system that continually evolves and increases its efficiency.

The communication infrastructure provides high-speed and reliable data exchange between agents, utilizing standardized NGVA protocols for compatibility with other platform systems. The interface with NGVA includes digital data buses that enable integration with onboard control, navigation, and communication systems, as well as unified exchange protocols to ensure interoperability with systems from other manufacturers and units.

Interaction between agents is facilitated through data exchange on threats and system status, coordination of actions to avoid conflicts and duplication, as well as joint learning and adaptation to new threats via machine learning mechanisms. Integration with the NGVA digital architecture allows for automatic transmission of incident information to centralized management systems to enhance crew situational awareness, synchronize actions with other systems, such as the fire control system, for a comprehensive response to threats, and optimize energy consumption and the distribution of computational resources through shared use of platform resources.

Direct interaction with the crew is conducted through human–machine interfaces, which display the system's status and threats on screens in the form of augmented reality symbols. These interfaces also provide options for manual intervention or adjusting system parameters, as well as issuing warnings and recommendations in critical situations. Integration with NGVA ensures interoperability and modularity, allowing for easy integration of new components and updates without significant changes to the architecture, as well as the ability for coherent interaction with systems from other vehicles and units in the interest of collective defense.

An important feature of the multi-agent system is its resilience to damage. If one or several agents fail, others can compensate for their functions, ensuring continuous protection. This is achieved through a decentralized architecture, where there is no single critical node on which the entire system depends. Enhanced reliability is provided by redundancy of critical functions and data transmission pathways, as well as automatic switching to backup agents within the same or other armored vehicle systems in the event of primary failures. Advanced update capabilities include the rapid deployment of new algorithms and protocols via network connections and support for modern security and data encryption standards.

Thus, the multi-agent system, integrated with the NGVA digital architecture, creates a highly efficient and adaptive protection system for armored vehicles. It combines intelligent technologies, reliable communications, and the ability to cooperate with other systems, which is critically important in modern combat conditions. A combat vehicle protected in this way does not passively absorb attacks but actively interacts with the environment, protecting itself and the crew. This not only enhances survivability but also provides an advantage on the battlefield through a swift and effective response to any threats.

3.3 The Concept of Improving Virtual Reality Technologies Based on LLM/LAM for Training and Exercises

3.3.1 A general view on the potential application of LLM/LAM in VR systems

The analysis of best practices in the use of virtual reality (VR) systems for military unit training (Figure 3.5) highlights the relevance of the task of further developing VR technologies. One important direction in this regard is the use of LLM/LAM capabilities. Within the proposed concept, a conglomerate of LLM/LAM of various architectures and purposes should operate in the VR environment. Specifically, they can be employed to recognize voice commands given by each soldier involved in the training to virtual avatars of civilians during the clearing of buildings in a settlement, or to fellow servicemen for action coordination, among other uses.

The integration of LLM into VR holds the potential for multiple replays of training episodes, which helps reinforce professional skills and master action strategies under conditions that closely resemble real-world scenarios. Video recordings of each individual's behavior, made during joint training, should be analyzed using AI-tracking based on neural networks like YOLO [2, 21] (more modern versions such as YOLO8 or YOLO10), followed by analysis using LLM to assess both absolute and relative dynamics of changes in posture, the position/orientation of weapons or tools, and more. In addition to a comprehensive analysis of participants' actions, this will allow for the identification of mistakes and provide feedback, leading to improved training efficiency.

Multimodal LLMs, such as GPT-4o, Claude 3.5 Sonnet, and others, can generate a variety of tactical training scenarios while eliminating risks to the health and safety of military personnel. Such LLMs should be considered an effective tool for managing the behavior of virtual agents and their interaction with real training participants, especially since LLMs are

Figure 3.5 Typical military unit training with virtual reality (photo by the author).

capable of performing functions as personal assistants (mentors). Moreover, the ability of LLMs to adjust training loads depending on the individual skill level of each service member allows for the creation of personalized training trajectories and the acquisition of relevant experience.

The synthesis of a safe virtual environment can be carried out using generative neural networks that are capable of directly creating fragments or individual scenes in a synthetic virtual world. A promising direction is the generation of images and videos for VR based on textual instructions, utilizing the generative capabilities of multimodal LLMs to transform written narratives into realistic video scenes [37, 38]. With tools like Sora from OpenAI, Runway Gen 3, or Luma AI, this process of video scene generation becomes more streamlined. The creative workflow should begin with the collaborative creation of a detailed text description, for example, with LLM o1 from OpenAI, which will include not only the visual elements of the future virtual scene but also the atmosphere, emotional tone, character interactions, and any specific actions that need to be depicted. For instance, if the text describes a calm setting on the streets of a quiet town, o1 should be aware of the time of day, weather, the presence of wildlife or people, transportation, and descriptions of all sounds and the behavior of elements such as trees, grass, water, and others. To assist in generating appropriate prompts, it is advisable to leverage not only the potential of o1 but also alternative multimodal LLMs.

After inputting the prompt generated by the LLM, a Sora-like model will analyze the instructions, identifying key visual components and narrative cues (prompts), and will sequentially generate a 3D video scene that includes the specified elements. As a result, the AI will transform a traditional VR scene from a simple static image into a dynamic environment with the potential for interactivity, as required by VR. This task is simplified by the development of specialized neural networks for synthesizing artificial worlds, particularly for the creation of video games. For example, the Vidu neural network can generate video not only with a specific person's face but also with any object. In the future, generative AI technologies will provide content synthesis for VR video not only in 3D format but also panoramically, with 360° coverage, allowing the user to look around and feel truly present in the surrounding virtual environment when viewed through a VR headset.

At the same time, the directing LLM algorithms must account for the depth and scale of the virtual space, creating a parallax effect when the user moves their head, contributing to a sense of immersion. The generation of VR video also involves recreating motion in the surrounding environment, such as the gentle rolling of waves or the rustling of leaves in trees, which should be smoothly looped to achieve a realistic effect. Moreover, if the text prompt specifies interaction or movement of characters in a particular scene fragment, the scene synthesis LLM agent will animate those characters accordingly, ensuring the development of the narrative or interactive elements with which the user can engage.

The expansion of video generator functionality is supported by the introduction of video editing capabilities. Specifically, this feature (video-to-video) is implemented in the Gen 3 Alpha Video editor from Runway. It allows users to upload their video clips and modify them using text prompts, changing the style, lighting, time of day, weather, adding new movements, etc. This video editing process is highly precise, utilizing unique visual effects and offering broad creative possibilities.

In this context, the idea of scaling the chain-of-thought (CoT) technology for image and video generation is promising, particularly for improving output quality. Traditionally, CoT is used for text processing, where the model gradually thinks through the request, analyzes intermediate conclusions, and arrives at a final decision [39]. However, visual information is more complex to the process due to its multidimensional nature and subjective quality criteria, which means that extending CoT technology to video generation can be approached in several ways.

First of all, it is worth noting that the chain of thought can be adapted for the sequential generation and analysis of intermediate stages in the creation of an image or video. At each stage, the model could evaluate the alignment of the current result with the initial prompt, compare key parameters (shapes, colors, composition), and decide whether to make adjustments or continue the process. Image generation can be broken down into several steps, where the model gradually adds details, as artificial intelligence does not simply generate an image or video based on text-defined requirements but thinks, analyzes, and refines each step, much like a human striving for perfection.

In the initial stage, artificial intelligence begins with a rough sketch, forming a simple composition that sets the basic parameters for the future image – object outlines, their spatial relationships, and proportions. After synthesizing the overall frame structure, colors, textures, lighting, and shadows are added. At each step, the model uses CoT to check the quality of intermediate results and, after analysis, autonomously decides on further optimization. If the composition is not precise enough or deviates from the user's defined expectations, the LLM makes the necessary adjustments and moves on to the next stage. Each new layer of information passes through the chain of thought, where, based on its own set of metrics, the model evaluates the degree of alignment with the desired outcome and, if needed, selects optimal methods to improve the result. Essentially, artificial intelligence operates like an artist, critically assessing each brushstroke and hue, deciding whether to make changes or further develop the image.

Another direction could be the use of the CoT for analyzing generated images and VR video scenes by comparing them with reference examples or the initial prompt. The model could independently identify deviations, such as an incorrectly chosen color palette or disproportionate shapes, and make adjustments without user intervention. A key feature of this technology is that the process is not limited to a single attempt or version. The model can create several variations of the image, analyzing them in terms of aesthetics, compliance with requirements, and the accuracy of detail reproduction.

The application of CoT in this case allows for a gradual approach toward the ideal result, executing a cycle of generation and self-critical analysis. Each step provides an opportunity for the LLM to improve itself by remembering the most successful thought chains and, if necessary, returning to key branching points, significantly enhancing the quality of the final image.

The process of generating multiple versions of images or videos should conclude with the automatic selection of the option that best aligns with the director's vision, based on various criterion parameters. In this way, the model evaluates its intermediate options and gradually improves them through a series of iterations to get as close as possible to video scenes or images that are more intuitively understandable for the user.

However, looking at the problem from another perspective, relying on just one chain of thought (CoT) may become a bottleneck when dealing with complex tasks that require fast processing and parallel analysis of multiple aspects of the image. This is where the idea of mixture of experts (MoE) [40–43] comes into play, adding a new dimension to the process. Instead of a single thought chain handling every detail, multiple expert models work in parallel, each specializing in its own aspect of the image. For example, one expert focuses on colors and textures, another on light and shadow, and a third on form and composition. These experts work simultaneously but not in isolation; each interacts with the others through separate chains of thought, analyzing their conclusions and making decisions about further actions.

A possible approach is to involve the same expert in several different thought chains that intersect, partially overlap, or are nested within each other. This functionality is achieved through data caching and scaling computational capabilities and memory resources allocated to the corresponding expert. Naturally, the allocation of these resources can be adaptive, depending on the tasks, the number of created chains, and energy consumption. Adaptive management, monitoring, and control of the chains of thought should be entrusted to a separate LLM within the MoE architecture.

This distributed approach significantly accelerates the process of generating or editing video scenes without compromising quality. Each expert contributes to the final result, and the chains of thought coordinate their efforts, adjusting their work in real time. This allows for the generation of complex images that meet the highest aesthetic and functional standards without sacrificing performance. The described generative LLM concept not only follows instructions but also thinks critically, refining its decisions at every stage by leveraging the power of parallel thought streams from different experts, unified into a harmonious creative process.

As a result, the user receives an intelligent system capable of visual self-improvement, where the chain of thought not only assists in image generation but also ensures a continuous cycle of enhancement through critical analysis and interaction with other expert systems. This opens new horizons in the field of generative art and VR environment synthesis, where artificial intelligence can not only respond to requests but also create realistic works that impress with their depth and precision.

Another critically important component of VR is audio, which adds true realism to the virtual experience. Multimodal LLMs, such as MusicGen by Meta AI, Suno, and others, can generate or select spatial soundtracks [44, 45] that align with the visual content, ensuring that sounds in the environment come from the appropriate source and change as the user looks around or interacts with the scene.

The resulting audio-enhanced VR video must be encoded in a standardized format compatible with the hardware and software of the VR training systems, allowing for seamless playback and interaction by different users. The final product will be a VR experience that brings the initial text to life, allowing immersion into a world created by words, interpreted, and reproduced through the ingenuity of AI, such as Sora. In this way, AR symbols can also be incorporated within the VR environment, simulating the use of equipment by soldiers, such as the integrated visual augmentation system (IVAS), optical sights, or binoculars with AR symbols, and other devices. VR technologies provide opportunities for simulating the operation of various types of weapons and specialized equipment, thereby expanding the scope of training and reducing the need for the use of real weapons and equipment. In this context, LLM-controlled agents in VR can integrate control over vehicles, UAVs, ground robotic platforms with simulated video data acquisition from them, maintenance and repair systems for equipment, and more.

Moreover, an important direction is the use of LLMs to assess the current cognitive load on a soldier operating in VR. This can help prevent negative health impacts and the development of any disorders during prolonged VR training sessions under conditions of exhaustion.

The implementation of joint training exercises via VR and AI for military personnel from different units and countries will significantly improve coordination and teamwork. Thus, the integration of multimodal LLMs and LAM into VR technologies for military purposes will enhance the qualification of servicemen while ensuring their safety and saving material resources.

3.3.2 The use of LAM for virtual training and education of soldiers

Given the capabilities of LAM, they can be considered a tool capable of helping soldiers automate the management of the virtual training process based on project management technologies, organize their training materials, plan the learning schedule, and assess progress in knowledge acquisition by interacting directly with training platforms.

The proposed concept of improving VR technology based on LLM/LAM capabilities primarily focused on enhancing the quality of perception of the virtual world by trainees. However, beyond the realism of representing inanimate objects and nature during such training, it is necessary to ensure interactive simulations in synthetic training environments (Figure 3.2) of soldiers from friendly units and the enemy, reproducing human actions in mixed reality through the so-called avatars. This will allow the creation of longer event scenarios during training, with branching outcomes depending on the decisions made by the trainees, and allow to conduct as many virtual trainings as possible.

Thus, the idea is to create a virtual training environment where all participants are represented by avatars. Each soldier, wearing virtual reality glasses, sees their comrades as avatars performing various actions (Figure 3.6).

The virtual environment is controlled by a multi-agent LAM or a collection of them, which interprets the commands and intentions of soldiers and translates them into actions for avatars in the virtual space. By automating avatar control through LAM, it becomes feasible to conduct training with only one real soldier who needs instruction, while the rest of the partners are simulated by avatars.

A typical virtual training scenario is implemented in several key stages. In the first stage, the training process is initiated:

- The real soldier enters the virtual environment using VR glasses and checks the functionality of tracking markers on their body and weapon.
- LAM automatically generates avatars that represent other soldiers and manages the preparation of the virtual environment for training, ensuring that all necessary virtual equipment and materials are correctly selected.

Figure 3.6 A synthetic environment within virtual reality (DALL-E3).

Let us consider an example of a typical request for LAM to manage avatars within a virtual tactical training scenario. This could be a set of prompt-instructions: "Find cover and take a defensive position; check your ammunition and report readiness for attack; patrol the perimeter and report any suspicious activity." These commands must be interpreted by specifically trained LAM and realized in the form of avatar actions in the virtual training environment, ensuring accuracy and realism in movements and interactions.

Another example of a more detailed prompt might describe the requirements for the entire training process: "Initiate the virtual training environment with the necessary equipment and materials for the military simulation. Listen to the soldier commander's orders through a voice interface or wait for their description via text input. Interpret instructions given to soldiers related to the training, such as 'assemble the rifle, take cover, secure the perimeter, and log observations.' Translate these instructions into actions for the avatars in the virtual environment, ensuring precise and realistic movements and interactions. Provide real-time feedback to the soldiers based on their actions, for example, informing them if their cover is insufficient or if their ammunition is running low. In the event of an emergency, such as a nearby virtual explosion threat, instruct the avatar to retreat or take necessary defensive measures. Allow multiple soldier avatars to interact and communicate within the virtual space. At the end of the training, guide the soldiers through the process of a virtual debriefing and ensure the security of any virtual equipment. Provide a summary of the training results and suggest areas for improvement or further training."

This prompt essentially governs the operation of the LAM at all stages of the training. It can be clarified and expanded with the addition of further explanations or constraints.

Returning to the description of the training stages, it should be noted that in the second stage, the execution of commands by the real participants begins:

- The soldier in training accompanies their actions with voice commands, which are interpreted by LAM. It then translates these commands into a sequence of actions performed by avatars in the virtual environment.
- Autonomous avatars respond to the actions and commands of the real soldier, creating the illusion of real team cooperation.

The next stage involves the real soldier receiving feedback from LAM, along with error messages, such as:

- Incorrect use of weapons or the wrong choice of weapon type for the specific situation.
- Failure to follow or violation of safety protocols while moving in a combat zone, such as using inappropriate routes that risk enemy encounters or exposure to a minefield.
- Misjudging the situation, such as underestimating the threat from the enemy or overestimating personal protection.
- Inappropriate movement within the team, disrupting tactical coordination with other soldiers, ignoring or failing to follow the commander's orders or mission instructions.
- Violating radio discipline or failing to relay critical information in a timely manner.
- Incorrect use of engineering or technical equipment, such as traps or mine detectors.
- Delayed application of medical assistance or improper handling of wounded comrades.

Depending on the scenario, the next stage involves collaborative interaction, during which the virtual avatars interact with each other and the real soldier, recreating realistic scenarios. The real soldier gains team-working experience, even if they are the only physical participant.

At the final stage of training, a summary is provided: LAM analyzes the actions taken and offers recommendations for improvement, while the soldier undergoing the training receives a report on their achievements and potential areas for further development. Based on LAM's capabilities, routine reporting tasks can be automated, such as data entry, report formatting, or planning for subsequent training sessions. With direct interfaces to databases and tactical tools, LAM can streamline the analysis of training results, helping to gather and organize information more effectively.

In the future, adaptive LAM-based assistants will personalize training content and delivery methods according to the learning styles and preferences of individual soldiers. LAM agents can take on the roles of organizing and conducting group briefings and seminars, adjusting to unforeseen changes in scenarios or programs. All of this is aimed at freeing up soldiers' time so that they can focus on gaining positive training experiences and discovering new tactical approaches.

The implementation of the described concept will enable training or participation in simulations that may be too risky, costly, or impractical in real life. This approach will provide a more immersive and interactive learning experience. The use of LAM in such applications can be particularly beneficial in remote learning situations, where soldiers lack access to physical training grounds or equipment. By using LAM to manage avatars, soldiers could quickly gain practical experience and develop skills that are difficult to acquire through traditional training methods.

This approach could also lead to new forms of collaborative interaction between soldiers from different geographical locations, working together in a single virtual space, controlling their avatars to conduct training exercises and solve tactical problems together. This would not only enhance the training experience but also promote the development of teamwork and communication skills.

3.4 Conclusion

Although the provided list of scenarios and use cases is far from exhaustive and covers only a small fraction of the possible directions for implementing LLMs in the military sphere, it illustrates the wide range of potential applications for these technologies. The analysis presented in this chapter emphasizes that the rapid development of LLMs, combined with their multimodal capabilities, opens up additional opportunities to enhance operational efficiency and decision-making at various levels. However, integrating LLMs into military structures should be approached with caution, ensuring compliance with international humanitarian law and legal norms. The development of local LLM systems for secure on-site data processing further highlights the critical need for robust security measures in military AI applications. As artificial intelligence technologies continue to evolve, the military's reliance on LLMs is likely to deepen, positioning these models as indispensable tools for achieving informational superiority and operational dominance.

References

[1] A. Barbu, 'Inteligenta artificial: cum vor schimba AI, Deep Learning si robotica domeniul militar', Bucuresti, Editura Militara, 178 p., 2023.

[2] V. Slyusar, M. Protsenko, A. Chernukha, V. Melkin, O. Biloborodov, M. Samoilenko, O. Kravchenko, G. Kalinichenko, A. Rohovyi, M. Soloshchuk, 'Improvement of the model for detecting objects on aerial photos and video in unmanned aerial systems', Eastern-European Journal of Enterprise Technologies, vol. 1, no. 9 (115), 2022, pp. 24–34, doi:10.15587/1729-4061.2022.252876.

[3] OpenAI, 'Introducing ChatGPT', November 30, 2022. [Online]. Available: https://openai.com/blog/chatgpt/.

[4] OpenAI, 'GPT-4 technical report,' *arXiv*, 2023. [Online]. Available: https://archive.org/details/gpt-4-technical-paper.

[5] OpenAI, 'GPT-4 technical report,' *arXiv*, 2024. [Online]. Available: https://arxiv.org/abs/2303.08774.

[6] H. Touvron, T. Lavril, G. Izacard, X. Martinet, M. Lachaux, T. Lacroix, B. Rozière, N. Goyal, E. Hambro, F. Azhar, A. Joulin, É. Grave, G. Lample, and L. Zettlemoyer, 'LLaMA: Open and Efficient Foundation Language Models,' *arXiv*, 2023. [Online]. Available: https://arxiv.org/abs/2302.13971.

[7] V. Slyusar, 'Large language models (LLM) in the military area', XXIII International Scientific and Technical Conference "Artificial Intelligence and Intellegent Systems" (AIIS'2023), 10 - 11 October, 2023. DOI:10.13140/RG.2.2.30196.94086.

[8] V. Slyusar, 'Reducing the Cognitive Burden of a Soldier with the Help of Personal AI and LLM Assistant', The LCGDSS Human System Integration (HSI) Symposium, 12 January, 2024. DOI:10.13140/RG.2.2.10264.57605/1.

[9] P. Georgiev, V. I. Le, et al., 'Gemini 1.5: Unlocking multimodal understanding across millions of tokens of context', *arXiv*, 2024. [Online]. Available: https://arxiv.org/abs/2403.05530.

[10] Anthropic, 'Claude 3.5 Sonnet', Jun. 20, 2024. [Online]. Available: http://www.anthropic.com/news/claude-3-5-sonnet.

[11] C. McKay, 'xAI Launches Grok-2 Models with Image Generation Capabilities', *Maginative,* Aug. 14, 2024. [Online]. Available: https://www.maginative.com/article/xai-launches-grok-2-models-with-image-generation-capabilities/.

[12] L. Jones, 'Microsoft Launches Phi-3.5 Series, A Trio of Open Source AI Models', *WinBuzzer,* Aug. 2024. [Online]. Available: https://winbuzzer.com/2024/08/21/microsoft-launches-phi-3-5-series-competing-with-google-and-openai-xcxwbn/.

[13] H. Liu, C. Li, Q. Wu, and Y. J. Lee, 'Visual instruction tuning', *arXiv*, 2023. [Online]. Available: https://arxiv.org/abs/2304.08485.

[14] T. Reid, 'Testing the new Llama 3.2 90B Vision model from Meta', Medium Daily, 2024. [Online]. Available: https://ai.gopubby.com/testing-the-new-llama-3-2-90b-vision-model-from-meta-d57392fe6a50.

[15] B. Lin, Y. Ye, B. Zhu, J. Cui, M. Ning, P. Jin, L. Yuan, 'Video-LLaVA: Learning United Visual Representation by Alignment Before

Projection', *arXiv,* 2023. [Online]. Available: https://arxiv.org/abs/2311.10122.

[16] *Qwen Team*, 'Qwen2-VL: To See the World More Clearly', Aug. 2024. [Online]. Available: https://qwenlm.github.io/blog/qwen2-vl/.

[17] OpenAI, 'OpenAI o1 System Card', Sept. 12, 2024. [Online]. Available: https://assets.ctfassets.net/kftzwdyauwt9/67qJD51Aur3eIc96iOfeOP/71551c3d223cd97e591aa89567306912/o1_system_card.pdf.

[18] M. Truth, 'Massive breakthrough in AI intelligence: OpenAI passes IQ 120', Sep. 2024. [Online]. Available: https://www.maximumtruth.org/p/massive-breakthrough-in-ai-intelligence.

[19] *Mensa Norway,* 'Mensa Norway IQ Test', 2024. [Online]. Available: https://test.mensa.no/Home/Test/en.

[20] V. Slyusar, 'The concept of aerial minefields', 16th scientific conference of Ivan Kozhedub Kharkiv National University of the Air Force, Kharkiv, KhNUPS, pp. 562 – 563, 2020. Available: https://slyusar.kiev.ua/XVI_conf_hnups_2.pdf.

[21] Y. Kondratenko, G. Kondratenko, A. Shevchenko, V. Slyusar, Y. Zhukov, M. Vakulenko, 'Towards Implementing the Strategy of Artificial Intelligence Development: Ukraine Peculiarities', CEUR Workshop Proceedings, 2023, vol. 3513, pp. 106–117. https://ceur-ws.org/Vol-3513/paper09.pdf

[22] Y. Kondratenko, A. Shevchenko, Y. Zhukov, M. Klymenko, V. Slyusar, G. Kondratenko, O. Striuk, 'Analysis of the Priorities and Perspectives in Artificial Intelligence Implementation', 13th International IEEE Conference "Dependable Systems, Services and Technologies" (DESSERT'2023), Greece, Athens, 8 p., October 13-15, 2023. DOI: 10.1109/DESSERT61349.2023.10416432.

[23] A. Shevchenko, Y. Kondratenko, V. Slyusar, G. Kondratenko, T. Yeroshenko, 'Analysis of the prospect domains in AI implementation: Nationals, NATO and Ukraine AI strategies', Research Tendencies and Prospect Domains for AI Development and Implementation, pp. 1–30, 2024. Available: https://www.riverpublishers.com/book_details.php?book_id=1163.

[24] S. Chen, 'Chinese scientists create and cage world's first AI commander in PLA laboratory', South China Morning Post, Sep. 20, 2024. [Online]. Available: https://www.scmp.com/news/china/science/article/3266444/chinese-scientists-create-and-cage-worlds-first-ai-commander-pla-laboratory.

[25] Y. Kondratenko, A. Shevchenko, Y. Zhukov, G. Kondratenko, O. Striuk 'Tendencies and Challenges of Artificial Intelligence Development and Implementation', Proceedings of the IEEE International Conference on Intelligent Data Acquisition and Advanced Computing Systems: Technology and Applications, IDAACS, 2023, pp. 221–226, Dortmund, 7 - 9 September, 2023. DOI10.1109/IDAACS58523.2023.10348800.

[26] R. Duro, Y. Kondratenko (Eds.), 'Advances in Intelligent Robotics and Collaborative Automation', River Publishers, Aalborg, Denmark, 2015, DOI:10.13052/rp-9788793237049.

[27] V. Slyusar, 'Application of neural network technologies for underwater munitions detection', Radioelectronics and Communications Systems, Vol. 65, No. 12, pp. 654–664, 2022. DOI:10.3103/S0735272723030020.

[28] T. Wasfy, P. Jayakumar, 'Next-generation NATO reference mobility model complex terramechanics – Part 1: Definition and literature review', Journal of Terramechanics, vol. 96, pp. 45-57, 2021. DOI: doi.org/10.1016/j.jterra.2021.02.002.

[29] Y. P. Kondratenko, V. I. Slyusar, M. B. Solesvik, N. Y. Kondratenko, and Z. Gomolka, 'Interrelation and inter-influence of artificial intelligence and higher education systems', Research Tendencies and Prospect Domains for AI Development and Implementation, pp. 31–58, 2024. Available: https://www.riverpublishers.com/book_details.php?book_id=1163.

[30] V.I. Slyusar, Y.P. Kondratenko, A.I. Shevchenko, T.V. Yeroshenko, 'Some Aspects of Artificial Intelligence Development Strategy for Mobile Technologies', Journal of Mobile Multimedia, Vol. 20_3, pp. 525–554, 2024. DOI: 10.13052/jmm1550-4646.2031.

[31] A. Jiang, A. Sablayrolles, A. Mensch, C. Bamford, D. Singh Chaplot, D. Casas, F. Bressand, G. Lengyel, G. Lample, L. Saulnier, L. Renard Lavaud, M.-A. Lachaux, P. Stock, T. Scao, T. Lavril, T. Wang, T. Lacroix, W. Sayed, 'Mistral 7B', *arXiv*, 2023. [Online]. https://arxiv.org/pdf/2310.06825.pdf.

[32] P. Lewis, E. Perez, A. Piktus, F. Petroni, V. Karpukhin, N. Goyal, H. Küttler, M. Lewis, W.-t. Yih, T. Rocktäschel, et al., 'Retrieval-Augmented Generation for Knowledge-Intensive NLP Tasks', Advances in Neural Information Processing Systems, vol. 33, pp. 9459–9474, 2020. [Online]. Available: https://arxiv.org/abs/2005.11401.

[33] T. Wieroński, 'Sztuczna inteligencja w strategicznych grach planszowych: czy algorytm może zastąpić człowieka?' Krakow, Wydawnictwa AGH, 2023, 80 str. ISBN: 9788367427500.

[34] B. Akesson; M. Amyot-Bourgeois; G. Ernis et al., 'Multi-Dimensional Data Farming: Extending Data Farming for Multi-Scale Decision Support by Integrating Novel AI Techniques', The NMSG Symposium "Simulation: Going Beyond the Limitations of the Real World" (STO-MP-MSG-207), Monterey, CA, USA, 19- 20 October, 2023. DOI: 10.14339/STO-MP-MSG-207.

[35] D. Ota, 'Towards Verification of NATO Generic Vehicle Architecture-Based Systems', in *Proceedings of the Twenty-First International Command and Control Research and Technology Symposium (21ST ICCRTS),* London, UK, 6 - 8 September, 2016. 22 p. [Online]. Available: https://www.researchgate.net/publication/309027098_Towards_Verification_of_NATO_Generic_Vehicle_Architecture-Based_Systems.

[36] Integris Composites. 'Integris Composites ABDS^{TM} Active Blast Mitigation System'. [Online]. Available: https://integriscomposites.com/vehicles/active-protection-technology/.

[37] Y. Li, M. Min, D. Shen, D. Carlson, L. Carin. (2018), 'Video Generation from Text', Proceedings of the AAAI Conference on Artificial Intelligence, 32(1). DOI:10.1609/aaai.v32i1.12233.

[38] X. Yang, T. Zhang, C. Xu, 'Text2Video: An End-to-end Learning Framework for Expressing Text With Videos', IEEE Transactions on Multimedia, vol. 20, no. 9, pp. 2360-2370, Sept. 2018. [Online]. Available: https://doi.org/10.1109/TMM.2018.2807588.

[39] J. Wei et al., 'Chain of Thought Prompting Elicits Reasoning in Large Language Models', *arXiv*, 2022. [Online]. Available: https://arxiv.org/abs/2201.11903.

[40] Z.-H. Zhou, 'Ensemble Methods: Foundations and Algorithms (Chapman & Hall/CRC Machine Learning & Pattern Recognition)', CRC Press, Taylor & Francis Group, Boca Raton, FL, USA, 2012.

[41] N. Shazeer, A. Mirhoseini, K. Maziarz, A. Davis, Q. Le, G. Hinton, J. Dean, 'Outrageously large neural networks: The sparsely-gated mixture-of-experts layer', *arXiv*, 2017. [Online]. Available: https://arxiv.org/pdf/1701.06538.

[42] Mixtral of experts A high quality Sparse Mixture-of-Experts. https://mistral.ai/news/mixtral-of-experts/.

[43] Z. Chen, Y. Deng, Y. Wu, Q. Gu, Y. Li, 'Towards Understanding Mixture of Experts in Deep Learning', 04 August, 2022, https://arxiv.org/abs/2208.02813.

[44] J. Copet, F. Kreuk, I. Gat, T. Remez, D. Kant, G. Synnaeve, Y. Adi, and A. Défossez, 'Simple and Controllable Music Generation', *arXiv*, 2024. [Online]. Available: https://arxiv.org/pdf/2306.05284.

[45] A. van den Oord, S. Dieleman, H. Zen, K. Simonyan, O. Vinyals, A. Graves, N. Kalchbrenner, A. Senior, K. Kavukcuoglu, 'WaveNet: A Generative Model for Raw Audio', *arXiv*, 2016. [Online]. Available: https://arxiv.org/abs/1609.03499.

4

Optimization-oriented Synthesis of Rule Bases of Intelligent Systems: Application Features for Complex Plants' Control

Yue Zheng[1], Jianjun Wang[2], Oleksiy Kozlov[3], Galyna Kondratenko[3], and Anna Aleksieieva[3]

[1]Yancheng Polytechnic College, China
[2]Yunzhou (Yancheng) Innovation Technology Co., Ltd, China
[3]Petro Mohyla Black Sea National University, Ukraine
E-mail: bsb@126.com; jianjun.wang@yunzhou-tech.com; kozlov_ov@ukr.net; halyna.kondratenko@chmnu.edu.ua; anna.aleksyeyeva@chmnu.edu.ua

Abstract

This chapter addresses the issue of research on an advanced method of optimization-oriented synthesis of rule bases (RBs) of intelligent systems, namely systems based on fuzzy logic. This method allows the creation of fuzzy systems with an optimal set of consequents and a reduced number of rules in RBs in terms of incomplete source information due to highly efficient sequential search procedures of structural-parametric optimization. The effectiveness studies of the considered method were carried out for two different intelligent control systems for such complex technical plants as a mobile robotic platform and a floating dock. The research results obtained validate the effectiveness of the presented advanced method of optimization-oriented synthesis, considering both the performance and the computational costs incurred, as well as the feasibility of its use for creating diverse intelligent systems.

Keywords: Intelligent systems, optimization-oriented synthesis, rule base, structural-parametric optimization, mobile robotic platform, floating dock.

DOI: 10.1201/9788743800989-4

4.1 Introduction

Artificial intelligence (AI) has achieved significant breakthroughs in recent years, dramatically enhancing its role in numerous technical and industrial domains [1–3]. One of the most notable achievements is the advancement of AI in autonomous systems, such as self-driving vehicles and industrial robotics [4–7]. These systems utilize sophisticated machine learning algorithms and computer vision techniques to navigate complex environments, make real-time decisions, and carry out tasks with high precision and minimal human intervention. For example, AI-driven autonomous vehicles are being refined to handle urban traffic, navigate through challenging weather conditions, and optimize routes for efficiency, all while adhering to safety standards [8–10].

Recent AI developments have also seen substantial progress in areas like predictive maintenance and smart manufacturing. AI algorithms are now capable of analyzing vast amounts of sensor data from industrial equipment to predict potential failures before they occur, reducing downtime and maintenance costs [11–13]. In smart factories, AI is being integrated into systems for quality control, supply chain optimization, and adaptive production processes, leading to higher efficiency and reduced waste [14, 15]. Moreover, AI technologies are being deployed in fields such as energy management, where they help optimize grid operations and enhance the integration of renewable energy sources [16, 17]. These advances illustrate AI's growing impact on enhancing operational efficiency, safety, and sustainability across a wide range of technical systems and complex objects.

Building on these advancements, AI technologies have also paved the way for more sophisticated intelligent control and decision-making systems [18–20]. These systems, designed to manage complex and dynamic environments, have become crucial in industries where traditional control methods may fall short due to uncertainty, variability, or incomplete information. Intelligent control systems leverage AI techniques, such as reinforcement learning, neural networks, and fuzzy logic, to adapt to real-time conditions, optimize performance, and make informed decisions without constant human oversight [21, 22]. This capability has significant implications for sectors ranging from autonomous vehicles and industrial automation to energy management and healthcare.

Fuzzy logic, in particular, has proven highly effective in intelligent control systems, especially when dealing with complex, non-linear, or poorly defined processes [23–25]. Unlike conventional binary logic systems, which operate in absolutes (true or false, on or off), fuzzy logic allows for a more nuanced approach by modeling uncertainty and imprecision. This approach is particularly useful in environments where data may be ambiguous or where precise mathematical modeling is difficult. For example, fuzzy logic controllers have been successfully applied to various domains such as automotive systems for real-time traction and stability control, industrial processes for regulating temperature and pressure, and smart grids for balancing power loads and integrating renewable energy sources [26–28].

The effectiveness of fuzzy logic-based systems is due in part to their flexibility and robustness in handling real-world uncertainties. They can process human-like reasoning, making them well-suited for applications where decision-making relies on heuristic or experiential knowledge rather than deterministic rules [23, 24]. Moreover, fuzzy control systems can be easily integrated with other AI techniques, such as neural networks and genetic algorithms, to enhance their adaptability and learning capabilities [29–31]. In practice, this means that systems employing fuzzy logic can quickly adjust to new conditions or changes in their operating environment, leading to higher performance, reduced error rates, and improved safety [32–34].

For instance, in the field of intelligent transportation, fuzzy logic controllers have been used to improve traffic management by dynamically adjusting traffic light sequences based on real-time traffic flow data, reducing congestion, and minimizing delays [35–37]. Similarly, in manufacturing, fuzzy logic-based systems are employed to optimize robotic path planning and improve the precision of automated assembly processes, enhancing overall productivity and product quality [38–40]. These examples underscore the significant benefits of intelligent control systems that incorporate fuzzy logic, demonstrating their capacity to deliver efficient, adaptive, and reliable solutions in complex and uncertain environments.

Despite the numerous efforts of scientists and researchers, the synthesis and design of highly effective fuzzy control and decision-making systems, taking into account various features of objects, remain a challenging problem. This complexity arises from the need to manage a vast range of variables, uncertainties, and dynamic conditions that are inherent in real-world applications. To address these challenges, optimization-oriented approaches have been successfully employed, focusing on refining various aspects of fuzzy systems such as their structure, linguistic terms (LTs), membership functions, rule bases, and adjustable coefficients [41–43]. These methods, which include search approaches, evolutionary algorithms, bio-inspired techniques, and hybrid optimization strategies, aim to fine-tune the parameters and enhance the overall performance of fuzzy control systems, providing more robust and adaptable solutions for complex environments [44–46]. This chapter is devoted to the issues of research and improvement of the method of optimization-oriented synthesis of rule bases of fuzzy systems, as well as the features of its application in the creation of control systems for complex technical objects.

The next sections of this chapter are organized as follows. Section 4.2 provides a brief discussion of the RB design problem and an in-depth exploration of the key steps of the optimization-oriented synthesis method for its solving in different types of fuzzy systems. It also includes improvements aimed at reducing the number of rules, alongside a graphical representation of the method's implementation. In Section 4.3, the focus shifts to the analysis of this method's efficiency and application in optimizing two distinct fuzzy control systems for complex technical facilities: a mobile robotic platform and a floating dock. Finally, Section 4.4 presents concluding remarks and outlines potential directions for future research.

4.2 Fuzzy System's Rule Base Designing: Peculiarities of the Challenge and the Optimization-oriented Method for Its Solution

4.2.1 Rule base designing challenge

One of the most challenging tasks in the synthesis and optimization of intelligent systems based on fuzzy logic, as outlined in [45, 46], is the development of highly efficient rule bases with an optimal set of consequents and a minimal number of rules, particularly when initial data is scarce and there is a high degree of uncertainty. This involves determining the antecedent vector $\mathbf{X}_A$, generating the consequent vector $\mathbf{X}_C$, and subsequently reducing the number of rules s. The total number of rules in a complete fuzzy system's rule base s_{full} is determined by the number of all possible combinations of the linguistic terms of the system's input variables [43, 44]. In a generalized fuzzy system, the rules consist of sets of antecedents paired with their corresponding consequents [44].

The antecedents of the rules are various combinations of LTs of the system's input variables [45]. For each rth rule in the rule base (where $r = 1, 2, \ldots, s$), the consequent LT_r is chosen from a set containing all possible consequents, which are ν linguistic terms of the output variable

$$\mathrm{LT}_r \in \{\mathrm{LT}_1, \mathrm{LT}_2, ..., \mathrm{LT}_\nu\}. \tag{4.1}$$

Thus, if we choose three linguistic terms for the output variable ($\nu = 3$), then the set can have the form, for example,

$$\mathrm{LT}_r \in \{\mathrm{LT}_1, \mathrm{LT}_2, \mathrm{LT}_3\} = \{\mathrm{S}, \mathrm{M}, \mathrm{L}\}, \tag{4.2}$$

if we choose $\nu = 5$, then

$$\mathrm{LT}_r \in \{\mathrm{LT}_1, \mathrm{LT}_2, \mathrm{LT}_3, \mathrm{LT}_4, \mathrm{LT}_5\} = \{\mathrm{VS}, \mathrm{S}, \mathrm{M}, \mathrm{L}, \mathrm{VL}\}, \tag{4.3}$$

where VS is very short; S is short; M is medium; L is long; VL is very long.

The vector of consequents $\mathbf{X}_\mathrm{C}$ of the rule base can be formed in various ways, so the task of synthesizing and optimizing the consequents reducing to finding the optimal vector (set) of consequents $\mathbf{X}_\mathrm{Copt}$ from the set of all possible alternatives, which ensures optimal performance indicators for the fuzzy system.

The vector of consequents $\mathbf{X}_{\mathrm{C}x}$ for the xth alternative version of the rule base can be generally represented as follows [45]:

$$\begin{gathered} \mathbf{X}_{\mathrm{C}x} = \{\mathrm{LT}_{x1}, \mathrm{LT}_{x2}, ..., \mathrm{LT}_{xr}, ..., \mathrm{LT}_{xs}\}, \\ \mathrm{LT}_{xr} \in \{\mathrm{LT}_1, \mathrm{LT}_2, ..., \mathrm{LT}_\nu\}, x \in \{1, 2, ..., \nu^s\}, \end{gathered} \tag{4.4}$$

where ν^s is the total number of possible variants of the vector $\mathbf{X}_\mathrm{C}$, determined as the number of linguistic terms ν of the output variable raised to the power of the total number of rules s in the rule base.

Thus, the task of creating a rule base with an optimal set of consequents is reduced to finding such a vector of consequents $\mathbf{X}_\mathrm{Copt} = \mathbf{X}_{\mathrm{C}x}$, where the value of the objective function J of the fuzzy system is optimal ($J \leq J_\mathrm{opt}$) [45]. This problem represents a high-dimensional discrete optimization challenge, requiring effective search methods that account for the specific characteristics of rule base consequents under conditions of information uncertainty. Solving this issue through an exhaustive search of all possible vectors $\mathbf{X}_{\mathrm{C}x}$ ($x = 1, 2, \ldots, \nu^s$) would necessitate calculating the objective function ν^s times, which, even for a rule base of modest size, would demand substantial computational and time resources [45].

For example, when synthesizing and optimizing a specific fuzzy system using existing computing tools, calculating the objective function takes 1 millisecond. If the rule base of this system has a fairly simple structure, namely 12 rules ($s = 12$) and 5 linguistic terms ($\nu = 5$) of the output variable, then with an exhaustive search of all possible vectors $\mathbf{X}_{\mathrm{C}x}$, the value of the objective function will need to be calculated 5^{12} times, which will take approximately 68 hours. If there are already 15 rules in this rule base, then the time of an exhaustive search will be almost 1 year (353.2 days).

4.2.2 Improved method of RB optimization-oriented synthesis

The optimization-oriented synthesis method proposed in [44] and studied in [46] allows for a relatively efficient solution to this complex problem while requiring only minimal computational and time resources. However, this method generates a complete rule base and does not allow to simultaneously reduce rules that have little impact on the system's performance during the synthesis process. As for the creation of a rule base with the optimal number of rules s_{opt} ($s_{\text{opt}} < s_{\text{full}}$), such an RB means a base containing only those rules that significantly affect the operation of the system. In order to identify and exclude rules from the RB that do not affect or have an insignificant impact on the process of functioning of the system, this chapter proposes to add a specialized rule reduction procedure to the considered method of optimization-oriented synthesis. This will fundamentally simplify further software and hardware implementation of the developed fuzzy logic system.

Thus, the proposed enhanced method facilitates the synthesis and optimization of rule bases by identifying the optimal set of consequents $\mathbf{X}_{\text{Copt}}$ and the reduced (optimal) number of rules s_{opt}. This ensures that the objective function for control and decision-making processes based on the system is optimized ($J \leq J_{\text{opt}}$). The method is particularly valuable for developing fuzzy systems under conditions where: (a) initial information is limited, leading to high uncertainty, (b) there is a large number of rules making expert-based rule base compilation less effective, and (c) varying levels of expert knowledge are involved.

The considered improved method generates the optimal vector of the RB consequents $\mathbf{X}_{\text{Copt}}$ through an iterative search process, sequentially selecting the consequents for each rule. Additionally, during the search for the $\mathbf{X}_{\text{Copt}}$ vector, rules that do not influence the system's performance are identified and subsequently removed from the rule base. The sequence of key computational procedures for the proposed method is visually depicted as a flowchart in Figure 4.1 . Additionally, the primary steps of this method are outlined in detail in the following text. This combination provides both a visual and textual understanding of the process flow.

Step 1. Initialization. The initial synthesis of the structure of the complete RB ($s = s_{\text{full}}$) is performed using the selected linguistic terms for the input variables, and a set of possible consequents $\text{LT}_1, \text{LT}_2, \ldots, \text{LT}_\nu$ for each rth rule is determined based on the previously selected ν linguistic terms of the output variable. The antecedents of the rules are formed by considering all possible combinations of the LTs of the input variables. The initial number

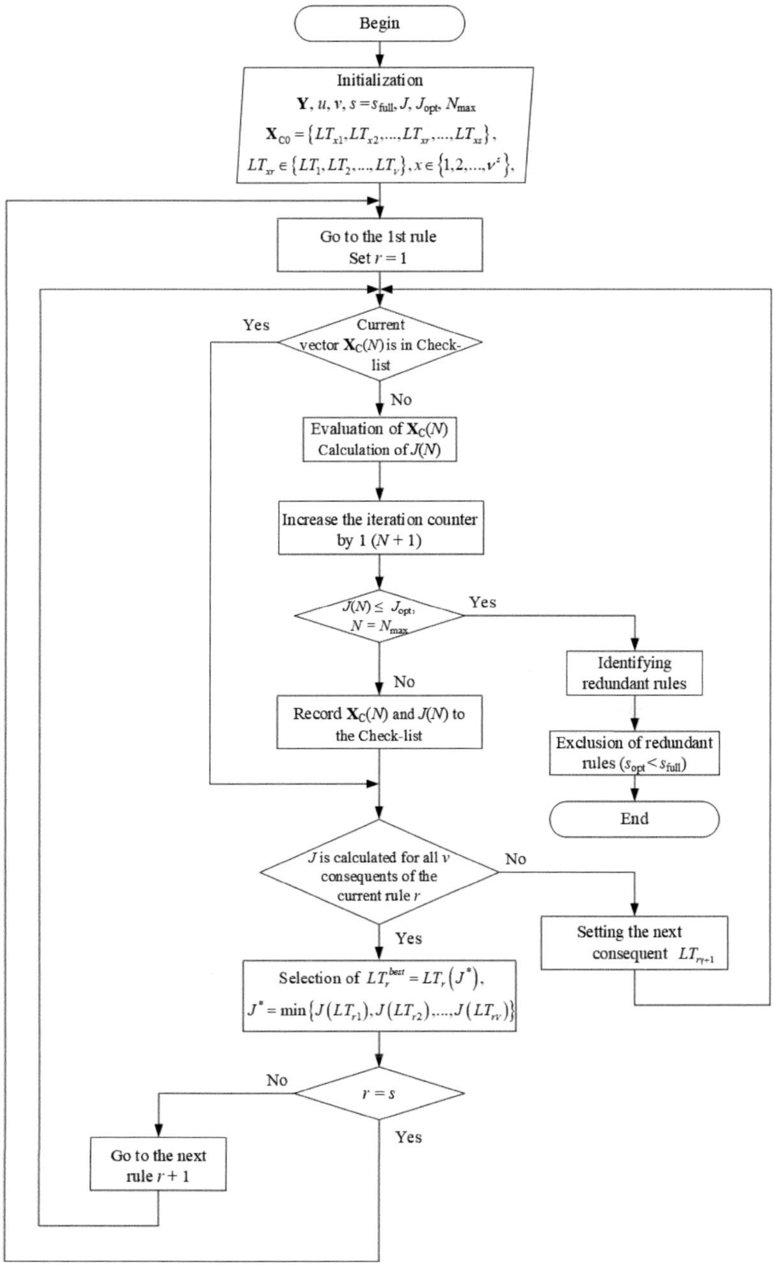

Figure 4.1 Flowchart of the improved method for the optimization-oriented synthesis of the fuzzy system's rule base.

of rules of the complete RB s_{full} corresponds to the total number of these combinations. At this stage, the input variable vector **Y** and the output variable u should already be defined. The initial vector of consequents $\mathbf{X}_{\text{C0}}$, in turn, is randomly generated and assigned in the system's RB. Additionally, the objective function J for evaluating the performance of the control or decision-making process is selected, along with its optimal value J_{opt} and the maximum number of iterations $N_{\max}$ for executing the proposed method.

Step 2. Transition to the first rule of the system's RB. The search process begins by moving to the first rule of the rule base to initiate the iterative procedures for identifying the optimal consequents' vector $\mathbf{X}_{\text{Copt}}$.

Step 3. Check-list verification. All vectors of the RB consequents $\mathbf{X}_{\text{C}}$, for which the objective function J has already been calculated during the method's execution, along with their corresponding J values, are recorded in the Check-list. At this stage, the Check-list is reviewed to avoid redundant calculations of the objective function for the system with the same vector $\mathbf{X}_{\text{C}}$. This step helps eliminate unnecessary iterations, the number of which equals $l(s_{\text{full}} - 1)$, where l represents the number of rounds of consecutive iterative procedures optimizing the RB rules from the 1st to the sth rule.

If the current consequent vector $\mathbf{X}_{\text{C}}$ is already listed in the Check-list, move directly to Step 7. If not, proceed to Step 4.

Step 4. Computation of the value of the objective function J using the current consequents vector $\mathbf{X}_{\text{C}}$. At this point, J is calculated for the system with the given $\mathbf{X}_{\text{C}}$ vector. Following this, the iteration counter is increased by 1.

Step 5. Verifying if the optimization of the consequents vector $\mathbf{X}_{\text{C}}$ is complete. The process is deemed complete if the optimal value of the objective function ($J \leq J_{\text{opt}}$) is achieved or the maximum number of iterations $N_{\max}$ has been reached. If this condition is met, proceed to step 10. Otherwise, continue to step 6.

Step 6. Recording the vector $\mathbf{X}_{\text{C}}(N)$ and its corresponding objective function $J(N)$ to the Check-list. At this point, the current vector $\mathbf{X}_{\text{C}}(N)$ and the associated value of the objective function $J(N)$ are logged into the Check-list.

Step 7. Verification of the completion of the optimization process for the current rule. The optimization process for the current rth rule is considered complete when the values of the objective function J for all ν possible consequents for this rule have been calculated. If this condition is met, proceed to step 8. Otherwise, assign the next consequent from the set of ν possible options to the current rule and return to step 3.

Step 8. Choosing the optimal consequent. In this step, identification of the consequent with the lowest value of the objective function J from the optimization calculations is performed for the current rth rule. This optimal consequent is then assigned to the rule.

Step 9. Verification of the rule number. At this stage, check whether all rules in the rule base ($r = s$) have been optimized. If so, proceed to step 2. If not, move on to the next rule ($r + 1$) and continue with step 3.

Step 10. Identification of rules that do not affect the process of system operation. At this stage, the rules are revealed, during the optimization of which the value of the objective function J did not change when all ν possible consequents were alternately changed. Since successive iterative optimization procedures of the RB rules from the 1st to the sth can be carried out l times (rounds) until finding the optimal vector $\mathbf{X}_{\mathrm{Copt}}$, in which $J \leq J_{\mathrm{opt}}$, the definition of non-essential (redundant) rules is carried out only on the last lth optimization round.

Step 11. Exclusion of rules that do not affect the process of system's operation. At this stage, the detected redundant rules (which do not affect the process of the system's operation) are excluded from the RB. As a result, the number of the RB rules will be reduced ($s_{\mathrm{opt}} < s_{\mathrm{full}}$).

Step 12. Finalization of the RB synthesis and optimization. Following this, further parametric optimization of the fuzzy system may be conducted, along with its hardware and software implementation for practical use in control and decision-making processes. This final implementation will benefit from a simplified hardware and software setup due to the reduced number of optimized RB rules ($s_{\mathrm{opt}} < s_{\mathrm{full}}$).

When applying the given improved method, it is advisable to set the maximum number of iterations N_{max} taking into account the following dependence:

$$N_{\mathrm{max}} = l \left[s_{\mathrm{full}} \nu - (s_{\mathrm{full}} - 1) \right]. \tag{4.5}$$

The number of optimization rounds l is selected experimentally for a specific RB depending on its size.

When a rule base with an established vector of consequents $\mathbf{X}_{\mathrm{C}}$ derived from expert knowledge is already available, the proposed method can be utilized to further optimize this RB, enhancing the system's efficiency and simplifying its hardware and software implementation by reducing the number of rules. Initially, at the first step, the vector of consequents $\mathbf{X}_{\mathrm{C0}}$ is set in the system's RB based on expert knowledge. The subsequent steps of the method are carried out as they would be without prior expert input. However, when an initial hypothesis regarding $\mathbf{X}_{C0}$ is available from experts, the iterative optimization procedures for the RB rules need only be performed once ($l = 1$), which significantly reduces the total number of iterations N_{max}.

As an example, Figure 4.2 provides a graphical representation of the application of the proposed method in the synthesis and optimization of a rule base consisting of nine rules ($s = 9$) with five possible consequents ($\nu = 5$) for each rule: BN (big negative), SN (small negative), Z (zero), SP (small positive), and BP (large positive). In turn, in Figure 4.2 , the notation γ represents the number of the consequent ($\gamma = 1, 2, \ldots, \nu$).

In particular, the antecedents of these nine rules are formed by the following combinations of LTs of the two input variables: (1) N & (AND) N; (2) N & Z; (3) N & P; (4) Z & N; (5) Z & Z; (6) Z & P; (7) P & N; (8) P & Z; (9) P & P.

The thick contour highlights the rule currently undergoing consequents optimization. The consequents assigned to the rules at this stage are shaded in gray, while the optimal (best) consequents, which have already been identified by the presented method and recorded during the optimization process, are marked in yellow.

Thus, at the initial stage, the vector of the RB consequents $\mathbf{X}_{C0}$ is randomly generated and has the following form:

$$\mathbf{X}_{C0} = \{Z, SN, BP, Z, SN, \ BN, SP, SN, Z\}. \tag{4.6}$$

Upon completing all optimization procedures with the developed improved method, the final optimal vector of consequents $\mathbf{X}_{Copt}$ for the considered fuzzy system is represented as follows:

$$\mathbf{X}_{Copt} = \{BN, BN, SN, SN, Z, SP, SP, BP, BP\}. \tag{4.7}$$

To simplify the visualization of the proposed method's operation, in this example, the procedure for eliminating unnecessary rules is not considered.

This method can be applied quite effectively to create rule bases for fuzzy systems (control and decision-making) of various types: Mamdani, Larsen, Takagi–Sugeno (zero-order), Tsukamoto, type-2 fuzzy systems, fractal fuzzy systems, etc. Moreover, the objective function can be calculated at each iteration using various approaches (using training samples, simulation models, various types of experimental data, reinforcement learning, etc.).

To assess the effectiveness and study the application features of the enhanced method for optimization-oriented RB synthesis using sequential

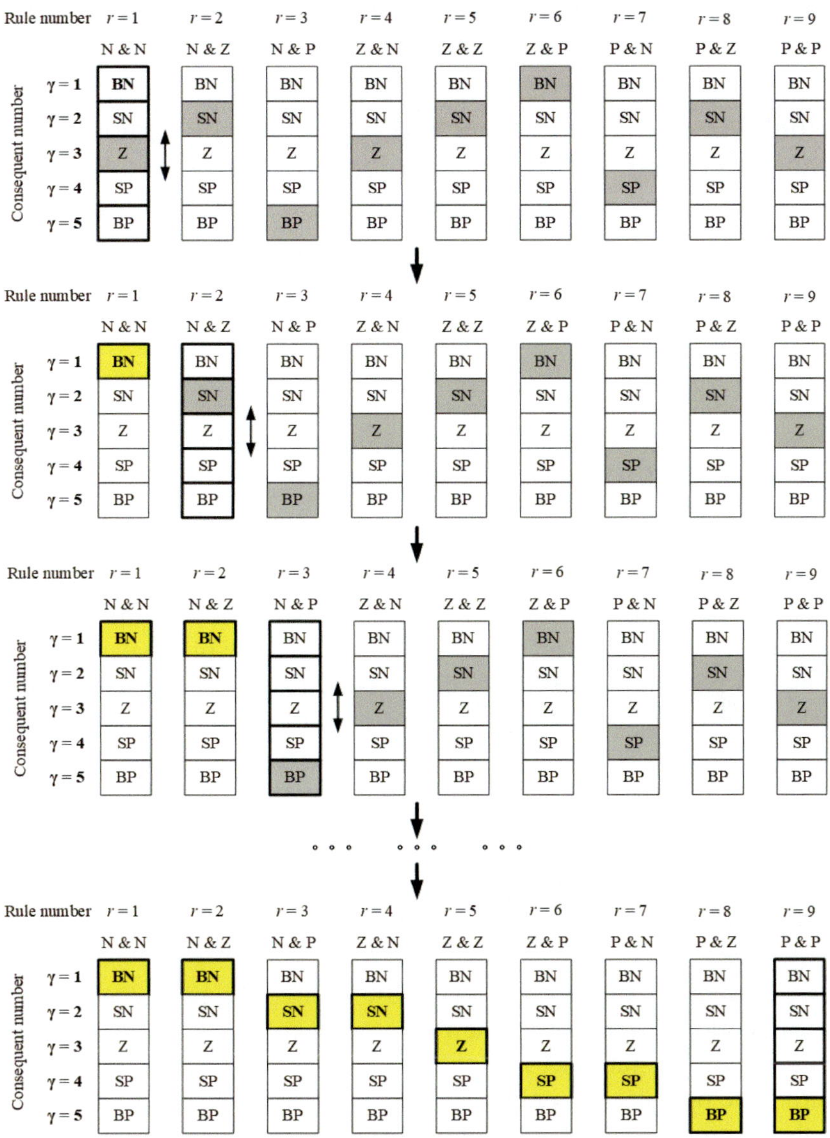

Figure 4.2 A graphic illustration of the implementation of the method for the optimization-oriented synthesis of the fuzzy system's RB based on sequential search procedures.

search procedures, in this chapter, we developed the rule bases of Mamdani-type fuzzy systems for: (a) controlling the speed of a mobile robotic platform and (b) controlling the draft of a floating dock designed for small-tonnage vessels.

4.3 Analysis of the Efficiency and Application Aspects of the Enhanced Method in Developing Rule Bases for Fuzzy Control Systems of Complex Technical Plants

4.3.1 Rule base designing for the fuzzy control system of the mobile robotic platform

The effectiveness of the enhanced RB synthesis method was evaluated through its application to the speed control system of a mobile robotic platform. A comprehensive description, including technical specifications, main parameters' values, and a mathematical model of this platform, can be found in [41, 46, 47]. This system features feedback based on the speed of movement over an inclined surface and employs a Mamdani-type controller. The input variables for the controller include speed control error ε_V, its time derivative $d\varepsilon_V/dt$, and the integral $\int \varepsilon_V dt$.

For this system, the error signal ε_V is fuzzified using five linguistic terms: (1) big negative (BN), (2) small negative (SN), (3) zero (Z), (4) small positive (SP), and (5) big positive (BP). For the fuzzification of the derivative and integral of the error, three linguistic terms are utilized: (1) negative (N), (2) zero (Z), and (3) positive (P). The output signal of the controller u_{FC} is represented by seven terms: (1) big negative (BN), (2) negative (N), (3) small negative (SN), (4) zero (Z), (5) small positive (SP), (6) positive (P), and (7) big positive BP. All chosen linguistic terms have triangular membership functions and are uniformly distributed across the working ranges of the input and output variables. The complete rule base of the controller consists of 45 rules ($s_{\text{full}} = 45$).

For comparative analysis, this study also utilizes the rule base of the controller developed from expert knowledge in paper [47]. A portion of this rule base is shown in Table 4.1 .

During the optimization-oriented synthesis of the controller's rule base using the improved method, the initial vector of consequents $\mathbf{X}_{C0}$ was generated randomly. The objective function J and the reference model for the dynamic behavior of the robotic platform are described by the same expressions as in [47]. The optimal objective function value was set to $J_{\text{opt}} = 0.1$, with a maximum iteration count of $N_{\max} = 813$ to allow for three complete optimization rounds of the rule base from the 1st to the sth

Table 4.1 Part of rule base of the fuzzy controller for the mobile robotic platform, synthesized from expert knowledge

Rule number	LTs of input variables			LTs of output variable
	ε_V	$d\varepsilon_V/dt$	$\int\varepsilon_V dt$	u_{FC}
1	BN	N	N	BN
6	BN	Z	P	N
17	SN	P	Z	Z
24	Z	Z	P	SP
29	SP	N	Z	Z
35	SP	P	Z	SP
40	BP	Z	N	P
45	BP	P	P	BP

rule ($l = 3$). To simulate all processes of movement of the robotic platform along an inclined metal plane, the same conditions were used as in paper [47]. It is worth noting that the objective function value for the rule base developed using expert knowledge is not optimal, standing at $J = 0.244$.

Figure 4.3 illustrates the graph depicting the variation in the objective function value J throughout the synthesis and optimization of the rule base using the proposed improved method. As shown in the figure, the optimization process achieved a minimum objective function value of $J_{\text{min}} = 0.091$, which is slightly better than the set optimal value of $J_{\text{opt}} = 0.1$.

The optimal vector of consequents $\mathbf{X}_{\text{Copt}}$, determined during the RB optimization-oriented synthesis process, is as follows:

$\mathbf{X}_{\text{Copt}} = \{$BN, BN, 0, 0, BN, BN, 0, BN, BN, BN, BN, N, N, 0, SN, 0, SN, SN, 0, N, SN, 0, Z, Z, SP, SP, P, SP, SP, SP, 0, P, P, SP, P, BP, 0, BP, BP, BP, BP, BP, BP, BP, BP$\}$.

In this instance, the consequents marked with zeros do not influence the speed control of the robotic platform (system functioning) and can be removed from the RB at step 11 of the proposed improved method. Consequently, it is recommended to exclude the following rules from the synthesized rule base with the optimal set of consequents: 3, 4, 7, 14, 16, 19, 22, 31, and 37. This results in a refined rule base with an optimal (reduced) number of rules $s_{\text{opt}} = 36$.

A portion of the rule base, developed and optimized using the proposed enhanced method, is presented in Table 4.2 .

Figure 4.4 illustrates the acceleration transient graphs of a mobile platform with a fuzzy system based on: 1 – a rule base developed from expert knowledge; 2 – a rule base developed using the proposed enhanced optimization-oriented synthesis method.

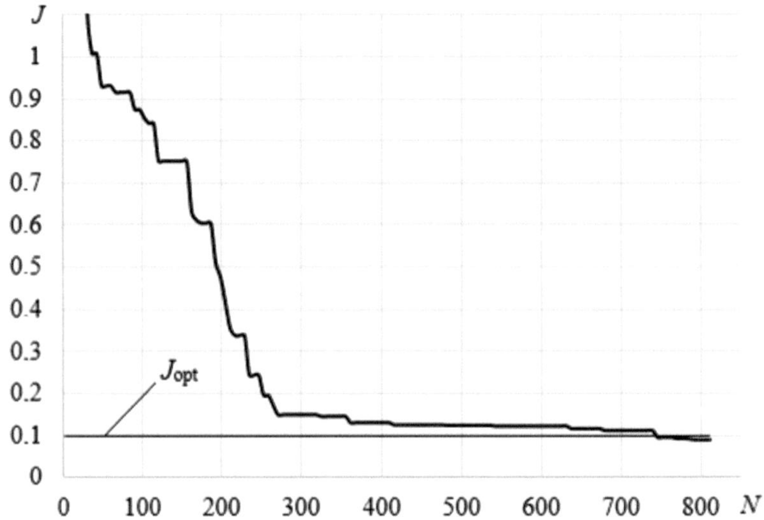

Figure 4.3 Graph depicting the variations in the objective function value J during the synthesis and optimization of the rule base for the mobile robotic platform.

Table 4.2 Part of rule base of the fuzzy controller for the mobile robotic platform, synthesized using the proposed enhanced method.

Rule number	LTs of input variables			LTs of output variable
	ε_V	$d\varepsilon_V/dt$	$\int\varepsilon_V dt$	u_{FC}
1	BN	N	N	BN
6	BN	Z	P	BN
17	SN	P	Z	SN
24	Z	Z	P	Z
29	SP	N	Z	SP
35	SP	P	Z	P
40	BP	Z	N	BP
45	BP	P	P	BP

Additionally, Table 4.3 provides a comparative analysis of the performance metrics for fuzzy speed control systems corresponding to the aforementioned transient processes.

As seen in Figure 4.4 and Table 4.3 , the speed control system of the robotic platform with an optimized rule base, developed using the proposed improved method, exhibits superior control quality compared to the system based on a rule base derived from expert knowledge. Specifically, the optimized RB reduced overshoot by 20.16%, decreased rise time by 37.2%, and shortened the overall transient time by 65.4%.

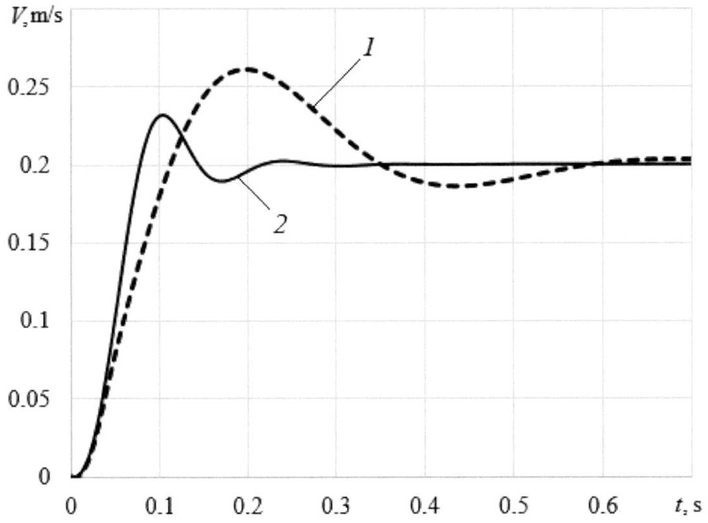

Figure 4.4 Acceleration transient graphs of a mobile robotic platform with a fuzzy speed control system.

Table 4.3 Comparative analysis of the performance metrics for the fuzzy control system of the mobile robotic platform.

Performance metrics	Fuzzy system's numerical values	
	Rule base developed from expert knowledge	Rule base developed using the proposed enhanced method
Objective function J	0.244	0.091
Total transient time, s	0.546	0.189
Rise time, s	0.121	0.076
Overshoot, %	35.43	15.27

The hardware and software implementation of the fuzzy controller with the optimized RB will be significantly simplified, as it contains nine fewer rules than the full rule base designed with expert input.

Furthermore, during the synthesis and optimization of the RB for a fuzzy speed controller, which achieved an optimal set of consequents and an optimal number of rules, the implementation of the proposed optimization-oriented synthesis method required minimal computational effort ($N_{max} = 813$), further demonstrating its high efficiency and demand.

Additionally, when comparing this control system with a similar one, the rule base of which is optimized using a genetic algorithm in study [47], it can be said that their transient characteristics practically coincide, but this system (optimized by the proposed improved method) has a smaller number of rules, which is a significant advantage.

4.3.2 Rule base development for the fuzzy control system of the floating dock

Shipbuilding and ship repair enterprises worldwide are continuously expanding their ship-lifting facilities to meet the growing demand for docking ships of various types and classes. In recent times, floating docks have become the most commonly used structures, as modern composite construction technologies allow for a significant reduction in both initial costs and production time [48]. However, docking operations with a floating dock are intricate and highly critical processes. A floating dock must maintain sufficient stability in any position, whether submerged or surfaced, with or without a vessel. The complexity of modern floating docks as multi-component technical systems underscores the need for specialized intelligent control systems to automate dock operations [48–50]. Therefore, in this work, the floating dock was selected as the second complex technical plant for study.

The effectiveness of the enhanced RB synthesis method was also evaluated through its application to the draft control system of a floating dock for small-tonnage vessels. A comprehensive description, including technical specifications, main parameters' values, and a mathematical model of this floating dock, can be found in [50]. This system features feedback based on the dock's immersion draft and employs a Mamdani-type controller. The input variables for the controller include speed control error ε_D, and its time derivative $d\varepsilon_D/dt$.

For this system, the error signal ε_D and its time derivative $d\varepsilon_D/dt$ are fuzzified using five linguistic terms each: (1) big negative (BN), (2) small negative (SN), (3) zero (Z), (4) small positive (SP), and (5) big positive (BP). The output signal of the controller u_{FC} is also represented by these five terms. All chosen linguistic terms have triangular membership functions and are uniformly distributed across the operating ranges of the input and output variables. The complete rule base of the controller consists of 25 rules ($s_{\text{full}} = 25$). In turn, these rules are determined by all possible combinations of LTs of two input variables.

For comparative analysis, this study also utilizes the rule base of the controller for the floating dock's draft developed from expert knowledge in paper [50]. This complete rule base is shown in Table 4.4 .

Table 4.4 Rule base of the fuzzy controller for the floating dock, synthesized from expert knowledge.

		Error time derivative $d\varepsilon_D/dt$				
		BN	**SN**	**Z**	**SP**	**BP**
Error signal ε_D	**BN**	BN	BN	BN	SN	SN
	SN	BN	BN	SN	SN	SN
	Z	SN	SN	Z	SP	SP
	SP	SP	SP	SP	BP	BP
	BP	SP	SP	BP	BP	BP

During the optimization-oriented synthesis of the draft controller's rule base using the improved method, the initial vector of consequents $\mathbf{X}_{C0}$ was also generated randomly. The objective function J and the reference model for the dynamic behavior of the submerging and surfacing processes of a floating dock are described by the same expressions as in paper [50]. The optimal objective function value was set to $J_{opt} = 2.2$, with a maximum iteration count of $N_{max} = 303$ to allow for three complete optimization rounds of the rule base from the 1st to the sth rule ($l = 3$). To simulate all processes of the submerging and surfacing of the floating dock, the same conditions were used as in [50]. It is also worth noting that the objective function value for the rule base developed using expert knowledge is not optimal, standing at $J = 2.843$.

Figure 4.5 illustrates the graph depicting the variation in the objective function value J throughout the synthesis and optimization of the rule base using the proposed improved method for the floating dock's draft control system. As shown in the figure, the optimization process achieved a minimum objective function value of $J_{min} = 2.148$, which is slightly better than the set optimal value ($J_{opt} = 2.2$).

The rule base, developed and optimized using the proposed enhanced method for the floating dock's control system, is presented in Table 4.5 .

In this instance, the consequents marked with zeros do not influence the draft automatic control process of the floating dock during its submerging and surfacing (system functioning) and can be removed from the RB at step 11 of the proposed improved method. Consequently, it is recommended to exclude the following rules from the synthesized rule base with the optimal set of consequents: 2, 5, 6, 10, 19, and 25. This results in a refined rule base with an optimal (reduced) number of rules $s_{opt} = 19$.

Figure 4.6 illustrates the graphs of the transients of submerging a floating dock with a fuzzy system based on: 1 – a rule base developed from

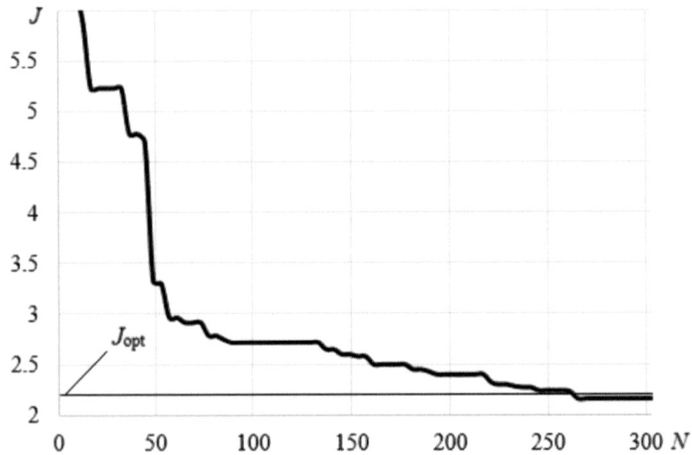

Figure 4.5 Graph depicting the variations in the objective function value J during the synthesis and optimization of the rule base for the floating dock's control system.

Table 4.5 Rule base of the fuzzy controller for the floating dock, synthesized using the proposed enhanced method

		Error time derivative $d\varepsilon_D/dt$				
		BN	**SN**	**Z**	**SP**	**BP**
Error signal ε_D	**BN**	BN	0	BN	BN	0
	SN	0	BN	BN	SN	0
	Z	BN	SN	Z	SP	BP
	SP	SP	SP	BP	0	BP
	BP	SP	BP	BP	BP	0

expert knowledge; 2 – a rule base developed using the proposed enhanced optimization-oriented synthesis method.

Additionally, Table 4.6 provides a comparative analysis of the performance metrics for fuzzy control systems of the floating dock draft corresponding to the aforementioned transients.

As shown in Figure 4.6 and Table 4.6 , the draft control system of the floating dock with an optimized rule base, developed using the improved optimization-oriented synthesis method, exhibits better control quality than the system based on expert knowledge. Specifically, the optimized rule base reduced the steady-state control error by 1.311% and shortened the total transient time by 9.16%. Moreover, the hardware and software implementation of the optimized controller will be somewhat simplified, as it contains six fewer rules compared to the full rule base designed using expert knowledge.

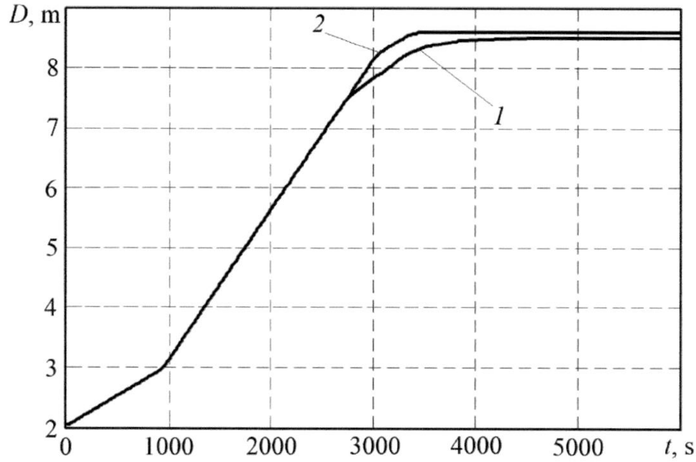

Figure 4.6 Transient graphs of submerging a floating dock with a fuzzy control system.

Table 4.6 Comparative analysis of the performance metrics for fuzzy control systems of the floating dock draft

Performance metrics	Fuzzy system's numerical values	
	Rule base developed from expert knowledge	Rule base developed using the proposed enhanced method
Objective function J	2.843	2.148
Total transient time, s	3765	3420
Steady-state error, %	2.124	0.813
Overshoot, %	0	0

During the synthesis and optimization of the rule base with the optimal set of consequents and the optimal number of rules for the fuzzy controller in the floating dock's draft control system, the implementation of the proposed improved optimization-oriented method did not require significant computational resources ($N_{max} = 303$), further demonstrating its efficiency. Additionally, to enhance the performance of the floating dock's draft control system, it would be beneficial to apply parametric optimization to the membership functions of the input and output variables' linguistic terms [50].

The research conducted on these two examples shows that the improved optimization-oriented method for rule bases synthesis is equally effective in creating fuzzy systems with an optimal set of consequents and an optimal (reduced) number of rules for various types of complex technical plants across different industries. This fully supports the method's suitability for designing intelligent systems of various types and configurations.

4.4 Conclusion

This study presented the challenges and advancements in the optimization-oriented synthesis of rule bases for fuzzy systems, along with insights into its application in developing control systems for complex technical plants. The developed method enables an iterative search for the optimal vector of RB consequents through a sequential evaluation of each rule's consequents, while also identifying and excluding rules that do not impact system performance. This process reduces the total number of rules to an optimal level, which as a result significantly simplifies software and hardware implementation and the total cost of the fuzzy system.

To generally evaluate the effectiveness and explore the application features of the enhanced optimization-oriented RB synthesis method, this chapter focuses on the development of fuzzy systems for two different technical plants from various industries: (a) a mobile robotic platform and (b) a floating dock designed for small-tonnage vessels. The computer simulation results demonstrated that the developed control systems for both the mobile robotic platform and the floating dock, utilizing optimized RBs of fuzzy controllers based on the proposed enhanced method, exhibit superior control quality and simplified hardware and software implementation compared to systems developed using expert knowledge. Specifically, for the robotic platform, overshoot, rise time, and total transient time were reduced by 20.16%, 37.2%, and 65.4%, respectively. Additionally, the optimized rule base for this system contains nine fewer rules ($s_{opt} = 36$) than the full RB ($s_{full} = 45$), which was synthesized using expert knowledge. For the floating dock, the steady-state error and total transient time were reduced by 1.31% and 9.16%, respectively, with the optimized RB containing six fewer rules ($s_{opt} = 19$) than the full RB ($s_{full} = 25$), also developed based on expert knowledge.

Future research will focus on exploring the application of this method in developing intelligent decision support systems for managing critical infrastructure facilities [51–54], medical diagnostics [55–63], robotics [7, 64–66], and transport logistics [25, 67–70]. Particular emphasis will be placed on systems with large-scale rule bases.

Acknowledgments

This work was sponsored by the National Foreign Expert Program (Grant No. G2022014114L).

References

[1] C.C. Aggarwal, 'Artificial Intelligence,' Springer International Publishing, 2021, 490 p. doi:10.1007/978-3-030-72357-6

[2] K. Knight, et al. (Eds.), 'Artificial Intelligence,' Second CCF International Conference, ICAI 2019, Xuzhou, China, Proceedings, Springer Singapore, 2019, 298 p. doi:10.1007/978-981-32-9298-7

[3] Y. Kondratenko, A. Shevchenko, Y. Zhukov, V. Slyusar, G. Kondratenko, M. Klymenko, O. Striuk, 'Analysis of the Priorities and Perspectives in Artificial Intelligence Implementation,' 2023 13th International Conference on Dependable Systems, Services and Technologies, DESSERT 2023, 2023, Athens, 13 – 15 October 2023, DOI 10.1109/DESSERT61349.2023.10416432

[4] B. Asmika, G. Mounika, P. S. Rani, 'Deep Learning for Vision and Decision Making in Self Driving Cars-Challenges with Ethical Decision Making,' 2021 International Conference on Intelligent Technologies (CONIT), Hubli, India, 2021, pp. 1-5, doi:10.1109/CONIT51480.2021.9498342

[5] D. Kalathil, et al., 'Self Driving Car using Neural Networks,' 2022 International Conference on Applied Artificial Intelligence and Computing (ICAAIC), Salem, India, 2022, pp. 213-217, doi:10.1109/ICAAIC53929.2022.9792595

[6] V. Slyusar, et al., 'Some Aspects of Artificial Intelligence Development Strategy for Mobile Technologies,' Journal of Mobile Multimedia, Vol. 20, Iss. 03, 2024, pp. 525–554. https://doi.org/10.13052/jmm1550-4646.2031

[7] R. Duro, et al. (Eds), 'Advances in intelligent robotics and collaborative automation,' River Publishers, Aalborg, 2015. doi:~https://doi.org/10.13052/rp-9788793237049

[8] S. Thrun, 'Toward robotic cars,' Communications of the ACM, Vol. 53, Iss. 4, 2010, pp. 99-106. https://doi.org/10.1145/1721654.1721679

[9] I. Goodfellow, Y. Bengio, A. Courville, 'Deep Learning,' MIT Press, 2016, 781 p.

[10] Y. Kondratenko, et al., 'Inspection mobile robot's control system with remote IoT-based data transmission,' Journal of Mobile Multimedia. Special issue "Mobile Communication and Computing for Internet of Things and Industrial Automation", Vol. 17, Is. 4, pp. 499-522, 2021. DOI: https://doi.org/10.13052/jmm1550-4646.1742

[11] J. Lee, B. Bagheri, H. A. Kao, 'A Cyber-Physical Systems architecture for Industry 4.0-based manufacturing systems,' Manufacturing Letters, Vol. 3, 2015, pp. 18-23. https://doi.org/10.1016/j.mfglet.2014.12.001

[12] A.I. Shevchenko, Y.P. Kondratenko, V.I. Slyusar, I.P. Atamanyuk, G.V. Kondratenko, T.V. Yeroshenko, 'Analysis of the prospect domains in AI implementation: Nationals, NATO and Ukraine AI strategies,' Y.P. Kondratenko, A.S. Shevchenko (Eds), Research Tendencies and Prospect Domains for AI Development and Implementation, River Publishers, 2024, pp. 1–30. https://www.riverpublishers.com/book_details.php?book_id=1163

[13] Y.P. Kondratenko, O.V. Korobko, O.V. Kozlov, 'Frequency Tuning Algorithm for Loudspeaker Driven Thermoacoustic Refrigerator Optimization,' K. J. Engemann, A. M. Gil-Lafuente, J. M. Merigo (Eds.), Lecture Notes in Business Information Processing, volume 115 of Modeling and Simulation in Engineering, Economics and Management, Springer-Verlag, Berlin, Heidelberg: 2012, pp. 270-279. https://doi.org/10.1007/978-3-642-30433-0_27.

[14] G. Hayduk, P. Kwasnowski, Z. Mikoś, 'Building management system architecture for large building automation systems,' 2016 17th International Carpathian Control Conference (ICCC), High Tatras, Slovakia, 2016, pp. 232-235, doi:10.1109/CarpathianCC.2016.7501100

[15] M. Ohlenbusch, et al., 'Installation and Control of Building Automation Systems Using Human-Robot-Interaction,' 2018 23rd International Conference on Methods & Models in Automation & Robotics (MMAR), Miedzyzdroje, Poland, 2018, pp. 493-497, doi:10.1109/MMAR.2018.8485854

[16] K. Zhou, C. Fu, S. Yang, 'Big data driven smart energy management: From big data to big insights,' Renewable and Sustainable Energy Reviews, Vol. 56, 2016, pp. 215-225. https://doi.org/10.1016/j.rser.2015.11.050

[17] M. Swarnkar, et al., 'Use of AI for development and generation of renewable energy,' 2023 IEEE Renewable Energy and Sustainable E-Mobility Conference (RESEM), Bhopal, India, 2023, pp. 1-5, doi: 10.1109/RESEM57584.2023.10236136

[18] Y. Kondratenko, et al. 'Tendencies and Challenges of Artificial Intelligence Development and Implementation,' in: Proceedings of the 12th IEEE International Conference on Intelligent Data Acquisition and Advanced Computing Systems: Technology and Applications,

IDAACS'2023, Vol. 1, 2023, pp. 221-226, IDAACS 2023, Dortmund, Germany, 7-9 September 2023. doi:10.1109/IDAACS58523.2023.103 48800
[19] W. Li, et al., 'Design of An Intelligent Control System for Underground Directional Drilling Trajectory in Coal Mines,' 2022 41st Chinese Control Conference (CCC), Hefei, China, 2022, pp. 2586-2590, doi: 10.23919/CCC55666.2022.9902602
[20] X. Xiong, 'Development of AI Intelligent Decision-Making System for Engineering Project Investment Cost Control based on Big Data Information Collection Algorithm,' 2022 International Conference on Edge Computing and Applications (ICECAA), Tamilnadu, India, 2022, pp. 172-175, doi:10.1109/ICECAA55415.2022.9936347
[21] H. Szczepaniuk, E. K. Szczepaniuk, 'Applications of Artificial Intelligence Algorithms in the Energy Sector,' Energies, Vol. 16, Iss. 1, 2023, 347. https://doi.org/10.3390/en16010347
[22] A. Rikalovic, et al., 'Intelligent Decision Support System for Industrial Site Classification: A GIS-Based Hierarchical Neuro-Fuzzy Approach,' in: IEEE Systems Journal, vol. 12, no. 3, pp. 2970-2981, 2018. doi: 10.1109/JSYST.2017.2697043.
[23] L.A. Zadeh, 'The concept of a linguistic variable and its application to approximate reasoning – I,' Information Sciences, Volume 8, Issue 3, 1975, pp. 199-249. https://doi.org/10.1016/0020-0255(75)90036-5
[24] L.A. Zadeh, 'The concept of a linguistic variable and its application to approximate reasoning – II,' Information Sciences, Volume 8, Issue 4, 1975, pp. 301-357. https://doi.org/10.1016/0020-0255(75)90046-8
[25] M. Solesvik, et al., 'Fuzzy decision support systems in marine practice,' in: Fuzzy Systems (FUZZ-IEEE), 2017 IEEE International Conference on Fuzzy Systems, pp. 1-6, 2017. DOI:10.1109/FUZZ-IEEE.2017.801 5471
[26] J. M. Mendel, 'Uncertain Rule-Based Fuzzy Systems: Introduction and New Directions, 2nd Edition,' Springer, 2017, 684 p.
[27] J. M. Mendel, 'Explainable Uncertain Rule-Based Fuzzy Systems,' Springer Cham, 2024, 580 p. https://doi.org/10.1007/978-3-031-35 378-9
[28] Y.P. Kondratenko, O.V. Kozlov, 'Combined Fuzzy Controllers with Embedded Model for Automation of Complex Industrial Plants,' in: S. N. Shahbazova, J. Kacprzyk, V. E. Balas, V. Kreinovich (Eds.), Recent Developments and the New Direction in Soft-Computing Foundations

and Applications, volule 393 of Studies in Fuzziness and Soft Computing, Springer, Cham, 2020, pp. 215-228. https://doi.org/10.1007/978-3-030-47124-8_18.

[29] Y. P. Kondratenko, et al., 'Synthesis and Research of Neuro-Fuzzy Model of Ecopyrogenesis Multi-circuit Circulatory System' Advance Trends in Soft Computing, Studies in Fuzziness and Soft Computing, Berlin, Heidelberg: Springer-Verlag, 2014, Vol. 312, pp. 1-14. https://doi.org/10.1007/978-3-319-03674-8_1

[30] G. Salazar, F. Rossomando, O. Camacho, 'An Adaptive Neuro-Fuzzy PID Controller Approach for thermal Systems: An Experimental Validation,' 2022 IEEE International Conference on Automation/XXV Congress of the Chilean Association of Automatic Control (ICA-ACCA), Curicó, Chile, 2022, pp. 1-5, doi:10.1109/ICA-ACCA56767.2022.10006148.

[31] I. K. Amin, et al., 'Adaptive Neuro-Fuzzy Controller for Grid Voltage Dip Compensations of Grid Connected DFIG-WECS,' 2019 IEEE International Electric Machines & Drives Conference (IEMDC), San Diego, CA, USA, 2019, pp. 2101-2106, doi:10.1109/IEMDC.2019.8785362

[32] O. Skakodub, O. Kozlov, Y. Kondratenko, 'Optimization of Linguistic Terms' Shapes and Parameters: Fuzzy Control System of a Quadrotor Drone,' in 2021 11th IEEE International Conference on Intelligent Data Acquisition and Advanced Computing Systems: Technology and Applications (IDAACS), 2021, pp. 566-571, doi:10.1109/IDAACS53288.2021.9660926.

[33] O.V. Kozlov, Y.P. Kondratenko, O.S. Skakodub, 'Information Technology for Parametric Optimization of Fuzzy Systems Based on Hybrid Grey Wolf Algorithms,' SN Computer Science, Volume 3, issue 6, 2022. 463. https://doi.org/10.1007/s42979-022-01333-4

[34] O.V. Kozlov, 'Optimal Selection of Membership Functions Types for Fuzzy Control and Decision Making Systems,' in: Proceedings of the 2nd International Workshop on Intelligent Information Technologies & Systems of Information Security with CEUR-WS, Khmelnytskyi, Ukraine, IntelITSIS 2021, CEUR-WS, Vol-2853, 2021, pp. 238-247. https://ceur-ws.org/Vol-2853/paper22.pdf

[35] M. F. T. Sim, A. A. Bandala, J. R. B. Del Rosario, 'An Intelligent Transport System (ITS): Fuzzy Logic Controller for Adaptive Cruise Control,' 2022 IEEE 14th International Conference on Humanoid, Nanotechnology, Information Technology, Communication and Control,

Environment, and Management (HNICEM), Boracay Island, Philippines, 2022, pp. 1-4, doi: 10.1109/HNICEM57413.2022.10109395
[36] M. Ramzanzad, H. Rashidy Kanan, 'A new method for design and implementation of intelligent traffic control system based on fuzzy logic using FPGA,' 2013 13th Iranian Conference on Fuzzy Systems (IFSC), Qazvin, Iran, 2013, pp. 1-4, doi:10.1109/IFSC.2013.6675630
[37] S. M. Odeh, 'Hybrid algorithm: Fuzzy Logic-Genetic Algorithm on traffic light intelligent system,' 2015 IEEE International Conference on Fuzzy Systems (FUZZ-IEEE), Istanbul, Turkey, 2015, pp. 1-7, doi: 10.1109/FUZZ-IEEE.2015.7338117
[38] L. Cherroun, M. Nadour, A. Kouzou, 'Type-1 and Type-2 Fuzzy Logic Controllers for Autonomous Robotic Motion,' 2019 International Conference on Applied Automation and Industrial Diagnostics (ICAAID), Elazig, Turkey, 2019, pp. 1-5, doi:10.1109/ICAAID.2019.8934997
[39] C. Le, and L. Zhenghua, 'Design of two-stage fuzzy controller for mobile robot using vision navigation,' 2016 IEEE Chinese Guidance, Navigation and Control Conference (CGNCC), Nanjing, China, 2016, pp. 872-877, doi:10.1109/CGNCC.2016.7828900
[40] A. Kouhkord, et al., 'Design of a Genetic based Optimized Fuzzy Logic Controller for Enhanced Trajectory Tracking Accuracy of a 3P Robot,' 2022 10th RSI International Conference on Robotics and Mechatronics (ICRoM), Tehran, Iran, Islamic Republic of, 2022, pp. 497-502, doi: 10.1109/ICRoM57054.2022.10025249
[41] Y.P. Kondratenko, et al., 'Bio-inspired optimization of fuzzy control system for inspection robotic platform: comparative analysis of hybrid swarm methods,' CEUR Workshop Proceedings, Vol. 3711, 2024, pp. 109-123. https://ceur-ws.org/Vol-3711/paper7.pdf
[42] V. Khattri, S. K. Nayak, 'A Review on Integrating Evolutionary Multiobjective Optimization in Developing Fuzzy Systems,' 2018 International Conference on Computational and Characterization Techniques in Engineering & Sciences (CCTES), Lucknow, India, 2018, pp. 252-257, doi:10.1109/CCTES.2018.8674108
[43] O.V. Kozlov, Y.P. Kondratenko, O.S. Skakodub, 'Intelligent Information Technology for Structural Optimization of Fuzzy Control and Decision-Making Systems,' in: Kondratenko, Y.P., Kreinovich, V., Pedrycz, W., Chikrii, A., Gil-Lafuente, A.M. (Eds.) Artificial Intelligence in Control

and Decision-making Systems, Studies in Computational Intelligence, Vol. 1087, Springer, Cham, 2023, P. 127-165. https://doi.org/10.1007/978-3-031-25759-9_7

[44] Y.P. Kondratenko, O.V. Kozlov, O.V. Korobko, 'Two Modifications of the Automatic Rule Base Synthesis for Fuzzy Control and Decision Making Systems,' in: Medina, J., Ojeda-Aciego, M., Verdegay, J.L., Pelta, D.A., Cabrera, I.P., Bouchon-Meunier, B., Yager, R.R. (Eds.) "Information Processing and Management of Uncertainty in Knowledge-Based Systems. Theory and Foundations", Book Series: Communications in Computer and Information Science, Vol. 854, 2018, Berlin, Heidelberg: Springer International Publishing, pp. 570-582. doi: 10.1007/978-3-319-91476-3

[45] O.V. Kozlov, 'Information Technology for Designing Rule Bases of Fuzzy Systems using Ant Colony Optimization,' International Journal of Computing, Vol. 20, Iss. 4, 2021, pp. 471-486. https://www.computingonline.net/computing/article/view/2434.

[46] O.V. Kozlov, Y.P. Kondratenko, 'Bio-Inspired Algorithms for Optimization of Fuzzy Control Systems: Comparative Analysis,' in: Y. P. Kondratenko, V. M. Kuntsevich, A. A. Chikrii, V. F. Gubarev (Eds.) "Advanced Control Systems: Theory and Applications", Series in Automation, Control and Robotics, River Publishers, Denmark, 2021. pp. 83-128. doi:10.1201/9781003337010-5

[47] O. Kozlov, Y. Kondratenko, 'Automatic Synthesis of Rule Bases of Fuzz Control Systems Based on Genetic Algorithms,' in: Shahbazova, S.N., Abbasov, A.M., Kreinovich, V., Kacprzyk, J., Batyrshin, I.Z. (Eds.) Recent Developments and the New Directions of Research, Foundations, and Applications, Studies in Fuzziness and Soft Computing, vol. 422, Springer, Cham, 2023, pp. 101-123. https://doi.org/10.1007/978-3-031-20153-0_9

[48] A. Apostolidis, J. Kokarakis, A. Merikas, 'Modeling the Dry-Docking Cost: The Case of Tankers,' Journal of Ship Production and Design, Vol. 28, No. 3, 2012, pp. 134-143.

[49] Wang Fang, 'Study on closed-loop gain shaping control of floating dock control system,' 2010 International Conference on Computer, Mechatronics, Control and Electronic Engineering, Changchun, China, 2010, pp. 53-55, doi:10.1109/CMCE.2010.5610388

[50] Y.P. Kondratenko, O.V. Kozlov, A.M. Topalov, 'Fuzzy Controllers for Increasing Efficiency of the Floating Dock's Operations: Design and Optimization,' in: V. M. Kuntsevich, V. F. Gubarev, Y. P. Kondratenko,

D. V. Lebedev, V. P. Lysenko (Eds.), Control Systems: Theory and Applications, Series in Automation, Control and Robotics, 2018, River Publishers, Gistrup, Delft, pp. 197-232. doi:10.1201/9781003337706-10

[51] M.V. Maksimov, S.N. Pelykh, R.L. Gontar, 'Principles of controlling fuel-element cladding lifetime in variable VVER-1000 loading regimes,' Atomic Energy, Vol. 112, Iss. 4, 2012, pp. 241-249. https://doi.org/10.1007/s10512-012-9552-3.

[52] S.N. Pelykh, M.V. Maksimov, 'The method of fuel rearrangement control considering fuel element cladding damage and burnup,' Problems of Atomic Science and Technology, Vol. 87, Iss. 5, 2013, pp. 84-90. https://vant.kipt.kharkov.ua/ARTICLE/VANT_2013_5/article_2013_5_84a.pdf

[53] Y.P Kondratenko, O.V. Kozlov, G.V. Kondratenko, I.P. Atamanyuk, 'Mathematical Model and Parametrical Identification of Ecopyrogenesis Plant Based on Soft Computing Techniques,' in: C. Berger-Vachon, et al. (Eds.), Complex Systems: Solutions and Challenges in Economics, Management and Engineering, Studies in Systems, Decision and Control, Vol. 125, Berlin, Heidelberg: Springer International Publishing, 2018, pp. 201-233. DOI: https://doi.org/10.1007/978-3-319-69989-9_13

[54] Y. Kondratenko, G. Kondratenko, A. Shevchenko, V. Slyusar, Y. Zhukov, M. Vakulenko, 'Towards Implementing the Strategy of Artificial Intelligence Development: Ukraine Peculiarities,' CEUR Workshop Proceedings, vol. 3513, 2023, pp. 106–117. https://ceur-ws.org/Vol-3513/paper09.pdf

[55] P. Chatterjee, et al., 'IoT-based decision support system for intelligent healthcare – applied to cardiovascular diseases,' in: 2017 7th International Conference on Communication Systems and Network Technologies (CSNT), Nagpur, India, pp. 362-366, 2017. doi:10.1109/CSNT.2017.8418567.

[56] I. Atamanyuk, et al., 'Calculation Method for a Computer's Diagnostics of Cardiovascular Diseases Based on Canonical Decompositions of Random Sequences,' CEUR Workshop Proceedings, Vol. 1356, 2015, pp. 108-120. http://ceur-ws.org/Vol-1356/paper_28.pdf

[57] I. Atamanyuk, et al., 'Computational method of the cardiovascular diseases classification based on a generalized nonlinear canonical decomposition of random sequences,' Scientific Reports 13, 59 (2023). https://doi.org/10.1038/s41598-022-27318-0

[58] O. Kozlov, et al., 'Comparative Analysis of Parametric Optimization Techniques: Fuzzy DSS for Medical Diagnostics,' in: S. Shahbazova, et al. (eds), Recent Developments and the New Directions of Research, Foundations, and Applications. Studies in Fuzziness and Soft Computing, vol. 423, 2023, pp. 193-201. Springer, Cham. https://doi.org/10.1007/978-3-031-23476-7_17

[59] A. Sheremet, et al., 'Diagnosis of Lung Disease Based on Medical Images Using Artificial Neural Networks,' 2021 IEEE 3rd Ukraine Conference on Electrical and Computer Engineering, UKRCON 2021 - Proceedings, 2021, pp. 561–566. DOI: 10.1109/UKRCON53503.2021.9575961

[60] A. Sokoliuk, et al., 'Machine Learning Algorithms for Binary Classification of Liver Disease,' in: 2020 IEEE International Conference on Problems of Infocommunications. Science and Technology (PIC S&T), 6-9 Oct. 2020, Kharkiv, Ukraine, Proceedings, Publ. IEEE, 2020, pp. 417-421. DOI:~10.1109/PICST51311.2020.9468051

[61] I. Sova, et al., 'Machine learning technology for neoplasm segmentation on brain MRI scans,' CEUR Workshop Proceedings, Vol. 2791, 2020, pp. 50–59. https://ceur-ws.org/Vol-2791/2020200050.pdf

[62] Y. Kondratenko, et al., 'Artificial Neural Networks for Recognition of Brain Tumors on MRI Images,' in: A. Bollin, et al. (eds), Information and Communication Technologies in Education, Research, and Industrial Applications. ICTERI 2020. Communications in Computer and Information Science, vol. 1308, 2021, pp. 119-140, Springer, Cham, DOI: https://doi.org/10.1007/978-3-030-77592-6_6

[63] Z. Gomolka, et al., 'Diagnosing Dyslexia in Early School-Aged Children Using the LSTM Network and Eye Tracking Technology,' Applied Sciences (Switzerland) 2024; 14(17):8004. https://doi.org/10.3390/app14178004

[64] A.N. Tkachenko, et al., 'Evolutionary adaptation of control processes in robots operating in non-stationary environments,' Mechanism and Machine Theory, Printed in Great Britain, Vol. 18, No. 4, 1983, pp. 275-278. DOI: 10.1016/0094-114X(83)90118-0

[65] I. Sidenko, et al., 'Machine Learning for Unmanned Aerial Vehicle Routing on Rough Terrain', in: Z. Hu, I. Dychka, M. He (eds), Advances in Computer Science for Engineering and Education VI, ICCSEEA 2023, Lecture Notes on Data Engineering and Communications Technologies, vol. 181, 2023, pp. 626–635. DOI:10.1007/978-3-031-36118-0_56

[66] Y. Kondratenko, et al., 'Machine Learning Techniques for Increasing Efficiency of the Robot's Sensor and Control Information Processing,' Sensors 2022, 22(3), 1062. https://doi.org/10.3390/s22031062

[67] S. Encheva, et al., 'Decision Support Systems in Logistics,' AIP Conference Proceedings 1060, 2008, pp. 254-256. https://doi.org/10.1063/1.3037065~

[68] Y.P. Kondratenko, et al., 'Synthesis of Intelligent Decision Support Systems for Transport Logistic,' in: Proceeding of the 6th IEEE International Conference on Intelligent Data Acquisition and Advanced Computing Systems: Technology and Applications, IDAACS'2011. Vol. 2 (Sept. 15-17, 2011, Prague, Czech Republic), 2011, pp.642-646. DOI: 10.1109/IDAACS.2011.6072847

[69] B. Werners, et al., 'Alternative Fuzzy Approaches for Efficiently Solving the Capacitated Vehicle Routing Problem in Conditions of Uncertain Demands,' in: C. Berger-Vachon, et al. (Eds.), Complex Systems: Solutions and Challenges in Economics, Management and Engineering, Book Series: Studies in Systems, Decision and Control, Vol. 125, Berlin, Heidelberg: Springer International Publishing, 2018, pp. 521-543. DOI: https://doi.org/10.1007/978-3-319-69989-9_31

[70] N. Ukhan, et al. 'ICT for planning and optimization of transport routes with time windows,' CEUR Workshop Proceedings, vol. 2740, 2020, pp. 365-372. https://ceur-ws.org/Vol-2740/20200365.pdf

5

The Nearest Results of Artificial Intelligence Application in Biology and Medicine: Development Trends and Implementation Risks

O. Mintser

Shupyk National Healthcare University of Ukraine, Ukraine
E-mail: o.mintser@gmail.com

Abstract

Against the incredibly rapid development of the theoretical foundations of the implementation of artificial intelligence (AI), its use in practical medicine is limited to a relatively small number of valuable areas. The purpose of the study is to conceptualize the reasons for limitations in the use of AI, as well as the prospects and risks of AI implementation. The main discussion results can be formulated in the following ways. (1) The emergence of AI opens a new era in biology and medicine and revolutionizes disease diagnosis, forecasting, and management strategies. (2) Despite the enormous potential of AI in healthcare, significant ethical, regulatory, technological, and technical challenges remain. The issues of constant changes in the clinical manifestations of the disease and problems of semantics deserve special attention. (3) Addressing issues related to data privacy, fragmentation of medical models and data, algorithmic biases, regulatory compliance, and inherent resistance to change is critical to AI's responsible and effective integration into healthcare. (4) Although the integration of AI promises significant advances in biology and healthcare, the latter are in continuous development and require additional research and clinical trials for confirmation.

DOI: 10.1201/9788743800989-5

Keywords: Artificial intelligence, large language models, deep learning, convolutional neural networks, image processing, digital pathology, Global Health.

5.1 Introduction

Artificial intelligence's emergence and widespread implementation in various sectors of the economy, science, and education have entirely changed our daily lives, significantly affecting how we perceive and process information. Today, fundamental language models (large language models – LLMs), some of which have over 500 billion parameters, have emerged. They were trained using massive amounts of unlabeled data with the help of self-supervision. LLMs already demonstrate remarkable capabilities that challenge human performance in completing complex tasks, such as answering intricate questions, creating coherent contexts, summarizing ideas, reasoning, and planning. Recent studies have shown that these systems can successfully generate new molecular structures with desired properties, predict protein–ligand interactions, and identify potential drug targets [1]. LLMs are also adapting to user prompts, leading to the emergence of a new in-demand profession: AI prompter or LLM psychologist. A notable trend in AI is its "democratization" [2], meaning that libraries, models, data, and computational resources are becoming more accessible, fostering community growth and collaboration. AI is also widely used in biomedical research [3, 4]. However, despite its rapid implementation, its use in practical medicine remains limited to a few specific areas. Generalizing the reasons for the relatively slow dissemination of AI ideas in medicine seems essential.

The purpose of the study is to conceptualize the reasons for the limitations of AI use, as well as the prospects and risks of AI implementation.

5.2 Short Analysis of State of the Art for AI in Medicine

Progress in the development of information processing methods has become particularly noticeable in the management of large datasets. New algorithms, technologies, and systems appeared. Nowadays, data processing is the manipulation of data with the help of a computer, which includes a number of procedures that are far from always formalized and standardized. Even the formation and transformation of the initial results into the desired form requires interpretation processes. Accordingly, the logic of using machine learning appeared. Machine learning (ML) is the study of specific computer algorithms that are built using a mathematical algorithm model from sample data, which, in turn, are used to generate predictions or decisions. Today, ML is actively integrated into various spheres of life [5, 6], first of all, for the creation of relevant databases, knowledge bases, and also for decision-making.

Deep learning (DL) is much more complex than ML. It involves the use of artificial neural networks with representation learning. It can also be seen as a form for automating predictive analytics, and thus DL is associated with a hierarchy of increasing complexity and abstraction, while ML algorithms remain a linear approach. Basically, DL simulates the complex neural networks of the human brain, allowing computers to autonomously detect patterns and make decisions based on large volumes of unstructured data [7, 8]. This direction has led to breakthroughs in various fields, from computer vision and natural language processing to diagnostic and predictive processes in healthcare.

A DL network usually consists of several layers of artificial neural networks, including an input layer, an output layer, and several hidden layers. Importantly, deep learning enables the creation of a set of computer models that enable rapid progress in image analysis. To date, DL algorithms in healthcare have reached an expert level in the detection of metastases of breast cancer and colorectal cancer carcinoma and have demonstrated high accuracy in screening for prostate cancer, as well as in the assessment of cancer of the breast, bladder, stomach, thyroid gland, etc. [9–12].

The most common DL method in digital pathology is convolutional neural networks (CNNs), which are designed to analyze insufficiently formalized data in large arrays, including color images. The period of decision-making is preceded by the period of training and its quality on a training sample of data with *a priori* known and verified conclusions [13–15]. Training high-quality CNNs requires large datasets for training, testing, and validation [16, 17]. In particular, the annotated ImageNet database containing more than a million non-medical images is used for deep learning of digital pathology [18, 19].

Another advantage of using CNNs for new tasks is the use of transfer learning, relying on previously trained CNNs to perform a new task. Not all CNN layers require retraining and adequate training performance can be achieved with smaller datasets. Although all CNNs have similar characteristics, their architecture differs, including size, sequence, number of layers and filters, number of parameters, and connections between CNN levels [20]. As a result, there are significant differences between different CNNs in terms of computational efficiency and performance. Many works adopted LeNet and AlexNet architectures with minor changes in the size of the penultimate output layer [21].

According to the data obtained in recent years, new elements have been introduced into the CNN architecture, which increase the efficiency of training while reducing the total number of training parameters. This strategy enables multi-level feature extraction [22, 23], increasing diagnostic accuracy. Another category of neural networks often used in digital pathology is recurrent neural networks (RNNs), which are commonly used to model sequential data where input and output parameters (as in feedforward neural networks) may vary in length.

Federated learning (FL), a machine learning method that allows you to train a model based on data stored on different devices without the need to share actual data, has become popular in recent years [24]. This approach allows you to train the model while preserving the privacy of user data at regional or even local levels. FL is an innovative approach to machine learning that moves model training to end-user devices instead of a centralized server-based training model. This approach provides a number of advantages and solves some of the problems associated with centralized learning. It offers several key advantages, such as data privacy, security, efficiency, and scalability, by keeping data locally and sharing only model updates over the communication network [25–27].

5.3 AI for Processing Medical Research Materials

A large-scale multicenter study, aimed at comparing the results of diagnostics with the help of artificial intelligence and with the participation of pathologists, was conducted by Mukhopadhyay S. with co-authors [28]. This study showed that the quality of primary diagnosis with digitized WSI (whole slide imaging) is not inferior to the results obtained using traditional microscopy methods. The introduction of digital scanners for histological preparations made it possible to develop strategies for quantitative histomorphometry. However, the problem of definition and segmentation of various histological elements remains quite difficult. For example, Irshad H. et al. analyzed a large number of works on segmentation of nuclei for histological analysis over the past 20 years [29]. Xu J. et al proposed a geodesic active contours (GAC) algorithm that uses mean shift clustering and normalized cuts (NCut) to identify common histological structures [30].

The algorithm begins by identifying all objects in the image that match the initial color sample. It then uses the GAC model's edge detection function based on the local color gradient structure tensor, which is obtained by computing the local minimum/maximum variation contributed by each color channel. This method is successfully used for segmentation of glandular areas in prostate biopsies. Although geodesic active contours have become viral tools for image segmentation, they are usually sensitive to model initialization. A second limitation of GAC models is that the edge detector function usually involves the use of a gray gradient; color images are usually converted to grayscale before calculating the gradient. However, using a grayscale gradient for color images results in broken edges and weak boundaries because the other channels are not used in the gradient calculation. To overcome these limitations, the authors applied a new GAC model, hierarchical normalized cuts (HNCut), which combines two powerful segmentation strategies, mean-shift clustering and normalized cuts. HNCut first involves identifying a color sample (usually a few pixels) from the object of interest. A multiscale normalized mean shift algorithm then quickly provides an initial accurate detection of all objects in the scene that match the colors in the sample. This detection result provides the initial outline of the GAC. The edge detection function of the GAC model uses a local texture tensor based on the color gradient obtained by computing the local minimum/maximum variation contributed by each color channel. The authors showed that the edge detection function based on the color gradient leads to more pronounced boundaries than the classical function based on the gray gradient [31].

The integration of HNCut's color gradient initialization scheme embodies five unique and novel attributes: (1) efficiency in segmenting multiple target structures; (2) ability to segment several objects from huge images; (3) minimal human interaction; (4) accuracy; and (5) reproducibility.

A quantitative and qualitative comparison of the HNCut-CGAC model with other state-of-the-art active contour schemes (including the hybrid active contour model (Paragios-Derish) and the region-based active contour model (Rousseau-Derish)) on 196 digitized prostate histopathological images shows that HNCut-CGAC performs better than current hybrid and regional active circuit methods.

It is interesting to note that image analysis is a cost-effective tool for relating complex features of tissue organization to molecular data and outcomes, and for resolving unclassified or heterogeneous cases. A study [32] showed that an image-based approach can substantiate a method for predicting colorectal cancer from standard slices using deep learning. The proposed technology classified samples previously unclassified by RNA expression profiling, reproduced expected correlations with genomic and epigenetic changes, and showed similar prognostic associations such as transcriptomic CMS. Thus, the prediction of an RNA expression classifier can be made based on images, opening the way to simple, inexpensive, and reliable biological stratification within routine workflows.

Pathomorphological examination of tissues is a key tool in the diagnosis of malignant tumors. Doctors have to manually analyze images of pathological tissue sections. This is not only time-consuming but also highly subjective, easily leading to misdiagnosis. It can be assumed that computer-aided image analysis has a much greater potential for more detailed detection, selection, and quantification of features compared to the capabilities of a pathologist.

Such analysis goes beyond manual capabilities and, most importantly, can create new diagnostic algorithms and predictive models. The latter are used in translational research and reveal new characteristics of the disease based on changes at the cellular and molecular levels [33]. However, although this approach has been successfully applied to detect and highlight glandular elements on histological images of normal colon tissue, the problem of using AI has not been fully resolved.

Automated diagnostic systems play an important role in the study of histological images and diagnostics. Various image processing and computer vision (CV) techniques are used to segment histological features, recognize cell types, and classify tissues for quantitative characterization, automated evaluation of histological images, and determination of the presence or absence of disease [20]. Given the complex procedure of histological imaging, machine learning involves several steps.

At the first stage, pre-processing of the image is performed, which includes color normalization to level the variability of the image caused by the peculiarities of material processing and staining of histological preparations. An important feature of the stage is the identification of markers for visual comparison of their positions, and adjacent tissue sections are adapted for their visualization with harmonized colors [34, 35].

The second stage is devoted to structure recognition and segmentation. The necessity of the stage is dictated by the heterogeneity and variability of structural elements in the same tissue, not to mention different organs. For this, specialized segmentation algorithms are used for various diseases, especially malignant neoplasms [36]. An important element of the analysis is cell nuclei, which are most susceptible to changes during pathological processes. Nuclear texture analysis (Euclidean distance map analysis), Hough transformation (recognition of graininess coefficients for circular textures), Laplacian

Gaussian filters, and other methods are used to assess the structure of nuclei and determine their size and shape, including a spectrum of probabilistic algorithms, determining the gradient in polar and graphic reductions, etc. [37].

When segmenting the glands, their variations in shape, size, elongation, as well as changes in decreasing tumor differentiation are taken into account [20]. The basis of gland analysis algorithms is the identification of nuclei and the value of the lumen of glandular structures.

In recent years, several deep learning algorithms have been developed specifically for segmentation tasks with relatively high speed and robust performance under various staining conditions [38], as they are virtually independent of staining intensity or manual functions [39]. Thus, deep-learning-based segmentation is expected to become an important tool for WSI analysis.

The next step in automated image processing is the selection of distinguishing features (characteristics) or biomarkers. It is clear that structural changes accompany the development of pathological processes, and these structural signs are essential for the diagnosis of the disease. For example, a carcinoma is characterized by abnormal growth that leads to increased nuclear density, changes in their size and structure, or a large number of mitotic cells in a small area that can be identified by automated methods. The initial list of symptoms is formed on the basis of descriptors (descriptions) from specialists in various fields of pathology [40, 41]. In personalized medicine, biomarkers are substances that doctors can measure in the body to help them determine whether a patient has a disease, how it develops the disease, or whether the treatment works, that is, to identify a specific subgroup of the population with diagnostic and prognostic conclusions. Examples of biomarkers are estrogen and progesterone levels, which allow the molecular subtype of breast cancer to be determined. The values of these phenotypic markers provide an opportunity to choose the right treatment and predict the outcome of treatment of patients with breast cancer. In a number of cases, current tests for biomarkers may not be reliable enough, but can be a source of additional information for further diagnosis or treatment.

Recently, a significant number of other biomarkers (cellular, subcellular, molecular) have been identified in certain types of cancer (tumor-associated cells [42]). The ordering, classification, and identification of complex biomarkers based on artificial intelligence enables the collection of clinical data and digital images [34], the definition of a system of quantitative characteristics according to the accepted criterion, and the provision of the best potential treatment prognosis [43].

It should be noted that AI algorithms can detect information that cannot be seen by the human eye and use it for prediction. Thus, the use of AI not only improves diagnosis but also predicts response to treatment, the presence of somatic mutations, and patient survival [44].

An important element of digital pathology is also the development of algorithms and functional approaches for the automated classification of tissues and structures [16]. Classification of structures can be improved by selecting appropriate regions of interest. Their choice is based primarily on the tasks of pathogistological diagnosis, which include determination of tumor size, histological type and subtype, characteristic features, degree of differentiation, presence of lymphovascular invasion, or damage to lymph nodes. In addition, the state of the resection margins and lymphocytic infiltration serve as factors that may become prognostically important under certain circumstances [45].

Quantitative feature modeling work for tissue classification in the context of digital pathology can be classified into two general categories: manual feature definition and unsupervised feature selection approaches, i.e., implementing a declarative or imperative strategy. In general, the imperative strategy refers to those cases that can be associated with specific measurable attributes of the image and have some degree of interpretation. Clearly, both strategies have strengths and weaknesses. Hand-crafted features typically provide greater transparency and may therefore be more intuitive to the end user – the pathologist or clinician, as the case may be. On the other hand, features that are not controlled and defined by the domain may seem more difficult to understand, since they include more fundamental, but not always visible, features related to the nature of the disease and its morphological manifestations in the tissues.

The use of deep learning techniques based on feature generation means that they can be quickly and efficiently applied to any problem. However, this is accompanied by difficulties in their interpretation. Finding ways to synergize the two sets of feature modeling approaches can provide an ideal combination of generalizability and compatibility for disease characterization and modeling in digital pathology. However, existing deep learning methods have certain limitations regarding the segmentation of pathological images of malignant tumors. This can be seen from the comparisons of the clustering-based method (they have high computational efficiency and are more sensitive to noise, which leads to low accuracy) and deep-learning-based segmentation methods (where it is difficult to achieve a balance between accuracy and segmentation efficiency [46]). Although CNN-based segmentation methods have higher accuracy, they are time consuming and memory intensive.

Summing up, let us emphasize that the achievements of digital pathology allow solving a number of tasks that are relevant for both pathologists and clinicians. These include assessment of diagnostic features, determination of disease probability, assessment of tumor differentiation (classification), differentiation of histological types of cancer, identification of new disease characteristics/signs, prediction of outcome, prediction of recurrence, and prediction of gene mutation status.

The results of AI usage in digital pathology allow us to conclude that computer image analysis provides excellent accuracy, reproducibility, and standardization in studies based on microscopic morphology, compared to classical histological research, as the amount of information contained within a cell exceeds what can be observed solely by a human specialist. The latest technologies have excellent potential for more detailed detection, extraction, and quantification of features compared to the evaluative capabilities of a human pathologist; they perform tasks that exceed manual capabilities and can generate new diagnostic algorithms and predictive models applied in translational research. As a result, they are able to identify new disease characteristics based on changes at the cellular and molecular levels.

Despite the reluctance of regulatory bodies to approve the use of scanned images for primary diagnostics, computer analysis and digital pathology will become critical tools in clinical decision-making in the near future.

5.4 AI Application in Healthcare Management

The significance of AI in hospital management goes beyond simple technological innovations; it represents a fundamental shift in how healthcare institutions operate by optimizing numerous aspects of hospital management, including administrative processes, clinical decision-making, and patient engagement. By utilizing machine learning, natural language processing, and other AI technologies, hospitals can streamline operations, improve patient outcomes, and ultimately redefine the standard of care [47, 48]. Moreover, the importance of AI in hospital management is highlighted by its potential to address long-standing issues in the healthcare sector, such as limited resources, rising costs, and the demand for personalized and efficient medical services [49]. The transformative impact of AI promises to expand the capabilities of healthcare workers and revolutionize the entire continuum of patient care [50].

In healthcare, the use of AI follows a conventionally established pattern. It begins with large volumes of data, their cleaning, and structuring [51, 52]. In the subsequent stages, machine learning algorithms extract metadata (goal-oriented information). This information is then used to generate valuable insights for solving a clearly defined problem in the medical system. The final stages include matching patient symptoms with the relevant model, discussing the insights with a physician, diagnosing the patient, predicting patient outcomes, and drug discovery. It is important to note the role of an assistant bot that can translate languages, transcribe notes, and organize images and files. The stages of AI model development in healthcare are presented in Figure 5.1.

Modern technologies have numerous adverse effects on mental health. Studies have identified the impact of AI on mental health, which included people with high levels of anxiety. This was characterized by feelings of uncertainty and concern about social connections, showing stronger reactions when interacting with AI systems. This includes both positive reactions, such as helping others, and adverse reactions, such as loneliness and insomnia. In an experiment involving 166 engineers from a Taiwanese biomedical company, who were surveyed for over three weeks, it was found that employees who interacted more frequently with AI systems were more prone to feelings of loneliness, insomnia, and increased alcohol consumption after work [53].

However, researchers from the University of Southern California (USC), in collaboration with the Defense Advanced Research Projects Agency (DARPA) and the US army, found that individuals suffering from post-traumatic stress and other forms of mental distress were more open to discussing their issues with devices that used virtual representations of real people, due to the fear of judgment. This study [54] provides promising results for the role of virtual assistants, leading to the collection of honest patient responses, which can help physicians diagnose and treat their patients more effectively and with better information.

Global developments in recent years have also been associated with changes in the severity of diseases.

Noncommunicable diseases (NCDs) have become virtually the leading cause of mortality, resulting in 200 million premature deaths, and are expected to cause another 150 million deaths over the next decade, the majority of which will occur in low- and middle-income countries [53, 55]. NCDs are typically multifactorial diseases, and their development is associated with several factors, including genetic and environmental, which complicate their effective prevention and treatment. They are exacerbated by four critical

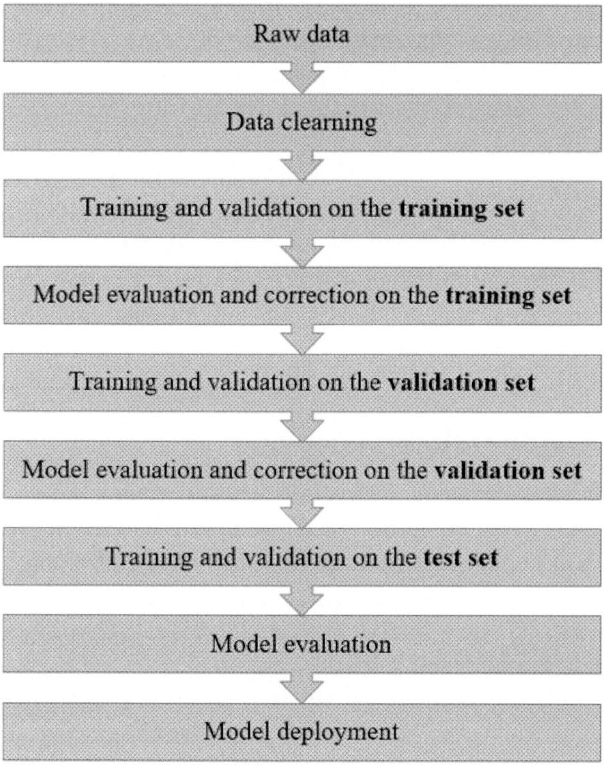

Figure 5.1 Stages of artificial intelligence model development in healthcare.

modifiable risk factors: tobacco use, harmful alcohol consumption, physical inactivity, and unhealthy diets [56]. In the United States, it was estimated that behavioral factors and genetic factors are the main contributors to premature death at 40% and 30%, respectively [57], and the role of public health awareness and intervention is exceptionally high [49].

In the search for new technologies, the potential of AI is noteworthy. It offers the ability to analyze large and complex datasets derived from patient lifestyle and clinical and biological data in ways that surpass the human capacity to comprehend [58]. Machine learning, natural language processing (NLP), robotics, virtual agents (chatbots), and speech analysis are just a few examples of AI applications used to improve public health [59]; for example, S.A.R.A.H. – the Smart AI Resource Assistant for Health. Sarah is a prototype of a digital health promoter available 24/7 in eight languages in video or text format. She can provide advice on how to relieve stress, eat healthily, and quit smoking and e-cigarettes, as well as offer information on several other health topics (https://www.who.int/campaigns/s-a-r-a-h). Alternatively, the STopobesity platform can offer personalized support to individuals with obesity (https://stop.publichealth.gwu.edu) and chatbots for personalized fitness strategies.

Monitoring processes are relatively well-prepared for the use of AI, but it was only recently that the FDA (US Food and Drug Administration) approved Kardiaband from AliveCor (in 2017) and the Apple Watch Series 4 (in 2018) for detecting atrial fibrillation. The use of smartwatches is the first step toward enabling people to collect personal health data and provide rapid intervention by patient support healthcare services.

5.5 AI in Research Data Processing

Biomedical research and medical practice are undergoing a revolutionary transformation due to the integration of artificial intelligence in these fields. This is most evident in radiomics, a field of medical image analysis, where the power of AI algorithms is used to extract complex information from medical images such as MRI, CT, and X-rays to facilitate early disease diagnosis and personalized treatment planning [60, 61].

Digital pathology (DP) is increasingly used in cancer diagnostics, providing additional tools for faster, higher-quality, and more accurate diagnoses. The practice of pathology diagnosis has undergone a tremendous transformation as new tools like digital images, advanced AI algorithms, and computer-assisted diagnostic methods are used to enhance the capabilities of computer histopathology and AI-supported diagnostics [62]. This opens the door to progress in precision cancer medicine. Automated whole-slide imaging scanners now reproduce high-quality diagnostic images of entire slides, and combining these images with innovative digital pathology tools allows for the integration of images into all aspects of pathology reporting, including anatomical, clinical, and molecular pathology.

The recent FDA approval of WSI scanners for primary diagnostics, as well as the approval of an AI prostate algorithm, has paved the way for the introduction of this exciting technology for primary diagnostic use.

Thus, it can be argued that machine learning methods have actively entered various fields of life [6, 37, 63, 64]. Among them, deep learning occupies a special place, as it is applied in many areas of healthcare and is an integral element and prerequisite for the development of digital pathology [37, 65]. Today, digital pathology is considered an effective tool for solving a number of educational, consultative, and clinical tasks. Almost half a century ago, results on the use of computerized image analysis of cells and chromosomes were published [66], and today, the introduction of digital processing and computer image analysis has experienced rapid development and gained popularity in cytological and pathohistological diagnostics.

Pathology is the cornerstone of cancer patient care. The need for accurate histological cancer diagnosis is increasing, as personalized cancer therapy requires precise diagnosis, staging, and biomarker assessment. In routine clinical practice, a pathohistological diagnosis is based on visual recognition, semi-quantitative determination, and integration of multiple morphological features in the context of the underlying disease process. Today, a fundamental limitation of histological diagnoses on hematoxylin and eosin-stained slides (in the era of "big data" processing technologies) is human interpretation.

To increase diagnostic accuracy and objective consistency between observers, most pathologists are trained to follow simple algorithmic decision trees that allow for the determination of a pathohistological diagnosis and the stratification of patients into reproducible groups based on tumor type and aggressiveness [37]. Even with these simplified algorithms based on binary conclusions and sufficiently different characteristics, inter-observer discrepancies still persist, even among expert specialists in narrow subfields, leading to diagnostic inconsistencies and potentially suboptimal patient care management.

Although systematic training and the use of standardized guidelines promote harmonization of the analytical process and increase diagnostic accuracy, pathohistological analysis is inherently limited by its subjective nature and individual differences in visual perception, data integration, and judgments between independent pathologists.

Additionally, over the past 50 years, several grading systems have been proposed in pathohistological diagnosis, allowing pathologists to evaluate tumors based on their appearance, such as the Gleason system for prostate cancer or the Nottingham system for breast cancer assessment [64]. These systems are informative tools for assessing disease heterogeneity and provide crucial information on prognosis and treatment decision-making. However, some systems that require quantitative analysis are too labor-intensive for routine clinical use.

Paradoxically, even with the use of molecular analysis strategies (which are generally more objective), existing limitations often complicate the final diagnosis or characterization of the biological factors of the disease process for predicting the clinical course.

These issues are further associated with the variability of accompanying diagnostic tests and biomarkers, often resulting from a lack of standardization, as well as spatial and/or temporal biological heterogeneity in samples [63]. It is also important to emphasize that most of the biological features used for analysis are continuous variables, and decision-making often requires reducing these characteristics to categorical and/or discrete options. Nevertheless, the determination of certain biomarkers is often one-dimensional and qualitative and does not account for the complex signaling and interactions between tumor cells, their microenvironment, etc. As a result, the pathologist still largely relies on simple approaches, such as decision trees, which use only a tiny fraction of the available knowledge from genomics, transcriptomics, and proteomics.

A powerful driver of DP development has been the implementation and active use of scanners, which have enabled the digitization of histological slides. This has significantly expanded the possibilities for remote consultations to obtain a "second opinion" in diagnosing complex cases and for multidisciplinary board meetings. Additionally, DP has addressed the issue of slide archiving, reducing the risk of damage and enabling the creation of cloud-based repositories of digital slides. This has set the stage for transforming the perception of DP not only as a powerful educational resource but also as a tool for generating new knowledge in medicine in general. Thanks to digital slide archives, several thousand slides and corresponding molecular genetic research results have become widely accessible, stimulating the development of tools for analyzing digital slides.

The combination of DP and machine learning methods has led to the widespread use of AI for the analysis of histological slides for diagnostic, prognostic, predictive, and other clinically significant purposes, including improving the efficiency of the pathohistological diagnostic workflow. Automated extraction of multiple visual and subvisual morphometric features from conventional hematoxylin and eosin-stained slides is complicated by sample selection challenges and tumor heterogeneity but can help overcome the limitations of subjective visual evaluation and integrate multiple measurements to analyze the complexity of tissue structural organization. These histopathological features can potentially be used along with other radiological, genomic, and proteomic parameters to provide a more objective, multidimensional, and functionally relevant diagnostic outcome.

To date, numerous digital pathology resources and certified AI solutions have been developed to objectify pathohistological research. Examples of potentially useful machine learning applications in practical terms include model-based evaluation of routine diagnostic features of pathological processes and diseases, as well as the ability to identify new features that expand understanding of disease. A significant factor in the development of this field has been the introduction of next-generation sequencing technologies and the availability of such data through open-source databases – for example, "The Cancer Genome Atlas" (CGA) and "The Gene Expression Omnibus" (GEO). This has not only expanded research capabilities in the development of genomics, transcriptomics, and other "omics" but also facilitated the creation of powerful models for more accurate cancer prediction. However, the rapid accumulation of new data and the development of the latest AI technologies require further formalization and systematization of technologies.

5.6 AI in Global Health Evaluation

The coronavirus pandemic of 2020–2021 was a landmark event that fundamentally altered our understanding of human health. It demanded that we rethink and change current healthcare paradigms without further delay. Health can no longer be understood solely in relation to humans (anthropocentric view); it must be considered on a global scale as a dimension that unites humans, animals, plants, and the environment based on the fact that the health of humans, animals, plants, and the environment are interconnected in an evolutionary interpretation of the biosphere [67].

This paradigm shift may seem relatively easy to understand, as it offers a perspective on health that has been available for some time and is generally well-founded. The more challenging aspect becomes the practical adoption of this paradigm and the acceptance of all its implications at the individual, societal, political, and economic levels. There is no doubt today that changes occurring in the first links of this interconnected chain of life (the environment and plant world) inevitably cause a domino effect: pathological manifestations are bound to affect animal and human health in the short or long term. This perspective, which inevitably prompts a view of health from a unified global perspective ("One Health"), is confirmed by the fact that several outbreaks of new infectious diseases caused by animal viruses have been observed over time as they occupy ecological niches free from other inhabitants [68].

Alongside the resurgence of serious bacterial infections caused by antibiotic resistance, this creates an epidemiological landscape of epidemic outbreaks and pandemic scenarios previously thought to be overcome [67, 69, 70, 71]. According to a new report from the World Economic Forum on the impact of global warming on health, addressing these new climate challenges and mitigating them will require comprehensive healthcare system transformation and global collaborative efforts among various stakeholders and sectors [72].

Global Health (GH) aims to improve healthcare for all people on the planet and eradicate all preventable diseases and deaths. The advent of artificial intelligence is innovatively reshaping healthcare practices and improving patient outcomes by handling vast amounts of health data – from medical records and clinical trials to genetic information – and analyzing it much faster than humans. As we previously emphasized, AI also helps improve medical imaging and diagnosis.

There is increased optimism about the use of AI applications at the local level, but the question remains unresolved as to whether these aspects can be scaled globally to advance healthcare services. It is also expected that health systems will face additional burdens due to climate impact. The analysis identifies floods and droughts as the main causes of climate-related mortality, with heat waves being the biggest cause of economic loss. It also forecasts the growth and spread of climate-sensitive diseases such as malaria and dengue [73].

The report highlights the urgent need for global strategies to reduce emissions and adapt healthcare infrastructure, advocating for joint efforts to transform healthcare systems in response to this escalating crisis [74]. While medicine today is capable of rapidly developing effective preventive, diagnostic, and therapeutic approaches (tests, drugs, vaccines), the discussed perspective introduces new bioethical challenges regarding the universality of care and disparities in access to this new approach to healthcare, as the new approach is likely to be more expensive and not all countries will be able to implement it quickly.

The very idea of One Health implies cultural changes that must be supported from the ground up rather than imposed from above. It should be noted that the ideas of One Health face significant implementation difficulties, as they require substantial changes in current medical, economic, social, and even ethical practices. Moreover, they are epistemologically indistinguishable from anthropocentric models, which place human health at the top of the hierarchy. In this context, environmental ethics can usefully engage in dialogue with health ethics, as the former provides a framework of theories related to the protection of natural objects and the use of natural resources.

Environmental ethics [75] represents a broader framework that can encompass the idea of One Health, as the latter has an ethical dimension. The arguments and theories put forward in environmental ethics can be used to evaluate humanity's impact on the planet, the protection humanity should provide it, and for what purpose. The main competing paradigms in question are anthropocentrism and ecocentrism, in which humanity's place in nature is understood differently. However, it is important to remember that ecological pragmatism represents a third option that should also be briefly presented.

In 2008, a new international collaboration in the field of health involving the Food and Agriculture Organization of the United Nations, the World Health Organization, and the World Organisation for Animal Health proposed with the World Bank a "Strategic Framework for Action at the Intersection of Animals, Humans, and Ecosystems" [76]. This document, titled "One Health," resonated widely. Already in November 2021, the High-Level Expert Group presented a new definition of "One Health," which was adopted by the Joint Tripartite Organization and the United Nations Environment Programme: One Health is a comprehensive approach aimed at achieving a sustainable balance and optimizing the health of humans, animals, and ecosystems.

It recognizes that the health of people, domestic and wild animals, plants, and the environment as a whole (including ecosystems) are closely connected and interdependent. This approach mobilizes multiple sectors, disciplines, and communities at various levels of society to work together to improve well-being and eliminate threats to health and ecosystems while addressing the collective need for clean water, energy, and air, safe and nutritious food, and taking actions on climate change and promoting sustainable development [77].

Since the COVID-19 pandemic began in early 2020, world leaders, global health experts, and human rights advocates have condemned the lack of global cooperation in combating an infectious pathogen that knows no borders [78]. In particular, global responses at various stages of the COVID-19 pandemic were marked by unjust and untimely distribution of pandemic response products. The 194 member states of the World Health Organization decided to draft a new international agreement to strengthen global collaboration in combating pandemics. On the other hand, the agreement stimulated the development of the "One Health" concept, as the new definition of health provides a more comprehensive view of the relationships between humans, animals, and the environment than its predecessors.

As part of this holistic approach, in March 2022, the UN Environment Programme officially joined the Joint Tripartite Agreement, which is now known as the Quadripartite Agreement. Expanding the scope to include the immediate environment of humans allows for a more complete definition of a health strategy. This has become more apparent compared to the current definition by the Health Commission, which emphasizes the multidisciplinary and transdisciplinary nature of the health definition rather than a holistic approach that focuses exclusively on human health.

An unconventional approach to One Health is proposed in [77], distinguishing two different relationships that arise in the traditional organism-environment dyad: interactive relationships and dynamic relationships. Such an approach complicates the use of AI. Dynamic relationships are the relationships between the organism and the external world, which can become part of (an extension of) the organism. Interactive relationships are the relationships between the extended organism and the external environment, which is part of the ecosystem. Dynamic relationships reflect the nature of the extended organism as resilient, meaning as a whole that has various temporal parts throughout its life [79].

The extended organism is built from the host organism and acquires external entities relative to it, which later undergo changes. While the extended organism consists of the organism and the dynamic environment, the extended organism interacts with another external environment – the interactive one. Like the traditional concept of the environment, the interactive environment includes conditions and circumstances with which the extended organism interacts and is understood as external, including physical, biological, and social domains [80, 81].

It is important to note that interactive relationships exist between the extended organism and other entities (biotic or abiotic), while dynamic relationships form the extended organism itself. In other words, the dynamic environment refers to the organism, while the interactive environment refers to the extended organism. These two different relationships can only be distinguished when the concept of biological individuality as a collective is accepted, as is the case with the extended organism. There is no direct solution to this issue when applying AI. In modern literature, the collective concept of individuality is often used [82, 83], and thus, the distinction between dynamic and interactive environments becomes apparent.

This new paradigm has led to many critical remarks, particularly in the ethical domain. For example, authors of studies [84, 85] have argued that regarding new infectious diseases originating from animals or zoonoses, ethical debates have been dominated by their threat to humans, while other infectious diseases caused by environmental conditions and their sources are often overlooked [84]. Not enough is being done to understand the ecological determinants that lead to pathogen spread, and thus, the potential of AI is partly lost.

In particular, immediate epidemic problem solutions are always available, specifically proposing endemic response measures rather than discussing epidemic preparedness and potential pandemics. The authors advocated for the possibility of herd immunity to propose a new approach to vaccination that could protect both human communities and the fauna with which they interact and often depend. For example, during the height of the Ebola virus outbreak, it was recommended to vaccinate only humans, but not wild primates, who were also heavily affected.

5.7 Challenges in Using and Implementing AI at the Current Stage of Healthcare Development

The routine use of AI for the diagnosis and treatment of diseases is hindered by the inability to quickly gather clinical material due to the constant changes in the set of symptoms of pathological processes and the methods for influencing them. While variations in pharmaceutical correction and the pathological process are obvious – since they are linked to the emergence of new drugs, clarifications of mechanisms of influence, and the discovery of side effects – changes in pathogenetic schemes are not as apparent and require explanation. The simplest logical structures exist for infectious processes. For example, when considering the dynamics of diagnostic and treatment procedures for COVID-19 in China, the most populous country in the world, scientific research was accumulated, providing evidence-based support for the official COVID-19 treatment guide. China's National Health Commission compiled, published, and updated a total of 10 versions of the "COVID-19 Patient Diagnosis and Treatment Protocol" over several years to better inform clinical doctors and staff for effective screening, diagnosis, management, treatment, and care for patients with severe acute respiratory syndrome coronavirus [86]. This article compares and summarizes all versions of the protocol regarding etiology and epidemiology, clinical manifestations and diagnosis, treatment and care, disease control and management, as well as presents detailed changes, additions, deletions, and clarifications of the protocols.

Ten years later, the ISHAM-ABPA working group reviewed the clinical practice guidelines for the diagnosis, classification, and treatment of allergic bronchopulmonary aspergillosis/mycoses (ABPA). An international panel of experts was convened to develop treatment recommendations for ABPA (caused by *Aspergillus* spp.) and allergic bronchopulmonary mycosis (ABPM; caused by fungi other than *Aspergillus* spp.) in adults and children, using a modified Delphi method. Consensus was defined as $\geq$70% agreement or disagreement. The terms "recommend" and "suggest" were used when the consensus was $\geq$70% and $<$70%, respectively [87]. At the same time, the authors themselves emphasize that there is no single test for diagnosing allergic bronchopulmonary aspergillosis, and the diagnosis is typically confirmed by a combination of clinical, radiological, and immunological data. Accordingly, they advocate the use of the revised 2024 diagnostic criteria proposed by the International Society for Human and Animal Mycology (ISHAM), which simplifies the previous diagnostic scheme.

Allergic bronchopulmonary aspergillosis (ABPA), a complex hypersensitivity reaction to colonization of the airways by *Aspergillus fumigatus*, can be difficult to differentiate from asthma or treatment-resistant cystic fibrosis. The ISHAM working group recently published revised diagnostic criteria for ABPA.

The strategy for managing intracerebral hemorrhage associated with direct Xa inhibitors has also changed [88]. As is known, for intracerebral hemorrhage associated with direct Xa inhibitors, either andexanet alfa or a four-factor prothrombin complex concentrate (PCC) is recommended, depending on the severity of the hemorrhage, local protocols, and availability (grade 2C). Andexanet may restore hemostasis more effectively than PCC, but it is associated with a higher risk of thrombosis.

The optimal strategy for discontinuing direct Xa inhibitors (apixaban, edoxaban, rivaroxaban) in acute intracerebral hemorrhage (ICH) has not been determined. In the ANNEXA-I study, which involved 530 patients with ICH related to Xa inhibitors, patients were randomly assigned to receive either andexanet alfa or standard therapy (usually including prothrombin complex concentrate). Those treated with andexanet had better hemostasis outcomes than those receiving standard therapy (67% vs. 53%). However, thrombotic events, including ischemic stroke and myocardial infarction, were more common with andexanet (10.3% vs. 5.6%). Thirty-day mortality and functional outcomes were similar. Based on these results, the authors individualize the choice of andexanet alfa or PCC for reversing direct Xa inhibitors in acute ICH and other life-threatening bleeds (previously, andexanet was preferred, as it reportedly restored hemostasis more effectively but with a higher risk of thrombosis).

It can be confidently assumed that further changes in the strategy for treating intracerebral hemorrhage will occur. This is evident from the basic rationale: "... thrombotic events, including ischemic stroke and myocardial infarction, were more common with andexanet (10.3% vs. 5.6%)." However, such statistics are inconclusive. The emergence of more convincing data will prompt further strategic changes. Similarly, the phrase "optimal strategy for reversing direct Xa inhibitors" remains unclear. The concept of optimality is not defined, and as such, there are insufficient grounds for altering patient management principles.

A major unresolved issue for AI implementation is the fragmentation of medical data and models. The development and deployment of a specific task (regression, classification, clustering, neural language processing, etc.) take considerable time and effort within one organization, but the results cannot be easily transferred for immediate use in another organization without recalibrating the data. Due to privacy concerns, data sharing between healthcare organizations is often unavailable or restricted, leading to data fragmentation that limits model reliability.

A second challenge is the creation of unbiased models. Bias is defined as a mistaken belief formed without the necessary knowledge or relevant understanding related to a process or object. Developing unbiased models in healthcare is associated with the notion of biased data.

AI systems are trained using part of the collected data (known as the training dataset), while the remaining data are reserved for testing (known as the testing dataset). Therefore, if the collected data are unbiased – targeting a specific race, gender, age group, or other factors – the resulting model will be unbiased, and the collected data must accurately reflect the population for whom they are intended.

Information accessibility refers to conditions in which people, regardless of their functional impairments or communication abilities, have access to information (data) in various formats and with the use of technologies. An accessible environment is a space of unlimited opportunities where there is no room for discrimination, and everyone's interests are considered.

5.8 Global Legislative Developments and Directives

In recent years, there has been a surge in documents addressing ethical principles for AI systems, and since the debut of ChatGPT in 2022, discussions about AI usage have continuously increased [89]. The number of scientific studies and clinical observations is also rising sharply. Today, it is rare to encounter an article without the use of AI. Heated debates continue over the issues of intellectual property theft via AI and cyberattacks involving AI [90]. Consequently, the question arises: Should AI be regulated, and how should this be done? It is important to justify the need for governmental guidelines, corporate commitments, and ethical guidelines [91–93].

A pivotal role in creating a regulatory framework for AI systems was played by the Toronto Declaration: "Protecting the right to equality and non-discrimination in machine learning systems" [94].

The preamble states: "As machine learning systems grow in capabilities and expand in use, we must learn about the impact of this technology on human rights. We recognize the potential of machine learning to promote human rights but are increasingly concerned about its ability to promote both intentional and unintentional discrimination against individuals or groups. We must urgently consider how these technologies affect people and their rights. In a world of machine learning systems, who will be accountable for harm to human rights?"

As the discussion on AI ethics continues, the Declaration is aimed at drawing attention to the relevant and existing international legal frameworks and human rights standards. These universal, mandatory, and applicable laws and standards provide the necessary tools to protect people from discrimination and to ensure inclusion, diversity, fairness, and equality. Human rights are universal, indivisible, interdependent, and interconnected.

In this context, accountability is viewed as a key enabler of ethical AI systems; however, accountability within AI is defined and considered from various perspectives depending on the goals of the different stakeholders involved in the AI pipeline [95, 96].

A key trend in the creation of a legal framework for AI can be seen in the adoption of stricter and mandatory legislative efforts. These efforts stem from concerns about the effects of unregulated social media experiments in recent years, which have led to unpredictable outcomes, such as the rampant spread of misinformation. The European Union is on the verge of adopting the first comprehensive legislative act, the AI Act, which promises to set a global standard for AI, similar to how the General Data Protection Regulation (GDPR) sets a standard for data privacy. The AI Act contains risk-based rules about when AI can and cannot be used, with strict penalties for non-compliance.

In the United States, the White House has issued an executive order to develop guidelines on AI safety. It is broader than the EU AI Act, covering everything from consumer fraud to weapons of mass destruction. The order requires AI companies to be more transparent about how their models work and set standards for labeling AI-generated content. Furthermore, the United States has already taken a decentralized approach by proposing its own laws, including the California Safe and Secure Innovation Act for advanced AI systems, aimed at protecting consumer privacy and promoting ethical standards in AI usage. Among the transparency, accountability, and public involvement provisions, the draft rules will require companies to conduct regular assessments of their AI systems for compliance.

The United Kingdom has taken a decidedly opposite stance with a pro-innovation approach to AI, which involves policies of non-binding principles governing AI's creation and use.

Proponents of AI legislation cite health, safety, fundamental human rights, democracy, the rule of law, and the environment as paramount. However, others are concerned that such legislation will stifle their domestic industries, conceding AI's profits and advantages to other, less scrupulous players [97]. Some argue that AI does not require new or separate regulation from traditional software, claiming that the only difference lies in the ratio of data-driven versus rule-driven outcomes, making AI behavior less transparent but not less deterministic.

A key issue is the logic of ethics and empathy in AI. Advocates of a more liberal approach to AI regulation argue that regulating empathy and ethics is not inherently an AI problem but is embedded in the historical data on which large language models are trained.

The way forward will require balance, but the best path will ensure that AI benefits all of humanity, regardless of country, status, or any other factor [98]. A popular framework in this regard is "Harmless, honest, and helpful AI." Initially proposed by the Anthropic team, this approach focuses on reinforcement learning from human feedback and controlled fine-tuning to align the model, eliminating inaccuracy, bias, and toxicity. This approach can also help create a high level of AI safety, as it can prevent harmful and incorrect conclusions and highlight vulnerabilities.

5.9 Conclusion

1. The emergence of AI opens a new era in biology and medicine, revolutionizing disease diagnosis, prognosis, and management strategies.

2. Despite AI's enormous potential in healthcare, significant ethical, regulatory, technological, and technical challenges remain, particularly concerning the constant evolution of clinical disease manifestations and semantic issues.
3. Addressing data privacy concerns, medical model and data fragmentation, algorithmic bias, regulatory compliance, and inherent resistance to change is critical for the responsible and effective integration of AI into healthcare.
4. While AI integration promises significant advancements in biology and healthcare, these fields remain in continuous development, requiring further research and clinical trials for validation.

References

[1] T. Guo et. al., 'What Indeed Can GPT Models Do in Chemistry? A Comprehensive Benchmark on Eight Tasks', Journal of Computer Science, 2023. https://arxiv.org/abs/2305.18365.

[2] I. G. Cohen, 'What should Chat GPT mean for bioethics?' Am. J. Bioeth, pp. 8–16, 23, 2023. DOI:10.1080/15265161.2023.2233357.

[3] Y. Kondratenko, A. Shevchenko, Y. Zhukov, G. Kondratenko, O. Striuk, 'Tendencies and Challenges of Artificial Intelligence Development and Implementation', Proceedings of the 12th IEEE International Conference on Intelligent Data Acquisition and Advanced Computing Systems: Technology and Applications, IDAACS'2023, Vol. 1, 2023, pp. 221–226, IDAACS 2023, Dortmund, Germany, 7-9 September 2023. DOI10.1109/IDAACS58523.2023.10348800

[4] Y. Kondratenko, A. Shevchenko, Y. Zhukov, V. Slyusar, M. Klymenko, G. Kondratenko, O. Striuk, 'Analysis of the Priorities and Perspectives in Artificial Intelligence Implementation,' 13th International IEEE Conference "Dependable Systems, Services, and Technologies" (DESSERT'2023), Greece, Athens, October 13-15, 2023. DOI10.1109/DESSERT61349.2023.10416432

[5] S. M. Anwar et al., 'Medical image analysis using convolutional neural networks: a review,' Journal of Medical Systems, 42, pp. 1–13, 2018. DOI:10.1007/s10916-018-1088-1.

[6] M. Cui, et al., 'Artificial intelligence and computational pathology,' Journal of Laboratory Investigation, 101(4), pp. 412–422, 2021. DOI: 10.1038/s41374-020-00514-0.

[7] N. Coudray et al., 'Classification and mutation prediction from non-small cell lung cancer histopathology images using deep learning,' Journal of Nature Medicine, 24(10), pp. 1559-1567, 2018. DOI:10.1038/s41591-018-0177.

[8] S. Ekins, 'The Next Era: Deep Learning in Pharmaceutical Research,' Journal of Pharmaceutical Research, 33(11), pp. 2594-2603, 2016. DOI: 10.1007/s11095-016-2029-7.

[9] B. Acs, et al., 'Not just digital pathology, intelligent digital pathology,' Journal of the American Medical Association Oncology, 4, pp. 403–404, 2018. DOI:10.1001/jamaoncol.2017.5449

[10] M. A. Aceves-Fernandez, 'Artificial Intelligence: Applications in Medicine and Biology,' London: IntechOpen, 140 p., 2019. DOI:10.5772/intechopen.77536

[11] Y. Socol, et al., 'Artificial intelligence in biology and medicine, and radioprotection research: perspectives from Jerusalem', J of Front Artif Intell, 6, p. 1291136, 2024. DOI:10.3389/frai.2023.1291136.

[12] V. Gulshan, et al., 'Development and validation of a deep learning algorithm for detection of diabetic retinopathy in retinal fundus photographs', Journal of the American Medical Association, 316, pp. 2402–2410, 2016. DOI:10.1001/jama.2016.17216.

[13] M. N. Gurcan, et al., 'Histopathological image analysis: a review,' Journal of IEEE Reviews in Biomedical Engineering, 2, pp. 147-171, 2009. DOI:10.1109/RBME.2009.2034865.

[14] C. Li, et al., 'A survey for breast histopathology image analysis using classical and deep neural networks,' Int. Conf. on Information Technologies in Biomedicine, Springer, 2019.

[15] Y. Xu, et al., 'Deep convolutional activation features for large scale brain tumor histopathology image classification and segmentation,' IEEE Int. Conf. on Acoustics, Speech and Signal Processing, Brisbane, 2015.

[16] A. L. S. Meirelles, et al., 'Building Efficient CNN Architectures for Histopathology Images Analysis: A Case-Study in Tumor-Infiltrating Lymphocytes Classification', Journal of Front Med (Lausanne), 9, p. 894430, 2022. DOI:10.3389/fmed.2022.894430.

[17] A. Madabhushi, et al., 'Image analysis and machine learning in digital pathology: Challenges and opportunities', Journal of Medical Image Analysis, pp. 170-175, 33, 2016. DOI:10.1016/j.media.2016.06.037.

[18] J. Barker, et al., 'Automated classification of brain tumor type in whole-slide digital pathology images using local representative tiles,' Journal

of Medical Image Analysis, 30, pp. 60-71, 2016. DOI:10.1016/j.media.2015.12.002.

[19] S. Wang, et al., 'Pathology Image Analysis Using Segmentation Deep Learning Algorithms', The American Journal of Pathology, 189(9), pp. 1686-1698, 2019, DOI:10.1016/j.ajpath.2019.05.007.

[20] N. Dimitriou, et al., 'Deep Learning for Whole Slide Image Analysis: An Overview,' Journal of Front Med (Lausanne), 6, p. 264, 2019. DOI: 10.3389/fmed.2019.00264.

[21] V. Slyusar, et. al. 'Improvement of the object recognition model on aerophotos using deep convolutional neural network,' Eastern-European Journal of Enterprise Technologies, 2(113), pp. 6–21, 2021. DOI:10.15587/1729-4061.2021.243094

[22] A. Esteva, et al., 'Dermatologist-level classification of skin cancer with deep neural networks?', Journal of Nature, 542, pp. 115–118, 2017, DOI:10.1038/nature21056.

[23] Y. Jing, et al., 'Deep Learning for Drug Design: an Artificial Intelligence Paradigm for Drug Discovery in the Big Data Era,' Journal of AAPS, 20(3), p. 58, 2018. DOI:10.1208/s12248-018-0210-0.

[24] J. Konečnỳ, et al., 'Federated optimization: Distributed optimization beyond the datacenter,' ArXiv, 2015. DOI:10.48550/arXiv.1511.03575.

[25] B. Yurdem, et al., 'Federated learning: Overview, strategies, applications, tools and future directions'. Heliyon, Volume 10, Issue 19, e38137, 2024, DOI:10.1016/j.heliyon.2024.e38137.

[26] N. Nishida, et al., 'Artificial intelligence models for the diagnosis and management of liver diseases,' Journal of Ultrasonography, 42(1), pp. 10-19, 2023. DOI:10.14366/usg.22110.

[27] R. Najjar, 'Redefining Radiology: A Review of Artificial Intelligence Integration in Medical Imaging,' Journal of Diagnostics (Basel), 13(17), p. 2760, 2023 DOI:10.3390/diagnostics13172760.

[28] S. Mukhopadhyay, et al., 'Whole slide imaging versus microscopy for primary diagnosis in surgical pathology: A multicenter blinded randomized noninferiority study of 1992 cases (Pivotal Study)', The American Journal of Pathology, 42, pp. 39–52, 2018. DOI:10.1097/PAS.0000000000000948.

[29] H. Irshad, et al., 'Methods for nuclei detection, segmentation, and classification in digital histopathology: a review-current status and future potential', IEEE Rev Biomed Eng, 7, pp. 97-114, 2014. DOI:10.1109/RBME.2013.2295804.

[30] J. Xu, et al., 'A high-throughput active contour scheme for segmentation of histopathological imagery,' Journal of Medical Image Analysis, Vol. 15, Is. 6, pp. 851-862, 2011. DOI:10.1016/j.media.2011.04.002.

[31] S. Wang, DM. Yang, R. Rong, X. Zhan, G. Xiao, 'Pathology Image Analysis Using Segmentation Deep Learning Algorithms. 'Am J Pathol. Sep;189(9), p. 1686-1698, 2019. DOI:10.1016/j.ajpath.2019.05.007.

[32] K. Sirinukunwattana, et al., 'Image-based consensus molecular subtype (imCMS) classification of colorectal cancer using deep learning,' Journal of Gut, 70(3), pp. 544–554, 2021. DOI:10.1136/gutjnl-2019-319866.

[33] M. Moscalu, et al., 'Histopathological Images Analysis and Predictive Modeling Implemented in Digital Pathology-Current Affairs and Perspectives,' Journal of Diagnostics (Basel), 13(14), p. 2379, 2023. DOI:10.3390/diagnostics13142379.

[34] P. C. Chen, et al., 'How to develop machine learning models for healthcare,' Journal of Nature Materials, 18(5), pp. 410-414, 2019. DOI: 10.1038/s41563-019-0345-0.

[35] E. Chousakos, et al., 'Topographical and Chronological Analysis of Thin Cutaneous Melanoma's Progressions: A Multicentric Study,' Journal of Cancers (Basel), 15(15), p. 3989, 2023. DOI:10.3390/cancers15153989.

[36] J. Calderaro, et al., 'Artificial intelligence-based pathology for gastrointestinal and hepatobiliary cancers,' Journal of Gut, 70(6), pp. 1183-1193, 2021. DOI:10.1136/gutjnl-2020-322880.

[37] M. J. Carr, et al., 'Sentinel lymph node biopsy in melanoma: beyond histologic factors,' Journal of Clinical & Experimental Metastasis, 39(1), pp. 29-38, 2022. DOI:10.1007/s10585-021-10089-9.

[38] S. Lin, et al., 'Accelerating Convolutional Networks via Global and Dynamic Filter Pruning,' Proceedings of the Twenty-Seventh Int. Joint. Conf. on Artificial Intelligence, Main track, 2018.

[39] M. Shao, et al., 'A dynamic CNN pruning method based on matrix similarity', Journal of Signal Image and Video Processing, 15(10), pp. 381–389, 2021. DOI:10.1007/s11760-020-01760-x.

[40] F. De Logu, et al., 'Recognition of Cutaneous Melanoma on Digitized Histopathological Slides via Artificial Intelligence Algorithm,' Journal of Frontiers in Oncology, 10, p. 1559, 2020. DOI:10.3389/fonc.2020.01559.

[41] E. Batista, 'Accountability and Empathy (Are Not Mutually Exclusive),' Executive Coaching, 2019. https://www.edbatista.com/2019/04/accoun

tability-and-empathy.html#:~:text=That%20widely%2Dheld%20ment al%20model,extension%2C%20of%20the%20leader' s20 (2021).

[42] A. Buja, et al., 'Prognosis for Cutaneous Melanoma by Clinical and Pathological Profile: A Population-Based Study,' Journal of Frontiers in Oncology, 11, p. 737399, 2021. DOI:10.3389/fonc.2021.737399.

[43] S. R. Alonso, et al., 'Progression in cutaneous malignant melanoma is associated with distinct expression profiles: a tissue microarray-based study,' The American Journal of Pathology, 164(1), pp. 193-203, 2004. DOI:10.1016/s0002-9440(10)63110-0.

[44] O. Mintser, et al., 'Incidence of BRAF mutations in cutaneous melanoma: histopathological and molecular analysis of a Ukrainian population,' Journal of Melanoma Management, MMT64, 10(1), 2023. DOI:10.2217/mmt-2023-0005.

[45] O. Mintser, et al., 'Artificial intelligence and next generation pathology: towards personalized medicine,' Journal of Proceedings of the Shevchenko Scientific Society, Medical sciences, 65(2), pp. 68-87, 2021. DOI:10.25040/ntsh2021.02.07.

[46] Z. Huang, Z. Ling, 'Medical assisted-segmentation system based on global feature and stepwise feature integration for feature loss problem-Biomed Signal Process Control 89, p. 105814. 2024. DOI:10.1016/j.bs pc.2023.105814'.

[47] S. V. Bhagat, et al., 'Navigating the Future: The Transformative Impact of Artificial Intelligence on Hospital Management - A Comprehensive Review,' Journal of Cureus, 16(2), e54518, 2024. DOI:10.7759/cureus .54518.

[48] S. B. Junaid, et al., 'Recent Advancements in Emerging Technologies for Healthcare Management Systems: A Survey,' Journal of Healthcare (Basel), 10(10), p. 1940, 2022. DOI:10.3390/healthcare10101940.

[49] T. Davenport, et al., 'The potential for artificial intelligence in healthcare,' Future Healthcare Journal, 6(2), pp. 94-98, 2019. DOI:10.7861/fu turehosp.6-2-94.

[50] 'Artificial intelligence (AI) in healthcare & hospitals,' 2023. https://ww w.foreseemed.com/artificial-intelligence-in-healthcare.

[51] M. H. Stanfill, et al., 'Health Information Management: Implications of Artificial Intelligence on Healthcare Data and Information Management,' Journal of Yearbook of Medical Informatics, 28(1), pp. 56-64, 2019. DOI:10.1055/s-0039-1677913.

[52] K. Basu, et al., 'Artificial Intelligence: How is It Changing Medical Sciences and Its Future?' Indian Journal of Dermatology, 65(5), pp. 365-370, 2020. DOI:10.4103/ijd.IJD_421_20.
[53] D. B. Olawade, et al., 'Using artificial intelligence to improve public health: a narrative review,' Journal of Frontiers in Public Health, 11, p. 1196397, 2023. DOI:10.3389/fpubh.2023.1196397.
[54] 'AI in mental Health: Applications, benefits & challenges,' Binariks. https://binariks.com/blog.
[55] T. Davenport, et al., 'The potential for artificial intelligence in healthcare,' Future Healthcare Journal, 6(2), pp. 94-98, 2019. DOI:10.7861/futurehosp.6-2-94.
[56] L. Lämmermann, et al., 'Managing artificial intelligence applications in healthcare: Promoting information processing among stakeholders,' International Journal of Information Management, Vol. 75, p. 102728, 2023. DOI:10.1016/j.ijinfomgt.2023.102728.
[57] R. Srivastava, 'Applications of Artificial Intelligence in Medicine,' Journal of Exploratory Research and Hypothesis in Medicine, 9(2), pp. 138-146, 2024. DOI:10.14218/ERHM.2023.00048.
[58] P. Rajpurkar, et al., 'AI in health and medicine,' Journal of Natural Medicines, 28(1), pp. 31-38, 2022. DOI:10.1038/s41591-021-01614-0.
[59] G. M. Lucas, et al., 'It's only a computer: Virtual humans increase willingness to disclose,' Journal of Computers in Human Behavior, 37, pp. 94-100, 2014. DOI:10.1016/j.chb.2014.04.043.
[60] K. Bera, et al., 'Predicting cancer outcomes with radiomics and artificial intelligence in radiology,' Journal of Nature Reviews Clinical Oncology, 19, pp. 132–146, 2022. DOI:10.1038/s41571-021-00560-7.
[61] P. Lee, C. Golberg, I. Kohane, 'The AI revolution in medicine: GPT-4 and beyond', Pearson Education Inc., 2023.
[62] S. Shafi, et al., 'Artificial intelligence in diagnostic pathology,' Journal of Diagnostic Pathology, 18, Art. No.109, 2023. DOI: 10.1186/s13000-023-01375-z.
[63] O. Abbas, et al., 'Cutaneous malignant melanoma: update on diagnostic and prognostic biomarkers,' The American Journal of Dermatopathology, 36(5), pp. 363-379, 2014. DOI: 10.1097/DAD.0b013e31828a2ec5.
[64] B. Acs, 'Artificial intelligence as the next step towards precision pathology,' Journal of Internal Medicine, 288(1), pp. 62-81, 2020. DOI: 10.1111/joim.13030.

[65] F. De Smet, et al., 'Next-Generation Pathology by Multiplexed Immunohistochemistry,' Journal of Trends in Biochemical Sciences, 46(1), pp. 80-82, 2021. DOI:10.1016/j.tibs.2020.09.009.

[66] J. M. S. Prewitt, 'Picture Processing and Psychopictorics,' Academic Press, Object enhancement and extraction, New York, pp. 75–149, 1970.

[67] V. A. Sironi, et al., 'The "One Health" approach in the face of Covid–19: How radical should it be?' Journal of Philosophy, Ethics, and Humanities in Medicine, 17(1), p. 3, 2022. DOI: 10.1186/s13010-022-00116-2.

[68] O. Mintser, A. Novyk, 'Information aspects of Health,' Monograph, Kyiv, Interservice, 2024, 204 p.

[69] O. A. Ogunseitan, 'One health and the environment: from conceptual framework to implementation science,' Environment: Science and Policy for Sustainable Development, 64 (2), pp. 11–21, 2022. DOI: 10.1080/00139157.2022.2021792.

[70] D. Schmiege, et al., 'One Health in the context of coronavirus outbreaks: A systematic literature review,' Journal of One Health, 10, p. 100170, 2020. DOI:10.1016/j.onehlt.2020.100170.

[71] H. Lerner, et al., 'The concept of health in one health and some practical implications for research and education: What is one health?' Journal of Infection Ecology & Epidemiology, Vol. 5, Is. 1, pp. 25300, 2015. DOI:10.3402/iee.v5.25300.

[72] 'Quantifying the Impact of Climate Change on Human Health,' World Economic Forum, Geneva, 2024. https://www.weforum.org/publications/quantifying-the-impact-of-climate-change-on-human-health.

[73] 'Global Risks Report', World Economic Forum, Geneva, 2023. https://www.weforum.org/publications/global-risks-report-2023.

[74] Intergovernmental Panel, 'Climate Change 2022: Impacts, Adaptation and Vulnerability,' 2022. https://www.ipcc.ch/report/ar6/wg2.

[75] J. Johnson, et al., 'More philosophical work needed in One Health on ethical frameworks and theory,' Journal of Medical Ethics, 46(10), pp. 705-706, 2020. DOI:10.1136/medethics-2020-106243.

[76] 'Contributing to one world, one Health. A Strategic Framework for Reducing Risks of Infectious Diseases at the Animal–Human–Ecosystems Interface,' Consultation Document. FAO, OIE, WHO, Coordination, U.S.I. UNICEF, World Bank, 2008. https://www.fao.org/3/aj137e/aj137e00.htm.

[77] Y. Friedman, 'Who is the biological patient? A new gradational and dynamic model for one health medicine,' History and Philosophy of the Life Sciences, 44(4), p. 61, 2022. DOI:10.1007/s40656-022-00540-9.

[78] M. Moss, 'The Pandemic accord: actualizing ambition in 2023,' https://s3.amazonaws.com/media.unfoundation.org/2022/12/Pandemic_Accord_Actualizing_Ambition_12_14_2022.pdf
[79] V. Triviño, et al., 'Holobionts: Ecological communities, hybrids, or biological individuals? A metaphysical perspective on multispecies systems,' Studies in History and Philosophy of Science Part C', Studies in History and Philosophy of Biological and Biomedical Sciences, Vol. 84, 2020. DOI:10.1016/j.shpsc.2020.101323.
[80] R. G. Wallace, et al., 'The dawn of Structural One Health: a new science tracking disease emergence along circuits of capital,' Journal of Social Science & Medicine, 129, pp. 68-77, 2015. DOI:10.1016/j.socscimed.2014.09.047.
[81] S. Viegas, 'Climate Change and the need of a One Health Approach – from science to policy,' European Journal of Public Health, Vol. 31, Is. Sup. 3, 2021. DOI:10.1093/eurpub/ckab164.271.
[82] J. Suárez, et al., 'A part-dependent account of biological individuality: why holobionts are individuals and ecosystems simultaneously,' Biological Reviews of the Cambridge Philosophical Society, Vol. 95, Is. 5. pp. 1308-1324, 2020. DOI:10.1111/brv.12610.
[83] S. Gissis, E. Lamm, A. Shavit, (Eds.), 'Landscapes of collectively in the life sciences,' Cambridge, MIT Press, pp. 1-432, 2017.
[84] Z. Lederman, et al., 'One health ethics: a response to pragmatism,' Journal of Medical Ethics, 46(9), p. 632-633, 2020. DOI:10.1136/medethics-2019-105859.
[85] Z. Lederman, et al., 'Stamping Out Animal Culling: From Anthropocentrism to One Health Ethics,' Journal of Agricultural and Environmental Ethics, 34(5), p. 27, 2021. DOI:10.1007/s10806-021-09868-x.
[86] Y. Wu, et al., 'Evolution and major changes of the diagnosis and treatment protocol for COVID-19 patients in China 2020-2023,' Journal of Healthcare Sciences, 2(3), pp. 135-152, 2023. DOI:10.1002/hcs2.45.
[87] R. Agarwal, et al., 'Revised ISHAM-ABPA working group clinical practice guidelines for diagnosing, classifying and treating allergic bronchopulmonary aspergillosis/mycoses,' European Respiratory Journal, 63(4), p. 2400061, 2024. DOI:10.1183/13993003.00061-2024.
[88] A. Dabi, et al., 'Reversal Strategies for Intracranial Hemorrhage Related to Direct Oral Anticoagulant Medications,' Journal of Critical Care Research and Practice, p. 4907164, 2018. DOI:10.1155/2018/4907164.
[89] A. Hegde, V. Agarwal, S. Rao, 'Ethics, Prosperity and Society: Moral Evaluation Using Virtue Ethics and Utilitarianism,' Proc. of the Twenty-Ninth Int. Joint Conf. on Artificial Intelligence, 2020.

[90] R. Srinivasan, et al., 'The Role of Empathy for Artificial Intelligence Accountability,' Journal of Responsible Technology, 9(12), p. 100021, 2021. DOI:10.1016/j.jrt.2021.100021.

[91] C. Canca, 'Operationalizing AI ethics principles,' Communications of the ACM Journal, 63(12), pp. 18-21, 2020. DOI:10.1145/3430368.

[92] J. Fjeld, et al., 'Principled Artificial Intelligence: Mapping Consensus in Ethical and Rights-Based Approaches to Principles for AI,' SSRN Electronic Journal, 1, 2020. DOI:10.2139/ssrn.3518482.

[93] T. Hagendorff, 'The Ethics of AI Ethics: An Evaluation of Guidelines,' Journal of Minds & Machines, 30, pp. 99–120, 2020. DOI:10.1007/s11023-020-09517-8.

[94] 'Toronto declaration: Protecting the right to equality and non-discrimination in machine learning systems,' Amnesty Int. and Access Now, Toronto, Canada, 2018.

[95] M. Wieringa, 'What to account for when accounting for algorithms: A systematic literature review on algorithmic accountability,' Proc. of the 2020 Conf. on Fairness, Accountability, and Transparency, Assoc. for Computing Machinery, New York, USA, 2020.

[96] F. A. Spanhol, et al., 'Breast Cancer Histopathological Image Classification Using Convolutional Neural Networks,' IEEE Int. Joint Conf. on Neural Networks, Vancouver, 2016.

[97] V. G. Rádi, 'Comparative Analysis of the AI Regulation of the EU, US and China from a Privacy Perspective,' 2023 46th MIPRO ICT and Electronics Convention (MIPRO), Opatija, Croatia, pp. 1446-1451, 2023. DOI:10.23919/MIPRO57284.2023.10159864.

[98] A. Bennetot, et. al., 'A Practical Guide on Explainable AI Techniques Applied on Biomedical Use Case Applications,' SSRN Electronic Journal, 2022. DOI:10.2139/ssrn.4229624.

6

Artificial Intelligence Technologies for Efficient Solving of Recognition Tasks

Ie. Sidenko[1], Y. Kondratenko[1, 2], I. Skarga-Bandurova[3], Y. Zhukov[4], and M. Saliutin[1]

[1]Petro Mohyla Black Sea National University, Ukraine
[2]Institute of Artificial Intelligence Problems, Ukraine
[3]Oxford Brookes University, United Kingdom
[4]C-Job Nikolayev, Ukraine
E-mail: ievgen.sidenko@chmnu.edu.ua; y_kondrat2002@yahoo.com; iskarga-bandurova@brookes.ac.uk; yuriy.zhukov@nuos.edu.ua; salyutin1@gmail.com

Abstract

This chapter investigates the practical application of artificial intelligence (AI) technologies in addressing various recognition challenges across multiply sectors. By focusing on convolutional and recurrent neural networks, we analyze their efficacy in tasks ranging from medical diagnosis and transportation logistics to military operations, and beyond. Through an analysis of successful implementations, this study highlights how AI enhances classification and recognition capabilities in real-world scenarios, specifically how AI is changing the future of security and remote sensing through the automation of recognition tasks. Additionally, we examine future prospects for AI development, identifying potential advancements and improvements to current technologies. This analysis contributes to the ongoing discourse on practical applications and future directions of AI technology, offering insights into how it can effectively solve complex recognition problems.

Keywords: Artificial intelligence, convolutional and recurrent neural networks, landmines identification, mask recognition, military objects classification, building segmentation.

DOI: 10.1201/9788743800989-6

6.1 Introduction

Object recognition in images and videos is increasingly critical in current technological landscape, as it enables the automation of processes and enhances the efficiency of various routine tasks. Applications range from large critical areas such as recognizing vehicle license plates on highways and identifying military equipment or objects in satellite images to smart home scenarios such as monitoring pets and ensuring home security [1–7]. In this chapter, we explore some recent applications of AI technologies in image recognition within the domains of security and remote sensing through a series of compelling case studies.

One of the important tasks today to protect human lives in conflict areas is the recognition and detection of landmines of the APHEL-1 type (anti-personnel high-explosive landmine). Military conflicts leave behind dangerous devices in the form of landmines of any type (anti-personnel, anti-tank, and "petal"). Mines, as a tool of destruction, cause significant damage to people and infrastructure, so eliminating this threat for civilian and military units has become one of the biggest global problems. Mines, regardless of their type and purpose, can be hidden in various places – on the ground, in bushes, or even in trees, making their detection and safe removal difficult [1–3]. That is why the development of intelligent systems for automated detection and recognition of landmines is becoming a priority task on the way to ensuring safety for both civilians and military units. The use of modern methods and technologies, in particular neural networks, can significantly facilitate this process and reduce the risk for people carrying out demining.

Recognition, detection, and localization of military vehicles are other vital tasks for surveillance, tracking, or security [8]. This requires high accuracy of vehicle identification and tracking so that they can be easily distinguished from non-military vehicles in the image. However, detecting military vehicles with high resolution and quality using close-range cameras is a very difficult task from a security point of view. Therefore, it is advisable to use satellite images of military vehicles for such tasks. This will allow to quickly fix their localization.

In the field of healthcare [9–11], we consider several tasks, including injury severity assessment and mask recognition. Injury severity assessment in resource-constrained environments highlights the potential of AI-driven UAV systems to provide real-time medical triage in disaster zones, optimizing emergency response despite limited computational resources.

Mask recognition on a person's face has proven effective in preventing the spread of various infections and diseases, as well as for personal protection when working with hazardous substances at enterprises. Therefore, in order to protect each other and themselves personally, each person must correctly wear a protective medical mask. However, some irresponsible people refuse to wear a mask despite all the dangers and consequences. Therefore, the development of a system for recognizing the presence of a mask on a person's face is a very important and urgent task [12, 13].

Next case study, provided in this chapter, is devoted to recognition of civil objects [14–16], especially buildings, which is also an important task, because the obtained information on the spatial distribution and changes of buildings has a wide range of applications in urban research, such as urban planning, disaster management, population estimation, and map updating. Local urban planning and natural resource management bureaus have spent a large amount of human and material resources to obtain accurate raster buildings. Space and airborne technologies provide abundant remote sensing images, which are increasingly important for obtaining information about buildings. At present, many government departments and industrial companies use manual methods to delineate building outline vector data from high-resolution remote sensing images to obtain vector maps that meet the requirements of surveying and mapping accuracy. Since manual annotation requires a lot of time and experience, it is beneficial to develop an efficient and reliable system to automatically form building outline polygons from remote sensing images.

Through these case studies, we highlight the transformative impact of visual AI technologies in enhancing security measures and advancing remote sensing capabilities, ultimately contributing to safer and more resilient societies.

6.2 Related Works and Problem Statement

Visual AI has significantly advanced the capabilities of image recognition systems operating in real time, particularly in the fields of security and remote sensing. Extensive research has been conducted to harness AI's potential in various applications, each addressing unique challenges and contributing to the enhancement of safety, efficiency, and precision. Below, we provide a detailed analysis of some applications deployed in these areas.

6.2.1 Landmine detection

Landmine detection continues to pose a significant challenge in ensuring safety in affected regions. Addressing this challenge requires advanced methods and AI technologies that can help accurately identify explosive devices, in particular APHEL-1 mines (Figure 6.1), which is particularly challenging due to their composition and mass [17–19]. Detecting an APHEL-1 mine is a complex task that lacks accurate tools due to its plastic base, making them not detectable by standard metal detectors. In addition, a very low mass of APHEL-1 mines introduces an additional layer of complexity for traditional detection methods [17, 19, 20].

Currently, various approaches employ combinations of hardware and software tools to address this challenge. Specifically, magnetic resonance technologies enable detecting the ferromagnetic properties of landmines. Infrared spectrum technology is also effective in detecting chemical signatures associated with explosive devices [17]. However, real-time detection remains hindered by environmental factors and the variability in mine deployment scenarios. To overcome these limitations, adapting mobile devices into

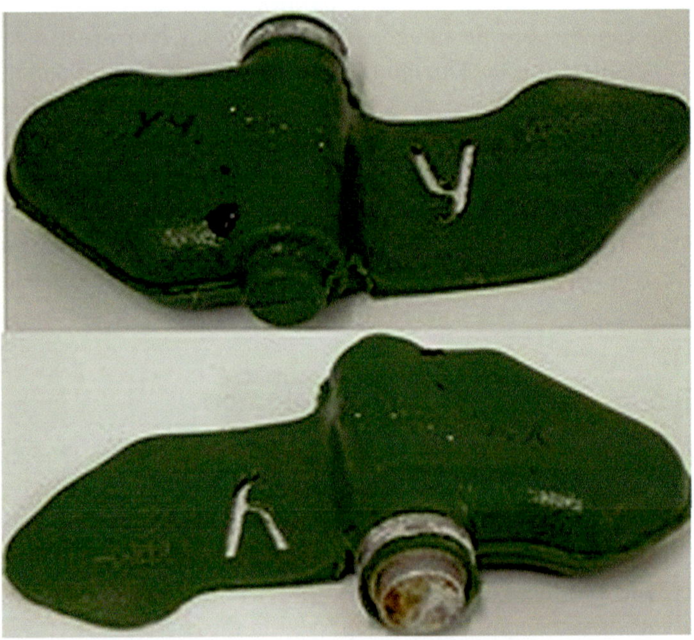

Figure 6.1 Landmine dummy APHEL-1.

contemporary landmine recognition systems can streamline the detection process, facilitate seamless integration with existing technologies, and promote widespread adoption, making the process more efficient and accessible for use in diverse operational contexts.

In the paper [17], the author proposes to optimize the use of unmanned aerial vehicles (UAVs) with lightweight multispectral and thermal infrared sensors for effective detection of landmine contamination in large areas. The method consists in using multispectral and thermal data obtained from an automated survey system to analyze and detect scattered landmines. The authors of the work [18] consider mine detection using a ready-made GPR (ground-penetrating radar) system; they use neural network models to improve geolocation, namely fast CNN and RNN. Fast CNN proved to be the best model for searching for explosive devices. The work [20] presents a solution for automatic detection and classification of buried objects using the convolutional neural network faster R-CNN. This approach allows you to distinguish anti-personnel mines with high accuracy.

The analyzed works are not narrowly focused on solving the problem of recognizing and detecting APHEL-1 mines and require additional expensive equipment for the implementation of such systems. Among the advantages of such systems, one can highlight good equipment with technologies that reveal a range of possibilities for solving the problem and the autonomy of the systems. Among the limitations, one can single out the high cost of equipment in the form of UAVs and infrared sensors, which are currently unavailable for testing in local conditions, and some studies only create models without practical implementation and the ability to make them cross-platform, which limits the use of such systems on a larger number of devices. These studies reflect various approaches to solving the problem of detecting and recognizing landmines, using various technological solutions and neural network models. Such an analysis creates a basis for further research in this area, aimed at developing a more effective and reliable APHEL-1 landmine detection and recognition system [17–19].

6.2.2 Military vehicle detection from aerial imagery

As satellite imagery has become very important in modern conflicts, the research direction of effectively using deep learning models to identify, recognize, and classify different types of military vehicles that can be found on the battlefield is relevant. Vehicle detection from aerial imagery has attracted attention worldwide. This is difficult due to the small size and variable orientation of the vehicles. Aerial imagery with complex backgrounds makes it difficult to recognize and classify objects [19].

The publication [21] considers the creation of a neural network capable of distinguishing between military and non-military equipment. Starting with videos containing a military vehicle, the VOTT tool was used to annotate it frame by frame to create a dataset. The collected dataset is annotated for two categories of vehicles (military and non-military). The images in the dataset contain multiple objects belonging to multiple classes. In total, this publication considers 13 classes, which are divided into 2 main categories.

In the study [22], the authors compared a state-of-the-art deep learning algorithm, namely faster R-CNN, and YOLOv3 for vehicle detection from aerial images. The researchers also studied the effect of hyperparameters on different algorithms and concluded that on a specific dataset, faster R-CNN performed better in terms of speed, while YOLOv3 performed better on a dataset with 320 × 320 input images.

A combined layer deep convolutional neural network method is proposed for vehicle recognition, and it is found that the new approach, which combines the upper and lower layers of deep convolutional neural networks, has demonstrated 16% and 6% improvement in accuracy and recall compared to traditional deep convolutional neural networks [23].

The study [24] proposes a technique to improve detection accuracy in remote sensing images by optimizing support blocks in faster R-CNN using ResNet-50 and ResNet-101 networks.

6.2.3 UAV visual detection and for emergency rescue missions

In recent years, the integration of AI with unmanned aerial vehicles (UAVs) has significantly advanced the capabilities of injury severity assessment, particularly in resource-constrained environments. UAVs offer unparalleled advantages in emergency response scenarios by providing real-time aerial surveillance, rapid data collection, and accessibility to otherwise inaccessible or hazardous areas. When combined with AI-driven image recognition technologies, UAVs can effectively support medical triage, optimize resource allocation, and enhance overall disaster management efforts.

The period from 2022 to 2024 has witnessed substantial progress in leveraging AI for injury severity assessment in UAV-collected imagery, particularly under resource-constrained conditions. Researchers have focused on developing lightweight deep learning models that can operate effectively on limited hardware, enabling real-time injury severity assessment on UAVs with limited computational resources [25]. Models such as YOLO, MobileNetV3, and EfficientNetB0 have been extensively explored due to their balance between accuracy and computational efficiency. Li et al. [26] explored the approach for small target detector in aerial images, achieving real-time performance with reduced memory usage. In [27], Kim et al. investigated the applicability of UAV photogrammetry and AI for the management of natural disaster.

MobileNetV3 is known for its optimized architecture, able to provide high accuracy while maintaining low latency. EfficientNetB0 scales model depth, width, and resolution systematically, enhancing performance without a proportional increase in computational demands [28]. Recent applications [29] have integrated EfficientNetB0 for injury severity classification, benefiting from its robust feature extraction capabilities. The integration of 5G technology with UAVs has significantly enhanced data transmission speeds and reliability, which are critical for real-time injury severity assessment. Lu et al. [30] proposed a UAV-based intelligent triage system that leverages 5G networks to facilitate swift data transfer between UAVs and medical response centers. This integration ensures that large volumes of image data can be transmitted with low latency, enabling timely decision-making and resource allocation during mass-casualty incidents such as war conflicts and natural disasters. Recent studies have focused on improving the accuracy and robustness of injury severity assessment through advanced image processing techniques. These include techniques like SOLO (segmenting objects by locations) used to achieve precise segmentation of injured individuals in aerial images and integration UAV systems with OpenPose or similar frameworks to detect human skeletons and assess postures. Lu et al. [30] explored unmanned aerial vehicle–based intelligent triage system in mass-casualty incidents. They developed an intelligent triage system based on two AI algorithms, namely OpenPose and YOLO where OpenPose was used to detect and analyze human postures.

Combining visual data with other sensory inputs such as thermal imaging and LiDAR has been explored to enhance injury severity assessment. This multi-modal approach allows for better detection under varying environmental conditions and improves the overall reliability of the assessment. For instance, Yoon and Cho [31] integrated thermal imaging with CNN-based models to improve detection in reduced visibility by leveraging thermal depth estimation for autonomous driving environments, ensuring consistent performance regardless of lighting and weather conditions. Other techniques such as model quantization, pruning, and the use of efficient inference engines like

TensorRT have been applied to reduce the computational load and enhance inference speeds. The family of YOLO models and their combinations with TensorRT on NVIDIA Jetson platforms was explored in [32], emphasizing that integration enables achieving significant reductions in inference time and memory usage without compromising accuracy.

Despite the advancements, several challenges still persist in deploying AI-driven injury severity assessment systems in resource-constrained environments. For example, UAVs operating in remote or disaster-stricken areas often have limited onboard processing capabilities that need models that are lightweight, energy efficient, and accurate to ensure real-time performance and efficient energy management. The models that operate on these vehicles must be robust and adaptable to maintain high performance across different scenarios. Seamlessly integrating AI-driven UAV systems with existing emergency response infrastructures and ensuring their scalability across different disaster scenarios and geographical regions remain a significant challenge.

6.2.4 Mask recognition

Mask recognition on human faces using AI methods has achieved promising results. However, existing methods need to be more robust in real-time environments. In addition, there are still insufficient suitable datasets and AI models for mask detection on human faces that can detect people without masks in real time, collect statistics, and notify relevant authorities.

The paper [33] examines the progress and challenges in masked face recognition (MFR), a field that gained prominence during the COVID-19 pandemic due to the widespread use of face masks. It reviews advancements in deep learning techniques for MFR, addressing the difficulties of identifying partially or fully covered faces. The survey highlights various methods, datasets, and evaluation metrics designed specifically for masked face scenarios. It identifies key challenges still faced by researchers and suggests potential directions for improving the technology. Overall, the paper provides a comprehensive resource for understanding the current state and future potential of face recognition in contexts of health crises and beyond.

The study [34] focuses on developing a facial recognition system capable of identifying individuals wearing face masks, a challenge heightened during the COVID-19 pandemic. Using a deep learning model for face mask detection and Procrustes analysis for measuring identity similarity, the system achieved an accuracy of 97.14% on a small dataset of 35 masked faces. The research evaluates system effectiveness through standard facial recognition performance metrics. While preliminary, the study highlights the potential of combining innovative techniques to improve masked face recognition. Future work could explore additional face mask detection methods and similarity analysis approaches to enhance system robustness.

The authors propose a straightforward method using machine learning tools like TensorFlow, Keras, OpenCV, and Scikit-Learn to identify whether individuals in images or videos are wearing masks. The system performs well in detecting masks on static and moving faces, demonstrating high accuracy. The study also fine-tunes parameters of a convolutional neural network (CNN) to optimize mask detection without overfitting. This approach offers a reliable solution for implementing mask detection in surveillance and public service settings [35].

The paper [36] addresses the challenges posed by face mask occlusion, which significantly impacts the accuracy of face recognition systems by obscuring over 75% of facial features. To overcome this, the authors propose an efficient method for generating synthetic mask data, eliminating the need for large-scale real-world masked face datasets. The method is versatile, functioning as a module that can be integrated into the training process of any masked face recognition model. Experiments on datasets like MLFW, MFR2, and RMFD demonstrate the approach's effectiveness and flexibility, achieving superior results compared to existing methods. This solution offers a practical advancement in enhancing face recognition systems under mask-wearing conditions.

Considering the above publications on mask recognition on a human face, we can conclude that currently existing neural network architectures provide a high recognition rate, but there is no comprehensive solution to provide the necessary functionality of such systems, in particular, maintaining statistics, sending messages, and cross-platform compatibility.

6.2.5 Buildings recognition

Automation of map construction has been studied by many researchers in recent years, mainly in the fields of cartography, geoinformatics, and computer science, especially computational geometry [37]. For example, Turker and Kok-San use a support vector machine (SVM) to identify built-up areas based on spectral bands and normalized difference vegetation index (NDVI).

CNNs can offer the best capabilities in cartography. With recent advances in semantic segmentation networks, the results of building contour generation have been significantly improved. These networks are usually fully convolutional networks (FCNs) and encoder–decoder architectures such as U-Net [38–39], SegNet [40–41], and FC-DenseNet [42–43], FCN has been shown to be efficient in processing large amounts of remote sensing data and provides reliable building segmentation results. SegNet is used to generate the first full-scale building area map for the United States. To improve the accuracy of large building segmentation, a U-Net-based architecture is proposed, where the original images and their down-sampled counterparts are taken as input to two branches with equal weights, an adversarial learning strategy is proposed to construct the extraction from remote sensing images, and FC-DenseNet is used as the base semantic segmentation network to generate accurate building footprints.

Deep learning techniques such as convolutional neural networks have greatly improved the performance of building segmentation of remote sensing images. However, images for building segmentation are often in the form of traditional orthophotos, where terrain displacement can lead to a significant offset between the roof contour and the building contour; such displacement poses serious challenges for obtaining accurate building contours, especially for high-rise buildings [44]. To address this problem, authors [45] proposed a new workflow for generating corrected building contours from traditional orthophotos. First, they use facade labels, which are efficiently and inexpensively prepared, together with roof labels to train a semantic segmentation network. Then, a well-trained network, using a modern version of EfficientNet as the backbone, extracts roof and facade segments of buildings from the input image. Experiments with aerial images covering a high-density residential area in Shanghai show that the proposed workflow can generate more accurate building contours than baseline methods, especially for high-rise buildings [44–46].

Analysis of publications and similar systems shows that convolutional and recurrent neural networks are effectively used for various types of object recognition tasks. However, despite the substantial progress in AI-driven image recognition for security and remote sensing applications, several challenges still exist, which hinder the effective deployment of these technologies. Among others, key issues identified in this review include resource constraints, demand for real-time processing, environmental variability, and data scarcity. Many applications, such as injury severity assessment in disaster zones, operate in environments with limited computational resources and energy availability while the vast majority of existing models require significant processing power and memory, making them unsuitable for deployment on edge devices like UAVs and remote cameras. Then, critical applications usually demand real-time or near-real-time processing to guarantee immediate decision-making and intervention. At the same time, the task of achieving high inference speeds without compromising accuracy remains a significant challenge, especially when dealing with high-resolution imagery and complex detection tasks. In addition, models must reliably operate in a variety of unpredictable environmental conditions, including changing lighting, scale, weather, and terrain, which in turn means that robustness and generalization issues must be addressed across all such scenarios. At the same time, obtaining high-quality annotated datasets for specialized applications such as mine detection or injury severity assessment is often challenging due to a variety of reasons such as data access, ethical or privacy concerns, limiting the ability of models to effectively learn and generalize. Although this chapter does not discuss this aspect in detail, we note that deploying AI-powered systems for real-time recognition and surveillance raises significant privacy and ethical issues. Therefore, it is essential to ensure that AI solutions are used responsibly and that data are handled in compliance with privacy regulations.

This chapter aims to explore solutions that optimize visual AI systems for deployment in resource-constrained environments, ensuring real-time performance and robustness across different scenarios. Through several case studies, including landmine detection, military vehicle detection, injury severity assessment, building detection, and mask detection, this research seeks to contribute to the development of more efficient, reliable, and scalable AI applications in security and remote sensing.

6.3 Artificial Intelligence Technologies

Progress in the development of neural network architectures and technologies creates new perspectives in various fields, in particular, for image processing [47, 48], especially with fuzzy logic [49–52], eye-tracking [53], transport logistics [54–56], control systems [57–59], robotic systems and navigation [60–67], and color information processing [68, 69]. They have a unique ability to quickly process information that may be difficult to understand or inaccessible to humans, or in complex or critical conditions. For example, the integration of computer vision [55, 70] and neural networks into systems allows automating the processes of identification and classification of mine threats, reduces risks for sapper groups, improves the efficiency of demining, and provides an opportunity to provide a person with an application that he can carry with him on his smartphone.

Currently, there are many neural network architectures [71–74]. Each architecture has its own design features and covers a certain percentage of tasks that it can solve with proper configuration. Convolutional neural networks (CNNs), as is known, differ from other types of neural networks in their high performance in image and natural language processing. Their structure includes three main layers: convolutional, union, and fully connected. The convolutional layer acts as the first stage in the sequence of operations of a convolutional network [5–7, 75–78]. After the convolutional layers, additional convolutional or pooling layers can be added, while the fully connected layer completes the structure under any conditions, performing the task of classifying the processed information. With each subsequent layer, the complexity of the neural network increases, allowing it to identify larger parts of the image. The initial layers are aimed at detecting simple elements such as colors, contours, and textures of the image. Passing through the CNN layers, the image data gradually recognizes more complex features or shapes of the object, reaching the level of identification of the desired object [17–19, 79, 80].

During the analysis of neural network architectures, it was noted that there is a difference between object detection and object tracking, so the implementation of the APHEL-1 mine recognition system requires algorithms that support not only the object detection format but also object tracking. Object tracking is an important area that has been studied and developed for many years. Today, many developments in this area are based on deep learning, which has advantages over standard algorithms, since neural networks can better approximate functions.

Among all known algorithms, YOLO is noted as one of the best in this area. Since the main idea of the application is to use a trained neural network model to recognize APHEL-1 mines in real time, using just an object detection algorithm is incorrect. Therefore, it is important to understand the difference between these two concepts [3, 19, 81–83].

Object detection is the identification of objects in an image/frame. That is, the algorithm or neural network identifies objects and fixes their position and bounding boxes. We are not talking about other frames at this time, and the algorithm works with only one. An example is shown in Figure 6.2.

Object tracking uses an alternative approach to solving its problem. The main goal of this process is not only to identify objects in the input frame but also to store and associate information from previous frames in order to track the movement of objects and preserve their uniqueness [84–85].

In the following video sequence, one frame was selected in which cars were recognized. Object tracking consists in recognizing all cars in this frame and counting their number. This will allow collecting statistical data on road congestion at any time (Figure 6.3).

That is, an object tracking includes object detection and other algorithms to understand which object in a new frame belongs to which one from the previous frame. YOLO is considered more efficient than many other algorithms for object detection. The developers of the YOLO architecture have provided a small graph (Figure 6.4) to compare the latest versions of YOLO with each other [81–83].

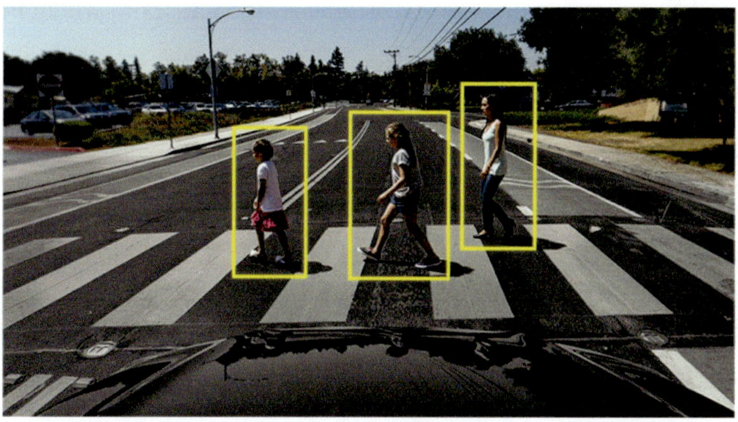

Figure 6.2 Example of object detection on one image frame.

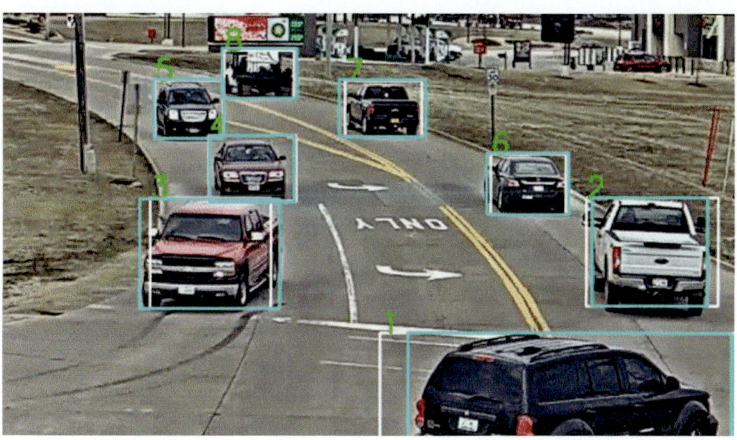

Figure 6.3 Example of object tracking working with car numbering.

There is a variety in the architectures of different object detector models. There are several types of neural network architectures designed for object detection. They are mainly divided into "two-level" ones, such as R-CNN, fast R-CNN, and faster R-CNN, and "one-level" ones, such as YOLO (Figure 6.5). However, there is one problem with the faster R-CNN algorithm and similar ones – they process the image not "as a whole," but only in separate regions, which leads to significant slowdown [75–78].

The architecture of YOLO in the first blocks does not differ significantly in "block logic" from other detectors: at the beginning, an input image is fed, then a CNN is used to create feature maps (note that YOLO uses its own CNN called Darknet-53), and then these feature maps are analyzed to determine the positions and sizes of bounding boxes, as well as the classes to which they belong [19, 81].

Android devices have a wide range of applications that use neural networks. From masks in Snapchat and Instagram to categorization of images in the smartphone gallery or cloud services, as well as improving the quality of photos in Google Camera – all these functions use neural networks. The future of mobile devices is inextricably linked with the development of

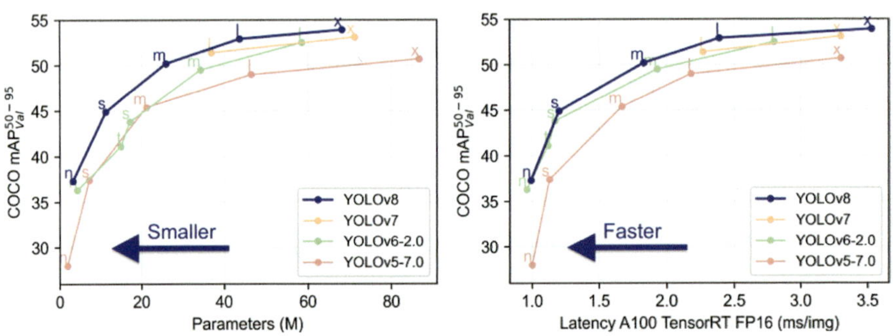

Figure 6.4 Real-time comparison of the latest YOLO models.

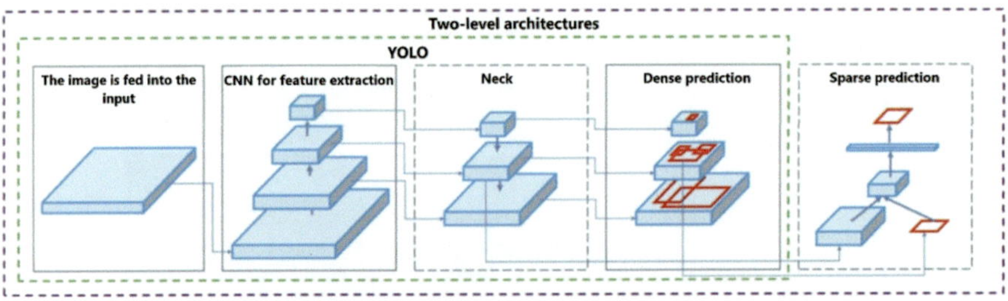

Figure 6.5 YOLO architecture.

neural networks and their integration into various applications, which helps to improve the user experience and increase the efficiency of applications. Various tools are used to implement neural networks in Android applications [82, 86–88].

To choose a topology for a convolutional neural network, you need to focus on the task set by the developer and the available data. There are stages that affect the need to choose the NN topology necessary for solving the task [5, 7, 19]:

- calculate the constraints in the given task (recognition accuracy, speed, and practicality);
- define the task to be solved using NN;
- examine the data and determine the input data (images, sounds, their size, format) and output data (number of classes).

About five years ago, NN was considered a very resource-intensive algorithm that required powerful computers for training and testing networks. But nowadays, NNs already work directly on mobile phones with low requirements for characteristics, and the AI built into the camera analyzes the environment, adapts the camera settings for better photo quality, and identifies objects in a matter of seconds. Therefore, for example, to solve the problem of recognizing a mask on a human face, MobileNetV2 technology was used, which uses a modern convolutional network architecture [89, 90].

The usual architecture of a convolutional NN is the following filter:

$$D_k \cdot D_k \cdot C_{\text{in}}, \tag{6.1}$$

where D_k is a convolution kernel size; C_{in} is a number of channels at the input.

The general calculation formula for the convolutional layer is

$$D_k \cdot D_k \cdot C_{in} \cdot D_f \cdot C_{\text{out}}, \tag{6.2}$$

where D_f is a height of the input layer of NN and C_{out} is the number of channels at the output.

Figure 6.6 shows the block structure of a convolutional NN, and next to it the block structure of MobileNet without modifications.

The MobileNet architecture has two parameters – α (width factor) and p (depth factor). The parameter α in this problem is responsible for a certain number of feature maps on each layer of the NN, and the resolution factor parameter is responsible for the spatial dimensions of the input data [89].

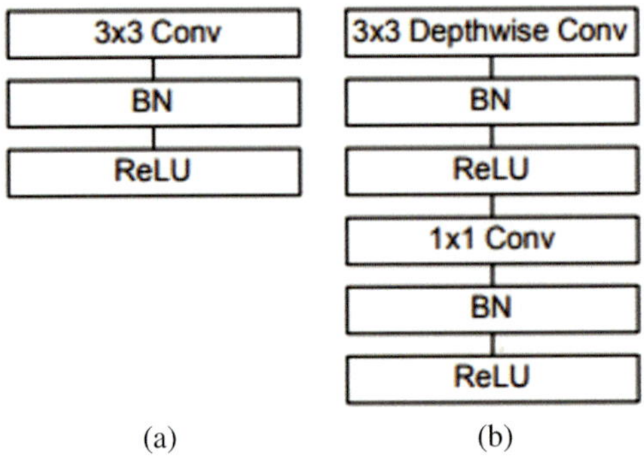

Figure 6.6 Structure of blocks of CNN (a) and MobileNet (b).

These parameters allow you to control the size of the NN: reducing the input parameters of the width and resolution factor reduces the recognition accuracy, but at the same time the neural network is trained much faster and the network memory consumption consumed during training is reduced [89, 90].

MobileNet has only three versions; the most stable is the second version of this architecture (MobileNetV2) – this is the next generation of convolutional NMs from Google. The MobileNetV1 structure is simple but less productive and has a smaller database on which the network was built [89, 90].

Comparing these versions of the MobileNet architecture, it can be seen that at the moment the networks have a higher recognition rate even on mobile phones without large expenditures of energy and device resources. The authors of this architecture also demonstrated that their SSDLite architecture, which is combined with a convolutional NM, has better results than the popular architecture for object recognition YOLOv2 (You Look Only Once) in terms of accuracy on the MS COCO dataset, while demonstrating a five-fold smaller size and greater speed [81–83, 89].

Another deep convolutional neural network architecture (XCeption) is effectively used for object recognition, in particular for vehicle detection and classification [91]. In XCeption, the data first passes through the input stream, then through the middle stream, which is repeated eight times, and finally through the output stream. Note that in Figure 6.7, after all the convolution and separable convolution layers, batch normalization is performed [92].

XCeption is an efficient architecture based on two main points: depth-separated convolution; key combinations between convolution blocks, as in ResNet.

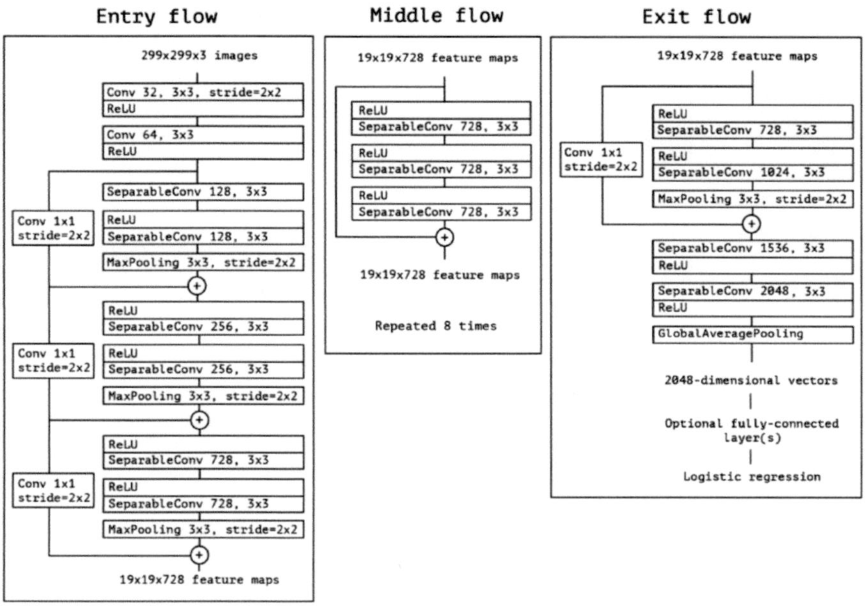

Figure 6.7 General architecture of XCeption.

The standard deep convolutional neural network architecture VGG (visual geometry group) is the foundation of innovative object recognition models. Designed as a deep neural network, VGGNet also outperforms the baseline on many tasks and datasets beyond ImageNet. It is also currently one of the most popular image recognition architectures [93]. Figure 6.8 shows the VGG architecture.

The VGG model, or VGGNet, which supports 16 layers, is also called VGG16, which is a convolutional neural network model. The VGG16 model achieves almost 92.7% accuracy on the top five ImageNet tests. ImageNet is a dataset consisting of over 14 million images belonging to almost 1000 classes. It was also one of the most popular models presented at ILSVRC-2014. It replaces large kernel-sized filters with multiple 3×3 kernel-sized filters one after the other, thus significantly improving AlexNet [94]. The VGG16 model was trained using Nvidia Titan Black GPUs for several weeks. VGGNet-16 supports 16 layers and can classify images into 1000 object categories, including keyboard, animal, pencil, mouse, etc. In addition, the model has an input image size of 224×224.

The concept of the VGG19 model (also VGGNet-19) is the same as VGG16, except that it supports 19 layers. The "16" and "19" refer to the

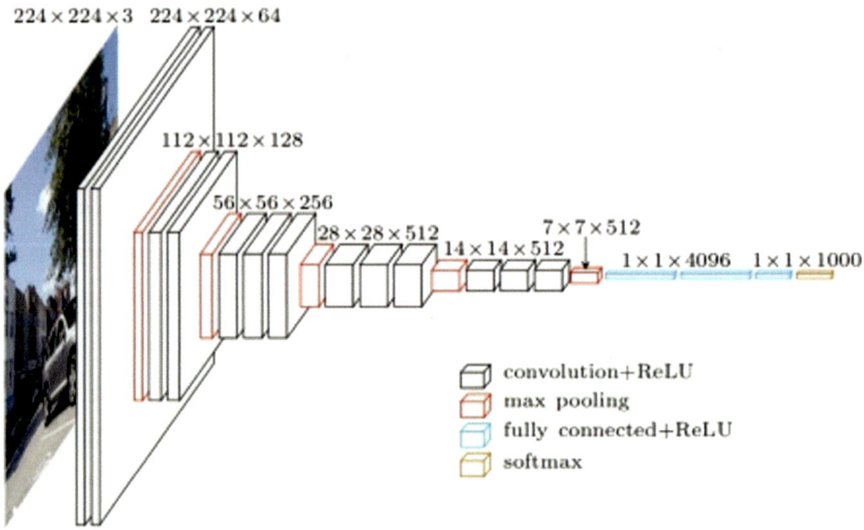

Figure 6.8 VGG architecture.

number of weight layers in the model (convolutional layers). This means that VGG19 has three more convolutional layers than VGG16 [93, 94]. The VGG network is built with very small convolutional filters. VGG-16 consists of 13 convolutional layers and three fully connected layers. VGGNet accepts an input image of size 224 × 224. The VGG convolutional layers use a minimum favorable field, i.e., 3 × 3, the smallest possible size that still captures up/down and left/right. In addition, there are also 1 × 1 convolutional filters that act as a linear transformation of the input data. Next comes the ReLU block, which is a huge innovation from AlexNet that reduces training time. ReLU stands for rectified linear unit activation function; it is a piecewise linear function that will output the input if it is positive; otherwise the output is zero. The convolution step is fixed at 1 pixel to preserve the spatial resolution after convolution (the step is the number of pixel shifts over the input matrix). All hidden layers in the VGG network use ReLU. VGG does not typically use local response normalization (LRN) because it increases memory consumption and training time. Also, it does not improve overall accuracy. VGGNet has three fully connected layers. Of the three layers, the first two have 4096 channels each, and the third has 1000 channels, 1 for each class [93].

Mask R-CNN is a CNN that is state-of-the-art in image segmentation [77, 78]. This variant of a deep neural network detects objects in an image and

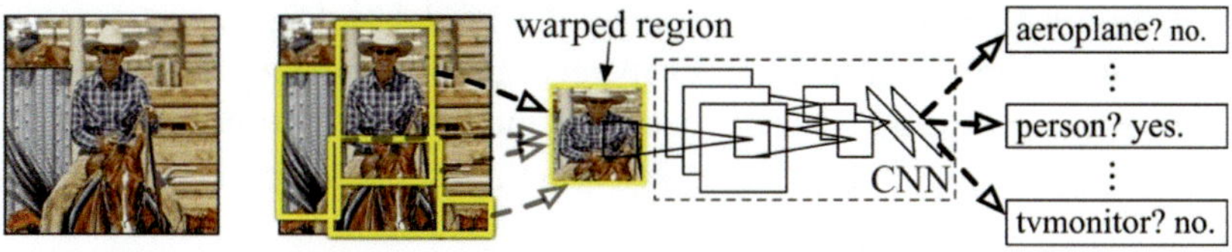

Figure 6.9 Mask R-CNN architecture concept.

creates a high-quality segmentation mask for each instance. This architecture uses frames in object regions, which then evaluate convolutional networks independently for all regions of interest (ROIs) to classify multiple image regions into a proposed class. The R-CNN architecture was developed to solve image detection problems. Furthermore, the R-CNN architecture forms the basis of Mask R-CNN, and it has been improved to what we know as faster R-CNN (Figure 6.9).

Faster R-CNN advances the data flow by learning the attention mechanism using a regional proposition network and the fast R-CNN architecture. The reason why "Fast R-CNN" is faster than R-CNN is because you do not have to pass 2000 propositions through the regions of the convolutional neural network every time. Instead, the convolution operation is performed only once for each image, and a feature map is created from it [77].

Mask R-CNN is an extension of faster R-CNN and works by adding a branch for predicting the object mask (region of interest) in parallel with the existing branch for recognizing the bounding box [78].

6.4 Case Studies: Data Preparation and Modeling Results

In this section, we demonstrate several case studies and discuss our results. Each case study outlines the data preparation methodologies and the specific modeling techniques employed to address unique challenges in resource-constrained environments.

6.4.1 Mines detection

In the process of training neural networks to solve the problem of object recognition, the availability of an appropriate dataset is a crucial factor, since it is the fundamental basis for the system's operation. To create a reliable model, a large amount of data is required that properly reflects the subject matter of the problem. The dataset allows the model to learn a variety of object variants, which in turn increases its recognition efficiency.

Before starting to train a neural network, the first thing to do is to have access to an appropriate dataset or to select an appropriate set of open data that meets a specific task.

Since one of the tasks is the recognition of APHEL-1 landmines, a search was conducted on the Kaggle resource in order to find an adequate dataset and assess its quality. However, when searching for an appropriate dataset, it was not possible to find a ready-made set that would meet the requirements. In such a situation, it seems advisable to create your own dataset that will fully meet the task.

As a result, a corresponding directory "LAND_PICTURES" was created and images of fields, deserts, and forests (where mines are most often found) were collected, as well as some images of urban environments (but they turn out to be rarer). Figure 6.10 shows an example of the collected images.

It is necessary to collect ready-made images of APHEL-1 mines in the ".png" format without a background for further use on other images. Images of APHEL-1 mines were downloaded from open resources and saved in the "PNG_MINES" directory (Figure 6.11). Since all images are in jpeg format, they cannot be directly used on other background images. To solve this problem, a script was created that automatically crops and converts images to png format. This significantly speeds up and automates the process without loss of quality and the need for manual editing in photo editors.

After creating two corresponding sets, you can proceed to creating the final dataset – images of the area with placed mines (Figure 6.12).

Figure 6.10 A dataset with an image of the terrain.

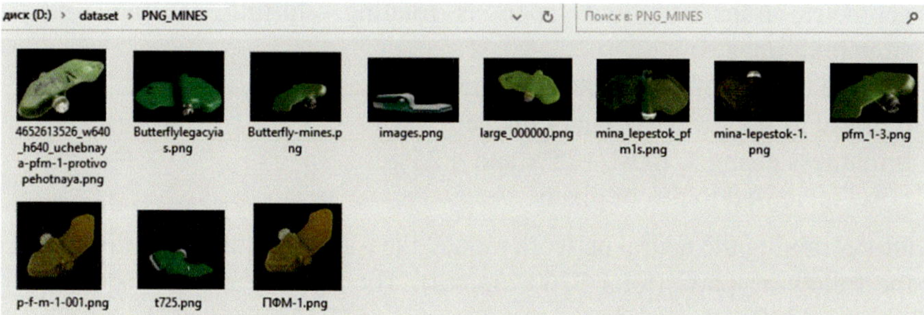

Figure 6.11 A created set of images of APHEL-1 mines.

Figure 6.12 Example of one image from the dataset.

Using the DALL-E 3 neural network, 9750 images were generated based on input images of the terrain and APHEL-1 mines. However, images alone are not enough for the neural network, so a supervised learning method based on a pre-trained dataset was chosen to solve the problem. This dataset contains input data along with expected output results, which allows the model to learn over time. The algorithm measures its accuracy using a loss function and adjusts until the error is minimized. To implement this process, the dataset was additionally annotated using the Computer Vision Annotation Tool resource [95].

As a result, after marking all images, additional files with the coordinates of the mine frame in each image were obtained. Given the complexity of the mine recognition task, since their location can be any, the dataset for this task was expanded using augmentation. Data augmentation is a method that consists in artificially increasing the volume of the training set by creating modified copies of the data based on existing ones. This includes making minor changes to the data or using deep learning to create new data. Among the augmentation methods that were used, the following can be noted:

- geometric transformations, such as rotating, shifting, scaling, and stretching images;
- random change of RGB color channels, contrast, and brightness;
- removal of part of the original image;
- brightness changed from −25% and +25%;
- noise increased to 5% of pixels.

Before training the neural network model, the training dataset was divided into the following parts (total 9760 images). The training set consisted of 8970 images (92%), the validation set consisted of 397 images (4%), and the testing set consisted of 393 images (4%). This approach to data distribution allows us to adjust the training parameters of the neural network, evaluate its performance on the validation set, and prevent overtraining.

In order to create an intelligent mine detection system APHEL-1, it is necessary to create your own CNN architecture. An initial model for training was developed. This is a convolutional neural network, which has the following architecture:

- Input layer "input_shape=(image_size[0], image_size[1], 3)," which defines the shape of the input data. In this case, input_shape is used, which indicates the size of the image that fits the model. image_size[0] and image_size[1] correspond to the width and height of the image, and 3 indicates three channels (often used for RGB images).
- Convolutional layers (Conv2D) with the RELU activation function. A sequence of Conv2D layers with the specified parameters (number of filters, convolution kernel size) performs image convolution to remove features. After that, the ReLU activation function is applied, which introduces nonlinearity into the network.
- Pooling layers (MaxPooling2D). These layers perform pooling, reducing the dimensionality of the resulting feature maps while preserving the most important features.
- The flatten layer reduces the feature map to a one-dimensional array using this layer for further use in the fully connected layer.
- Fully connected layer (Dense). The last layer in the architecture has one neuron with Sigmoid activation, which is used for binary classification (the output value is close to 0 or 1).

For training, 200 epochs were selected in the network and an image of size 640 × 640 was fed as input.

The neural network was trained for 406 minutes, and the resulting data show that the classification accuracies for both classes ("no_mine" and "mine") are 88% and 85%, respectively. However, the model identified only 70% of the images without mines and 60% of the images with mines. This means that it misclassified some of the images and did not detect all the mines. The overall accuracy of the model is 80%, which is a good result due to the difficulty of recognizing a mine on the ground with similar texture and color to the ground on which the mine is located. The f1-score indicators, which take into account the balance between accuracy and completeness, are 83% for the class "no_mine" and 82% for the class "mine" (Table 6.1).

Based on the visualized test results, the neural network was able to recognize only three mines out of seven; note that the third mine was recognized with a small percentage (only 57%, which is very low when the minimum threshold is 70%). Therefore, from the obtained visualized and text data, we can conclude that the model may need additional settings or optimization to ensure better accuracy and ability to correctly recognize mines in the input image, and it was decided to switch to the YOLO architecture, namely YOLOv8 nano. This architecture consists of 225 layers, which contain a total of 3,011,043 parameters. The architecture is built from a sequence of layers using different types of convolutions, concatenations, and convolutional operation blocks. The network has a deep structure, which allows it to detect objects of various sizes and complexity in images at high speed, using 8.9 giga FLOPs of computation [81–83].

According to the latest data of the final epoch, there is a noticeable decrease in the average error in predicting the coordinates of the object, which indicates increased accuracy. Improvements in other parameters are also noted: the average error value from 63.7 fell to 0.43, and the tracking error value decreased from 4.074 to 0.8832, which indicates the effectiveness of the model. An important stage during training was data validation. Looking at the training graphs (Figure 6.13), we can see that the model error decreased at each epoch on both the training and validation datasets. Let us display the graphs of the model training accuracy on the test and validation datasets. The precision (B) metric measures the percentage of objects identified by

Table 6.1 The part of the process of training a developed CNN with the YOLO architecture.

Epoch	Time (sec)	Loss	Accuracy	Validation loss	Validation accuracy
1	122	0.3072	0.8647	0.1015	0.9728
2	121	0.1083	0.9641	0.0534	0.9837
3	124	0.0774	0.9784	0.0433	0.9864
4	122	0.0624	0.9781	0.0367	0.9878
5	124	0.0590	0.9801	0.0340	0.9891

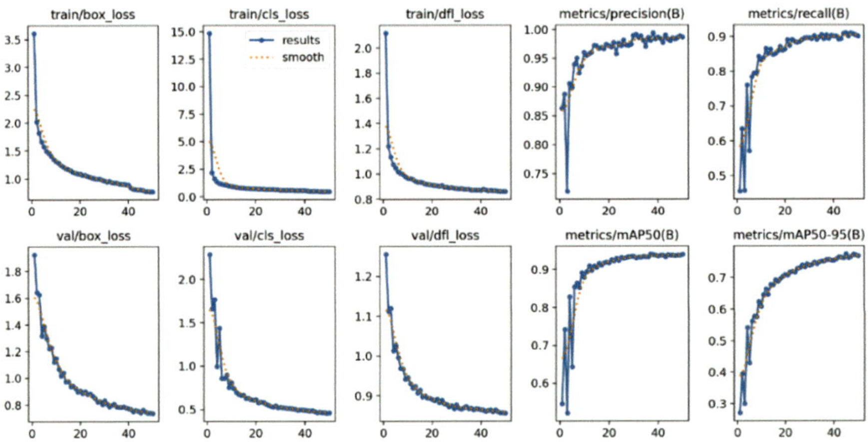

Figure 6.13 Model training metrics on 50 epochs.

the model as APHEL-1 mines that are actually such. The recall (B) metric measures the percentage of real APHEL-1 mines that were detected by the model. The accuracy of the measurements increases over 50 epochs. mAP50 (B) indicates the average accuracy when using a confidence threshold of 50%, and mAP50-90 (B) indicates the average accuracy from 50% to 95% of the confidence threshold. The graphs also show the increase in the accuracy of detecting APHEL-1 mines. After that, it was decided to run the neural network on test images (397 images) after data validation (Figure 6.14). We will load augmented images, i.e., processed with a black and white filter, blend them (i.e., take four images and combine their parts), and change the brightness of the image from −25% to +25%.

As a result, in very complex images where the mine is located in the leaves, the mine was accurately recognized; it is very difficult for the human eye to detect it, because it is very similar in color palette and is hidden among the leaves.

After creating the first CNN, it was found that a conventional neural network without any modifications on average demonstrates results at the level of 50%–60% on simple images. For this reason, it was decided to switch to the ready-made YOLOv8n [96] architecture and train the model for 50 epochs without further adjustments. This approach showed significantly better results, which allows us to conclude that using an already pre-trained model is more effective than developing our own convolutional neural network. Modification and optimization are needed, because most often when importing the model to the device that will process it, the developer will face

Figure 6.14 Testing the model on test data.

many problems. The previous model showed good results but still needs to be improved and optimized. Among all these methods, model quantization was chosen. Model quantization is a popular deep learning optimization technique in which model data – both network parameters and activations – is converted from a floating-point representation to a lower-precision representation, such as using 8-bit integers. There are different types of quantization; in this case, float32 to float16 was used.

To train the quantized YOLOv8n model, the Google Collab service was chosen, where the created dataset, all libraries, and code were imported. The number of epochs was also increased to 100 due to the possibility of losing recognition accuracy.

With 100 epochs, the neural network was trained for 5.5 hours, and the model weighs 6.3 megabytes. Let us review the training process to see the graphs (according to Figure 6.15).

Comparing the values at the final epochs, the following data can be obtained: at 50 epochs, the loss of recognition of the object in the image (box_loss) was 0.766, and at 100 epochs the error decreased to 0.62113.

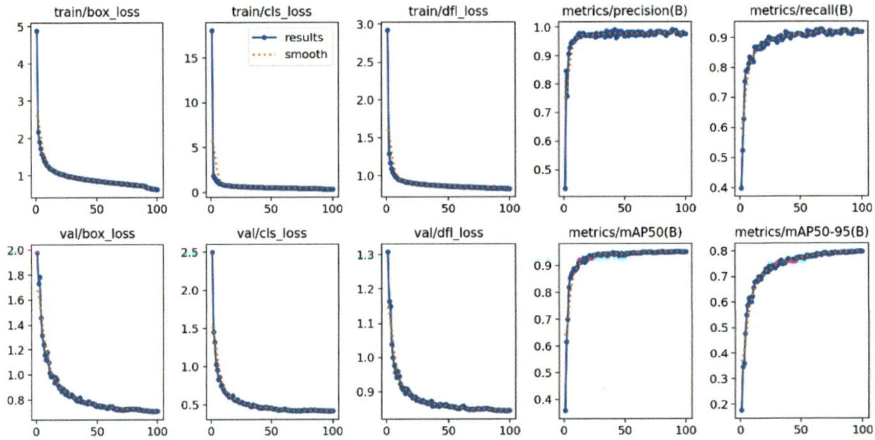

Figure 6.15 Metrics of the quantum model learning process.

All other graphs also show a noticeable improvement; quantization accelerated the training of the neural network and allowed not to lose accuracy at 100 epochs, but even on the contrary, to improve the recognition accuracy. Quantization helped to improve training using the YOLOv8n trained model, but one graph is not enough, so the operation of the neural network was checked using a test dataset, which will be provided to the neural network to detect mines in images.

We test the system on augmented data (according to Figure 6.16).

On augmented images, the neural network produces an accuracy of 89%–90% on average, and also processes images without misclassification on images where there are no mines. Quantization in neural networks is an important optimization method that provides an optimal balance between accuracy and resources. This approach allows you to reduce the amount of memory required to store model parameters and computational costs during inference. After that, an application was developed that can use the created models. In order to develop a mobile version of the neural network model, you first need to convert it from the "best_model.pt" format to "best_model.pb." After this operation, you can proceed to creating an application, where the optimized version of the neural network model is loaded and the following application is obtained at the output, which uses the Android device's camera (according to Figure 6.17).

After building the project, the imported model was tested on separate test files. Analyzing the operation of the Android application, we can conclude

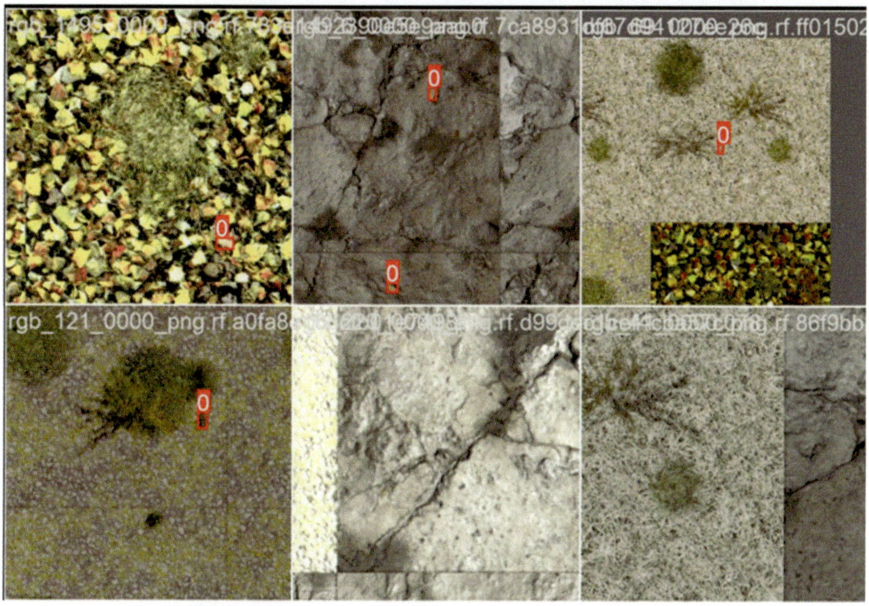

Figure 6.16 Testing the model on augmented data.

that on average, on a Redmi Note 9 device with a weak MediaTek Helio G85 processor, the camera produced 35–45 frames per second during the operation of the application. After quantizing the model, the weights were changed from fp32 to fp16, and it was noticed that the speed of the model improved and even on weak specifications it gives a good result, but the accuracy dropped to 85% maximum, which is a good result.

The main task during the development of the intelligent system for detecting landmines APHEL-1 was to create an accurate and reliable neural network model that would allow it to be used on mobile devices, or any others that have a modern processor and the Android operating system. Therefore, it was decided to compare the model data with each other using the metrics of the trained neural networks.

The first convolutional neural network model (Table 6.2) showed poor training results due to the outdated architecture and the small number of layers used for training. Another problem was the use of 200 epochs for training; this approach forced the neural network to retrain and detect individual areas in the image and the background, but not the mines themselves. Also, this architecture does not support object tracking, which creates a problem

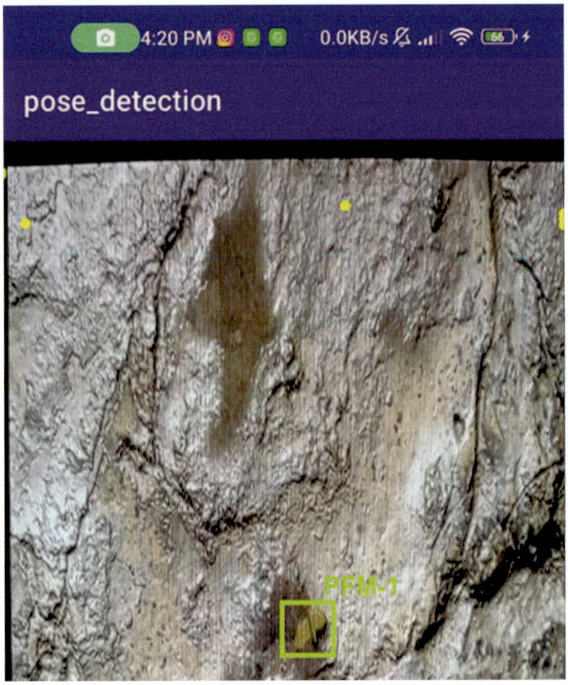

Figure 6.17 The result of mine recognition using the smartphone camera.

Table 6.2 Comparison of trained neural network models.

Model	box_loss	cls_loss	dfl_loss	Precision	Recall	Epochs
CNN	1.0252	0.9463	1.5602	0.841	0.752	200
YOLOv8	0.7411	0.4343	0.8832	0.937	0.94	50
Quantized YoloV8	0.6211	0.3445	0.8257	0.951	0.948	100

for using this neural network in real time due to unoptimized use of device resources. Therefore, it was decided to abandon this architecture.

The second model was a modern trained architecture YOLOv8n. Having carefully identified all the specifications and types of the model, 50 epochs were selected for training. It showed better results and had the ability to validate the input data after each epoch to detect problems such as overtraining and errors in the input data. After testing, it was noticed that this model has a good recognition rate, but it is very heavy even for a modern machine; so it was decided to move on to creating a third model.

The third model is YOLOv8 nano with quantization. Instead of using fp32, the weights were converted to fp16 format, and instead of 50 epochs, 100 were conducted. The result was the same accuracy as in the previous second model (YOLOv8), but the third model is smaller in size, which reduces the amount of memory required for its storage and speeds up calculations, which allowed it to be run on Android devices. This information indicates that the use of the third model is suitable for the task of detecting APHEL-1 landmines.

6.4.2 Injury severity assessment in resource-constrained environments

To simulate a resource-constrained environment typical of UAV deployments, the experiments were conducted on the following hardware: edge device (NVIDIA Jetson Nano Developer Kit, Quad-core ARM A57 @ 1.43 GHz, 128-core Maxwell GPU, 4 GB LPDDR4, 16 GB eMMC storage), and development workstation (CPU Intel Core i9-10900K, GPU NVIDIA RTX 3090, 64 GB memory DDR4, and 1 TB NVMe SSD storage).

For this study, a new custom war trauma dataset (WTDS) was developed based on UAV-captured aerial images of war traumas (Figure 6.18). Data were annotated in collaboration with medical professionals to assign injury severity levels based on the Abbreviated Injury Scale (AIS) [97] and Ten Second Triage Tool (TST) [98], focusing on visible indicators without measuring physiological vital signs. The dataset includes 6,000 images that encompass various injury scenarios, lighting conditions, and environmental settings and 5 classes (minor injury, 820 cases; moderate injury, 936 cases; serious injury, 988 cases; severe injury, 1233 cases; and critical and maximal (currently untreatable), 2023 cases). Data were split at a 70:15:15 rate, which corresponds to the percentage for training, validation and testing. Data

Figure 6.18 Fragment of the war trauma dataset (WTDS).

augmentation techniques included rotation, scaling, flipping, and brightness adjustment to enhance dataset diversity and improve model generalization.

The model selection was based on our previous study [99] and grounded on the following requirements: (1) low computational footprint to be suitable for resource-constrained hardware; (2) high precision in classifying injury severity; and (3) ability to process data with minimal latency. Based on these assumptions, MobileNetV3 [100], an optimized CNN tailored for embedded vision applications that can balance accuracy and efficiency, was selected as a benchmark model and compared with four other architectures. We leveraged pre-trained weights from MobileNetV3 trained on ImageNet datasets to expedite training and improve generalization. The model was fine-tuned using transfer learning with a batch size of 32, Adam optimizer, categorical cross-entropy as a loss function, dropout layers with a rate of 0.3, and L2 weight decay and trained 50 epochs. The learning rate was initially set to 0.001 with a scheduler, reducing it by a factor of 0.1 upon the plateau. A grid search was conducted to optimize hyperparameters, focusing on learning rate, batch size, and dropout rates. A five-fold cross-validation was employed to ensure the robustness of the model. Each fold was trained and validated independently, and the results were aggregated to provide a performance assessment. The model performance was evaluated on the edge device to ensure it meets real-time and resource constraints. In addition to standard evaluation metrics, inference time, which is the time taken to process and classify each image, was evaluated.

To contextualize the performance of MobileNetV3, we conducted a comparative analysis with other deep learning models under identical experimental conditions. The results are shown in Table 6.3.

MobileNetV3 demonstrated the best balance of accuracy and speed. The highest accuracy among tested lightweight models while maintaining a reasonable inference time (45 ms per image) makes it the best option for real-time applications in resource-constrained environments. Next, EfficientNetB0, with slightly lower accuracy and slower inference, demonstrated a competitive alternative to MobileNetV3. ResNet50 was included in this comparison due to being more accurate on some benchmarks. However, for UAV

Table 6.3 Comparative performance of different models for injury severity assessment.

Model	Parameters	FLOPs	FPS	Accuracy	Inference time
MobileNetV3	5.4M	219M	22	92.5%	45 ms/image
ResNet50	25.6M	4.1G	6.7	88.3%	150 ms/image
EfficientNetB0	5.3M	390M	16.7	90.1%	60 ms/image
SqueezeNet	1.24M	1.24G	33	85.6%	30 ms/image

deployment, this model can be considered unsuitable due to its high computational demands and slower inference speed. SqueezeNet provides the fastest inference but at the cost of significantly lower accuracy, making it less suitable for precise injury severity assessments. Finally, YOLOv5 (small) strikes a balance but falls slightly behind MobileNetV3 in both accuracy and speed.

To further enhance MobileNetV3 performance, we applied several optimization techniques to the edge device. They included model quantization and model pruning. Post-training quantization was performed to reduce the model size and improve inference speed without substantial loss in accuracy. As a result, the model size was reduced from 20 to 5 MB, inference time was decreased to 35 ms per image, and the accuracy rate was maintained at 91.8%. Structured model pruning enabled reduction of model parameters by 30% with further decreased inference time to 30 ms per image. Accuracy slightly decreased to 91.0%, which is within acceptable limits for real-time applications.

To understand the contribution of different components in the MobileNetV3 architecture, we conducted ablation studies focusing on the impact of depthwise separable convolutions [101] and the effect of neural architecture search (NAS) [102]. Replacing standard convolutions with depth-wise separable convolutions resulted in model parameters reduced by 50%, floating point operations per second (FLOPs) reduced by 70% and accuracy maintained within 1% of the baseline. Utilizing NAS to optimize the network architecture led to improved accuracy by 2% compared to manually designed counterparts and enhanced inference speed due to optimized layer configurations.

The experimental results demonstrated that the optimized MobileNetV3 architecture ensures a good balance between accuracy and computational efficiency, making it a suitable solution for deployment on edge devices such as UAVs. This finding has significant practical implications, as it suggests that MobileNetV3 could be a valuable tool for real-time injury severity assessment in resource-constrained environments. At the same time, it should be mentioned that different UAVs may have varying hardware specifications, which requires additional tuning and optimizations tailored to specific devices.

Visual results reveal high true positive rates across all injury severity classes with minimal misclassifications, particularly between adjacent severity levels "serious injury" and "severe injury." The most effectively distinguished cases were between minor and critical injuries, even in challenging environmental conditions. We also found that misclassifications primarily occurred in scenarios with occlusions or poor lighting. To improve model training, we are considering incorporating advanced augmentation techniques, such as generative adversarial networks, to create synthetic injury images. Future enhancements also include combining visual data with other sensory inputs (e.g., thermal imaging, LiDAR, etc.) to enhance the accuracy of injury assessment and adaptive learning mechanisms to boost the system's efficacy and applicability in diverse operational scenarios.

6.4.3 Medical mask detection

To train and test the selected neural network model for recognizing a medical mask on a human face [6, 7, 103, 104], a Python script was created, which includes the following parameters:

- img_path – parameter for the path to the dataset on which the NN will be trained;
- epochs – number of epochs for training;
- num_photo_per_epoch – number of photos per epoch;
- name_model – name for the trained model.

Inside this script, an object of the MobileNetV2 class is also used, which contains a ready-made architecture of the CNN.

For training the NN, a ready-made dataset was loaded, consisting of images of people "with a mask" and "without a mask." The collected dataset consists of 1920 images, divided into two classes required for future training (Figure 6.19): with_mask – 966 images of people with a mask on their faces;

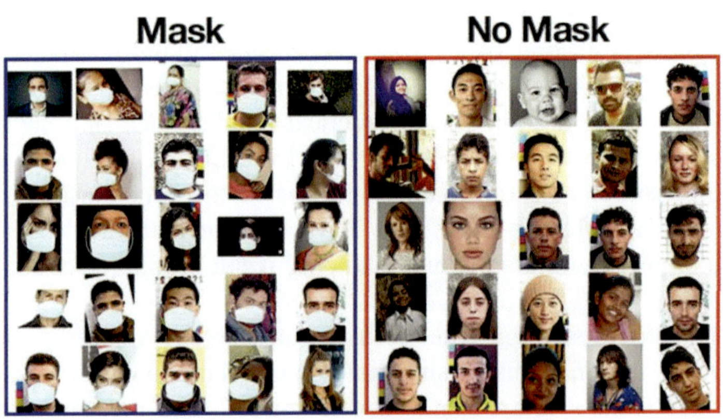

Figure 6.19 Dataset for NN training.

without_mask – 954 images of people without a mask on their faces. After running the code, data collection begins and the NN training process begins (Table 6.4). The system for recognizing masks on a person's face is also equipped with additional functionality. The first function is an administrator or security guard notifier about an intruder. This function can be implemented using TelegramBotApi – a built-in HTTP-based interface created specifically for developers from the popular Telegram messenger, which is designed for writing bots. After creating the bot, this API token is written to the system configuration file and is used further for its control. The bot notifies the administrator or security guard in the telegram (as specified by a specific user_id in the system settings). Also, through this bot, if necessary, the user can find out the general statistics at any time by simply entering the necessary command. The result of the robot's work is shown in Figures 6.20 and 6.21.

Table 6.4 The part of the process of training a developed CNN with the MobileNetV2 architecture.

Epoch	Time (sec)	Loss	Accuracy	Validation loss	Validation accuracy
1	77	0.5515	0.7500	0.2302	0.9891
2	55	0.2159	0.9625	0.0982	0.9891
3	55	0.1158	0.9813	0.0603	0.9891
4	55	0.0796	0.9841	0.0451	0.9964
5	57	0.0610	0.9916	0.0342	1.0000

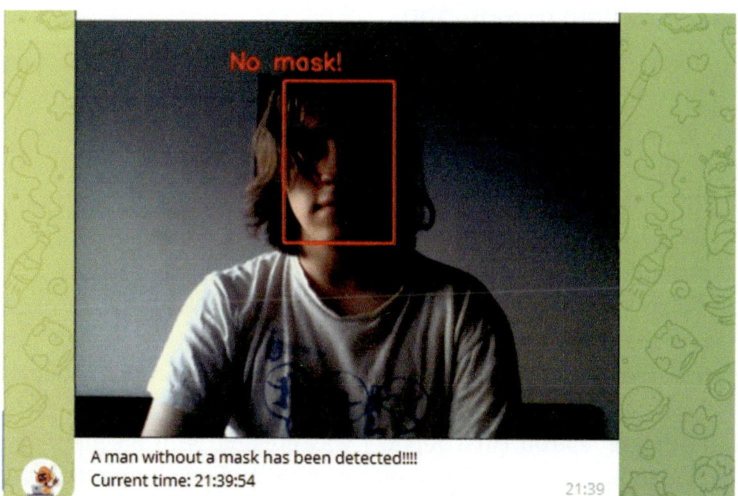

Figure 6.20 The result of the bot's work.

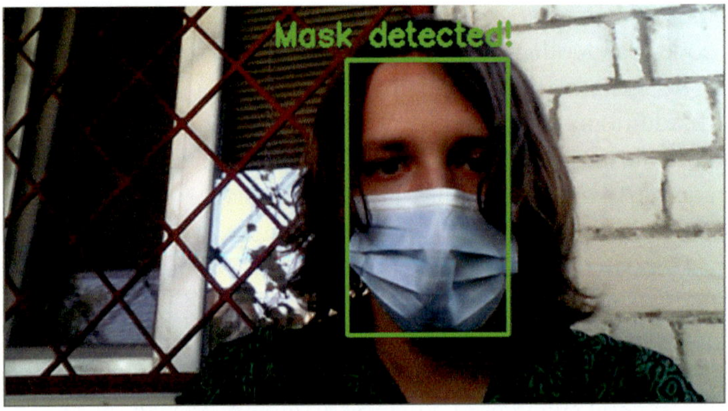

Figure 6.21 Face recognition result in a mask.

The developed system has a simple and user-friendly interface, after passing visual testing [105]. It contains complete information on choosing a trained NN model, setting up the camera, and connecting a telegram bot to notify the administration or security of a person without a mask. A database was developed specifically for the system to maintain statistics on the number of people with or without a mask, which the user can access via the telegram bot.

6.4.4 Military vehicle recognition

For military vehicle recognition, Tensorflow was used, which has a handy utility known as image_dataset_from_directory, which allows you to work with a dataset that is already on the cloud. The dataset was divided into training and validation data, namely 20% of the data was allocated for validation and 80% for training. In total, the MSTAR dataset offers 8 classes of military vehicles from 9466 images. 7573 images were allocated for training, and validation will be performed on 1893 images. The image size is 128 × 128, with a batch size of 32. Since all images were black and white, it was necessary to set the color mode to grayscale [8, 106–107].

For training, images and their corresponding labels were used, as depicted in Figure 6.22.

A multilayer perceptron (first model) was created with an input layer, three hidden layers with ReLU activation function, and one output layer.

For the second model, a convolutional neural network with three convolutional layers with an output space dimension (i.e., the number of output filters

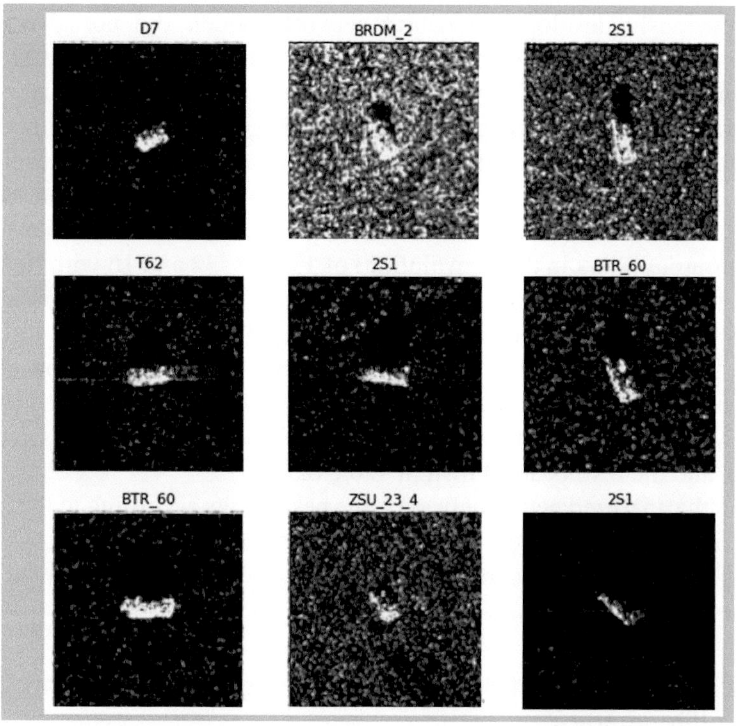

Figure 6.22 Training data and their corresponding labels.

in the convolution) of 32 was used with ReLU activation functions and one hidden layer of size 128 with ReLU activation function.

For the third model, a CNN with three convolutional layers with an output space dimension (i.e., the number of output filters in the convolution) of 10, 20, and 30 was used with ReLU activation functions and an output layer with Softmax activation function.

For the fourth model, a neural network with XCeption [90] architecture was used. At the beginning of this model, an input layer of size 128 and data augmentation were added and an output layer of size 8 and a Softmax activation function were added.

For the fifth model, a neural network with the VGG19 architecture was used. Using the Keras functionality, the weights for this model were pre-trained for ImageNet. At the beginning of this model, an input layer of size 128 and data augmentation were added and an output layer of size 8 and a Softmax activation function were added [93].

The previously developed 5 neural network models did not give the desired results in terms of object recognition accuracy. Therefore, a sixth convolutional neural network model was created, taking into account the architectural features, advantages and disadvantages of previous models, existing studies on object recognition in satellite images, taking into account the characteristics of the dataset used. The developed model has data augmentation, four convolutional layers with output space dimensions (i.e. the number of output filters in the convolution) of 128, 64, 32 and 16 with ReLU activation functions and kernel sizes of 5, 4, 3 and 2, respectively, two fully connected layers with output space dimensions of 1024 and 128 with ReLU activation functions, and an output layer with output space dimension of 8 with Softmax activation function.

To solve the corresponding problem, six neural network models were developed, and the results are shown in Table 6.5.

Among the analyzed neural networks, the best results according to the relevant metrics (bold underlined values) were shown by sixth model (CNN3), which was able not only to learn on the dataset used but also to recognize an image that was not in the dataset.

6.4.5 Building identification and contour segmentation from satellite images

For the task of building identification and segmentation, a new dataset was created by merging publicly available images and official building photos. Below is an example of images from the dataset (Figure 6.23).

After the dataset has been generated, the images from it need to be prepared for further use. Next, two neural networks will be implemented based on two architectures U-Net and Mask R-CNN [67–78]. Different annotations are used for them. To annotate images for the Mask R-CNN architecture,

Table 6.5 Metrics of developed neural network models.

ANN architectures	**Final metrics**					
	Loss	**CA**	**MCC**	**F2**	**AUC**	**Epochs**
MLP (the 1st model)	0.43	0.84	0.82	0.84	0.99	61
CNN1 (the 2nd model)	3.15	0.58	0.57	0.57	0.83	15
CNN2 (the 3rd model)	1.44	0.51	0.45	0.51	0.85	16
XCeption (the 4th model)	3.34	0.47	0.42	0.43	0.80	17
VGG19 (the 5th model)	2.45	0.33	0.19	0.30	0.70	27
CNN3 (the 6th model)	**0.12**	**0.94**	**0.93**	**0.94**	**0.99**	37

Figure 6.23 Example images from the dataset.

the web application Makesense.ai was used, a free, open-source online photo labeling tool that supports the following labeling types: rectangles, lines, points, and polygons (Figure 6.24).

The programming language was chosen as Python, as one of the most modern and promising programming languages for implementing neural networks. For the implementation and training of Mask R-CNN, the necessary dependencies were established [77, 78].

The created application has two modes, namely training and main. If the training mode is started, the application will train the weight coefficients of neurons on the training sample, which is located in the application directory, according to the neural network settings. The training results are presented in Table 6.6.

Table 6.6 The part of the process of training a developed CNN with the Mask R-CNN architecture.

Epoch	Time (sec)	Loss	Accuracy	Validation loss	Validation accuracy
27	4	1.1875	0.9251	0.2103	0.9702
28	4	1.0488	0.9305	0.1905	0.9755
29	4	1.1164	0.9353	0.1856	0.9812
30	4	1.1379	0.9476	0.1720	0.9895

As you can see, the final accuracy is about 95%; this accuracy will be improved later. After successfully training the scales, you can choose the main mode of operation, which is started using the main.py file. This mode will process all images located in the test folder in the application directory. Examples of the program in this mode are shown in Figure 6.25.

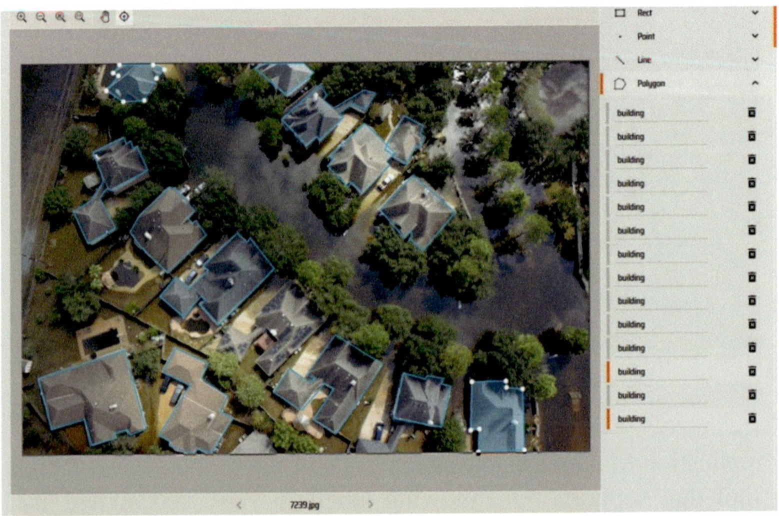

Figure 6.24 Example of labeling and annotating buildings in the makesense.ai application.

Figure 6.25 Results of the developed building contouring application.

As a result, the effectiveness of using such convolutional network architectures as U-Net and Mask R-CNN was investigated. Convolutional neural networks were created and configured in the Python programming language on selected architectures to form the contour of buildings. Several implementations of convolutional neural networks were created on different architectures and configured to work with the selected dataset. The developed application has an accuracy of 89%, so it can be used with full confidence in the results. The created system can be integrated into any work terminal. In this way, it is possible to provide experts with software for forming the contour of buildings. This will help save a lot of time on manual annotation.

6.5 Conclusion

This chapter explores how artificial intelligence (AI) technologies can be effectively applied to address various recognition challenges across multiple fields. It emphasizes the use of convolutional and recurrent neural networks to tackle tasks such as the healthcare sector, military applications, and cartography. By reviewing successful applications, the study showcases AI's ability to improve classification and recognition in real-world contexts. It also examines future possibilities for advancing AI technologies to enhance their capabilities further. This analysis adds to the ongoing discussion about the practical uses and future potential of AI in solving complex recognition problems.

The study demonstrated the effective use of various neural network architectures for recognizing and classifying landmines and military equipment, which is very important for the military and ordinary citizens, recognizing masks on a person's face, which is important for the healthcare sector, as well as identifying and segmenting building contours when mapping damaged structures.

References

[1] Y. Liu, Y. Li, G. Chen, H. Gao, "An Edge-end Based Fast Car License Plate Recognition Method', International Conference on Big Data & Artificial Intelligence & Software Engineering (ICBASE), pp. 394–397, Bangkok, Thailand, 30 October - 01 November, 2020, doi:10.1109/ICBASE51474.2020.00090.

[2] V. Lytvyn, N. Oleksiv, M. Nazarkevych, "Tanks detection and recognition based on custom dataset model", IEEE 4th International Conference on Smart Information Systems and Technologies (SIST),

pp. 583–586, Astana, Kazakhstan, 15–17 May, 2024, doi:10.1109/SIST61555.2024.10629455.

[3] M. S. Hasan, F. Fahim, A. A. Farabi, F. Rahman,, "A Comparison between YOLOV7 and YOLOV5-based detection of Combat Targets and Camouflaged Militia", 4th International Conference on Sustainable Technologies for Industry 4.0 (STI), pp. 1–6, Dhaka, Bangladesh, 17-18 December, 2022, doi:10.1109/STI56238.2022.10103281.

[4] I. Sidenko, et. al., "Hybrid neural network and genetic algorithm combination for recognition and avoidance of vehicle obstacles", P. Geril, S. Bhonsale, eds. Industrial Simulation Conference'2024, EUROSIS-ETI, Valencia, Spain, 2024.

[5] Y. P. Kondratenko, A. I. Shevchenko (Eds.), "Research Tendencies and Prospect Domains for AI Development and Implementation", River Publishers: Gistrup, pp. 1–154, 2024.

[6] I. Sidenko, G. Kondratenko, O. Heras, Y. Kondratenko, "Neural Technologies for Objects Classification with Mobile Applications", Journal of Mobile Multimedia, 20(03), pp. 727–748, 2024, doi:10.13052/jmm1550-4646.2039.

[7] G. Kondratenko, I. Sidenko, M. Saliutin, Y. Kondratenko, "Mobile Recognition of Image Components Based on Machine Learning Methods", Journal of Mobile Multimedia, 20(03), pp. 699–726, 2024, doi: 10.13052/jmm1550-4646.2038.

[8] O. Kovaliv, et. al., "Neural Network Architectures for Recognizing Military Objects on Satellite Images", IEEE 12th International Conference on Intelligent Data Acquisition and Advanced Computing Systems: Technology and Applications (IDAACS), pp. 175–180, Dortmund, Germany, 07-09 September, 2023, doi:10.1109/IDAACS58523.2023.10348905.

[9] A. Sheremet, et. al., "Diagnosis of Lung Disease Based on Medical Images Using Artificial Neural Networks", IEEE 3rd Ukraine Conference on Electrical and Computer Engineering (UKRCON), pp. 561–565, Lviv, Ukraine, 26-28 August, 2021, doi:10.1109/UKRCON53503.2021.9575961.

[10] Z. Gomolka, et. al., "Diagnosing Dyslexia in Early School-Aged Children Using the LSTM Network and Eye Tracking Technology", Applied Sciences (Switzerland), 14(17):8004, 2024, https://doi.org/10.3390/app14178004.

[11] A. Sokoliuk, et. al., "Machine Learning Algorithms for Binary Classification of Liver Disease", IEEE International Conference on Problems

of Infocommunications. Science and Technology (PIC S&T), pp. 417–421, Kharkiv, Ukraine, 06-09 October, 2020, doi:10.1109/PICST51311.2020.9468051.

[12] V. M. Opanasenko, S. Fazilov, S. S. Radjabov, S. S. Kakharov, "Multilevel Face Recognition System", Cybernetics and Systems Analysis, vol. 60, No. 1, pp. 146–151, 2024, doi:10.1007/s10559-024-00655-w.

[13] V. M. Opanasenko, S. K. Fazilov, O. N. Mirzaev, S. S. Kakharov, "An Ensemble Approach To Face Recognition In Access Control Systems", Journal of Mobile Multimedia, 20(3), pp. 749–768, 2024, doi:10.13052/jmm1550-4646.20310.

[14] Z. Q. Wang, et. al., "Fully Convolutional Network for Recognition of Small Buildings in Aerial Images", Fifth International Workshop on Earth Observation and Remote Sensing Applications (EORSA), pp. 1–5, Xi'an, China, 18-20 June, 2018, doi:10.1109/EORSA.2018.8598558.

[15] T. Chawla, D. Kumar, V. Kukreja, "An Enhanced YOLOV5 Model for Gateways Recognition in Heritage Buildings", 2nd International Conference on Edge Computing and Applications (ICECAA), pp. 736–740, Namakkal, India, 19-21 July, 2023, doi:10.1109/ICECAA58104.2023.10212376.

[16] P. Bezak, "Building recognition system based on deep learning", Third International Conference on Artificial Intelligence and Pattern Recognition (AIPR), pp. 1–5, Lodz, Poland, 19-21 September, 2016, doi:10.1109/ICAIPR.2016.7585230.

[17] J. Baur, et. al., "Applying Deep Learning to Automate UAV-Based Detection of Scatterable Landmines", Remote Sens., 12(5):859, 2020, doi:10.3390/rs12050859.

[18] O. A. Pryshchenko, et. al., "Implementation of an Artificial Intelligence Approach to GPR Systems for Landmine Detection", Remote Sens., 14(17):4421, 2022, doi:10.3390/rs14174421.

[19] D. Munteanu, et. al., "Sea Mine Detection Framework Using YOLO, SSD and EfficientDet Deep Learning Models", Sensors, 22(23):9536, 2022, doi:10.3390/s22239536.

[20] V. Kafedziski, S. Pecov, D. Tanevski, "Detection and Classification of Land Mines from Ground Penetrating Radar Data Using Faster R-CNN", 26th Telecommunications Forum (TELFOR), pp. 1–4, Belgrade, Serbia, 20-21 November, 2018, doi:10.1109/TELFOR.2018.8612117.

[21] F. Kamran, M. Shahzad, F. Shafait, "Automated Military Vehicle Detection from Low-Altitude Aerial Images", Digital Image Computing: Techniques and Applications (DICTA), pp. 1–8, Canberra, ACT, Australia, 10-13 December, 2018, doi:10.1109/DICTA.2018.8615865.

[22] A. Ammar, et. al., "Aerial Images Processing for Car Detection using Convolutional Neural Networks: Comparison between Faster R-CNN and YoloV3", arXiv:1910.07234, doi:10.3390/electronics10070820.

[23] Q. Tan, et. al., "Vehicle Detection in High Resolution Satellite Remote Sensing Images Based on Deep Learning", IEEE Access, 8, pp. 153394–153402, 2020, doi:10.1109/ACCESS.2020.3017894.

[24] D. Kumar, X. Zhang, H. Su, S. Wei, "Accurate Object Detection Based on Faster R-CNN in Remote Sensing Imagery", 6th Asia-Pacific Conference on Synthetic Aperture Radar (APSAR), pp. 1–6, Xiamen, China, 26-29 November, 2019, doi:10.1109/APSAR46974.2019.9048519.

[25] J. Yin, et. al., "A Data Augmentation Method for War Trauma Using the War Trauma Severity Score and Deep Neural Networks", Electronics, 10(21):2657, 2021, doi:10.3390/electronics10212657.

[26] Y. Li, et. al., "AID-YOLO: An Efficient and Lightweight Network Method for Small Target Detector in Aerial Images", Electronics, 13(17):3564, 2024, doi:10.3390/electronics13173564.

[27] S. Kim, et. al., "Disaster Damage Investigation Using Artificial Intelligence and Drone Mapping", Int. Arch. Photogramm. Remote Sens. Spatial Inf. Sci., XLIII-B3-2022, pp. 1109–1114, 2022, doi:10.5194/isprs-archives-XLIII-B3-2022-1109-2022.

[28] M. Tav, Q. V. Le, "EfficientNet: Rethinking Model Scaling for Convolutional Neural Networks", arXiv:1905.11946, doi:10.48550/arXiv.1905.11946.

[29] N. Almufadi, H. F. Alhasson, "Classification of Diabetic Foot Ulcers from Images Using Machine Learning Approach", Diagnostics, 14(16):1807, 2024, doi:10.3390/diagnostics14161807.

[30] J. Lu, et. al., "Unmanned aerial vehicle based intelligent triage system in mass-casualty incidents using 5G and artificial intelligence", World J Emerg Med., 14(4), pp. 273–279, 2023 doi:10.5847/wjem.j.1920-8642.2023.066.

[31] S. Yoon, J. Cho, "Deep Multimodal Detection in Reduced Visibility Using Thermal Depth Estimation for Autonomous Driving", Sensors, 22(14):5084, 2022, doi:10.3390/s22145084.

[32] D. K. Alqahtani, A. Cheema, A. N. Toosi, "Benchmarking Deep Learning Models for Object Detection on Edge Computing Devices", arXiv:2409.16808, doi:10.48550/arXiv.2409.16808.

[33] M. Mahmoud, M. S. Kasem, H-S. Kang, "A Comprehensive Survey of Masked Faces: Recognition, Detection, and Unmasking", Applied Sciences, 14(19):8781, 2024, doi:10.3390/app14198781.

[34] M. S. Mazli Shahar, L. Mazalan, "Face Identity for Face Mask Recognition System", IEEE 11th IEEE Symposium on Computer Applications & Industrial Electronics (ISCAIE), pp. 42–47, Penang, Malaysia, 03-04 April, 2021, doi:10.1109/ISCAIE51753.2021.9431791.

[35] G. Kaur, "Face Mask Recognition System using CNN Model", Neuroscience Informatics, 2(3):100035, 2021, doi:10.1016/j.neuri.2021.100035.

[36] K. Guo, C. Zhao, J. Wang, "A fast mask synthesis method for face recognition", Vis. Intell., 2(25), 2024, doi:10.1007/s44267-024-00060-z.

[37] J. Sun, J. Xue, G. Li, J. Liu, "A Novel Map Representation for Automatic Construction of Topological Map and Lane-Level Route Planning", China Automation Congress (CAC), pp. 7885–7890, Chongqing, China, 17-19 November, 2023, doi:10.1109/CAC59555.2023.10450231.

[38] Y. Kondratenko, et. al., "Artificial Neural Networks for Recognition of Brain Tumors on MRI Images", in: A. Bollin, et al. (Eds.) Information and Communication Technologies in Education, Research, and Industrial Applications. ICTERI 2020. Communications in Computer and Information Science, vol. 1308, pp. 119–140, Springer, Cham, 2020, doi:10.1007/978-3-030-77592-6_6.

[39] I. Sova, et. al., "Machine Learning Technology for Neoplasm Segmentation on Brain MRI Scans", CEUR Workshop Proceedings, vol. 2791, pp. 50–59, 2020, https://ceur-ws.org/Vol-2791/2020200050.pdf.

[40] D. X. Ascar, D. Judson, S. K. Pittala, "SegNet Approach for Vehicle License Plate Localization", 17th International Conference on Information Technology Trends (ITT), pp. 113–117, Abu Dhabi, United Arab Emirates, 25-26 November, 2020, doi:10.1109/ITT51279.2020.9320883.

[41] R. Kavya, et. al., "Lane Detection and Traffic Sign Recognition from Continuous Driving Scenes using Deep Neural Networks", 2nd International Conference on Smart Electronics and Communication

(ICOSEC), pp. 1461–1467, Trichy, India, 07-09 October, 2021, doi: 10.1109/ICOSEC51865.2021.9591927.

[42] X. Duan, et. al., "High-Capacity Image Steganography Based on Improved FC-DenseNet", IEEE Access, vol. 8, pp. 170174–170182, 2020, doi:10.1109/ACCESS.2020.3024193.

[43] M. Deaconu, D. Popescu, L. Ichim, "Automatic Detection of Blood Vessels in Retinal Images Using FC-DenseNet Neural Networks", 25th International Conference on System Theory, Control and Computing (ICSTCC), pp. 449–454, Iasi, Romania, 20-23 October, 2021, doi:10.1 109/ICSTCC52150.2021.9607051.

[44] M. Pathak, et. al., "A Robust EfficientNet Architecture for Brain Tumor Classification and Identification Using MRI Image", 11th International Conference on Intelligent Systems and Embedded Design (ISED), pp. 1–5, Dehradun, India, 15-17 December, 2023, doi:10.1109/ISED5938 2.2023.10444597.

[45] Q. Chen, et al., "Extracting Rectified Building Footprints from Traditional Orthophotos: A New Workflow", Sensors, 22(1):207, 2022, doi:10.3390/s22010207.

[46] R. D. Bhosale, D. M. Yadav, "Analysis of EfficientNet Family Models by Retraining for Tuberculosis Detection from Chest X-Ray Images", Second International Conference on Informatics (ICI), pp. 1–6, Noida, India, 23-25 November, 2023, doi:10.1109/ICI60088.2023. 10420853.

[47] O. Striuk, et. al., "Generative Adversarial Neural Network for Creating Photorealistic Images", 2020 IEEE 2nd International Conference on Advanced Trends in Information Theory (ATIT), pp. 368–371, Kyiv, Ukraine, 25-27 November, 2020, doi:10.1109/ATIT50783.2020.93493 26.

[48] I. Khortiuk, et. al., "Scoring system based on neural networks for identification of factors in image perception", CEUR Workshop Proceedings, vol. 2604, pp. 993–1003, 2020, https://ceur-ws.org/Vol-26 04/paper66.pdf.

[49] D. Mikhov, et. al., "Fuzzy Logic Approach to Improving the Digital Images Contrast", IEEE 2nd Ukraine Conference on Electrical and Computer Engineering (UKRCON), pp. 1183–1188, Lviv, Ukraine, 02-06 July, 2019, doi:10.1109/UKRCON.2019.8879961.

[50] Y. Pomanysochka, et. al., "Soft Computing Techniques for Noise Filtration in the Image Recognition Processes", IEEE 2nd Ukraine

Conference on Electrical and Computer Engineering (UKRCON), pp. 1189–1195, Lviv, Ukraine, 02-06 July, 2019, doi:10.1109/UKRCON.2019.8879910.

[51] Y. Pomanysochka, et. al., "Noise Filtration in the Digital Images Using Fuzzy Sets and Fuzzy Logic", CEUR Workshop Proceedings, vol. 2403, pp. 63–72, 2019, https://ceur-ws.org/Vol-2403/paper8.pdf.

[52] O. Striuk, Y. Kondratenko, "Cross-Domain Reconfigurable GAN with Fuzzy Components for Anomaly Detection", 13th International Conference on Dependable Systems, Services and Technologies (DESSERT), pp. 1–5, Athens, Greece, 13-15 October, 2023, doi: 10.1109/DESSERT61349.2023.10416521.

[53] I. Sidenko, et. al., "Eye-tracking technology for the analysis of dynamic data", IEEE 9th International Conference on Dependable Systems, Services and Technologies (DESSERT), pp. 479–484, Kyiv, Ukraine, 24-27 May, 2018, doi:10.1109/DESSERT.2018.8409181.

[54] I. Sidenko, et. al., "Machine Learning for Unmanned Aerial Vehicle Routing on Rough Terrain", Z. Hu, I. Dychka, M. He (Eds.), Advances in Computer Science for Engineering and Education VI. ICCSEEA 2023. Lecture Notes on Data Engineering and Communications Technologies, vol. 181, pp. 626–635, Springer, Cham, 2023, doi:10.1007/978-3-031-36118-0_56.

[55] V. Zinchenko, et. al., "Computer Vision in Control and Optimization of Road Traffic", IEEE Third International Conference on Data Stream Mining & Processing (DSMP), pp. 249–254, Lviv, Ukraine, 21-25 August, 2020, doi:10.1109/DSMP47368.2020.9204329.

[56] R. Leizerovych, et. al., "IoT-complex for Monitoring and Analysis of Motor Highway Condition Using Artificial Neural Networks", IEEE 11th International Conference on Dependable Systems, Services and Technologies (DESSERT), pp. 207–212, Kyiv, Ukraine, 14-18 May, 2020, doi:10.1109/DESSERT50317.2020.9125004.

[57] Y. P. Kondratenko, V. M. Kuntsevich, A. A. Chikrii, V. F. Gubarev (Eds.), "Advanced control systems: Theory and applications", River Publishers: Gistrup, pp. 1–441, 2021, ISBN: 9788770223416, DOI: 10.1201/9781003337010.

[58] Y. P. Kondratenko, V. M. Kuntsevich, A. A. Chikrii, V. F. Gubarev (Eds.), "Recent Developments in Automatic Control Systems", River Publishers: Gistrup, pp. 1–492, 2022, ISBN: 978-877022673-8, 978-877022674-5.

[59] V. M. Kuntsevich, et. al. (Eds.), "Control Systems: Theory and Applications", pp. 1–326, River Publishers, Gistrup, Delft, 2018, https://www.riverpublishers.com/book_details.php?book_id=668.

[60] Y. P. Kondratenko, A. Roshanineshat, D. Simon, "Safe navigation of an autonomous robot in dynamic and unknown environments", Y. P. Kondratenko, V. M. Kuntsevich, A. A. Chikrii, V. F. Gubarev (Eds.), Recent Developments in Automatic Control Systems, pp. 261–288, Gistrup, 2022, https://www.taylorfrancis.com/chapters/edit/10.1201/9781003339229-13/safe-navigation-autonomous-robot-dynamic-unknown-environments-yuriy-kondratenko-arash-roshanineshat-dan-simon.

[61] Y. Zheng, et. al., "Research progress in surface water quality monitoring based on remote sensing technology", International Journal of Remote Sensing, 45:7, pp. 2337–2373, 2024, doi:10.1080/01431161.2024.2327086.

[62] Y. Kondratenko, et. al., "Machine Learning Techniques for Increasing Efficiency of the Robot"s Sensor and Control Information Processing", Sensors, 22(3), 1062, 2022, doi:10.3390/s22031062.

[63] V. Timchenko, et. al., "Decision Support System for the Safety of Ship Navigation Based on Optical Color Logic Gates", CEUR Workshop Proceedings, vol. 3347, pp. 42–52, 2022, https://ceur-ws.org/Vol-3347/Paper_4.pdf.

[64] Y. Kondratenko, S Sidorenko, "Ship Navigation in Narrowness Passes and Channels in Uncertain Conditions: Intelligent Decision Support" P. Shi, J. Stefanovski, J. Kacprzyk (Eds.), Complex Systems: Spanning Control and Computational Cybernetics: Foundations. Studies in Systems, Decision and Control, vol. 414, pp. 475–493, Springer, Cham, 2022, https://doi.org/10.1007/978-3-030-99776-2_24.

[65] R. Duro, et. al. (Eds.), "Advances in intelligent robotics and collaborative automation", River Publishers, Aalborg, 2015, doi:10.13052/rp-9788793237049.

[66] Y. Zhukov, O. Zivenko, "Ship Operation Analysis and Optimization via Mobile Application", Journal of Mobile Multimedia, 20(03), pp. 627–650, 2024, doi:10.13052/jmm1550-4646.2034.

[67] Y. D. Zhukov, B. N. Gordeev, A. V. Zivenko, "Polymetric sensing of intelligent robots", IEEE 7th International Conference on Intelligent Data Acquisition and Advanced Computing Systems (IDAACS), pp. 880–884, Berlin, Germany, 12-14 September, 2013, doi:10.1109/IDAACS.2013.6663053.

[68] V. Timchenko, et. al., "Logical Platforms for Mobile Application in Decision Support Systems Based on Color Information Processing", Journal of Mobile Multimedia, 20(3), pp. 679–698, 2024, doi:10.13052/jmm1550-4646.2037.

[69] V. L. Timchenko, et. al., "Why Color Optical Computing?" N. H. Phuong, V. Kreinovich (Eds.), Deep Learning and Other Soft Computing Techniques. Studies in Computational Intelligence, vol. 1097, pp. 227–233, Springer, Cham, 2023, doi:10.1007/978-3-031-29447-1_20.

[70] I. Sidenko, T. Misiuk, G. Kondratenko, Y. Kondratenko, "Objects segmentation in augmented reality environment", CEUR Workshop Proceedings, vol. 2870, pp. 959–968, 2021, https://ceur-ws.org/Vol-2870/paper72.pdf.

[71] Y. Kondratenko, et. al., "Analysis of the Priorities and Perspectives in Artificial Intelligence Implementation", 13th International Conference on Dependable Systems, Services and Technologies (DESSERT), pp. 1–8, Athens, Greece, 13-15 October, 2023, doi:10.1109/DESSERT61349.2023.10416432.

[72] V. Slyusar, et. al., "Some Aspects of Artificial Intelligence Development Strategy for Mobile Technologies", Journal of Mobile Multimedia, 20(3), pp. 525–554, 2024, doi:10.13052/jmm1550-4646.2031.

[73] Y. Kondratenko, et. al., "Tendencies and Challenges of Artificial Intelligence Development and Implementation", IEEE 12th International Conference on Intelligent Data Acquisition and Advanced Computing Systems: Technology and Applications (IDAACS), pp. 221–226, Dortmund, Germany, 07-09 September, 2023, doi:10.1109/IDAACS58523.2023.10348800.

[74] Y. P. Kondratenko, et. al., "Towards Implementing the Strategy of Artificial Intelligence Development: Ukraine Peculiarities", CEUR Workshop Proceedings, vol. 3513, pp. 106–117, 2023, https://ceur-ws.org/Vol-3513/paper09.pdf.

[75] E. D. Cherpanath, et al., "Food Image Recognition and Calorie Prediction Using Faster R-CNN and Mask R-CNN", 9th International Conference on Smart Computing and Communications (ICSCC), pp. 83-89, Kochi, Kerala, India, 17-19 August, 2023, doi:10.1109/ICSCC59169.2023.10335053.

[76] G. Priyadharshini, D. R. Judie Dolly, "Comparative Investigations on Tomato Leaf Disease Detection and Classification Using CNN, R-CNN, Fast R-CNN and Faster R-CNN", 9th International Conference

on Advanced Computing and Communication Systems (ICACCS), pp. 1540–1545, Coimbatore, India, 17-18 March, 2023, doi:10.1109/ICACCS57279.2023.10112860.

[77] H. Tahir, M. Shahbaz Khan, M. Owais Tariq, "Performance Analysis and Comparison of Faster R-CNN, Mask R-CNN and ResNet50 for the Detection and Counting of Vehicles", International Conference on Computing, Communication, and Intelligent Systems (ICCCIS), pp. 587–594, Greater Noida, India, 19-20 February, 2021, doi:10.1109/ICCCIS51004.2021.9397079.

[78] T. Peng, F. Wen, "Photovoltaic Panel Fault Detection Based on Improved Mask R-CNN", IEEE International Conference on Control, Electronics and Computer Technology (ICCECT), pp. 1187–1191, Jilin, China, 28-30 April, 2023, doi:10.1109/ICCECT57938.2023.10140742.

[79] F. C. Zegarra, J. Vargas-Machuca, A. M. Coronado, "Comparison of CNN and CNN-LSTM Architectures for Tool Wear Estimation", IEEE Engineering International Research Conference (EIRCON), pp. 1–4, Lima, Peru, 27-29 October, 2021, doi:10.1109/EIRCON52903.2021.9613659.

[80] M. A. Prameswari, M. Dwi Sulistiyo, A. F. Ihsan, "Classification of Handwritten Sundanese Script via Transfer Learning on CNN-Based Architectures", 3rd International Conference on Electronic and Electrical Engineering and Intelligent System (ICE3IS), pp. 401–406, Yogyakarta, Indonesia, 09-10 August, 2023, doi:10.1109/ICE3IS59323.2023.10335382.

[81] R. Hamzah, et. al., "Comparing modified Yolo V5 and Faster Regional Convolutional Neural Network performance for Recycle Waste Classification", IEEE International Conference on Automatic Control and Intelligent Systems (I2CACIS), pp. 415–419, Shah Alam, Malaysia, 29-29 June, 2024, doi:10.1109/I2CACIS61270.2024.10649835.

[82] K. Xiong, Q. Li, Y. Meng, Q. Li, "A Study on Weed Detection Based on Improved Yolo v5", 4th International Conference on Information Science and Education (ICISE-IE), pp. 1–4, Zhanjiang, China, 15-17 December, 2023, doi:10.1109/ICISE-IE60962.2023.10456396.

[83] Y. Qi, H. Sun, "Defect Detection of Insulator Based on YOLO Network", 9th International Conference on Electronic Technology and Information Science (ICETIS), pp. 232–235, Hangzhou, China, 17-19 May, 2024, doi:10.1109/ICETIS61828.2024.10593675.

[84] S. Manzoor, et. al., “Qualitative Analysis of Single Object and Multi Object Tracking Models”, 22nd International Conference on Control, Automation and Systems (ICCAS), pp. 1539–1545, Jeju, Republic of Korea, 27 November - 01 December, 2022, doi:10.23919/ICCAS5566 2.2022.10003784.

[85] A. S. B. Sadkhan, S. R. Talebiyan, N. Farzaneh, “An Investigate on Moving Object Tracking and Detection in Images”, 1st Babylon International Conference on Information Technology and Science (BICITS), pp. 69–75, Babil, Iraq, 28-29 April, 2021, doi:10.1109/BI CITS51482.2021.9509887.

[86] J. Li, et. al., “Research on Intelligent Recognition Solution of Tobacco Disease on Android Platform”, International Conference on Automation, Robotics and Computer Engineering (ICARCE), pp. 1–4, Wuhan, China, 16-17 December, 2022, doi:10.1109/ICARCE55724.2022.100 46516.

[87] M. Khalid, A. Ashraf, W. H. Bangyal, M. Iqbal, “An Android Application for Unwanted Vehicle Detection and Counting”, International Conference on Human-Centered Cognitive Systems (HCCS), pp. 1–6, Cardiff, United Kingdom, 16-17 December, 2023, doi:10.1109/HCCS 59561.2023.10452502.

[88] L. B. Damahe, et. al., “Object Detection using YOLO to Search Project Details”, International Conference on Emerging Trends in Engineering and Medical Sciences (ICETEMS), pp. 432–435, Nagpur, India, 18-19 November, 2022, doi:10.1109/ICETEMS56252.2022.10093629.

[89] M. J. Y. Sutayco, M. V. C. Caya, “A Comparative Study of MobileNetv2 and VGG-16 Convolutional Neural Network Architectures for Identification of Medicinal Mushrooms”, IEEE 15th International Conference on Humanoid, Nanotechnology, Information Technology, Communication and Control, Environment, and Management (HNICEM), pp. 1–6, Coron, Palawan, Philippines, 19-23 November, 2023, doi:10.1109/HNICEM60674.2023.10589123.

[90] K. Dong, C. Zhou, Y. Ruan, Y. Li, “MobileNetV2 Model for Image Classification”, 2nd International Conference on Information Technology and Computer Application (ITCA), pp. 476–480, Guangzhou, China, 18-20 December, 2020, doi:10.1109/ITCA52113.2020.00106.

[91] N. An, “Xception Network for Weather Image Recognition Based on Transfer Learning”, International Conference on Machine Learning and Intelligent Systems Engineering (MLISE), pp. 330–333,

Guangzhou, China, 05-07 August, 2022, doi:10.1109/MLISE57402.2022.00072.

[92] X. Zhu, et. al., "Simplified-Xception: A New Way to Speed Up Malicious Code Classification", 9th International Conference on Information, Cybernetics, and Computational Social Systems (ICCSS), pp. 111–116, Nanjing, China, 02-04 June, 2023, doi:10.1109/ICCSS58421.2023.10269891.

[93] D. Upadhyay, M. Manwal, V. Kukreja, R. Sharma, "Deep Learning-based VGGNet, GoogleNet, and DenseNet121 Models for Cervical Cancer Prediction", 5th International Conference for Emerging Technology (INCET), pp. 1–6, Belgaum, India, 24-26 May, 2024, doi: 10.1109/INCET61516.2024.10593267.

[94] L. Y. Win Lwin, A. N. Htwe, "Image Classification for Rice Leaf Disease Using AlexNet Model", IEEE Conference on Computer Applications (ICCA), pp. 124–129, Yangon, Myanmar, 27-28 February, 2023.

[95] B. Pande, et. al., "A Review of Image Annotation Tools for Object Detection", International Conference on Applied Artificial Intelligence and Computing (ICAAIC), pp. 976–982, Salem, India, 09-11 May, 2022, doi:10.1109/ICAAIC53929.2022.9792665.

[96] H. Tang, Y. Jiang, "An Improved YOLOv8n Algorithm for Object Detection with CARAFE, MultiSEAMHead, and TripleAttention Mechanisms", 7th International Conference on Computer Information Science and Application Technology (CISAT), pp. 119–122, Hangzhou, China, 12-14 July, 2024, doi:10.1109/CISAT62382.2024.10695221.

[97] T. A. Gennarelli, E. Wodzin (Eds.), "The Abbreviated Injury Scale 2005 - Update 2008", Barrington, IL: Association for the Advancement of Automotive Medicine, 2008.

[98] NHS England, "Ten Second Triage Tool", [online] www.england.nhs.uk, available at: https://www.england.nhs.uk/long-read/ten-second-triage-tool/.

[99] Y. Boltov, I. Skarga-Bandurova, M. Derkach, "A Comparative Analysis of Deep Learning-Based Object Detectors for Embedded Systems", IEEE 12th International Conference on Intelligent Data Acquisition and Advanced Computing Systems: Technology and Applications (IDAACS), pp. 1156–1160, Dortmund, Germany, 07-09 September, 2023, doi:10.1109/IDAACS58523.2023.10348642.

[100] A. Howard, et. al., "Searching for MobileNetV3", IEEE/CVF International Conference on Computer Vision (ICCV), pp. 1314–1324, Seoul, Korea (South), 27 October - 02 November, 2019, doi:10.1109/ICCV.2019.00140.

[101] F. Chollet, "Xception: Deep Learning with Depthwise Separable Convolutions", IEEE Conference on Computer Vision and Pattern Recognition (CVPR), pp. 1800–1807, Honolulu, HI, USA, 21-26 July, 2017, doi:10.1109/CVPR.2017.195.

[102] R. Pengzhen, et. al., "A Comprehensive Survey of Neural Architecture Search: Challenges and Solutions", ACM Comput. Surv., 54(4), pp. 1–34, 2021, doi:10.1145/3447582.

[103] D. Chumachenko, et. al., "Forecasting of COVID-19 Epidemic Process in Ukraine and Neighboring Countries by Gradient Boosting Method", E. Faure, et. al. (eds) Information Technology for Education, Science, and Technics. Lecture Notes on Data Engineering and Communications Technologies, vol. 178, pp. 503–514 Springer, Cham, 2023, doi:10.1007/978-3-031-35467-0_30.

[104] B. Brosnan, I. Skarga-Bandurova, T. Biloborodova, I. Skarha-Bandurov, "An Integrated Approach to Automated Diagnosis of Cervical Intraepithelial Neoplasia in Digital Histology Images", Stud. Health. Technol. Inform., 302, pp. 615–616, 2023, doi:10.3233/SHTI230220.

[105] K. Ivanova, et. al., "Artificial intelligence in automated system for web-interfaces visual testing", CEUR Workshop Proceedings, vol. 2604, pp. 1019–1031, 2020, https://ceur-ws.org/Vol-2604/paper68.pdf.

[106] O. Striuk, et. al., "Implementation of Generative Adversarial Networks in Mobile Applications for Image Data Enhancement", Journal of Mobile Multimedia, 19(3), pp. 823–838, 2023, DOI:10.13052/jmm1550-4646.1938.

[107] M. Tetyana, et. al., "Computer Vision Mobile System for Education Using Augmented Reality Technology", Journal of Mobile Multimedia, 17(4). pp. 555–576, 2021, 10.13052/jmm1550-4646.1744.

7

Hierarchical Decision Support System for Increasing Maritime Safety Based on Optical Color Computing Architecture

V. Timchenko[1], V. Kreinovich[2], Y. Kondratenko[3,4], and I. Demidov[1]

[1]Admiral Makarov National University of Shipbuilding, Ukraine
[2]University of Texas at El Paso, USA
[3]Petro Mohyla Black Sea National University, Ukraine
[4]Institute of Artificial Intelligence Problems, Ukraine
E-mail: vl.timchenko58@gmail.com; admildemidov@gmail.com; vladik@utep.edu; y_kondrat2002@yahoo.com

Abstract

This chapter presents the basic principles of constructing logical components of the architecture of optical color computing based on estimating the dispersion of truth operands.

The structures of elementary additive and subtractive logical coloroids as the components of multi-level hierarchical networks of logical inference of decisions are determined. To implement the proposed optical architecture, a real-time changing multifactor database was generated to assess the safety of navigation in limited water areas with heavy vessel traffic. A three-level decision support system has been developed to control traffic safety and organize port ship maintenance. Possible logical operations for obtaining estimates for a specific set of input data are modeled and the effectiveness of the proposed approach due to the speed and parallelism of optical color computing is assessed.

Keywords: Decision support system, navigation safety, color set, color optical computing.

DOI: 10.1201/9788743800989-7

7.1 Introduction

The development and implementation of artificial intelligence (AI) methods, means, and algorithms is one of the most important research problems at the modern stage of technological progress [1–3]. AI influences the different fields of human activity and significantly increases the efficiency of existing and newly designed control and decision-making systems [4, 5]. AI can help to solve complex management problems of the control objects, which function in uncertainty and non-stationary conditions [6–8]. There are many successful cases of AI implementation in robotics [5, 9–13], control systems of ships, unmanned aerial vehicles and underwater moving objects [14–16], transport logistics [17–23], shipbuilding and ship repairing [24–27], and other industrial domains [28, 29].

Special attention should be paid to AI development and implementation for improving efficiency of decision-making processes [30–32] in uncertainty.

The problem of increasing productivity of computer computing is an urgent problem in almost all aspects of the application of decision support systems (DSS) in conditions of extremely large, real-time changing input data. Published works [33–39] in this direction show the energy efficiency (a) of the optical architecture, the structural possibility of parallel computing (b), the high speed of information processing (c), the resistance of computer networks to interference (d), etc. The main idea underlying most directions for creating optical logic gates is using various implementations of nonlinear transformations of light radiation based on the optical effects of diffraction, interference, and polarization. Due to significant nonlinearity, these approaches aim to achieve the states necessary for binary calculations [0; 1]. Difficulties along this path are primarily associated with the high technological complexity of implementation at the nanoscale level. At the same time, computing performance increases significantly with the development of optical technologies [40, 41].

In the tasks of decision support systems, we operate with qualitative information. If you use classical linguistic terms [16, 42, 43], then they need to be converted into a numerical fuzzy set, and then into binary codes. Further logical operations are performed by the software in binary code, and the resulting decision must be converted back into a fuzzy set and then into a linguistic term for the decision-maker (Figure 7.1). These transformations involve the use of a large number of bits and require more logic elements to process this data and, as a result, the more complex the computational design is.

Applying a logical calculation scheme that directly uses fuzzy sets as input and output information is more effective and for logical operations to derive solutions. In the works [44, 45], it is proposed to use a light quantum of a certain color as a fuzzy set of input information (Figure 7.2). A sufficiently developed and simply technologically implementable optical architecture of the main logical operations OR, AND, NOT, NOR, and NAND allows the use of the proposed solution for constructing logical networks for outputting decisions in DSS, including for increasing the safety of navigation in limited water areas [46].

The principles for constructing a DSS for managing the safety of various technological processes should include the following universal positions:

- determination of an array of main factors, as well as their component parameters that form the safety of the process;
- ranking of each factor according to the importance of its impact on safety;
- formation of an array of expert assessments of navigation safety;
- formalization of possible decisions of a human operator (dispatcher).

Basic logical rules for logical derivation of decisions (estimates):

- selection of structural constructions of hierarchical multi-level inference networks;

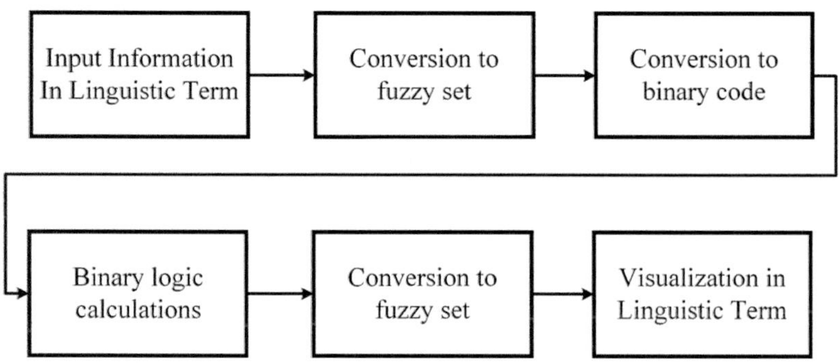

Figure 7.1 Block diagram of inference of decision for classical fuzzy computing.

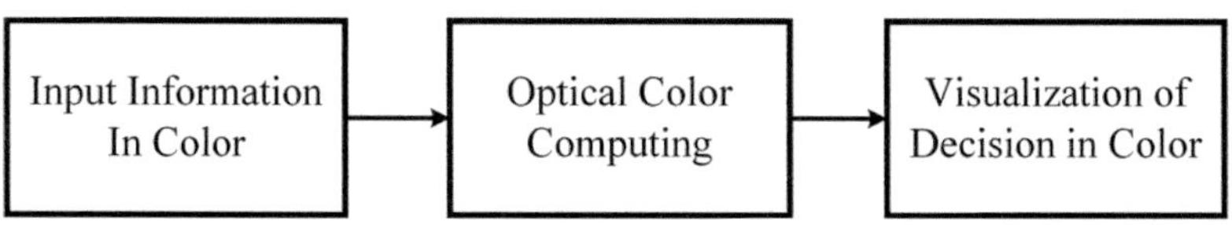

Figure 7.2 Block diagram of inference of decision for optical color computing.

- assessing the effectiveness of decision-making processes in terms of the truth of decisions made by the system.

The increasing intensity of maritime traffic, accounting for more than 80% of global cargo turnover, requires the development and improvement of hierarchically organized systems for automated control of vessel traffic in limited water areas. Such systems are built on the interaction of a human operator and an automated control system in the process of developing solutions that ensure the safety of navigation in the conditions of the occurrence of non-standard scenarios and the impact on the ship of intensive random external disturbances.

The relevance of scientific research in the field of improving human–machine systems is determined by the significant influence of the human factor, in particular the psychophysical state of the human operator, on the safety of navigation.

The formation of DSS expert systems includes various inference mechanisms based on certain rules, precedents, forming a matrix of ranked evaluations etc. [47–48]. The formation of decisions under conditions of uncertainty is based on a qualitative assessment of factors and their component parameters using a large sample of statistical data and probabilistic methods of analysis.

Solving navigation safety problems using decision-making systems is based on the following methods:

- risk-based approaches to assessing safety factors [49];
- concepts of changing the pace of maneuvering and robust-optimal control when moving along a given trajectory [50, 51];
- dynamic games in the DSS navigation safety navigator [52];
- modified method of high-speed obstacles for the synthesis of a ship collision avoidance system [53, 54];
- algorithm for joint trajectory planning of sea surface vessels [55];
- autonomous decision-making scheme with iterative observation and inference to prevent multi-ship collisions [56];
- use of associative memory in intelligent ship control [57, 58];
- a hybrid algorithm for optimizing oncoming ship trajectories based on dynamic windows [59];
- use of templates for ship route plans using data from automatic information systems [60] and other works [61, 62].

The theory of fuzzy sets and fuzzy logic is widely used in the formation of databases of qualitative information and logical inference systems [63–65].

Development of a decision support system in transport logistics problems, when planning the trajectories of vessels in limited water areas under conditions of increased traffic intensity and significant external disturbances is considered in the works [66–68].

In [46], the authors proposed a DSS structure with the formation of an input database for a group of Mykolaiv seaports (four in total, including one river port), which have one of the longest approach estuary channels at 30 miles. The Liman Rybosol was built in the mid-nineteenth century by Dutch engineers with a width of 100 m and a depth of about 11 meters, with the prevailing depths in the canal not exceeding 4.5 meters. The total number of ship calls in favorable years is more than 4,000 ships per year.

The formation of the assessment database on the main factors influencing the safety of navigation in this water area was possible based on (a) the authors' more than 10 years of experience operating the bunkering fleet [69–72] in this water area (as well as in other seaports of the Black Sea coast of Ukraine), and (b) a detailed analysis of navigation safety based on a survey of captains and chief engineers of more than 40 different vessels.

For a sufficiently narrow sea channel, the safety problem is extremely relevant, and, thus, the DSS system for the dispatch service for regulating vessel traffic has increased the level of navigation safety. At the same time, the proposed DSS operates with a limited amount of input data and requires optimization of computational structures in terms of increasing the efficiency of logical decisions made.

The development of the DSS is based on the computational optical architecture proposed by the authors [45, 73–80], which effectively uses the information quantum of the input data as a specific color of the light emitter as a fuzzy variable. The optical architecture is technologically quite simply implemented on the properties of additive and subtractive color transformation using light filters and allows you to synthesize multi-component computational structures for the logical derivation of solutions.

The purpose of this work is to analyze the logical operations of DSS, determine the optimized structures of optical logic gates (coloroids), and, on their basis, synthesize multi-level networks for making complex decisions to improve navigation safety in large seaport facilities.

7.2 Basic Principles of Optical Color-Logic Computing

Consider logical solutions, for example, based on expert ratings, and form a system for identifying the primary and secondary colors as a combination of

Table 7.1 Degrees of confidence.

Color	Degrees of confidence
$\{R\} = \{N\}$	"no"
$\{G\} = \{YN\}$	"probably yes"
$\{B\} = \{Y\}$	"yes"
$\{W\} = \{R\} + \{G\} + \{B\} = \{YYNN\}$	"positive decision"
$\{C\} = \{G\} + \{B\} = \{YYN\}$	"very probably yes"
$\{M\} = \{R\} + \{B\} = \{NY\}$	"probably no"
$\{Yel\} = \{R\} + \{G\} = \{NNY\}$	"very probably no"
$\{Blc\} = \{W\} - \{R\} - \{G\} - \{B\} = \{0\}$	"no decision"

positive *Y (yes)* and negative *N (no)* expert ratings and possible solutions. Interpretations of combinations of basic colors can be naturally associated with the combinations of the corresponding degrees of confidence (Table 7.1).

The operations of addition and subtraction of color, given in Table 7.1, can be naturally interpreted as the operations of union (disjunction) and intersection (conjunction) of sets (logical statements, operations).

7.2.1 Principles of forming decision inference structures

A hierarchical system implies a hierarchy of the importance of decisions. Naturally, the first level of the hierarchy involves less important decisions and, possibly, less trained, low-skilled, and low-rated experts. The basic 12-component single-level logical coloroid [73] proposed in the work has in its structure a blocking decision of the most responsible experts (for example, those bearing personal responsibility of some kind), since it assumes a final decision at the output.

Two-level solution inference moves the final solution to the second level of the hierarchy and naturally builds its structure around the basic 12-component blocking coloroid.

Let us consider and analyze possible options for the logical structures of the third block of color filters of the basic coloroid. With three consecutive color filters of the form {Yel, M, C} for seven possible information quanta at the output of the second block of color filters: {W}, {R}, {G}, {B}, {Yel}, {M}, {C}, we get a blocking result – the output signal {Blc}, i.e., lack of solution (Figure 7.3).

We have three intersecting sets, of which the first two allow only the set {R}, and the second two only the set {B}, thus blocking any of the input sets,

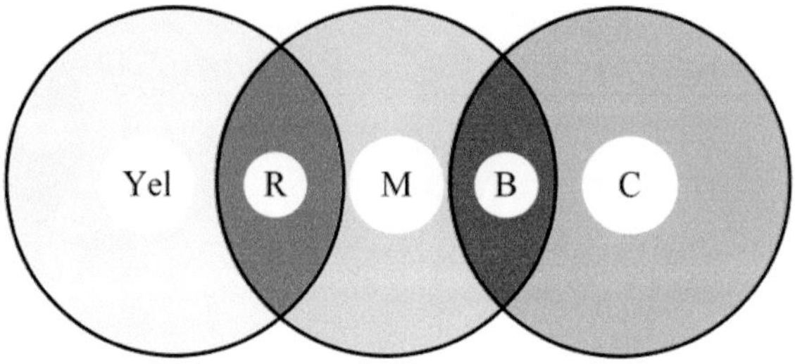

Figure 7.3 Sequence of three color filters.

for example, for {W}

$$\text{diag }(\text{R}, \text{G}, \text{B}) \times \text{diag }(\text{R}, \text{G}, 0) \times \text{diag }(\text{R}, 0, \text{B}) \times (0, \text{G}, \text{B}) = \text{diag }(0,\ 0,\ 0)\,.$$

Without taking into account the placement in the third block, which does not affect the output estimate, we have for color filters the number of combinations

$$A = (n + k - 1)!/k!(n - 1)! = 10.$$

For seven different combinations of input sets, the total number of combinations reaches 70, from which a significant number is blocking for at least one input set. Since we want to optimize the architecture of optical channels, we will consider other possible structures of the third block of the logical coloroid.

For three combinations of two color filters {Yel, M} {Yel, C} {M, C} (Figure 7.4), 21 output estimates (with repetitions) will look like this:
input set {W}:

$$\text{diag }(\text{R}, \text{G}, \text{B}) \times \text{diag }(\text{R}, \text{G}, 0) \times \text{diag }(\text{R}, 0, \text{B}) = \text{diag }(\text{R},\ 0,\ 0)\,,$$
$$\text{diag }(\text{R}, \text{G}, \text{B}) \times \text{diag }(\text{R}, \text{G}, 0) \times \text{diag }(0, \text{G}, \text{B}) = \text{diag }(0,\ \text{G},\ 0)\,,$$
$$\text{diag }(\text{R}, \text{G}, \text{B}) \times \text{diag }(\text{R}, 0, \text{B}) \times \text{diag }(0, \text{G}, \text{B}) = \text{diag }(0,\ 0,\ \text{B})\,,$$

input set {R}:

$$\text{diag }(\text{R}, 0,\ 0) \times \text{diag }(\text{R}, \text{G}, 0) \times \text{diag }(\text{R}, 0, \text{B}) = \text{diag }(\text{R},\ 0,\ 0)\,,$$
$$\text{diag }(\text{R}, 0,\ 0) \times \text{diag }(\text{R}, \text{G}, 0) \times \text{diag }(0, \text{G}, \text{B}) = \text{diag }(0,\ 0,\ 0)\,,$$
$$\text{diag }(\text{R}, 0,\ 0) \times \text{diag }(\text{R}, 0, \text{B}) \times \text{diag }(0, \text{G}, \text{B}) = \text{diag }(0,\ 0,\ 0)\,,$$

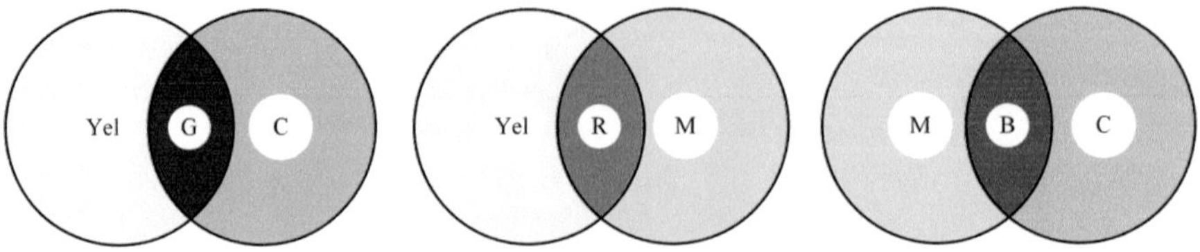

Figure 7.4 Combinations of two color filters.

input set $\{G\}$:

$$\mathrm{diag}\ (0, G,\ 0) \times \mathrm{diag}\ (R, G, 0) \times \mathrm{diag}\ (R, 0, B) = \mathrm{diag}\ (0,\ 0,\ 0),$$
$$\mathrm{diag}\ (0, G,\ 0) \times \mathrm{diag}\ (R, G, 0) \times \mathrm{diag}\ (0, G, B) = \mathrm{diag}\ (0,\ G,\ 0),$$
$$\mathrm{diag}\ (0, G,\ 0) \times \mathrm{diag}\ (R, 0, B) \times \mathrm{diag}\ (0, G, B) = \mathrm{diag}\ (0,\ 0,\ 0),$$

input set $\{B\}$:

$$\mathrm{diag}\ (0,\ 0,\ B) \times \mathrm{diag}\ (R, G, 0) \times \mathrm{diag}\ (R, 0, B) = \mathrm{diag}\ (0,\ 0,\ 0),$$
$$\mathrm{diag}\ (0,\ 0,\ B) \times \mathrm{diag}\ (R, G, 0) \times \mathrm{diag}\ (0, G, B) = \mathrm{diag}\ (0,\ 0,\ 0),$$
$$\mathrm{diag}\ (0,\ 0,\ B) \times \mathrm{diag}\ (R, 0, B) \times \mathrm{diag}\ (0, G, B) = \mathrm{diag}\ (0,\ 0,\ B),$$

input set $\{Yel\}$:

$$\mathrm{diag}\ (R, G,\ 0) \times \mathrm{diag}\ (R, G, 0) \times \mathrm{diag}\ (R, 0, B) = \mathrm{diag}\ (R,\ 0,\ 0),$$
$$\mathrm{diag}\ (R, G, 0) \times \mathrm{diag}\ (R, G, 0) \times \mathrm{diag}\ (0, G, B) = \mathrm{diag}\ (0,\ G,\ 0),$$
$$\mathrm{diag}\ (R, G, 0) \times \mathrm{diag}\ (R, 0, B) \times \mathrm{diag}\ (0, G, B) = \mathrm{diag}\ (0,\ 0,\ 0),$$

input set $\{M\}$:

$$\mathrm{diag}\ (R, 0, B) \times \mathrm{diag}\ (R, G, 0) \times \mathrm{diag}\ (R, 0, B) = \mathrm{diag}\ (R,\ 0,\ 0),$$
$$\mathrm{diag}\ (R, 0,B) \times \mathrm{diag}\ (R, G, 0) \times \mathrm{diag}\ (0, G, B) = \mathrm{diag}\ (0,\ 0,\ 0),$$
$$\mathrm{diag}\ (R, 0, B) \times \mathrm{diag}\ (R, 0, B) \times \mathrm{diag}\ (0, G, B) = \mathrm{diag}\ (0,\ 0,\ B),$$

input set $\{C\}$:

$$\mathrm{diag}\ (0, G,\ B) \times \mathrm{diag}\ (R, G, 0) \times \mathrm{diag}\ (R, 0, B) = \mathrm{diag}\ (0,\ 0,\ 0),$$
$$\mathrm{diag}\ (0, G, B) \times \mathrm{diag}\ (R, G, 0) \times \mathrm{diag}\ (0, G, B) = \mathrm{diag}\ (0,\ G,\ 0),$$
$$\mathrm{diag}\ (0, G, B) \times \mathrm{diag}\ (R, 0, B) \times \mathrm{diag}\ (0, G, B) = \mathrm{diag}\ (0,\ 0,\ B).$$

For three single filters (Figure 7.5) $\{Yel\}$, $\{C\}$, and $\{M\}$, we will also have 21 combinations (with repetitions) of output estimates:

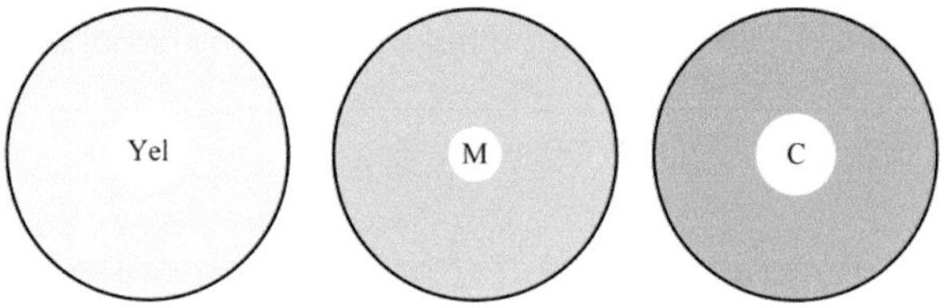

Figure 7.5 Three single filters.

input set $\{\mathrm{W}\}$:

$$\operatorname{diag}\ (\mathrm{R},\mathrm{G},\mathrm{B})\times\operatorname{diag}\ (\mathrm{R},\mathrm{G},0)=\operatorname{diag}\ (\mathrm{R},\mathrm{G},0)\,,$$
$$\operatorname{diag}\ (\mathrm{R},\mathrm{G},\mathrm{B})\times\operatorname{diag}\ (0,\mathrm{G},\mathrm{B})=\operatorname{diag}\ (0,\mathrm{G},\mathrm{B})\,,$$
$$\operatorname{diag}\ (\mathrm{R},\mathrm{G},\mathrm{B})\times\operatorname{diag}\ (\mathrm{R},0,\mathrm{B})=\operatorname{diag}\ (\mathrm{R},0,\mathrm{B})\,.$$

And then sequentially, for the remaining input sets,

$$\{R\}\to\{R\},\{0\},\{R\};\{G\}\to\{G\},\{G\},\{0\};\{B\}\to\{0\},\{B\},\{B\};$$
$$\{Yel\}\to\{Yel\},\{G\},\{R\};\{M\}\to\{R\},\{B\},\{M\};\{C\}\to\{G\},\{C\},\{B\}.$$

Let us take the quantitative assessment of truth as 1, and falsehood (the statement that a situation is dangerous when it is truly unsafe) as 0. For a comparative assessment of the reliability of the received *n* assessments (for example, a group of experts assesses the safety of a situation: "really safe," "very likely safe," "probably safe," "probably dangerous," "very likely dangerous," "dangerous"). Based on the quantitative ratio of the Y/N operands to the safety truth, we compose the following expressions for the average values of *E* and the root-mean-square estimate *D*:

$$E=\frac{k}{n},\tag{7.1}$$

$$D=\left[(1-E)^2\right],\tag{7.2}$$

where k is the number of ratings Y.

For simplicity of presentation, we will further give quantitative estimates in relation to the complete truth of statements about complete safety. Naturally, in the general case, we can accept the statement about danger as true and carry out the corresponding calculations in reverse order.

Completely identical color scores naturally result in a zero standard deviation. It is also natural to assume that the optimized structure of the elementary coloroid will have to assume the minimum value of the standard deviation

$$D \to \min.$$

7.2.2 Toolkit for generating output structure components

In the works [46, 73, 74], elementary and basic structures of logical inference are proposed, as well as further in the works [76, 77] the principles of forming coloroid networks for decision support systems. The main focus is on the initial stage of the formation of the optical color architecture of logical calculations for ordinary and complex (complex) solutions.

At the same time, the development of optical color computing and color networks for decision support systems with a large amount of input information requires a more detailed study of the components of the computing architecture, in particular sequential and parallel input of information.

In general, the components of additive information input (the first block of the basic coloroid) can include n input channels (Figure 7.6). However, taking into account the fundamental property of color logic – the principle of idempotence, with a significant number of channels, this will lead to ignoring identical quanta of color information.

Let us consider the structure of an elementary additive coloroid with three inputs, adopted in the basic coloroid.

With input quanta, for example,

$$\{R\} + \{R\} + \{R\} = \{R\},$$

we have an output estimate {R}. In the Y/N operands, this will be written as

$$\{N\} + \{N\} + \{N\} = \{N\},$$

and to clarify the decision in this case, the color quantum is separated and, suppose, sent to a subtractive coloroid (Figure 7.7) with assessments, for

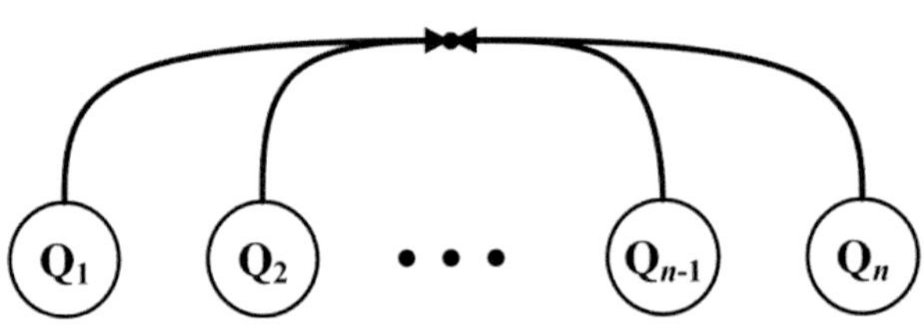

Figure 7.6 Operation of unification (disjunction) of N color sets **Q**.

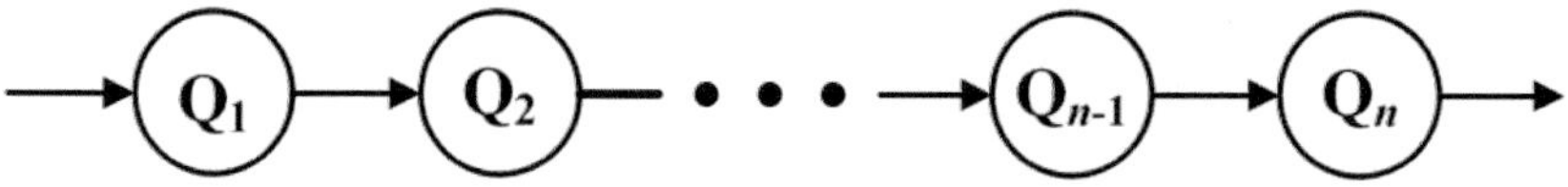

Figure 7.7 Operation of intersections (conjunction) of N color sets $\mathbf{Q}$ sequentially.

example, from a group of experts of a higher classification (i.e., possibly bearing personal, criminal, or administrative responsibility).

Let us consider the options for combinations of logical outputs and note that, in accordance with the principles of optical transformation of color radiation, the presence of only one filter C in the subtractive coloroid will block the logical output as an empty quantum Blc. The closest combination of color filters, including C, according to estimates to $\{R\}$, is Yel, Yel, C, which gives in the operands NNY, NNY, YYN with the ratio Y/N, E, D, which we define as a criterion for assessing the truth (1, 2) of a logical conclusion, $\{$ratio 4/5; $E = 0.4$; $D = 0.36\}$. Taking into account the ratio of the three input quanta, ratio 0/3, we obtain a total $\{$ ratio 4/8; $E = 0.33$; $D = 0.45\}$. This shows that it is advisable to use the additive coloroid output as the final one for the evaluation in this example – $\{R\}$.

Further, for the input color quanta after logical summation

$$\{\mathrm{R}\} + \{\mathrm{R}\} + \{\mathrm{G}\} = \{\mathrm{Yel}\}$$

and

$$\{\mathrm{R}\} + \{\mathrm{G}\} + \{\mathrm{G}\} = \{\mathrm{Yel}\},$$

we will have formulas in the operands, respectively,

$$\mathrm{N} + \mathrm{N} + \mathrm{YN} = \mathrm{NNNY},$$
$$\mathrm{N} + \mathrm{YN} + \mathrm{YN} = \mathrm{NNNYY},$$

or approximately at the NNY output for both output estimates with operand ratios: $\{$ratio 1/3; $E = 0.25$; $D = 0.56\}$, $\{$ratio 2/3; $E = 0.4$; $D = 0.36\}$, respectively.

Let us evaluate the possibilities of refining (increasing the truth) logical estimates with an increase in the number of input quanta, taking into account the influence of the idempotence property. Suppose for four input quanta, the combination

$$\{\mathrm{R}\} + \{\mathrm{R}\} + \{\mathrm{R}\} + \{\mathrm{G}\} = \{\mathrm{Yel}\}$$

with $\{$ratio 1/4; $E = 0.2$; $D = 0.64\}$, and for five

$$\{\mathrm{R}\} + \{\mathrm{R}\} + \{\mathrm{R}\} + \{\mathrm{R}\} + \{\mathrm{G}\} = \{\mathrm{Yel}\}$$

$-\{$ratio 1/5; $E = 0.17$; $D = 0.69\}$.

We can conclude that having the same output quantum Yel, the input quanta combine the ratio of the operands for a given combination with an increasingly confidently negative evaluation, which is not reflected in the output quantum and, then, the expansion of the number of inputs in one elementary coloroid to more than three is idempotent. This conclusion also supports the principle of an ordinary solution W, as the minimum necessary combination of the three main RGB color quanta (Figure 7.8).

Circuit structures [74] have been proposed that allow, with solidary (equal) estimates, for example, RRR or BBB, for an elementary additive coloroid with three inputs, to separate the ordinary solidary solution, respectively, R and B, turning off the further logical evaluation procedure in the basic coloroid of the form (Figure 7.9).

Thus, we can assume the feasibility of using parallel elementary additive coloroids with an increasing input quanta number in decision support systems.

A similar approach can be extended to parallel structures of subtractive coloroids with a combination, for example, in three branches, of two filters M, M, and twice Yel, Yel with an input quantum B (Figure 7.10). With this combination, we will have a ratio for the output quantum when summing up all the truth operands $\{$ratio 7/10; $E = 0.41$; $D = 0.35\}$ (taking into account the value of the input quantum). With a decrease in the number of parallel branches to two with the same filters (Figure 7.11). Then, with the same quantum at the output, the output ratio will be 5/6 $\{$for $E = 0.45$; $D = 0.3\}$. For one branch (Figure 7.12), we have a ratio 3/2 $\{$for $E = 0.6$; $D = 0.16\}$.

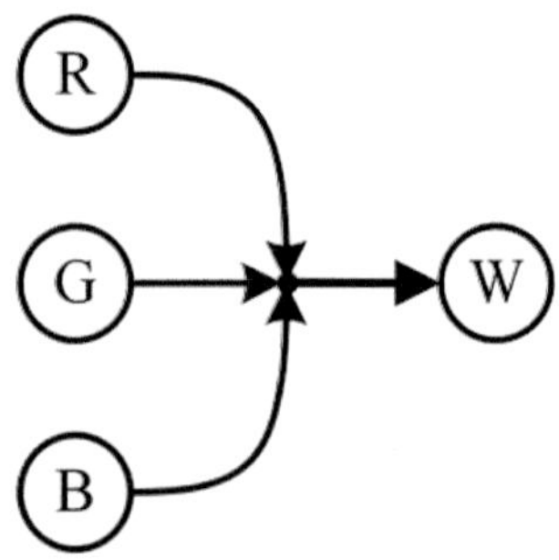

Figure 7.8 Optical transformation RGB.

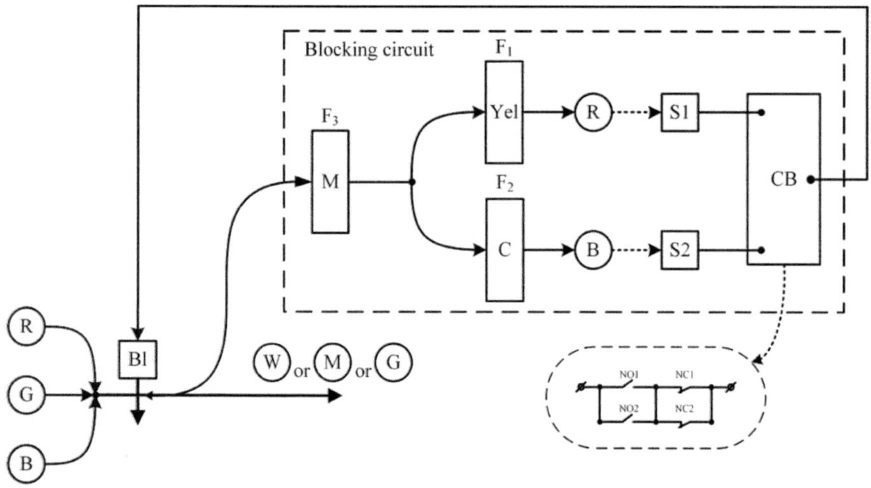

Figure 7.9 Optical schemes of summing coloroid with blocking circuit for RGB input.

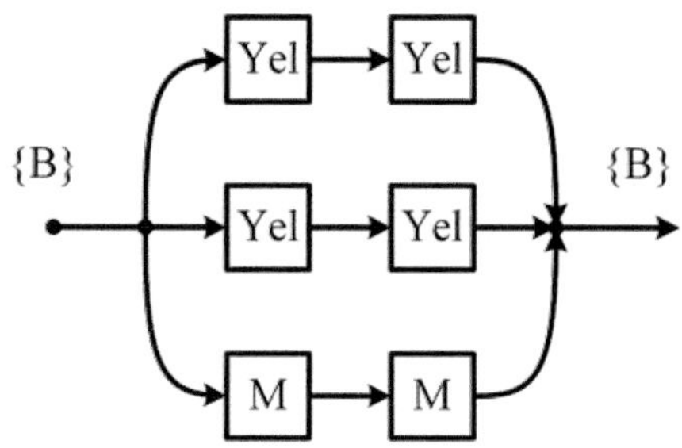

Figure 7.10 Subtractive coloroid with combination in three branches.

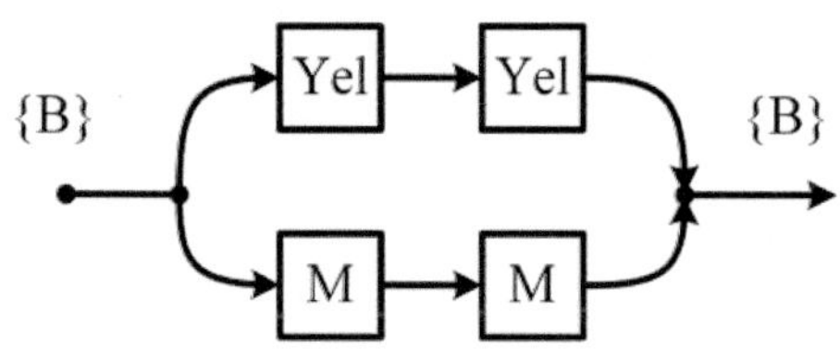

Figure 7.11 Subtractive coloroid with combination in two branches.

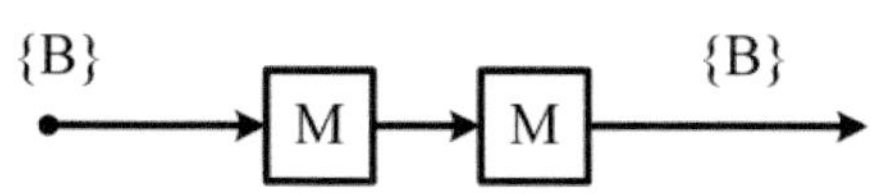

Figure 7.12 Subtractive coloroid with single branch.

Thus, with an increase in the number of parallel branches with possible negative or, for other combinations, positive assessments with a negative input, the number of alternative assessments increases while maintaining the value of the output quantum of information. This suggests, if it is feasible to limit alternatives, the use of three parallel branches in the base coloroid.

The third block of the basic coloroid includes a sequential channel for the subtractive transformation of the color quantum of information. The proposed scheme (Figure 7.13) uses the structure of three color filters, assuming, among other things, that it fully implements the minimum possible optical structure of the blocking solution for any input color set in the form of a combination of Yel, M, C with ratio 4/4 $\{$for $E = 0.5$; $D = 0.25\}$.

Extremely opposite estimates will be for the combinations Yel, Yel, Yel with $\{$ratio 3/6; $E = 0.33$; $D = 0.45\}$ and C, C, C with $\{$ratio 6/3; $E = 0.67$; $D = 0.11\}$, which miss the extreme input estimates, R and B, respectively. Since the principle of idempotence also applies to the logical operation of conjunction, which indicates that it is inappropriate to increase the number of color filters in a separate serial optical channel of the base coloroid (Figure 7.14).

In general, we can draw a general conclusion about the structure of the basic logical coloroid:

- it is advisable to limit the number of additive input quanta, parallel subtractive branches, color filters in a serial subtractive channel to no more than three positions;
- the number of subtractive parallel branches is determined by the need to form two or three alternative conclusions depending on the expected proximity in the ratio of estimates (if the estimated estimates are close, then two branches are sufficient, and if the estimates are not close, we form three).

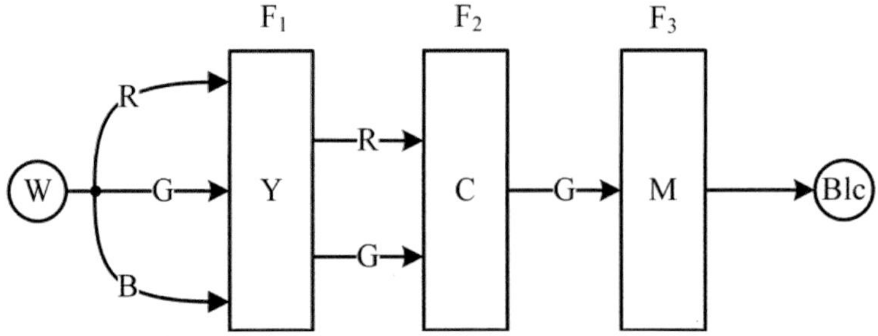

Figure 7.13 Blocking optical structure.

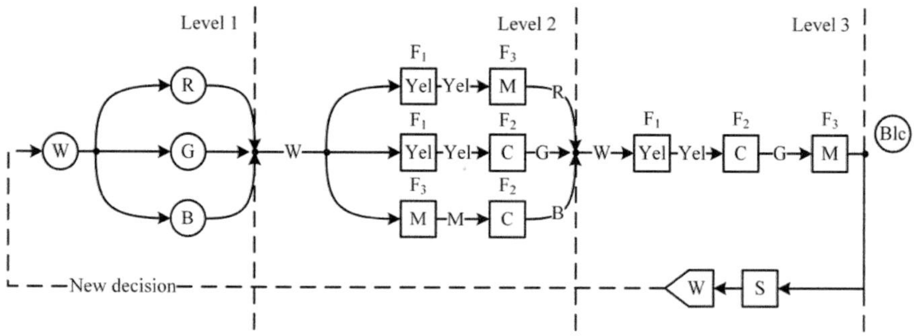

Figure 7.14 Basic logical coloroid.

7.3 Synthesis of a Decision Support System to Improve Navigation Safety in Marine Terminals

7.3.1 Formation of a fuzzy color database that determines the safety of navigation

In this work, a DSS with an expanded database has been developed for large infrastructure marine facilities with significantly more intense vessel traffic. Thus, the seaport, for example, of Rotterdam has about 30,000 ship calls per year (about 80 ships daily), which implies a much more intense traffic of vessels than considered in the work [46]. We will consider increasing the base of input information by more than two times, introducing additional estimates that affect the safety of navigation. Thus, the assessments presented in Tables 7.2 – 7.5 were formed, including assessments of weather conditions and channel conditions, technical characteristics of the vessel, conditions and qualifications of the crew, pilotage and dispatch services.

7.3.2 Optical structure of dispatch decision support systems to improve navigation safety

Let us model the process of logical derivation of the assessment of permission for a vessel to enter the sea channel and port territory. In accordance with the data in Tables 7.2 – 7.5, we assume the following input set:

Input set = {**B, G, R, B, G, B, M, M, M, C, Yel, M, Yel, C, M, Yel, C, M, C, M, Yel, M, M, M, C**},

where *Factor 1*: Visibility, excellent, **B**; *Factor 2*: Average wind, **G**; *Factor 3*: Night, **R**; *Factor 4*: Ice conditions, **B**; *Factor 5*: Spring, **G**; *Factor 6*:

Table 7.2 Weather and channel conditions.

Factor	**Level of danger**	**Factor**	**Level of danger**
1.Wind speed		4. Ice conditions, sm	
Light wind (1–4 m/c)	**B**	0–5	**B**
Moderate wind (4–11 m/s)	**G**	5–20	**G**
Strong wind (11–17 m/s)	**R**	>20	**R**
2.Time of day		5.Season	
Daylight	**B**	Summer, Spring, Autumn	**B**
Dark time of day	**G**	Winter	**G**
Night	**R**		
3. Visibility, m		6. A pilot on board, years of experience	
< 500	**R**	>5	**B**
500–2000	**G**	2–5	**G**
> 2000	**B**	0–1	**R**

Table 7.3 Characteristics of the specific vessel and other vessels in the canal.

Factor	**Level of danger**	**Factor**	**Level of danger**
7. Average length, m		10. Availability of ships in a canal with a length of more than 300 m	
<200	**C**	No	**C**
200-300	**M**	1–2	**M**
≥ 300	**Yel**	>2	**Yel**
8. Factor 8. Average draft, m		11. Age of the vessel, years	
<15	**C**	0–7	**C**
15-25	**M**	7–15	**M**
>25	**Yel**	>15	**Yel**
9. Average width, m		12. Number of oncoming vessels in canal	
< 25	**C**	No	**C**
25–40	**Yel**	1–4	**M**
> 40	**M**	>4	**Yel**

Experienced Pilot, **B**; *Factor 7*: Average length, **M**; *Factor 8*: Average draft, **M**; *Factor 9*: Average width, **M**; *Factor 10*: There are no vessels over 300 m, **C**; *Factor 11*: Vessel age, low, **Yel**; *Factor 12*: Number of oncoming vessels, average, **M**; *Factor 13*: 1–2 years before renovation, **Yel**; *Factor 14*: Continuous operation time – 6 months, **C**; *Factor 15*: Captain, more than five years of experience, **M**; *Factor 16*: Senior mechanic, less than three years of experience, **Yel**; *Factor 17*: Ballast, Excellent, **C**; *Factor 18*:

Table 7.4 Technical condition of the vessel and crew characteristics.

Factor	Level of danger	Factor	Level of danger
13. Time until scheduled ship repairs		16. Senior mechanic qualification, years	
5–4	**C**	>10	**B**
3–2	**M**	5–10	**C**
<1	**Yel**	<5	**G**
14. Time of continuous work of the crew, month		17. Full crew	
1–6	**C**	Excellent	**C**
>6	**M**	Good	**M**
<1	**Yel**	Satisfactory	**Yel**
15. Captain's experience, years		18. Availability of ballast	
>10	**C**	Excellent	**C**
5–10	**M**	Good	**M**
<5	**Yel**	Satisfactory	**Yel**

Table 7.5 Type of vessel and cargo, weather forecast, and other additional information.

Factor	Level of danger	Factor	Level of danger
19. Vessel type		22. Type of propulsion system: one propeller + rudder, three propellers + rudder (two propellers, azipod)	
Bulker	**C**	Three propellers + rudder, two propellers, azipod	**C**
Passenger	**M**	One propeller + rudder	**M**
Tanker	**Yel**	23.Qualification of dispatch service	
20. Type of cargo		Excellent	**C**
Bulk	**C**	Good	**M**
General	**M**	24. Total number of ships in the channel	
Oil/fuel	**Yel**	<5	**C**
21. The condition of the vessel is average		5–10	**M**
Good	**C**	>10	**Yel**
Satisfactory	**M**	25. General weather forecast	
Partially satisfactory	**Yel**	Favorable	**B**
		Permissible	**C**
		Threatening	**G**

Average completeness, Good, **M**; *Factor 19*: Bulker, **C**; *Factor 20*: General cargo, **M**; *Factor 21*: The condition of the vessel is average, **Yel**; *Factor 22*: Type of propulsion system, **M**; *Factor 23*: The dispatch service is highly qualified, **M**; *Factor 24*: Number of ships, average, **M**; *Factor 25*: Prognosis is favorable, **C**.

I hieratical network:

- coloroid Col_1^{I}, for input set $\{$R, G, B$\}$:

$$\mathrm{diag}\ (\mathrm{R},0,0)+\mathrm{diag}\ (0,\mathrm{G},0)+\mathrm{diag}\ (0,0,\mathrm{B})=\mathrm{diag}\ (\mathrm{R},\mathrm{G},\mathrm{B}),$$

filters $\{$M, C$\}$

$$\mathrm{diag}\ (\mathrm{R},\mathrm{G},\mathrm{B})\times\mathrm{diag}\ (\mathrm{R},0,\mathrm{B})\times\mathrm{diag}\ (0,\mathrm{G},\mathrm{B})=\mathrm{diag}\ (0,\ 0,\ \mathrm{B}),$$

filters $\{$M, Yel$\}$

$$\mathrm{diag}\ (\mathrm{R},\mathrm{G},\mathrm{B})\times\mathrm{diag}\ (\mathrm{R},0,\mathrm{B})\times\mathrm{diag}\ (\mathrm{R},\mathrm{G},0)=\mathrm{diag}\ (\mathrm{R},\ 0,\ 0),$$

filters $\{$M, M$\}$

$$\mathrm{diag}\ (\mathrm{R},\mathrm{G},\mathrm{B})\times\mathrm{diag}\ (\mathrm{R},0,\mathrm{B})\times\mathrm{diag}\ (\mathrm{R},0,\mathrm{B})=\mathrm{diag}\ (\mathrm{R},\ 0,\ \mathrm{B}),$$

disjunction

$$\mathrm{diag}\ (0,\ 0,\mathrm{B})+\mathrm{diag}\ (\mathrm{R},0,\ 0)+\mathrm{diag}\ (\mathrm{R},0,\mathrm{B})=\mathrm{diag}\ (\mathrm{R},\ 0,\ \mathrm{B}),$$

- coloroid Col_2^I, for input set $\{$B, G, B$\}$:

$$\mathrm{diag}\ (0,\ 0,\ \mathrm{B})+\mathrm{diag}\ (0,\mathrm{G},0)+\mathrm{diag}\ (0,\ 0,\mathrm{B})=\mathrm{diag}\ (0,\ \mathrm{G},\ \mathrm{B}),$$

filters $\{$Yel, C$\}$

$$\mathrm{diag}\ (0,\mathrm{G},\mathrm{B})\times\mathrm{diag}\ (\mathrm{R},\ \mathrm{G},0)\times\mathrm{diag}\ (0,\mathrm{G},\mathrm{B})=\mathrm{diag}\ (0,\ \mathrm{G},\ 0),$$

filters $\{$C, M$\}$

$$\mathrm{diag}\ (0,\mathrm{G},\mathrm{B})\times\mathrm{diag}\ (0,\mathrm{G},\mathrm{B})\times\mathrm{diag}\ (\mathrm{R},0,\mathrm{B})=\mathrm{diag}\ (0,\ 0,\ \mathrm{B}),$$

filters $\{$Yel, M$\}$

$$\mathrm{diag}\ (0,\mathrm{G},\mathrm{B})\times\mathrm{diag}\ (\mathrm{R},\mathrm{G},0)\times\mathrm{diag}\ (\mathrm{R},0,\mathrm{B})=\mathrm{iag}\ (0,\ 0,\ 0),$$

disjunction

$$\mathrm{diag}\ (0,\ \mathrm{G},\ 0)+\mathrm{diag}\ (0,\ 0,\mathrm{B})+\mathrm{diag}\ (0,\ 0,\ 0)=\mathrm{diag}\ (0,\ \mathrm{G},\ \mathrm{B}),$$

- II hieratical network, Col^{II} for input set $\{$M, C$\}$:

$$\mathrm{diag}\ (\mathrm{R},\ 0,\ \mathrm{B})+\mathrm{diag}\ (0,\ \mathrm{G},\mathrm{B})=\mathrm{diag}\ (\mathrm{R},\ \mathrm{G},\ \mathrm{B}),$$

filters {C, M}

$$\text{diag } (\text{R}, \text{G}, \text{B}) \times \text{diag } (0, \text{G}, \text{B}) \times \text{diag } (\text{R}, 0, \text{B}) = \text{diag } (0,\ 0,\ \text{B}),$$

filters {Yel, M}

$$\text{diag } (\text{R}, \text{G}, \text{B}) \times \text{diag } (\text{R}, \text{G}, 0) \times \text{diag } (\text{R}, 0, \text{B}) = \text{diag } (\text{R},\ 0,\ 0),$$

disjunction

$$\text{diag } (0,\ 0,\ \text{B}) + \text{diag } (\text{R},\ 0,\ 0) = \text{diag } (\text{R},\ 0,\ \text{B}),$$

filters {M, M, C}

$$\text{diag } (\text{R}, 0, \text{B}) \times \text{diag } (\text{R}, 0,\ \text{B}) \times \text{diag } (\text{R}, 0, \text{B}) \times \text{diag } (0, \text{G}, \text{B}) = \text{diag } (0,\ 0, \text{B}),$$

$\{\text{B}\} \rightarrow$ **Final Decision**.

This is quite consistent with the final decision (Figure 7.15) "**Ship enters port**."

Using simple operand counting, we get:

- for the first hierarchical level – the first basic coloroid – {ratio 9/9; $E = 0.5$; $D = 0.25$}; second coloroid – ratio {ratio 12/8; $E = 0.6$; $D = 0.16$};
- for the second hierarchical level – {ratio 9/8; $E = 0.53$; $D = 0.22$}.

Let us simulate the decision of the DSS when the estimate "Average number of vessels" changes to "a significant number of vessels in the canal," i.e., M $\rightarrow$ Yel in the second filter of the left branch of the second level we get the result

- II hieratical network, Col^{II} for input set {M, C}:

$$\text{diag } (\text{R},\ 0,\ \text{B}) + \text{diag } (0,\ \text{G}, \text{B}) = \text{diag } (\text{R},\ \text{G},\ \text{B}),$$

filters {C, Yel}

$$\text{diag } (\text{R}, \text{G}, \text{B}) \times \text{diag } (0, \text{G}, \text{B}) \times \text{diag } (\text{R}, \text{G}, 0) = \text{diag } (0,\ \text{G},\ 0),$$

filters {Yel, M}

$$\text{diag } (\text{R}, \text{G}, \text{B}) \times \text{diag } (\text{R}, \text{G}, 0) \times \text{diag } (\text{R}, 0, \text{B}) = \text{diag } (\text{R},\ 0,\ 0),$$

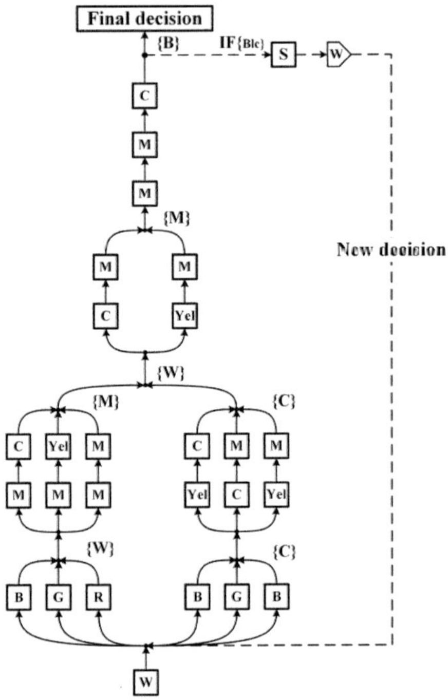

Figure 7.15 Modernized logical operations for a two-level coloroid.

disjunction

$$\text{diag }(0, \text{G}, 0) + \text{diag }(\text{R}, 0, 0) = \text{diag }(\text{R}, \text{G}, 0),$$

filters $\{\text{M, M, C}\}$

$$\begin{aligned} &\text{diag }(\text{R}, \text{G}, 0) \times \text{diag }(\text{R}, 0, \text{B}) \times \text{diag }(\text{R}, 0, \text{B}) \times \text{diag }(0, \text{G}, \text{B}) \\ &\qquad = \text{diag }(0, 0, 0), \\ &\{\text{Blc}\} \to \textbf{Final Decision } (\text{NoDecision}). \end{aligned}$$

For the second hierarchical level, we get ratio 9/9, a negative decision (Figure 7.16) on “Vessel entry into port.”

The absence of a solution presupposes the launch of a search for a new solution until the situation with the number of ships in the canal changes to an average level. Of course, the DSS interacts with the dispatch service operator, who makes the final decision. The proposed fuzzy data base is illustrative in nature and requires taking into account the interdependence

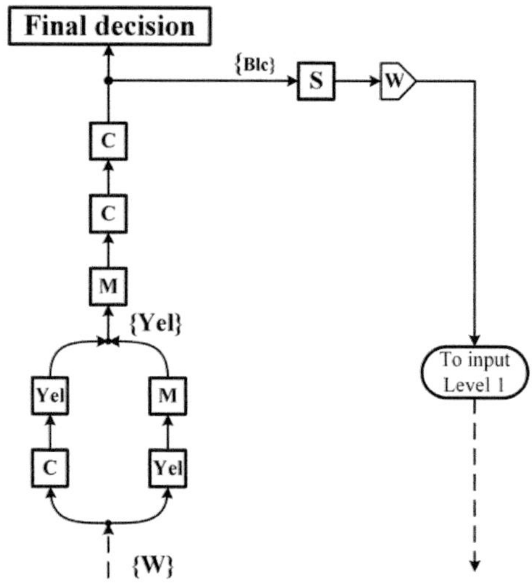

Figure 7.16 Combination of the second level of logical inference without the final decision.

of security factors and the characteristics of the specific task of creating a decision support system.

Further, suppose the dispatch service needs to control, for example, three vessels in one loading area for a given period of time, including maneuvering, mooring, and preparation for loading. Therefore, it is advisable to propose, based on the resulting assessment of the condition of an individual vessel (output assessment in Figure 7.17), to evaluate the parameters of the safe condition of the loading area. Let us introduce additional risk factors that vary in the range of low Yel, medium M, and high C safety ratings, for example, let us assume:

1. Qualification and completeness of the mooring crew **C**.
2. Availability of tugs in the area **C**.
3. Preparation of the cargo pier site **Yel**.
4. Readiness of cargo mechanisms **M**.
5. Qualification of cargo mate **M**.
6. Preparation of port ship maintenance services **M**.
7. Readiness of coastal rescue services **C**.

To process input signals from three neighboring ships, we use an optical structure with two subtractive parallel branches (Figure 7.17) and the absence of a search function for a new solution, performing the functions of the general state of the loading area.

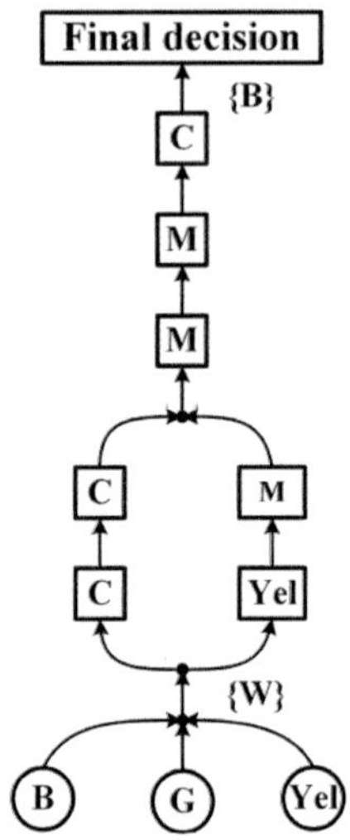

Figure 7.17 Optical structure for assessing the condition of the loading zone.

Logical operations of the logical derivation of the assessment, for example, taking into account assessments of the state of individual vessels $\{$B, G, Yel$\}$, will take the form

$$\mathrm{diag}\ (0,\ 0,\ \mathrm{B}) + \mathrm{diag}\ (0,\ \mathrm{G}, 0) + \mathrm{diag}\ (\mathrm{R},\ \mathrm{G}, 0) = \mathrm{diag}\ (\mathrm{R},\ \mathrm{G},\ \mathrm{B}),$$

filters $\{$C, C$\}$

$$\mathrm{diag}\ (\mathrm{R}, \mathrm{G}, \mathrm{B}) \times \mathrm{diag}\ (0, \mathrm{G}, \mathrm{B}) \times \mathrm{diag}\ (0, \mathrm{G}, \mathrm{B}) = \mathrm{diag}\ (0,\ \mathrm{G}, \mathrm{B}),$$

filters $\{$Yel, M$\}$

$$\mathrm{diag}\ (\mathrm{R}, \mathrm{G}, \mathrm{B}) \times \mathrm{diag}\ (\mathrm{R}, \mathrm{G}, 0) \times \mathrm{diag}\ (\mathrm{R}, 0, \mathrm{B}) = \mathrm{diag}\ (\mathrm{R},\ 0,\ 0),$$

disjunction

$$\mathrm{diag}\ (0, \mathrm{G},\ \mathrm{B}) + \mathrm{diag}\ (\mathrm{R},\ 0,\ 0) = \mathrm{diag}\ (\mathrm{R},\ \mathrm{G},\ \mathrm{B}),$$

filters $\{$M, M, C$\}$

$$\mathrm{diag}\ (\mathrm{R}, \mathrm{G}, \mathrm{B}) \times \mathrm{diag}\ (\mathrm{R}, 0,\ \mathrm{B}) \times \mathrm{diag}\ (\mathrm{R}, 0, \mathrm{B}) \times \mathrm{diag}\ (0, \mathrm{G}, \mathrm{B}) = \mathrm{diag}\ (\mathrm{B},\ 0,\ 0)$$

We get an assessment of the general condition in this case "**safe**."

7.4 Conclusion

The chapter presents the principles of forming the optical architecture of color logic calculations for decision-making problems. The analysis of combinations of logical operations based on the relations of true and false operands made it possible to determine the rational structural constructions of universal optical gates (coloroids) as components of multi-level networks for making complex decisions.

An elementary additive coloroid is defined by a structure with three input color sets, subject to the constraints imposed by the idempotence property of logical operations, and the use of a combination of RGB input sets as a solution in the face of contradictions. The latter seems important when forming ordinary decisions in "simple" decision-making problems. Also, the concept of ordinary solutions with structural logical inference is proposed to be used for joint positive (B, B, B) and negative (R, R, R) input estimates.

An elementary subtractive coloroid is proposed, taking into account the introduction of a certain number of alternative solution branches, which is determined by the parameters of the problem being solved. The expediency of limiting the optical structure to three parallel branches of subtractive logical operations is formulated, taking into account the idempotence rule and the possible large number of alternative contradictory estimates.

Based on the developed optical structures of logic gates as basic coloroids, it is possible to implement multi-level parallel high-speed logical processes in DSS.

To implement the proposed optical architecture in decision-making problems, a multi-object infrastructure facility (a large seaport) with a large number of input fuzzy information changing in real time was considered. A database of input data has been developed in the form of certain factors that determine the safety of navigation and the functioning of port facilities.

Factors including parameters of sea vessels, weather conditions, sea shipping channel, port structures, and services are transformed into color fuzzy information sets.

A multi-level hierarchically structured decision support system is proposed, and examples of logical operations presented in matrix form are modeled for various input estimates of safety factors. The synthesized decision support system operates in real time, allows you to expand, almost unlimitedly, input information, including expert information, and implements safe decision-making trajectories.

Further development of multi-level hierarchical decision-making systems based on the proposed principles for the formation of an optical computing architecture is interesting for such infrastructure facilities as large airports, which require a much larger volume of input information that determines flight safety. Such advantages of the optical color logic architecture as speed, parallel computing structures, dynamic, operator-friendly visualization of color information suggest significant prospects for the proposed approach.

References

[1] A.I. Shevchenko, et al., "Analysis of the prospect domains in AI implementation: Nationals, NATO and Ukraine AI strategies", in: Y.P. Kondratenko, A.I. Shevchenko (Eds), Research Tendencies and Prospect Domains for AI Development and Implementation, 2024, pp. 1–30. https://www.scopus.com/record/display.uri?eid=2-s2.0-85202988430&origin=resultslist

[2] Y. Kondratenko, et al., "Analysis of the Priorities and Perspectives in Artificial Intelligence Implementation," 2023 13th International Conference on Dependable Systems, Services and Technologies, DESSERT 2023, 2023, Athens, 13 – 15 October 2023, DOI:10.1109/DESSERT61349.2023.10416432

[3] V. Slyusar, et al., "Some Aspects of Artificial Intelligence Development Strategy for Mobile Technologies," Journal of Mobile Multimedia, 2024, 20(3), pp. 525–554. DOI: 10.13052/jmm1550-4646.2031

[4] Y. Kondratenko, et al., "Tendencies and Challenges of Artificial Intelligence Development and Implementation," Proceedings of the IEEE International Conference on Intelligent Data Acquisition and Advanced Computing Systems: Technology and Applications, IDAACS, 2023, pp. 221–226, Dortmund, 7 - 9 September 2023. DOI:10.1109/IDAACS58523.2023.10348800

[5] A.N. Tkachenko, et al., "Evolutionary adaptation of control processes in robots operating in non-stationary environments," Mechanism and Machine Theory, Vol. 18, No. 4, Printed in Great Britain, 1983, pp. 275–278. DOI:10.1016/0094-114X(83)90118-0

[6] I.P. Atamanyuk, et al., "The Algorithm of Optimal Polynomial Extrapolation of Random Processes," In: K.J. Engemann, A.M. Gil-Lafuente, J.L. Merigo (Eds.), Modeling and Simulation in Engineering, Economics and Management, International Conference MS 2012, New Rochelle, NY, USA (May 30 – June 1, 2012), Proceedings, Lecture

Notes in Business Information Processing, Volume 115, Springer, 2012, pp. 78–87. DOI:10.1007/978-3-642-30433-0_9

[7] V. Vychuzhanin, et al., "Cognitive-impulse model for assessing complex technical systems survivability," CEUR Workshop Proceedings, Vol. 2711, 2020, pp. 571–585. https://ceur-ws.org/Vol-2711/paper44.pdf

[8] I. Atamanyuk, et al., "Method of polynomial predictive control of fail-safe operation of technical systems," Proc. XIIIth International Conference "The Experience of Designing and Application of CAD Systems in Microelectronics", CADSM 2015, Polyana-Svalyava, Ukraine, 19-23 Febr., 2015, pp. 248–251. DOI:10.1109/CADSM.2015.7230848

[9] R. Duro, et al. (Eds), "Advances in intelligent robotics and collaborative automation," River Publishers, Aalborg, 2015. doi:https://doi.org/10.13052/rp-9788793237049

[10] Y.P. Kondratenko, A. Roshanineshat, D. Simon, "Safe navigation of an autonomous robot in dynamic and unknown environments," In: Y.P. Kondratenko, V.M. Kuntsevich, A.A. Chikrii, V.F. Gubarev (Eds.), "Recent Developments in Automatic Control Systems," River Publishers, Gistrup, 2022, pp. 261–288. https://www.taylorfrancis.com/chapters/edit/10.1201/9781003339229-13/safe-navigation-autonomous-robot-dynamic-unknown-environments-yuriy-kondratenko-arash-roshanineshat-dan-simon

[11] O. Kozlov, et al., "Swarm Optimization of Fuzzy Systems for Mobile Robots with Remote Control," Journal of Mobile Multimedia, 2023, 19(3), pp. 839–876. https://journals.riverpublishers.com/index.php/JMM/article/view/14975

[12] Y. Kondratenko, et al., "Machine Learning Techniques for Increasing Efficiency of the Robot's Sensor and Control Information Processing," Sensors 2022, 22(3), 1062. https://doi.org/10.3390/s22031062

[13] Y.P. Kondratenko, et al., "Slip displacement sensors for intelligent robots: Solutions and models," Proceedings of the 2013 IEEE 7th International Conference on Intelligent Data Acquisition and Advanced Computing Systems, IDAACS 2013, Volume 2, art. no. 6663050, 2013, pp. 861–866. DOI:10.1109/IDAACS.2013.6663050

[14] I. Sidenko, et al., "Machine Learning for Unmanned Aerial Vehicle Routing on Rough Terrain," In: Z. Hu, I. Dychka, M. He (Eds) Advances in Computer Science for Engineering and Education VI. ICCSEEA 2023. Lecture Notes on Data Engineering and Communications Technologies, Vol. 181, Springer, Cham, 2023, pp. 626–635. DOI: 10.1007/978-3-031-36118-0_56

[15] O. Kozlov, et al., "Intelligent IoT-based Control System of the UAV for Meteorological Measurements," Journal of Mobile Multimedia, 2024, 20(3), pp. 555–596. DOI:10.13052/jmm1550-4646.2032
[16] O. Skakodub, et al., "Optimization of Linguistic Terms' Shapes and Parameters: Fuzzy Control System of a Quadrotor Drone," Proceedings 11th IEEE International Conference on Intelligent Data Acquisition and Advanced Computing Systems: Technology and Applications, IDAACS 2021, Vol. 1, Cracow, 22-25 September 2021, 176232, 2021, pp. 566 – 571. DOI:10.1109/IDAACS53288.2021.9660926
[17] S. Encheva, et al., "Decision Support Systems in Logistics," AIP Conference Proceedings 1060, 2008, pp. 254–256. DOI:10.1063/1.30 37065
[18] G.V. Kondratenko, et al., "Fuzzy models for capacitative vehicle routing problems in uncertainty," In: Proc. 17th International DAAAM Symposium "Intelligent Manufacturing and Automation: Focus on Mechatronics & Robotics," Vienna, Austria, 8 -11 November 2006, 103204, 2006, pp. 205–206.
[19] B. Werners, et al., "Alternative Fuzzy Approaches for Efficiently Solving the Capacitated Vehicle Routing Problem in Conditions of Uncertain Demands," In: C. Berger-Vachon, et al. (Eds.), Complex Systems: Solutions and Challenges in Economics, Management and Engineering, Studies in Systems, Decision and Control, Vol. 125, Springer International Publishing, Berlin, Heidelberg, 2018, pp. 521–543. DOI:https://doi.org/10.1007/978-3-319-69989-9_31
[20] N. Ukhan, et al., "ICT for planning and optimization of transport routes with time windows," CEUR Workshop Proceedings, Vol. 2740, 2020, pp. 365–372. https://ceur-ws.org/Vol-2740/20200365.pdf
[21] Y. Kondratenko, et al., "Fuzzy and Evolutionary Algorithms for Transport Logistics Under Uncertainty," Advances in Intelligent Systems and Computing, Volume 1197, AISC, 2021, pp. 1456–1463, International Conference on Intelligent and Fuzzy Systems, INFUS 2020, Istanbul, Turkey, 21-23 July 2020; 242349. DOI:10.1007/978-3-030-51156-2_169
[22] Y.P. Kondratenko, et al., "Comparative Analysis of Evaluation Algorithms for Decision-Making in Transport Logistics," In: M. Jamshidi, V. Kreinovich, J. Kazprzyk (Eds) Advance Trends in Soft Computing, Series: Studies in Fuzziness and Soft Computing, Volume 312, 2014, pp. 203–217. DOI:10.1007/978-3-319-03674-8_20

[23] Y.P. Kondratenko, et al., "Synthesis of Intelligent Decision Support Systems for Transport Logistic," Proceeding of the 6th IEEE International Conference on Intelligent Data Acquisition and Advanced Computing Systems: Technology and Applications, IDAACS'2011. Vol. 2 (Sept. 15-17, 2011, Prague, Czech Republic), 2011, pp. 642–646. DOI:10.1109/IDAACS.2011.6072847
[24] Y. Zhukov, et al., "Polymetric sensing of intelligent robots," 2013 IEEE 7th International Conference on Intelligent Data Acquisition and Advanced Computing Systems (IDAACS 2013), 2013, pp. 880–884, DOI:https://doi.org/10.1109/IDAACS.2013.6663053.
[25] Y.D. Zhukov, O.V. Zivenko, "Intelligent polymetric systems industrial applications," CEUR Workshop Proceedings, vol. 2762, 2020, pp. 122–137. https://ceur-ws.org/Vol-2762/paper8.pdf
[26] Y.P. Kondratenko, et al., "Towards Implementing the Strategy of Artificial Intelligence Development: Ukraine Peculiarities," CEUR Workshop Proceedings, Vol. 3513, 2023, pp. 106–117. https://ceur-ws.org/Vol-3513/paper09.pdf
[27] Y. Zhukov, O.Zivenko, "Ship Operation Analysis and Optimization via Mobile Application," Journal of Mobile Multimedia, 20(03), 2024, pp. 627–650. https://doi.org/10.13052/jmm1550-4646.2034
[28] Kondratenko, Y., Kuntsevich, V.M., Chikrii, A.A., Gubarev, V. (Eds), "Advanced control systems: Theory and applications," River Publishers, Gistrup, 2021, pp. 1–441. ISBN: 9788770223416, DOI:10.1201/9781003337010
[29] Kondratenko, Y.P., Kuntsevich, V.M., Chikrii, A.A., Gubarev, V.F. (Eds), "Recent Developments in Automatic Control Systems," River Publishers, Gistrup, 2022, pp. 1–492. ISBN: 978-877022673-8, 978-877022674-5
[30] Y. Kondratenko, S. Sidorenko, "Ship Navigation in Narrowness Passes and Channels in Uncertain Conditions: Intelligent Decision Support," In: P. Shi, J. Stefanovski, J. Kacprzyk (Eds) Complex Systems: Spanning Control and Computational Cybernetics: Foundations, Studies in Systems, Decision and Control, Vol 414, Springer, Cham, 2022, pp. 475–493. https://doi.org/10.1007/978-3-030-99776-2_24
[31] M. Solesvik, et al., "Joint Digital Simulation Platforms for Safety and Preparedness," In: Y. Luo Y. (Ed) Cooperative Design, Visualization, and Engineering. CDVE 2018,' Lecture Notes in Computer Science, Vol. 11151, Springer, Cham, 2018, pp. 118–125. DOI:https://doi.org/10.1007/978-3-030-00560-3_16

[32] Y.P. Kondratenko, V.L. Timchenko, "Increase in Navigation Safety by Developing Distributed Man-Machine Control Systems," Proceedings of the Third (1993) International Offshore and Polar Engineering Conference, Vol. 2, Singapore, 6-11 June 1993, Code 18719, 1993, pp. 512-519.

[33] A. Sanjeev, et al., "Non-contact optical wave front shaping for focusing light and high-resolution imaging inside and behind biological scattering medium," In: M. R. Douglass, et al.(Eds.), Emerging Digital Micromirror Device Based Systems and Applications XI, Article 1093204, Proceedings of SPIE - The International Society for Optical Engineering, Vol. 10932, SPIE, 2019. https://doi.org/10.1117/12.2507797

[34] D. Azhigulov, et al., "High-speed thermally tuned electro-optical logic gates based on micro-ring resonators," Optical and Quantum Electronics, 52, 2020, Article 412. https://doi.org/10.1007/s11082-020-02526-y

[35] Z. Zhu, et al., "Multifunctional and multichannels all-optical logic gates based on the in-plane coherent control of localized surface plasmons," Optics letters, 45(23), 2020, pp. 6362–6365. DOI:10.1364/OL.402085.

[36] C. Qian, et al., "Performing optical operators by a diffractive neural network," Light Sciences and Applications, 9, 59, 2020. https://doi.org/10.1038/s41377-020-0303-2

[37] V. Jandieri, et al., "Functional all-optical logic gates for true time-domain signal processing in nonlinear photonic crystal waveguides," Optics Express, 28(12), 2020, pp. 18317–18331. https://doi.org/10.1364/OE.395015

[38] L. Caballero, et al., "Photonic crystalintegrated logic gates and circuits," Optics Express, 30(2), 2022, pp. 1976–1993. https://doi.org/10.1364/OE.444714

[39] D. A. Miller, et al., "Environmental assessment of optical and electronic computing systems," Nature Sustainability, 6(6), 2023, pp. 756–764.

[40] M. Matuszewski, et al., "Role of all-optical neural networks", Phys. Rev. Applied, Vol. 21, Issue 1, 014028, 2024. DOI:https://doi.org/10.1103/PhysRevApplied.21.014028

[41] N. L. Kazanskiy, M. A. Butt, S. N. Khonina, "Optical Computing: Status and Perspectives," Nanomaterials, 12(13), 2171, 2022. DOI:10.3390/nano12132171.

[42] L. Zadeh, "The role of fuzzy logic in modeling, identification and control," Modeling, 15(3), 1994, pp.191–203. DOI:https://doi.org/10.4173/mic.1994.3.9

[43] V. Kreinovich (Ed), "Uncertainty Modeling," Studies in Computational Intelligence, vol. 683, Springer, Cham, 2017, pp. 1–292. DOI:https://doi.org/10.1007/978-3-319-51052-1

[44] V.L. Timchenko, Y.P. Kondratenko, V. Kreinovich, "Why color optical computing?" In: Phuong, N.H., Kreinovich, V. (Eds) Deep Learning and Other Soft Computing Techniques, Studies in Computational Intelligence, vol. 1097, Springer, Cham, 2023, pp. 227–233. https://doi.org/10.1007/978-3-031-29447-1_20

[45] V. Timchenko, Y. Kondratenko, O. Kozlov, V. Kreinovich, "Fuzzy color computing based on optical logical architecture," In: C. Kahraman, et al. (Eds) Intelligent and Fuzzy Systems, INFUS 2023, Lecture Notes in Networks and Systems, vol. 758, Springer, Cham, 2023, pp. 491–498. https://doi.org/10.1007/978-3-031-39774-5_55

[46] V. Timchenko, Y. Kondratenko, V. Kreinovich, "Decision support system for the safety of ship navigation based on optical color logic gates," CEUR Workshop Proceedings, Vol. 3347, 2022, pp. 42–52. https://ceur-ws.org/Vol-3347/Paper_4.pdf

[47] M. Gil, K. Wróbel, J. Montewka, F. Goerlandt, "A Bibliometric Analysis and Systematic Review of Shipboard Decision Support Systems for Accident Prevention," Safety Science, Vol. 128, 2020, 104717. https://doi.org/10.1016/j.ssci.2020.104717

[48] M. D'Arcy, P. Fazli, D. Simon, "Safe Navigation in Dynamic, Unknown, Continuous, and Cluttered Environments," In: 2017 IEEE International Symposium on Safety, Security and Rescue Robotics (SSRR), Shanghai, China, 2017, pp. 238–244. DOI:10.1109/SSRR.2017.8088169

[49] T. Degre, "The importance of a risk-based approach to maritime safety," Recherche, Transports Sécurité, Vol. 78, 2003, pp. 21–32. https://doi.org/10.1016/S0761-8980(03)00004-9

[50] A. Nagasawa, "Quantitative assessment of marine traffic environment by using the maneuverings pace concept," Ninon kokai gakkai ronbunshu, J. Jap. Inst. Navig., 1998, pp. 93–101.

[51] V.L. Timchenko, et al., "Robust stabilization of Marine Mobile Objects on the Basis of Systems with Variable Structure of Feedbacks," J. of Automation and Information Sciences, Vol. 43, No. 6, New York: Begel House Inc., 2011, pp. 16–29. DOI:10.1615/JAutomatInfScien.v43.i6.20

[52] J. Lisowski, "Dynamic games methods in navigator decision support system or safety navigation," Advances in Safety and Reliability, Vol. 2, London-Singapore, Balkema Publishers, 2005, pp. 1285 – 1292.

[53] Y. Huang, et al., "Ship collision avoidance methods: State-of-the-art," Safety Science, Vol. 121, 2020, pp. 451–473. https://doi.org/10.1016/j.ssci.2019.09.018

[54] T.A. Johansen, T. Perez, A. Cristofaro, "Ship collision avoidance and COLREGS compliance using simulation-based control behavior selection with predictive hazard assessment," In: IEEE Transactions on Intelligent Transportation Systems, vol. 17, no. 12, 2016, pp. 3407–3422. DOI:10.1109/TITS.2016.2551780

[55] C. Tam, R. Bucknall, "Cooperative path planning algorithm for marine surface vessels," Ocean Engineering, Vol. 57, 2013, pp. 25–33. https://doi.org/10.1016/j.oceaneng.2012.09.003

[56] T. Wang, Q. Wu, J. Zhang, B. Wu, Y. Wang, "Autonomous decision-making scheme for multi-ship collision avoidance with iterative observation and inference," Ocean Engineering, Vol. 197, 2020, 106873. https://doi.org/10.1016/j.oceaneng.2019.106873

[57] Ning–Shou Xu, et al., "Associative memory–based intelligent control of ship steering systems," In: Proceedings of the 3-rd European Control Conf., Roma, Italy, 1995, pp. 1625–1630.

[58] K. Naus, "Drafting route plan templates for ships on the basis of AIS historical data," The J. of Navigation, Vol. 73, Issue 3, 2020, pp. 726–745. DOI:https://doi.org/10.1017/S0373463319000948

[59] E.F. Wilthil, A.L. Flåten, E.F. Brekke, M. Breivik, "Radar-based maritime collision avoidance using dynamic window," In: 2018 IEEE Aerospace Conference, Big Sky, MT, USA, 2018, pp. 1–9. DOI:10.1109/AERO.2018.8396666

[60] S. Li, J. Liu, R. Negenborn, F. Ma, "Optimizing the joint collision avoidance operations of multiple ships from an overall perspective," Ocean Engineering, Vol. 191, 2019, 106511. https://doi.org/10.1016/j.oceaneng.2019.106511

[61] J. Zhang, S. Yu, Y. Yan, "Fixed-time output feedback trajectory tracking control of marine surface vessels subject to unknown external disturbances and uncertainties," ISA Transactions, Volume 93, 2019, pp. 145–155. https://doi.org/10.1016/j.isatra.2019.03.007

[62] V.L. Timchenko, D. O. Lebedev, "Algorithmic Procedures Synthesis of Robust-Optimal Control for Moving Objects," In: Y.P. Kondratenko, V.M. Kuntsevich, A.A. Chikrii, V.F. Gubarev (Eds.), Recent

Developments in Automatic Control Systems, River Publishers, Gistrup, 2022, pp. 289–323. eBook ISBN: 9781003339229
[63] E. Köse, et al., "Expert system for monitoring dynamic stability of small craft," IEEE J. of Oceanic Engineering, Vol. 20, No. 1, 1995, pp. 13–22. DOI:10.1109/48.380250
[64] T. Tran, et al., "A vessel management expert system," In: Proceedings of the Institution of Mechanical Engineers, Part M: Journal of Engineering for the Maritime Environment, Volume 216, Part 2, 2002, pp. 161-771. DOI:10.1243/147509002762224379
[65] E. Kim, J. Park, J. Kim, S. Kim, "Color Decision System based on Deep Learning and Fuzzy Inference System," In: 2018 Joint 10th International Conference on Soft Computing and Intelligent Systems (SCIS) and 19th International Symposium on Advanced Intelligent Systems (ISIS), Toyama, Japan, 2018, pp. 236–239, doi:10.1109/SCIS-ISIS.2018.00049
[66] R. Szlapczynski, J. Szlapczynska, "A method of determining and visualizing safe motion parameters of a ship navigating in restricted waters," Ocean Engineering, Vol. 129, 2017, pp. 363–373. https://doi.org/10.1016/j.oceaneng.2016.11.044
[67] Kubo Masayoshi, et al., "Safety evaluation of ship entering a harbor under severe wave conditions," In: Proceedings of the 10th International Offshore and Polar Engineering Conference, Seattle, Washington, USA, Int. Soc. Offshore and Polar Eng., ISOPE-I-00-369, 2000, pp. 330–336.
[68] I. Norstad, K. Fagerholt, G. Laporte, "Tramp ship routing and scheduling with speed optimization," Transportation Research Part C: Emerging Technologies, Vol. 19, Issue 5, 2011, pp. 853–865. https://doi.org/10.1016/j.trc.2010.05.001
[69] T.A. Altameem, et al., "Computer Decision Making System for Increasing Efficiency of Ship's Bunkering Process," In: Annals of DAAAM for 2010 & Proceeding of the 21th Int. DAAAM Symp. "Intelligent Manufacturing and Automation", (20-23 Oct., 2010, Zadar, Croatia), Published by DAAAM International, Vienna, Austria, 2010, pp. 0403–0404. https://www.daaam.info/Downloads/Pdfs/proceedings/proceedings_2010/20540_Annals_1_head.pdf
[70] Y.P. Kondratenko, G.F. Romanovsky, D.M. Pidopryhora, et al., "Optimal planning of cargo operations at bunkering tankers with respect to dynamical character of their parameter restrictions," In: IFAC Proceedings Volumes (IFAC-PapersOnline), Volume 37, Issue 10, 2004, pp. 239–244. https://doi.org/10.1016/S1474-6670(17)31738-X

[71] A. Topalov, et al., "A Mobile Application of a Decision Support System for Ballasting a Floating Dock," Journal of Mobile Multimedia, Volume 20, Issue 03, 2024, pp. 597–626. https://doi.org/10.13052/jmm1550-4646.2033

[72] M. Solesvik, et al., "Fuzzy decision support systems in marine practice," In: 2017 IEEE International Conference on Fuzzy Systems (FUZZ-IEEE), Naples, Italy, 2017, pp. 1–6. DOI:10.1109/FUZZ-IEEE.2017.8015471

[73] V. Timchenko, Y. Kondratenko, V. Kreinovich, "The architecture of optical logical coloroid with fuzzy computing," CEUR Workshop Proceedings, Vol. 3373, 2023, pp. 638–648. https://ceur-ws.org/Vol-3373/paper44.pdf

[74] V. Timchenko, V. Kreinovich, and Yu. Kondratenko, "Color optical computing: visualization, numbers, alphabet," CEUR Workshop Proceedings, Vol-3790, 2024, pp. 123–132. https://ceur-ws.org/Vol-3790/paper11.pdf

[75] V.L. Timchenko, Y.P. Kondratenko, V. Kreinovich, "Interval-Valued and Set-Valued Extensions of Discrete Fuzzy Logics, Belnap Logic, and Color Optical Computing," In: S. Massanet, et al. (Eds), Fuzzy Logic and Technology, and Aggregation Operators. EUSFLAT AGOP 2023. Lecture Notes in Computer Science, Volume 14069, Springer, Cham, 2023, pp. 297–303. https://doi.org/10.1007/978-3-031-39965-7_25

[76] V. Timchenko, Y. Kondratenko, V. Kreinovich, "Logical Platforms for Mobile Application in Decision Support Systems Based on Color Information Processing," Journal of Mobile Multimedia, Volume 20, Issue 3, 2024, pp. 679–698. doi.org/10.13052/jmm1550-4646.2037

[77] _V. Timchenko, V. Kreinovich, Y. Kondratenko, V. Horbov, "Effectiveness Evaluations of Optical Color Fuzzy Computing," In: Research Tendencies and Prospect Domains for AI Development and IDAACS, River Publishers, 2024, pp.129–150. DOI:10.1201/9788770046947-7

[78] Y.P. Kondratenko, A.I. Shevchenko (Eds), "Research Tendencies and Prospect Domains for AI Development and Implementation," River Publishers, 2024, pp. 1–155. ISBN: 978-877004692-3, 978-877004693-0. https://www.riverpublishers.com/book_details.php?book_id=1163

[79] V. Timchenko, Y. Kondratenko, V. Kreinovich, "Implementation of Optical Logic Gates Based on Color Filters", In: Z. Hu, I. Dychka, M. He (eds) Advances in Computer Science for Engineering and Education VI. ICCSEEA 2023. Lecture Notes on Data Engineering and

Communications Technologies, Vol. 181, Springer, Cham, 2023, pp. 126–136. DOI:10.1007/978-3-031-36118-0_12

[80] Timchenko, V., Kondratenko, Y., Kreinovich, V. Logical Decision Networks Based on the Optical Coloroids. Proceedings of the IEEE International Conference on Intelligent Data Acquisition and Advanced Computing Systems: Technology and Applications, IDAACS, 2023, pp. 1194–1199, Dortmund, 7 - 9 September 2023. DOI:10.1109/IDAACS 58523.2023.10348692

8

Artificial Intelligence: Effective Socionics Models of Psycho-Informational Processes and Quantum Computers

A. V. Bukalov

International Institute of Socionics, Ukraine
E-mail: 123@socionic.info

Abstract

The creation of a full-fledged multifunctional artificial intelligence is impossible without understanding mental processes and the nature of consciousness. This review of theoretical and experimental studies of the quantum nature of the psyche and consciousness is based on the author's results showing the connection between quantum and mental processes. Numerous studies confirm the quantum nature of mental processes and consciousness. The author introduced the concept of an elementary unit (quantum) of consciousness and proposed a formula for calculating the degree of consciousness of any living organism. Analysis of the presented data leads to the conclusion that adequate modeling and reproduction of mental processes with the manifestation of consciousness and multifunctional intelligence is possible only on quantum computers with a structure corresponding to the real structure of the psyche. It is well described by the extended information model of the psyche, proposed by the author, in socionics (or psychoinformatics) as the theory of information metabolism. Socionics is a science about the information interaction of the psyche with the outside world, the models of which are effectively used in practice in psychology, psychiatry, aviation, astronautics, management, pedagogy, sports, etc., because they adequately describe mental processes, differences in the strategies of behavior and thinking of people. The author significantly developed the basic socionic model,

DOI: 10.1201/9788743800989-8

introducing the coordinating function of consciousness and the description of the internal structure of mental functions, and showed that the hierarchy of these functions can be modeled as a special system from a number of specialized quantum processors. This provides the basis for the development of a fundamentally new architecture of future quantum systems of artificial intelligence.

Keywords: Artificial intelligence, neural network, psycho-informational processes, quantum psyche, consciousness, socionics, type of information metabolism, quantum computer, model of the psyche.

8.1 Introduction

The successful creation of artificial intelligence (AI) systems raises new questions about the further fruitful development of this area. Currently, AI is beginning to be widely used in a wide variety of areas of human activity [1–5]. We can state that a new technological and information revolution is beginning in all areas of service, business, technology, and industry. The issue of creating AI that can have intelligence and even consciousness is already on the agenda. However, significant problems arise along this path. This is due to the fact that the nature and relationship between consciousness and matter, psyche, and body are one of the most complex and intriguing mysteries not only of science but also of human cognition in general.

The emergence of cybernetics in the 20th century as the science of control and communication, as well as computers, made it possible to simulate a range of information processes with the goal of creating artificial intelligence, even to attempts to imitate the functioning of the brain using computer models simulating millions of interacting neurons.

Existing systems are improving in pattern recognition or imitating some aspects of logical analysis, acting as a human assistant in information processing. However, nothing similar to manifestations of consciousness is observed in such systems and models, despite the continuous increase in computing power. At the same time, researchers in the field of creating artificial intelligence do not have a clear understanding of the nature of the processes and phenomena of the psyche, consciousness, and mind, which are supposed to be reproduced in modeling.

Therefore, the question of the nature of consciousness and psyche cannot be considered resolved today, despite all the successes of neurophysiological and computational approaches. Moreover, the modern idea of the special nature of consciousness arose and is developing within the framework of quantum physics, the success of which, as we know, has revolutionized not only the scientific picture of the world but also the flow of new technologies. Even Niels Bohr, the creator of the theory of the atom, considered obvious analogies between descriptions of quantum and mental processes [6].

The purpose of this chapter is to show how understanding the quantum nature of the psyche and consciousness will allow us to create the architecture of new quantum computers, the artificial intelligence of which will be able to fully reproduce the phenomena of the psyche and consciousness. The next sections of this chapter are organized as follows.

Section 8.2 provides a brief discussion of ours and a number of other theoretical and experimental studies that show quantum aspects of mental processes, pattern recognition, and decision-making. Since the late 1980s, the author has been developing the concept of the quantum nature of the psyche. Having examined a number of correspondences between quantum and mental processes, the author came to the conclusion that full-fledged modeling of consciousness and thinking is possible only on a quantum basis. The results of other researchers over the past 35 years confirm this conclusion.

Section 8.3 focuses on the analysis of quantum aspects of the physics of life, including direct experimental evidence, as well as the author's work on coherent processes in living organisms. The concept of an elementary cellular quantum of consciousness is introduced, and a formula for determining the value of consciousness in any living organism is proposed. Of particular interest is also the connection we discovered between the degree of development of the brain and consciousness of an organism and the rate of neutral mutations in its genome. All this leads us to the conclusion that consciousness has a primary quantum nature and is closely connected with the phenomenon of life.

Section 8.4 is devoted to the neuroholographic model of mental processes and mental functions and processes, which was proposed by the author and has received experimental confirmation. The neuroholographic model reveals the features of the work of mental functions that process various aspects of the information flow, as well as the mechanisms of extroversion–introversion. It is concluded that socionic models of mental functions can be used to create a new architecture of multifunctional quantum computers.

Section 8.5 describes the models of organization of mental functions that are developed in the theory of information metabolism – socionics or psychoinformatics and are successfully used for practical purposes in working with people. In addition to the basic model of A. Augustinavichute, an extended model of the psyche (model B) proposed by the author, including the control function of consciousness, is also considered.

Section 8.6 examines the author's model B in more detail, including internal parameters – dimensions of mental functions of information metabolism and the function of consciousness. Such models are effectively used in practice in psychology, psychiatry, aviation, astronautics, management, pedagogy, sports, etc., since they adequately describe mental processes, differences in behavioral strategies, and thinking of people.

Finally, Section 8.7 presents concluding remarks and outlines potential directions for future research, which open up the possibility of building more advanced artificial intelligence systems, in the form of quantum computers with a fundamentally new architecture. Such systems will be able to adequately reproduce the phenomena of the psyche and consciousness.

8.2 Descriptive Analysis of Quantum Properties in Mental Processes

Research on quantum mental processes explores cognitive phenomena – such as information processing in the brain, language, decision-making, memory, concept formation, judgment, and perception – through the lens of quantum theory's mathematical framework. These studies are not contingent on assumptions about the quantum nature of brain processes; instead, they adopt a phenomenological and empirical approach, making their findings experimentally verifiable in psychological research.

The application of quantum formalisms to mental processes emerged during the 1980s and 1990s in the works of researchers such as D. Aerts [7] and his collaborators [8], J. Broekaert, E. Finkelstein, A. Bukalov [9], S. Smets, E. Atmanspacher [10], P. Bordley, and A. Khrennikov [11]. This research direction gained significant momentum in the late 2000s with the publication of numerous articles in leading psychological journals, as well as monographs and textbooks. Viewing the psyche as a macroquantum phenomenon at a systemic level reveals that it inherently exhibits all the characteristics of quantum laws, including the fundamental complementarity between particle-like and wave-like descriptions. This perspective has been emphasized by prominent figures such as D. Bohm, N. Bohr, R. Feynman, E. Finkelstein, I. Tsekhmistro, A. Bukalov, etc. [9–13].

Analyzing the quantum properties of the psyche naturally leads to distinguishing its corpuscular and wave components. In humans, this duality corresponds to the interplay between rational and irrational aspects of cognition. For instance, the principles of mathematical logic, which assert that a formal description of an object can render it meaningless or that a meaningful object may resist formal description, are mirror extreme cases of the uncertainty principle. In quantum mechanics, measuring a particle's momentum with infinite precision precludes determining its position and vice versa. Similarly, the complementarity of formal and semantic descriptions reflects the dynamic relationship between verbal, logical-formal thinking, and non-verbal, intuitive-semantic cognition.

This interplay between formal and semantic descriptions of objects, as well as their corresponding cognitive processes, was also evident in the foundational debate between formalism (led by D. Hilbert) and intuitionism (advocated by L. Brouwer) in mathematics [14]. These discussions highlighted the inherent incompatibility yet complementarity of the different modes of understanding and representation in human thought.

The emergence and realization of a thought can be likened to the measurement process in quantum mechanics. Psychologists and philosophers such as W. James and H. Bergson have likened the continuous stream of consciousness to the modern depiction of a physical vacuum, composed of virtual quanta of physical fields and particles – transient, semi-real entities that arise and vanish. Similarly, a thought, analogous to an elementary particle, exhibits both "corpuscular" and "wave-like" properties. When attention is focused on a specific "particle" of thought, it is effectively isolated from the broader continuum of the mental vacuum. This isolated thought grows and gains weight, though it simultaneously loses some of its prior characteristics, particularly when translated into verbal expression.

In this process, the superposition of the thought particle's states with the quantized, virtual continuum of consciousness collapses, isolating a distinct state. This selected state represents one of the intrinsic states of consciousness, which functions as a measuring instrument. This mechanism reflects the selective and subjective nature of consciousness, driven by predispositions and orientations toward particular solutions. Such phenomena suggest the feasibility of defining a wave function (Ψ) that encapsulates the dynamics of the psyche [13]. Logical operations within consciousness reduce the wave function, compressing the thought's wave packet and anchoring it in a fixed state. However, focusing on specific aspects of thought inherently leads to the exclusion of others, presenting challenges in self-reflection and introspection.

From an evolutionary standpoint, abstract, formally logical thinking in its advanced form likely emerged in humans only when the brain could afford its resource-intensive nature, as such intellectual activity suppresses instinctual and automatic neural processes. The trajectory of thought is non-linear, interacting associatively (or interfering) with other thoughts, much like vacuum virtual particles in quantum systems. The path to a specific goal is indeterminate, as the thought's progression becomes entangled, fragmented, and dispersed across the associative mental landscape. This description aligns closely with quantum interference of alternatives, as described by the Feynman path integral [13].

The verbal or "corpuscular" components of the psyche are inherently discrete, contrasting with the holistic nature of gestalt images and the indivisibility of mental acts. This indivisibility mirrors the central tenet of quantum mechanics concerning the integrity of quantum phenomena. Consequently, recognizing the psyche as a quantum mechanical system offers explanations for many cognitive paradoxes and phenomena.

The quantum characteristics of the psyche can also be examined through the lens of holographic principles of brain function, as proposed by K. Pribram [15] and others. Under this framework, the quantum mechanical properties described above – such as superposition of mental and emotional states, and interference of probability amplitudes for thoughts or actions – naturally emerge. Additionally, in this interpretation, the unconscious aspect of the psyche, which remains unobservable, can be regarded as a "quantum vacuum". However, this mental vacuum is not without structure; it embodies a hierarchy of symmetries akin to those found in quantum vacuum fields [13].

In any component of the psyche, there exists a wave-particle duality, grounded in a profound physical basis. This duality arises because the psyche, in whole or in significant part, serves as a reflection of the universe as a reality and, to some extent, as a model or reproduction of it. Consequently, the psyche's representation of external phenomena adheres to quantum mechanical principles, mirroring the fundamental laws of nature. This implies that the psyche not only reflects the phenomena of the external world but also the governing laws of these phenomena. In turn, this reflection exhibits isomorphism with fundamental physical principles.

The question of why two distinct hemispheres of the brain exist can thus be answered as follows: the inherent complementarity of observed reality necessitated the development of a quantum modeling substrate within the mind, employing the same governing principles [16]. This necessity is underscored by the holographic nature of information processing observed within brain structures.

Research in the domain of Quantum Cognition aligns with the quantum paradigm, which posits that the mechanisms of information processing in a complex system such as the brain – accounting for the contextual dependence of information and probabilistic reasoning – can be mathematically articulated through quantum information theory and quantum probability theory. Importantly, this field does not seek to elucidate how the macroscopic, seemingly classical neural brain facilitates quantum-like behavior. Instead, it focuses on the effects themselves, demonstrating that various cognitive phenomena are better described by quantum information theory and quantum probability than by their classical counterparts. The quantum probability perspective advanced by C.A. Fuchs and colleagues [17] further reinforces this quantum framework, particularly in modeling decision-making processes.

Contextuality plays a central role here, as quantum mechanics is inherently contextual [18]. Quantum systems lack objective properties that can be defined independently of the context of specific measurements, as highlighted by N. Bohr [6]. This contextual nature implies the presence of incompatible mental variables, along with a violation of the classical law of total probability and the occurrence of interference effects. For example, experiments on decision-making in players reveal that when participants are unaware of the outcome of the first round, most refuse to engage in a second round. Conversely, when informed of the results, players were generally willing to proceed, regardless of whether they won or lost. This outcome deviates from classical probability theory but can be accounted for by the quantum interference effect, akin to the explanation of results in the double-slit experiment in quantum physics [19].

Such deviations from classical rational expectations in decision-making under uncertainty lead to well-documented paradoxes in behavioral economics. Human behavior under these uncertain conditions is elucidated through quantum aspects such as superposition, interference, contextuality, and the incompatibility of non-commuting operators [8].

Similar quantum effects are also observed in *memory* processes [20]. Quantum probability provides a novel framework for explaining common human *errors* in probability estimation, including conjunction and disjunction errors [21]. For instance, the Liar Paradox represents a contextual paradox. It can be demonstrated that the alternating "true–false" states in this paradox are represented within a complex Hilbert space, with their oscillatory behavior dynamically described by the quantum Schrödinger equation [22]. Furthermore, the use of quantum entanglement has been proposed to model the semantics of combinations of various concepts [23]. The principle of quantum superposition is employed to explain how new concepts emerge when pre-existing concepts are combined [24].

J. A. Hampton proposed [25] that the combination of two concepts can be represented within a quantum Fock space, where deviations from classical theory are attributed to contextual interactions, superposition, interference, and entanglement [7, 8, 24]. Furthermore, cognitive testing of specific concept combinations has demonstrated that quantum entanglement emerges between individual concepts, leading to violations of Bell's inequalities [25].

In the domain of *perception*, it is well-documented that stimuli with ambiguous interpretations often result in fluctuating perceptions over time. Quantum models have been developed to predict the durations of these fluctuations and their dependency on measurement frequency. Additionally, quantum theory has been employed to model Gestalt perception, accounting for interference effects observed during measurements involving ambiguous figures [10]. E. Conte provided experimental evidence supporting the quantum interference effect and the existence of a wave function at the perceptual–cognitive level. This was achieved through studies involving ambiguous figures, cognitive anomalies such as delusional conjunctions, emotive–cognitive conflicts, and the observation of ambiguous figures following cognitive tasks. These findings suggest that the quantum properties of consciousness are rooted in the fundamental quantum principle of superposition of states in quantum mechanics [26].

In *economics and finance*, several studies indicate that the information processing of market agents adheres to the principles of quantum information theory and quantum probability [27]. For instance, Bohm's model of stock price dynamics conceptualizes stock prices as quantum potentials shaped by the expectations of financial market participants [28].

Additionally, some researchers employ the theory of open quantum systems to model decision-making as the dynamic interaction of mental states with the surrounding environment. This approach equates the mathematical description of the decision-making process with the dynamics of decoherence [11].

8.3 Quantum Dimensions in the Physics of Living Systems

In the 1980s, a novel scientific direction emerged in the works of Prof. S. P. Sit'ko and his colleagues in Kyiv [29]. This field, termed the "physics of the alive," was developed in conjunction with the application of microwave resonance therapy (MRI) as part of quantum medicine. From its inception, the physics of living systems has been examined through a quantum lens. This new approach addressed unresolved questions concerning the synchronization of processes in billions of cells, the mechanisms underlying tissue cell differentiation, and the realization of genetic information during organismal development [30].

H. Fröhlich, a pioneer in quantum superconductivity theory, was the first to propose a physical explanation for the stable existence of macroscopic living organisms [31]. He introduced the concept of biological coherence, suggesting that it enables effective long-range interactions. Fröhlich highlighted that natural oscillations of protoplasmic membranes in cells, determined by their physical properties, occur in the frequency range of $10^{(10 \div 11)}$ Hz. These oscillations, when energized, become sources of electromagnetic radiation within the millimeter-wave range [17].

The practical exploration of biological coherence began in 1982 when S. P. Sit'ko and collaborators identified the characteristic frequencies of the human body in the millimeter electromagnetic wave spectrum [29]. Subsequent experiments demonstrated health improvements in patients exposed to low-intensity electromagnetic radiation at approximately 50 GHz, targeted at biologically active points (BAPs). The findings suggested that each cell could act as an active center contributing to the coherent electromagnetic field of the entire organism.

The physics of living systems posits that living organisms represent the fourth level of quantum organization in nature, succeeding the nuclear, atomic, and molecular levels. In this framework, a self-consistent potential, analogous to a laser potential in the millimeter-wave range, facilitates biological coherence through effective long-range interactions. The defining characteristic of living organisms is their ability to function as quantum mechanical entities, distinguishing them fundamentally from non-living matter.

Additional studies have demonstrated that under specific conditions, even light quanta interacting with organic molecules at room temperature can give rise to a quantum hybrid superfluid liquid capable of frictionless movement [32]. A biological cell is similarly conceptualized as a system performing quantum information processing, functioning as a hypersonic molecular quantum phonon computer, with the brain envisioned as a network of such quantum computers [33]. This idea was initially proposed and developed by E. A. Liberman and collaborators [33]. Independently, R. Penrose and S. Hameroff, building on H. Fröhlich's work, introduced a related hypothesis linking consciousness to quantum mechanical oscillations in the cytoskeletal microtubules of cells, forming the foundation of the "theory of quantum neurocomputing" [34, 35]. However, as R. Penrose noted, such a framework is insufficient without the collective quantum state extending across large, multicellular regions of the brain to coordinate global mental processes [36].

By synthesizing the contributions of H. Fröhlich, E. Liberman, R. Penrose, S. Sit'ko, and others, the author deduced that these findings pertain to a unified phenomenon involving coherent oscillations of diverse origins within the frequency range of 50–100 GHz in both individual cells and multicellular organisms [37]. Research into the optical properties of axons further supports the possibility of photon transmission across macroscopic distances within the brain. For instance, axons approximately 2 millimeters in length can transmit between 46% and 96% of the biophotons they receive. With the brain generating over 10^9 biophotons per second, this suggests potential for quantum entanglement among these photons, facilitating quantum communication [38]. Such communication, however, necessitates not only optical channels but also mechanisms for encoding, receiving, and processing quantum information, effectively functioning as quantum processors.

Moreover, an analysis of the observation process in conventional quantum mechanics led several prominent physicists to conclude that the consciousness of the observer is integral to the measurement process. This perspective is supported by the principle of quantum mechanics that emphasizes the inseparability of the object and the measuring apparatus, along with the relativity of boundaries between them, as articulated in von Neumann's theorem regarding the arbitrary placement of the boundary between the observed system and the observer's consciousness [39]. Even in scenarios where a microscopic quantum event is amplified into a macroscopic one, its measurement ultimately depends on the observer's consciousness. The measuring apparatus extends to the retina and neural structures responsible for processing incoming information, but the quantum measurement process is completed only when it is realized by the observer's internal "Self." While this view might be dismissed as a formal abstraction, the role of consciousness is further underscored by the observer's active decision in selecting what to observe and how to observe it. This interpretation has been supported by leading quantum mechanics experts, including von Neumann, E. Schrödinger, F. London, E. Bauer, E. Wigner, R. Penrose, and M. Mensky, who explored the idea of wave packet reduction by the observer's consciousness.

Experimental studies have provided *direct evidence that the brain utilizes quantum computational processes*. Researchers from Trinity College in Dublin, through magnetic resonance imaging (MRI) measurements of proton spins, observed correlations between these quantum measurements and short-term memory performance and levels of awareness. This suggests that quantum processes contribute to cognitive and conscious brain functions [40]. Their work was grounded in quantum mechanics principles, particularly the notion that if known systems interacting with an unknown system exhibit quantum entanglement, the unknown system must also possess quantum characteristics. Importantly, electrophysiological signals, such as heart rate evoked potentials, are not detectable by MRI; thus, their observation was attributed to the entanglement of proton spins within the brain's fluids. Consequently, the researchers inferred that brain functions inherently involve quantum phenomena.

Additionally, their findings substantiated the non-classical nature of mental processes, challenging earlier assertions that quantum properties could not persist in the brain's warm and aqueous environment [40]. This aligns with the Integrated Information Theory of Consciousness proposed by G. Tononi [41], which seeks to identify the conditions and mechanisms underlying consciousness based on its observable properties. If these properties, as emerging evidence suggests, align with quantum mechanical principles, then the mechanisms of consciousness must be quantum in nature and reliant on quantum material substrates.

We also proposed a reasonable hypothesis regarding the existence of the fundamental unit or quantum of psyche and consciousness, equating this quantum to the consciousness of a single cell, regarded as the basic unit of life [37]. This idea is supported by research and neural network modeling of intelligent behaviors exhibited by single-celled organisms such as amoebas and ciliates. The identification of a neuron-like ribosomal r-protein network functioning as a "molecular brain" [42] and investigations into the cognitive capabilities of prokaryotes, including associative learning and problem-solving [43], further reinforce this hypothesis.

The quantification of a living organism's consciousness, denoted as Ψ, can be expressed using the logarithm of the number of neurons (or dendrites) Z, relative to a single cell, adhering to established principles in information theory.

$$\Psi = b \cdot \ln Z, \tag{8.1}$$

where b is a numerical coefficient [37].

This formula is in agreement with the Weber–Fechner psychophysical law, which establishes a logarithmic relationship between the intensity of a stimulus and the magnitude of a subjective sensation and the corresponding logarithmic relationship when encoding information in neurons [44]. Since the phenomenon of consciousness is associated with the presence of subjective experience, formula (8.1) proposed by us can be considered as a generalization of psychophysical and corresponding physiological laws for assessing the value of consciousness of living organisms.

Our research has also revealed that the logarithm of the evolutionary increase in neuron count or brain mass among primates – corresponding to the growth of mentality and consciousness – is inversely proportional to the logarithm of the experimentally determined frequency of neutral mutations in the genomes of organisms ranging from *Drosophila* to primates and humans [45]. This relationship (Figure 8.1) illustrates that the evolutionary enhancement of informational order in the psyche and consciousness counterbalances the rise in genomic entropy at the quantum biochemical level:

$$S(mutation) = \text{const} - I(brain) \tag{8.2}$$

$$S(mutation) + I(brain) = \text{const}, \tag{8.3}$$

where $S(mutation)$ is the mutational entropy of the genome, and $I(brain)$ is the information content of the brain, directly proportional to the mass of the brain or the number of neurons.

This finding highlights a fundamental principle: the conservation of the sum of information and entropy within living organisms as information systems. However, understanding the quantum properties of psyche and consciousness likely requires more than the electromagnetic structure identified by S. P. Sit'ko. While this structure provides a coherent electromagnetic framework, it is insufficient to account for the complexity of consciousness, quantum computation, and thought processes. It is best regarded as one substructure within the broader quantum system of the organism, facilitating interaction and integration with molecular biological mechanisms.

To realize a complete quantum system capable of supporting psyche and consciousness, an additional substrate may be necessary. One possibility is a quantum condensate of light elementary particles [14]. Modern physics and astrophysics concepts, along with experimental evidence, suggest the existence of such particles – such as "dark matter," "dark energy," axions, or sterile neutrinos. These quantum structures, while distinct from biological components, could be physically interconnected with them. According to our hypothesis, these structures play a significant role in mental phenomena and consciousness, operating in conjunction with biological processes [46].

This framework may also explain extraordinary phenomena, such as individuals functioning with brains missing up to 90%–95% of neurons [47]. Furthermore, self-awareness, as demonstrated through experiments like the "mirror test," has been observed in ants [48], which possess only 250,000 neurons compared to humans' 86 billion. These findings suggest that the mere

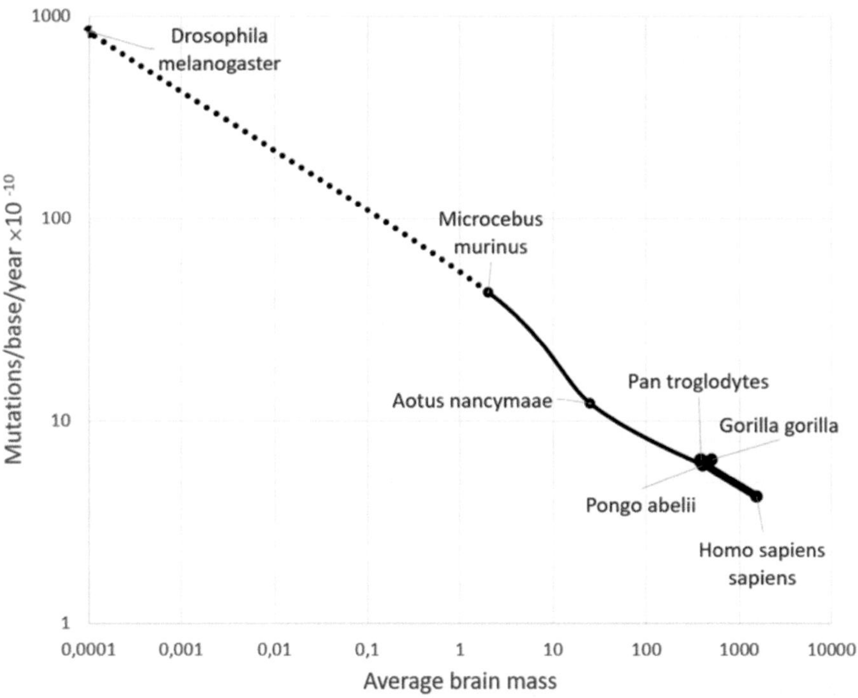

Figure 8.1 Dependence of mutation rate on brain mass (in logarithmic scales).

number of neurons has limited influence on the emergence of self-awareness. In contrast, artificial neuron-like systems, despite their millions of elements, remain devoid of self-awareness.

This leads us to the conclusion that consciousness has a primary quantum nature and is closely related to the phenomenon of life.

8.4 Holographic Model of Consciousness

8.4.1 The emergence of holographic models and their specificity

One of the earliest non-mechanistic models of consciousness is the holographic model proposed by K. Pribram [15], which highlights the significance of wave processes in shaping consciousness and thought. Building on this approach, another holographic model was developed by interpreting the Jung–Augustinavichute mental functions as cognitive organs [49]. This model provides a framework for understanding the interplay between sensory information and cognitive processes.

The model is grounded in neurophysiological findings [50], which indicate that the brain receives information about external and internal realities through two distinct systems: the specific system and the non-specific system. These systems transmit signals from receptors and lower neural centers to the cerebral cortex, facilitating the assessment of both the physical parameters of stimuli and their biological significance. The synthesis of these inputs at the cortical level represents one of the foundational stages of higher nervous activity.

The specific system processes discrete information that is tied to sensory modalities, adhering to the projection principle across the cerebral cortex [50]. This system transmits objective, physical characteristics of stimuli without consideration of their biological relevance, enabling precise analysis of stimuli based on their intrinsic properties. Consequently, such information is classified as specific.

In contrast, the non-specific system conveys information that is more abstract in nature. As signals pass through the brainstem, they lose their specificity in terms of sensory modality due to their delocalization within the cerebral cortex, thereby exiting the projection field of the corresponding sensory analyzers. However, as these signals traverse the emotional and motivational centers of the limbic system and hypothalamus, they acquire a new dimension of meaning, specifically their biological significance. Thus, while the non-specific system does not preserve sensory specificity, it conveys information that is highly specific in terms of its relevance to the organism's activities and survival. In this sense, non-specific information pertains to the biological role of stimuli, reflecting their importance in guiding behavior and physiological responses.

This leads to the distinction between two types of signals: one conveying "objective" information and the other "subjective" information, shaped by internal desires, motivations, and biological needs [50]. In this context, it is worth highlighting C. G. Jung's characterization of extraversion as a tendency to prioritize the perception of objective external data, subordinating subjective elements to this process, in contrast to introversion, which emphasizes reliance on the inner world of thoughts, desires, and emotions, subordinating external data accordingly [51].

Consequently, we proposed associating the neurophysiological mechanisms responsible for transmitting and processing specific information with the mental process of extraversion, while linking the mechanisms for non-specific information processing to the mental process of introversion. This framework is part of a new holographic model (Figure 8.2) [12, 14,

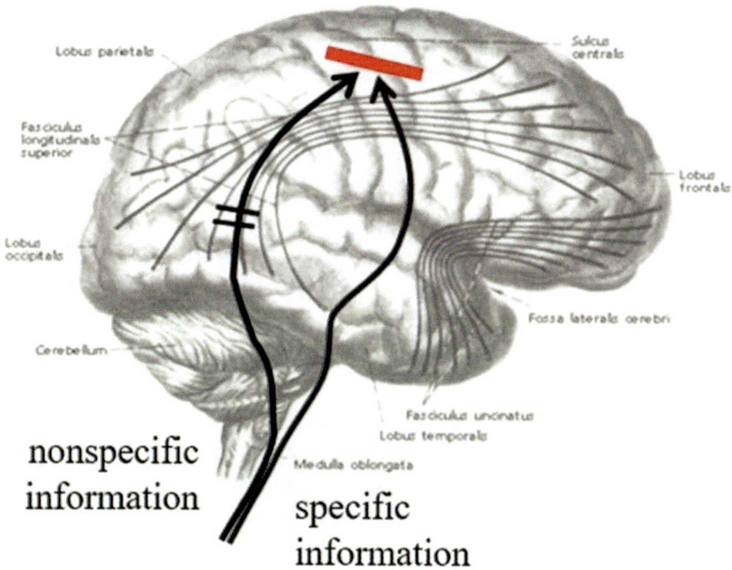

Figure 8.2 Conceptual holographic approach to brain data processing.

49, 52, 53]. A key aspect of this model, which incorporates the holographic memory concept developed by G. I. Shulgina [54] as a specific case, has been validated through neurophysiological studies exploring the mechanisms underlying extraversion and introversion [53].

8.4.2 The principles and mechanism of holography

Let us consider the effects of holography in detail. If a coherent beam of light emitted by a source (laser) is split into two beams using a semi-transparent reflective plate (Figure 8.3) and one of the beams illuminates an object, and then brings the first beam together with beam 2 reflected by the object, these beams will interact with each other (interfere). As a result, a three-dimensional image of the object illuminated by beam 2 will appear in the area of interaction of the beams.

Thus, in the wave holographic process, all information about the object from which it was read is transferred and restored. In this case, beam 1, which remains unchanged in its characteristics and creates a coherent background, is called the reference beam, and beam 2, interacting with the object, is called modulated, since it is modulated by information about the object with which it interacted.

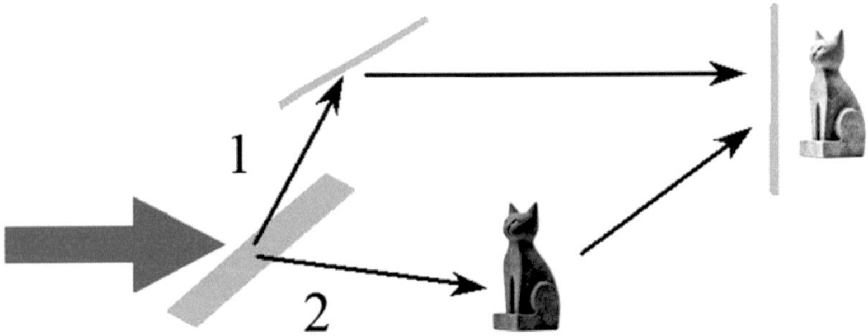

Figure 8.3 Mechanism of holography.

The principles of holography are applicable to any wave processes, for example, acoustic ones. We consider the processes of information processing in the brain as a consequence of the flow of wave coherent processes, the reflection of which are the known rhythms of the brain.

8.4.3 Functions of information metabolism in holographic model

The correspondence between the functions of information metabolism (FIM) and neural structures has been considered in socionics and neurophysiology since 1989 [49, 52, 55, 56]. This subsection represents a development of the neuroholographic model of the FIM operation proposed by the author in 1995–2009 [49–57].

FIM themselves can be considered from various points of view, including as an analogue of biodynamic organs (according to Bernstein), which were formed in the course of evolution. FIMs apparently have a neurophysiological correlate in the form of neural ensembles that integrate information processed in the cerebral cortex [57]. The deep basis of these structures is apparently neural networks, the identified functionality of which is in good agreement with the work of the mental functions of information metabolism described in the typology of C. G. Jung and socionics [58–60]. The presence of various functional subsystems in the brain allows for the existence of various types of intelligence, both predominantly left-hemisphere with a leading rational function (*logic* or *ethics*), and predominantly right-hemisphere with a leading irrational function (*intuition* or *sensing*).

The functions of information metabolism act as fixed (in the configuration space of brain states) areas of interaction and interference of coherent wave processes, including specific and non-specific components that interfere with each other in information aspects in the FIM, evolutionarily distinguished and

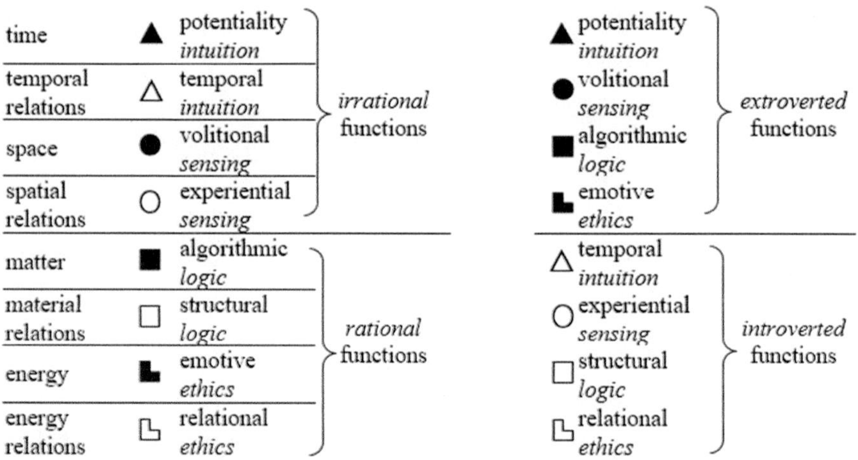

Figure 8.4 The functions of information metabolism perceive and process various aspects of reality.

differentiated for the flow of these processes. We will consider them in more detail in Section 8.5.

Then the mechanism of *extroversion* of the FIM of the *potentiality intuition, volitional sensing, algorithmic logic, emotive ethics* looks like this: the information entering these FIMs is modulated by data from external reality, and its receipt corresponds to the movement of specific information in the neurophysiological sense. In this case, non-specific information, passing through the subcortical structures, reticular formation, etc., is used by extroverted FIM only as a supporting information flow, ignoring its subjective, motivational, including special biological, content. Thus, *extroverted* functions fall under the power of objective processes of the surrounding world. In contrast to this process, for *introverted* FIM (*temporal intuition*, *experiential sensing*, *structural logic*, *relational ethics*) specific, objective information is associated with the supporting wave information flow, and non-specific, subjective information is associated with the information process modulated by subjective, including biological, human needs.

Thus, if for *extroverted* FIM non-specific information is only a background for isolating objective information from the surrounding reality, then for *introverted* FIM objective information is a background for isolating subjective reality and its predominance in the mental processes of perception. This model (Figure 8.5) is fully consistent with the findings of neurophysiologists that for the emergence of a subjective image or sensation and the

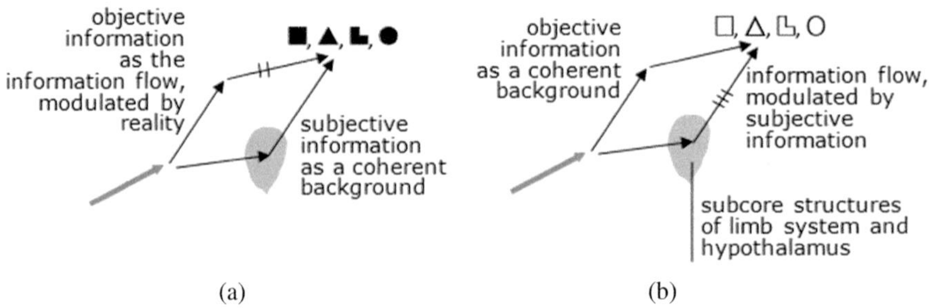

Figure 8.5 Objective (a) and subjective (b) informational flows.

transition of a physiological process into a psychological one, a synthesis of two types of information about the stimulus is necessary: its physical parameters and informational significance. This is the central point of the act of perception. In this case, sensory information corresponds to the "objective" properties of the stimulus, and information associated with motivation and personality attitude gives perception a "subjective" aspect" [50].

In addition, our model includes the holographic model of memory by G. I. Shulgina [50] as a special case. But the model of G. I. Shulgina describes only the *extroverted* form of memory. The new model describes both the extroverted and introverted forms of not only memory but also information processing.

From the proposed model, it naturally follows that introverts are oriented toward the inner, subjective world, have a greater sensitivity to the perception of transpersonal experience, archetypes, etc. An example of this is C. G. Jung himself as a deep introvert. We should also note that Jung himself defined the archetypes of the collective unconscious as psychic correlates of instincts [51]. And instinctive behavior is precisely what determines is subcortical structures associated with non-specific information.

In contrast, bright extroverts prefer to rely on objective data from the outside world, experiments, etc. An example of such an approach is I. P. Pavlov.

However, due to the presence of both objectifying and subjectivizing functions in the FIM system, any person is capable of perceiving both objective and subjective reality with greater or lesser success.

Note that the proposed model apparently allows us to describe the origin of a number of mental illnesses, such as autism, schizophrenia, hysteria, neuroticism, etc. Thus, autism can arise from a partial blocking of objective information flow to extroverted functions.

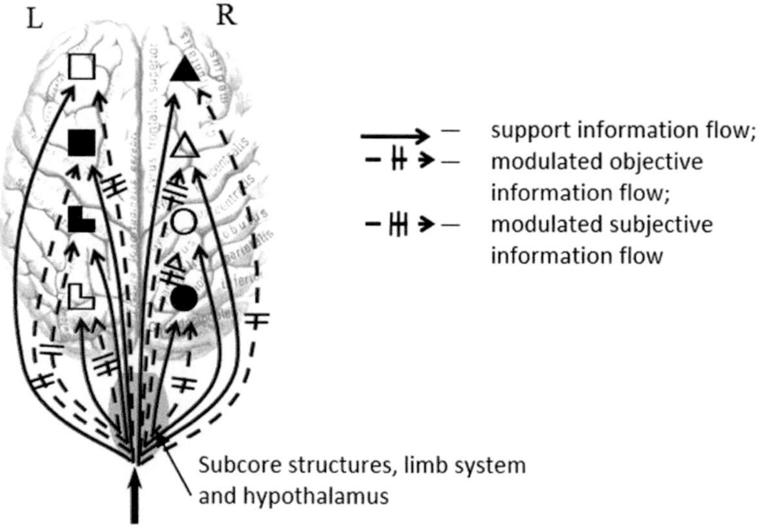

Figure 8.6 The general holographic model of FIM in relation to the hemispheres of the brain.

The general holographic model of FIM in relation to the hemispheres of the brain is shown in Figure 8.6. Of course, secondary information processes and auxiliary connections are not taken into account here.

Note also that each FIM probably has a mirror image in the opposite hemisphere. In this way, subdominant FIM arise. It is possible that the signs of these subdominant FIMs are opposite to those of the dominant functions. Then the complete system of dominant and subdominant FIM is described by the 16-component model B [49].

8.4.4 Distortion of C. G. Jung's concept of extroversion–introversion by H. J. Eysenck and his followers

H. J. Eysenck, having borrowed the concept of extroversion–introversion from C. G. Jung, significantly simplified it, reducing it to observable aspects of activity–inactivity, sociability–non-communicability, differences in temperaments [61], etc. At the same time, the fundamental difference between extroverts and introverts according to Jung, associated with the objective–subjective form of mental processes, was completely ignored. Ignoring this circumstance leads to a systematic failure to distinguish between fundamentally different situations: physiologically conditioned differences between extroverts and introverts, on the one hand, and situationally emerging, or developed, modes of mental functioning, on the other hand, which in lexical models (for example, in the Big Five [62, 63]) are interpreted as extroversion or introversion. Moreover, supporters of lexical models often believe that as a result of life evolution, extroverts can become introverts or vice versa. However, this point of view is clearly erroneous and demonstrates a superficial and limited approach to the description of these traits, since H. J. Eysenck already discovered clearly expressed physiological differences in the reactions of extroverts and introverts [61]. It is obvious that such innate differences cannot be changed at the will of a person or by changing the mode of his activity and communication. I. Trofimova in her works [63] also gave a detailed analysis of lexical models and showed their inconsistency with physiological data and dependence on social and subjective aspects.

8.4.5 Experimental confirmation of Jung's concept and the neuroholographic model

Jung's original approach to identifying and describing the characteristics of extroversion and introversion directly suggests deep and fundamental differences in the functioning of the psyche of extroverts and introverts. This approach was largely ignored by Eysenck and his followers. Most modern psychological tests and lexical models describe these differences very superficially. But the neuroholographic model we proposed and based on neurophysiological data exactly corresponds to Jung's ideas. Moreover, it is experimentally verifiable.

And indeed, in 2010, neurophysiological studies were conducted that confirmed the correctness of the ideas of C. Jung and, at the same time, our neuroholographic model. A. A. Cherninsky et al. [64], in their work, studied changes in the electroencephalography (EEG) recordings of people presented with various olfactory stimuli in the form of essential oil odors, as well as the dependence of such changes on the level of extra/introversion of the person. The authors found that introverted persons had a higher level of non-specific brain activation. This was accompanied by a decrease in the power of low-frequency EEG components in the parietal, occipital and temporal cortex of the cerebral hemispheres. At the same time, an increase in the level of coherence of high-frequency spectrum oscillations demonstrates an increase in internal associative processes. In turn, extroverted subjects showed lower levels of non-specific brain activation [64].

Thus, the direct experimental data obtained are completely consistent with the key aspect of our holographic model of the extroversion–introversion mechanism and confirm Jung's original opinion on this issue.

In particular, the authors found higher reactivity of introverts compared to extroverts, and they associated these differences with "intense activation of mechanisms of directed attention in introverts." Extroverts and introverts were also distinguished by specific dynamics of EEG indicators, which indicated generalized non-specific cerebral activation in introverts, and a number of other indicators.

Thus, in full accordance with the concept of C. G. Jung, introverts turned out to be more reactive to the described stimulation. At the same time, they showed a predominance of intensification of internal associative processes. In turn, extroverts showed a predominance of processes of analysis of external sensory information [64].

These data fully correspond to the neuroholographic model proposed by us. We also note that the obtained experimental results confirm the fundamental incompleteness of the ideas of H. Eysenck and his numerous followers about the nature and manifestations of introversion and extroversion, which was noted in the works of A. Augustinavichute [65] in the early 80s of the 20th century, as well as by other authors.

8.4.6 The need for quantum computers to simulate mental processes

Thus, the obtained data confirm both Jung's primary concept, on which the information model of the psyche in socionics is based, and, in fact, once again – the peculiarities of information processing according to the neuroholographic model we proposed, based on well-established neurophysiological data.

In this regard, the question arises about the nature of wave holographic processes, on which the model and the work of the psyche as a whole are based. After all, quantum coherent radiation, which is created by a laser, is used to implement holographic processes in optics. However, the nervous system and the brain as a whole are not quantum systems, although a number of studies within the *Quantum Cognition direction* demonstrate a number of quantum patterns in the work of the psyche.

Psychologists and physicists working in this direction state dozens of experimental confirmations of the work of quantum features of mental processes. But at the same time they cannot offer a satisfactory model linking the clearly non-quantum neurophysiological structure of the brain and the quantum behavior of the psyche. However, it is easy to notice that the neuroholographic model we have proposed already to some extent links the work of neural structures and the observed quantum features of mental processes. At the same time, if we take into account the existence of a coherent electromagnetic framework of the organism with characteristic frequencies of about 50 GHz, discovered in 1981–1988 and studied by S. P. Sit'ko et al. [29], then this will be the next step to explaining the implementation of a number of coherent phenomena in the body and nervous system. However, the electromagnetic nature of this framework cannot explain all the phenomena of coherence and quantum phenomena of mental processes, since external magnetic, electromagnetic fields have almost no effect on the work of the psyche itself. Therefore, the third step, fully explaining the observed experimental phenomena, can be the study of the entire hierarchy of all possible coherent fields that can exist in the body and cause quantum-wave synchronization of all processes – from intracellular – to neural ensembles and the brain as a whole [20, 37, 49].

Holographic models provide a strong theoretical framework for explaining observed phenomena, yet the capacity of neural substrates alone to facilitate holographic processes remains uncertain. This uncertainty arises because such processes depend on quantum coherence, which necessitates an appropriate quantum substrate. Neural structures, being macroscopic and non-quantum, inherently exhibit high entropy. While they are connected to wave-like quantum holographic processes, their role appears limited in directly generating these processes. Instead, neural structures may function more as classical transitional systems for the input and output of information relative to quantum processes and substrates. Consequently, the holographic model described here can be classified as phenomenological, offering a physiological projection of more fundamental quantum structures that underlie mental processes.

This distinction highlights challenges in simulating thinking processes on traditional computers, where the inherent limitations of classical computing systems prevent them from replicating the unique characteristics of consciousness. However, ongoing advancements in quantum computing, which utilize qubits within quantum cells containing dozens or even hundreds of quantum-correlated particles, offer a promising alternative. These systems integrate microscopic quantum mechanisms with macroscopic classical input–output interfaces, a setup analogous to the relationship between quantum substrates and neural structures within the biophysical quantum paradigm.

Quantum computers thus hold greater potential for modeling certain aspects of psyche and consciousness. Achieving this, however, would require quantum computers to be designed as systems of at least eight specialized processors, each tasked with handling distinct components of the overall information flow, much like the specialized divisions within the human psyche. A central processor would oversee and integrate these components, mirroring the integrating role of consciousness. In fields such as *socionics* or psychoinformatics, which study information metabolism in the psyche, models of such structures are well-established [49, 66]. Leveraging these models could guide the development and realization of advanced quantum computers capable of more effectively replicating cognitive and conscious processes.

8.5 Information Metabolism Models of Psyche in Socionics and Psychoinformatics

Our research in the field of socionics (psychoinformatics) as the theory of information metabolism and information structure of psyche [48, 64] allows us to propose a new concept for the creation of multifunctional quantum computers with a new architecture that will allow us to model mental processes, including consciousness.

Socionics, also referred to as psychoinformatics, *is characterized by its robust and empirically verifiable information models of the psyche.* These models elucidate the mechanisms through which the psyche perceives, processes, and interprets diverse types of information to make decisions. As a result, socionics-based methodologies are applied across various domains, including the training of pilots and air traffic controllers [67], astronaut selection, enhancing team efficiency in management [68], psychotherapy, sports psychology, astronautics, civil aviation, education, sociology, political science, and the modeling of cognitive processes [14, 49, 66]. Over the past three decades, these approaches and conclusions have been extensively validated through experimentation and practical applications [69].

The construction of socionic information models involves identifying eight fundamental subsystems responsible for processing different aspects of the information flow. These subsystems, which represent the core mechanisms for information exchange and processing in the psyche, are referred to as mental functions in psychological terms. In socionics, they are specifically defined as functions of information metabolism (FIM).

Each component of the information flow corresponds to a distinct function of information metabolism (FIM) (Figure 8.4), which defines an individual's capacity to perceive and interpret specific aspects of the world. These FIMs generate unique mental representations and conceptual frameworks, forming a kind of "grammar" that shapes a person's interactions with the world, including their relationships with others. Nature equips individuals with the ability to develop these functions, enabling them to receive, process, and produce information.

Each FIM functions as an information processing subsystem, effectively acting as a specialized processor designed to address a specific category of problems. Depending on the structure of the task, various configurations of the eight FIMs can integrate into a unified information processing system, facilitating the efficient resolution of multidimensional problems with high speed and accuracy. Additionally, each FIM correlates with specific bodily functional systems and extensive neural networks.

For example, the default mode network (DMN), also referred to as the operational rest network or the target-negative network, is active during states of rest, self-reflection, dreaming, meditation, or light dozing. It aligns with the concept of the "intuition of possibilities." Conversely, the task-positive network (TPN), or the operational problem-solving network, which is activated during flow states and intense focus on complex tasks, corresponds to the "intuition of time."

The *sensing* aspect of socionics, which governs bodily functions and interactions with the external world, is one of the most extensively studied by physiologists. It involves systems for regulating sensitivity (*experiential sensing*) and motor control pathways (*volitional sensing*), including the peripheral nervous system. This system comprises motor units (nerves and muscle fibers controlling shape, speed, and strength), muscle spindles (sensors with adjustable sensitivity to length and speed for reflex activation), and reflex-activating receptors, among others.

The *logic* aspect corresponds to functional systems involving neural networks that include place neurons, head direction neurons, grid coordinates, and border neurons. These systems form the foundation for logical structures, which are further developed within the cerebral cortex.

The *emotive ethics* aspect (or "feeling") is linked to the activity of the functional system associated with the assessment of the achievement or non-achievement of the goal formed by the feedback acceptor.

Empathy-related mechanisms, such as mirror neurons, have already been studied quite well. The corresponding FIM for this system is known as *relational ethics* [70].

At the level of human psychology, nature implements 16 fundamental combinations of the eight FIMs, resulting in 16 types of information metabolism (TIMs), which represent distinct forms of intelligence. These TIMs evolved over time and collectively constitute a psycho-informational social system referred to as the *Socion* [49, 65]. Each TIM is characterized by its unique mode of information perception and processing, behavioral strategies, and decision-making approaches.

Socionics also examines the *types of informational interactions* between these types of information metabolism, predicting and describing intertype relationships and their interactions with the external environment. Optimal interaction between human operators and technical systems is particularly significant in control systems for complex processes, such as those found in nuclear power plants and transportation systems. When considering human–system interactions, it is possible to define the informational type of a given system and identify various potential interactions with the person. These interactions can range from harmonious to conflicting. By considering these dynamics, it becomes feasible to create systems that are more human-friendly and can interact optimally with their operators. Such systems can be adapted for interaction with specific individuals [49, 70].

Current artificial intelligence systems [1–5] and robotic systems [71] are capable of modeling, though primarily only in part, three of the eight subsystems:

- Algorithmic- and structural-logical processes (at the algorithm and program level)
- Empirical sensing (gathering data from sensors) and pattern recognition
- Control of actuators.

Holistic intelligence comprises at least eight distinct subsystems, making it evident that genuine artificial intelligence must incorporate at least five additional information-processing subsystems. These subsystems serve as analogues for corresponding functions of information metabolism (Figure 8.7) [49, 65].

Our investigations suggest that FIMs may be regarded as specialized quantum or quasi-quantum processors [49].

This perspective aligns with the framework of Quantum Cognition, wherein R. Blutner and E. Hochnadel demonstrated that the formalization of psychological-type theory, as proposed by C. G. Jung, Myers-Briggs, and A. Augustinavichute, through quantum mechanics, leads to the derivation of 16 personality types [72]. These personality types correspond to the socionic types of information metabolism.

The advancement of the A-Model results in the eight-component A–B–Model (Augustinavichute–Bukalov), which includes an integrative function of consciousness [73].

This consciousness function (Figure 8.8) governs the operations of all FIMs by adapting their activity to various operational modes required for

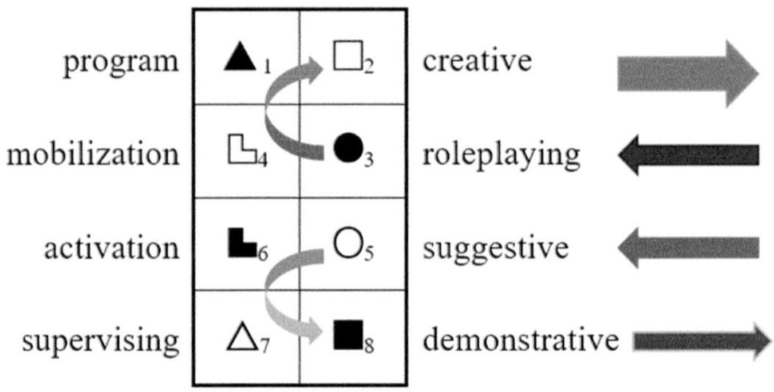

Figure 8.7 Representation of the intuitive logical extravert A-model: FIMs and information flow pathways.

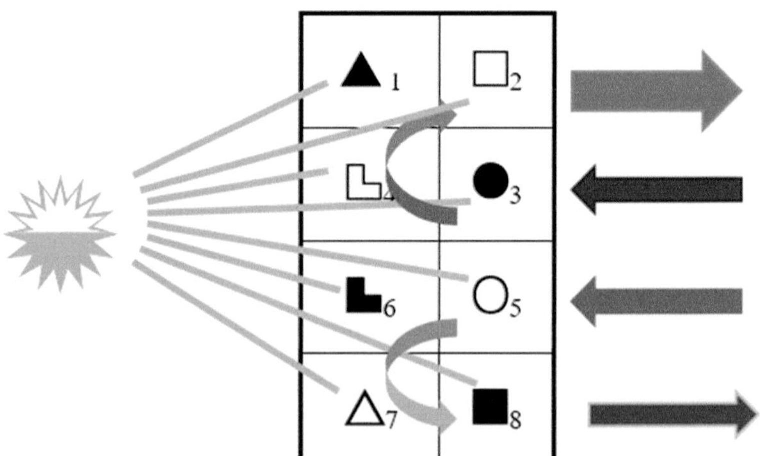

Figure 8.8 Consciousness function as the controller of FIM mode transitions.

addressing diverse, particularly non-standard, challenges in the external environment.

8.6 Dimensionality of FIM and the Hierarchy of Memory, Attention, and Thinking Volumes

The dimensionality of a function defines the upper limit on the number of operational units it can encompass, while the quantity of units that are activated reflects the degree of development of that particular function, as well as the overall maturity of the personality.

The internal quantization of the psycho-informational space – encompassing memory, attention, and thinking – yields a characteristic spectrum for the number of operational cells. This spectrum corresponds to A. Bukalov's magic series: 6(7), 10(11), 16(17), 26(27), 42(43) [74]. The first term in this sequence, Miller's number 7 ± 2, represents the capacity of human short-term memory (RAM) and aligns closely with the Fibonacci sequence, exhibiting golden ratios between neighboring terms [49, 74]. Expanding the foundational A-Model produces a more differentiated 16-component B-Model, augmented with the integrative function of consciousness [73], which enhances the flexibility and descriptive scope of the human psyche.

In Figure 8.9, each vector associated with the dimension of a mental function corresponds to distinct amounts of attention, thinking, and memory. For example, a one-dimensional fourth function **(4)** involves only the personal experience vector *Ex*, with a capacity of $N_4 =$ **6(7)** operational cells (including an additional unit for the integrating function of consciousness).

A two-dimensional third function **(3)**, defined by vectors *Ex* (personal experience) and *Nm* (learned norms and rules), has a capacity of $N_3 =$ **10 (11)** cells.

The three-dimensional second function **(2)** adds the situation vector *Sm* to *Ex* and *Nm*, with a total capacity of $N_2 =$ **16 (17)** cells.

Finally, the four-dimensional first function **(1)** integrates *Ex*, *Nm*, *Sm*, and globality *G*, resulting in a maximum capacity of $N_1 =$ **26 (27)** cells.

In the functions of the vital ring **(5)–(8)**, the mental vectors change direction (indicated by dashes), shifting the mode of operation from information production to consumption. This transition activates similar vital vectors (depicted by light lines). To describe conscious activity at this stage, it is sufficient to consider mental vectors alone.

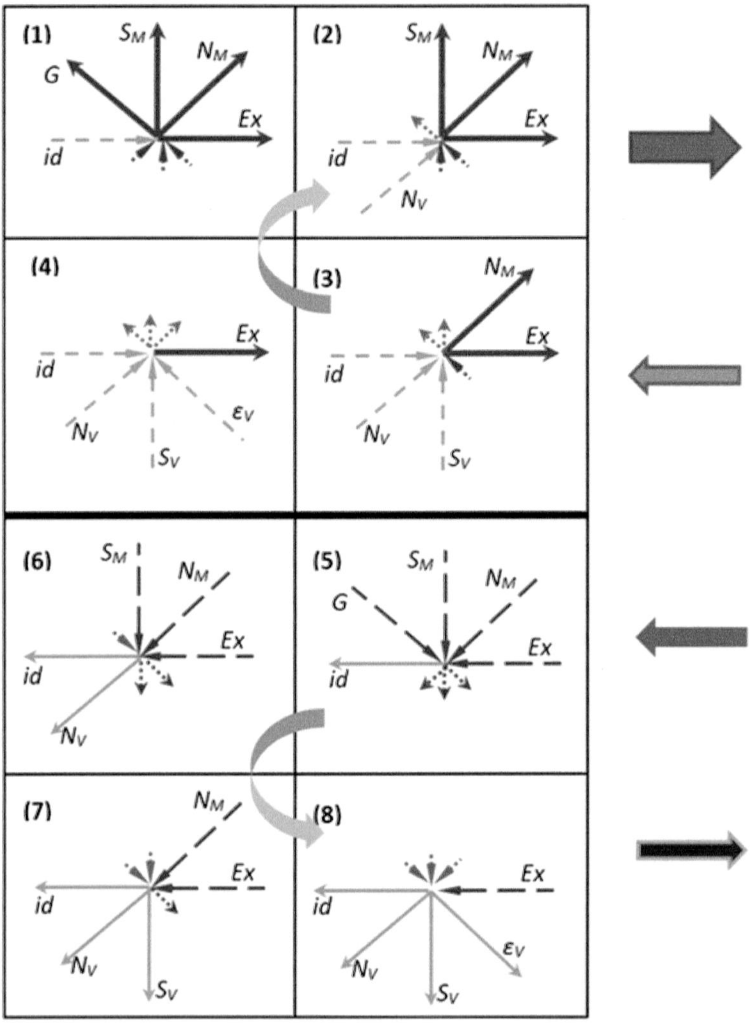

Figure 8.9 Dimensions of functions of informational metabolism and information input/output channels.

The factorial of the number of operational cells interacting within each function-processor approximates the number of combinations that mental functions can execute. For instance, the combinatorial capacity is $\boldsymbol{W_1 = N_1!}$ $= \mathbf{27! \approx 10^{28}}$ for the **(1)** function; $\boldsymbol{W_2 = N_2!} = \mathbf{17! \approx 3.6{\cdot}10^{14}}$ for the **(2)** function; $\boldsymbol{W_3 = N_3!} = \mathbf{17! \approx 4{\cdot}10^{7}}$ for the **(3)** function, and $\boldsymbol{W_4 = N_4!} = \mathbf{7!}$ $= \mathbf{5040}$ for the **(4)** function.

In real individuals, not all operational cells may be fully activated, leading to variations in the level of mental development, abilities, talents, and skills across people. In apes, the number of operational cells is 2–3 times fewer than in humans, accounting for the disparity in cognitive capabilities between humans and apes [49].

8.7 Conclusion

A conceptual and theoretical examination of the psyche, consciousness, and thought processes highlights their quantum nature. This conclusion is supported by direct experimental evidence. Consequently, effective modeling of mental processes, including consciousness, appears feasible only through quantum computers, where quantum mechanisms interact with classical, macroscopic structures and processes. However, such computers must mirror natural systems in structure. At the same time, information models of the psyche developed in socionics provide a robust framework for explaining numerous observable aspects of human cognition and behavior. These models could serve as a foundation for designing complex quantum multiprocessor computer architectures, replicating the mental functions of information metabolism and managing various facets of incoming information streams. The capabilities and sophistication of each function are determined by the parametric dimensions of its operational space and the number of operational cells within it. There is substantial evidence suggesting that the interactions among these cells are quantum in nature and realizable in specific quantum systems. Current technological advancements seem to enable the creation of such systems, bringing us closer to simulating human cognition.

Our analysis of the psyche, consciousness, and thinking confirms their quantum characteristics and processes, as corroborated by experimental findings. We have considered a number of quantum processes in living organisms, including the creation of the concept of elementary cellular consciousness and the hierarchy of consciousness of multicellular living organisms. We have also proposed a formula for assessing the value of consciousness or the level of awareness of any living organism. The quantum neuroholographic model proposed by us describes a number of mental processes well and its key aspect – the nature of the mechanisms of extroversion–introversion has been confirmed by neurophysiologists. These findings further support the premise that the accurate simulation of mental processes, including consciousness, is attainable only with quantum computers, where quantum structures and processes integrate with macroscopic, classical structures, and processes.

We demonstrated that such computers must emulate natural systems in design. Furthermore, the extended informational socionic model of the psyche (Model B) we developed offers a comprehensive description of observed aspects of human thought and behavior. This model could underpin the architecture of advanced quantum multiprocessor systems that replicate the structure of mental functions of information metabolism, handling diverse aspects of informational inputs. Our research also revealed that the capacity and development of each function are dictated by the parametric scope of its operational space and the interaction among operational cells. Evidence indicates that these interactions are inherently quantum and feasible within specific quantum systems. Contemporary technologies appear capable of realizing such systems, thereby enabling progress toward replicating human cognitive processes.

References

[1] Y. Kondratenko, A. Shevchenko, Y. Zhukov, G. Kondratenko, O. Striuk, 'Tendencies and Challenges of Artificial Intelligence Development and Implementation', Proceedings of the IEEE International Conference on Intelligent Data Acquisition and Advanced Computing Systems: Technology and Applications, IDAACS, 2023, pp. 221–226, Dortmund, 7-9 September 2023. https://doi.org/10.1109/IDAACS58523.2023.10348800.

[2] Y. Kondratenko, A. Shevchenko, Y Zhukov, V. Slyusar, G. Kondratenko, M. Klymenko, O. Striuk, 'Analysis of the Priorities and Perspectives in Artificial Intelligence Implementation', 2023 13th International Conference on Dependable Systems, Services and Technologies, DESSERT 2023, 2023, Athens, 13–15 October 2023, https://doi.org/10.1109/DESSERT61349.2023.10416432.

[3] A.I. Shevchenko, Y.P. Kondratenko, V.I. Slyusar, I.P. Atamanyuk,, G.V. Kondratenko, T.V. Yeroshenko, 'Analysis of the prospect domains in AI implementation: Nationals, NATO and Ukraine AI strategies. Research Tendencies and Prospect Domains for AI Development and Implementation', 2024, pp. 1–30.

[4] Y. Kondratenko, G. Kondratenko, A. Shevchenko, V. Slyusar, Y. Zhukov, M. Vakulenko, 'Towards Implementing the Strategy of Artificial Intelligence Development: Ukraine Peculiarities', CEUR Workshop Proceedings, 2023, 3513, pp. 106–117.

[5] V. Slyusar, Y. Kondratenko, A. Shevchenko, T. Yeroshenko, 'Some Aspects of Artificial Intelligence Development Strategy for Mobile Technologies', Journal of Mobile Multimedia, 2024, 20(3), pp. 525–554. https://doi.org/10.13052/jmm1550-4646.2031.

[6] Niels Bohr, 'Essays 1932-1957 on atomic physics and human knowledge', Woodbridge, Conn.: Ox Bow Press. 1958.

[7] D. Aerts, J. Broekaert, L. Gabora, S. Sozzo, 'Quantum structure and human thought', Behavioral and Brain Sciences, 2013, 36 (3), pp. 274–276.

[8] D. Aerts, 'Quantum particles as conceptual entities: A possible explanatory framework for quantum theory', Foundations of Science, 2009, (14), pp. 361–411.

[9] A.V. Bukalov, 'Consciousness and physical universe', Physics of consciousness and life, Cosmology and Astrophysics, 2001, 1(1), pp. 5–9. https://physics.socionic.info/index.php/physics/article/view/234.

[10] H. Atmanspacher, T. Filk, H. Romer, 'Quantum zeno features of bistable perception', Biological Cybernetics, 2004, (90), pp. 33–40.

[11] M. Asano, I. Basieva, A. Khrennikov, M. Ohya, I. Yamato, 'Non-Kolmogorovian Approach to the Context-Dependent Systems Breaking the Classical Probability Law', Foundations of Physics, 2013, 43 (7), pp. 895–911.

[12] A.V. Bukalov, 'Consciousness and physical world: the changing states of consciousness and transpersonal psychology', Physics of consciousness and life, Cosmology and Astrophysics, 2001, 1(4), pp. 9–20. https://physics.socionic.info/index.php/physics/article/view/259.

[13] A.V. Bukalov, 'Psychics, living processes and quantum mechanics — a phenomenological approach', Physics of consciousness and life, Cosmology and Astrophysics, 2001, 1(1), pp. 22–32. https://physics.socionic.info/index.php/physics/article/view/236.

[14] A.V. Bukalov, 'On the possible quantum nature of consciousness and psyche', Psychology and socionics of interpersonal relationships', 2017, (9–10), pp. 5–40. https://library.socionic.info/o-vozmozhnoj-kvantovoj-prirode-soznaniya-i-psihiki.

[15] K. Pribram, 'Languages of the brain; experimental paradoxes and principles in neuropsychology', Englewood Cliffs, NJ: Prentice-Hall, 1971.

[16] A.V. Bukalov, 'Problem of consciousness and quantum modeles of mentality', Psychology and socionics of interpersonal relationships',

2016, (11–12), pp. 6–78. https://publishing.socionic.info/index.php /psychology/article/view/2190/2202.
[17] C.M. Caves, C.A. Fuchs, R. Schack, 'Quantum probabilities as Bayesian probabilities', Physical review A, 2002, 65(2), p. 022305.
[18] M. Van den Noort, S. Lim, P. Bosch, 'On the need to unify neuroscience and physics', Neuroimmunology and Neuroinflammation, 2016, (3), pp. 271–273.
[19] J. Busemeyer, P. Bruza, 'Quantum Models of Cognition and Decision', Cambridge: Cambridge University Press, 2012.
[20] P. Bruza, K. Kitto, D. Nelson, C. McEvoy, 'Is there something quantum-like about the human mental lexicon?', Journal of Mathematical Psychology, 2009, 53(5), pp. 362–377.
[21] P. La Mura, 'Projective expected utility', Journal of Mathematical Psychology, 2009, 53(5), pp. 408–414.
[22] J.S. Trueblood, J.R. Busemeyer, 'A quantum probability account of order effects in inference', Cognitive science, 2011, (8), pp. 1518–1552.
[23] D. Widdows, S. Peters, 'Word Vectors and Quantum Logic: Experiments with negation and disjunction', Eighth Mathematics of Language Conference, 2003, pp. 141–154.
[24] A. Tversky, D. Kahneman, 'Extensional versus intuitive reasoning: The conjunction fallacy in probability judgment', Psychological Review, 1983, (90), pp. 293–315.
[25] J.A. Hampton, 'Disjunction of natural concepts', Memory & Cognition, 1988, (16), pp. 579–591.
[26] E. Conte, A. Khrennikov, O. Todarello, R. De Robertis, A. Federici, J.P. Zbilut, 'On the possibility that we think in a quantum mechanical manner: An experimental verification of existing quantum interference effects in cognitive anomaly of Conjunction Fallacy', Chaos and Complexity Letters, 2011 (4), pp. 123–136.
[27] E. Haven, A. Khrennikov, 'Quantum Social Science', Cambridge University Press, 2012.
[28] O. Choustova 'Quantum probability and financial market', Information Sciences, 2009, 179(5), pp. 478–484, https://doi.org/10.1016/j.ins.2008 .07.001.
[29] S.P. Sit'ko, Eu.A. Andreyev, I.S. Dobronravova, 'The Whole as a Result of Self-Organization', Journal of Biological Physics, 1988, (16), p. 71.
[30] I.S. Dobronravova, 'Physics of the alive as a phenomenon of postnonclassical science', Physics of the alive, 2001, 9(1), pp. 85–95.

[31] Herbert Fröhlich, Friedrich Kremer (eds), 'Coherent Excitations in Biological Systems. Proceedings in Life Sciences', Springer-Verlag. 1983. https://doi.org/10.1007/978-3-642-69186-7.

[32] Giovanni Lerario et al. 'Room-temperature superfluidity in a polariton condensate', Nature Physics, 2017, (05 June). https://doi.org/10.1038/nphys414.

[33] E.A. Liberman, 'Molecular quantum computers', Biophysics, (5), 1989.

[34] S. Hameroff, R Penrose, 'Orchestrated reduction of quantum coherence in brain microtubules: A model for consciousness', Mathematics and Computers in Simulation, 1996, 40(3–4), pp. 453-480. https://doi.org/10.1016/0378-4754(96)80476-9.

[35] S. Hameroff, R Penrose, 'Reply to seven commentaries on "Consciousness in the universe: Review of the 'Orch OR' theory"', Physics of Life Reviews, 2014, 11 (1), pp. 94–100. https://doi.org/10.1016/j.plrev.2013.11.013.

[36] R. Penrose, 'Shadows of the Mind: A Search for the Missing Science of Consciousness', Oxford University Press, 1994.

[37] A.V. Bukalov, Modeling the behavior of unicellular organisms and the hypothesis of the elementary cellular quantum of consciousness. Intracellular biocomputers, consciousness and the electromagnetic frame of a living organism', Proc. of XIV Internat. Conf. on Applied Biophysics, Bionics and Biocybernetics, 2021. https://doi.org/10.13140/RG.2.2.22559.23206.

[38] S. Kumar, K. Boone, J. Tuszynski, P.E. Barclay, C. Simon, 'Possible existence of optical communication channels in the brain', Scientific Reports, 2016, (6), p. 36508. https://doi.org/10.1038/srep36508.

[39] J. Von Neumann, 'Mathematische Grundlagen der Quantenmechanik', Berlin: Springer, 1932.

[40] Christian Matthias Kerskens et al. 'Experimental indications of non-classical brain functions', Journal of Physics Communications, 2022. https://doi.org/10.1088/2399-6528/ac94be.

[41] G. Tononi, 'An information integration theory of consciousness', BMC Neuroscience, 2004, 5 (1), p. 42. https://doi.org/10.1186/1471-2202-5-42.

[42] Y. Timsit, S.P. Grégoire, 'Towards the idea of molecular brains', Int J Mol Sci, 2021, 22(21), p. 11868.

[43] W.B.Jr. Miller, A.S. Reber, P. Marshall, F. Baluška, 'Cellular and Natural Viral Engineering in Cognition-Based Evolution', Communicative

& Integrative Biology, 2023, (16), pp. 1. https://doi.org/10.1186/1471-2202-5-4210.1080/19420889.2023.2196145.

[44] G. Scheler, 'Logarithmic distributions prove that intrinsic learning is Hebbian', F1000Research, 2017, 6:1222. https://doi.org/10.12688/f1000research.12130.2.

[45] A.V. Bukalov, 'Evolutionary development of the human brain and psyche and the rate of mutations in the genome', Physics of consciousness and life, Cosmology and Astrophysics, 2019, (3-4), pp. 5–10. https://physics.socionic.info/index.php/physics/article/view/520.

[46] A.V. Bukalov, 'Intracellular biocomputers, consciousness and the electromagnetic frame of a living organism', Proc. of XIV Internat. Conf. on Applied Biophysics, Bionics and Biocybernetics, 2021. https://www.researchgate.net/publication/360261868_Intracellular_biocomputers_consciousness_and_the_electromagnetic_frame_of_a_living_organism.

[47] L. Feuillet, H. Dufour, J. Pelletier, 'Brain of a white-collar worker', Lancet, 2007, 370 (9583), p. 262. https://doi.org/10.1186/1471-2202-5-4210.1016/S0140-6736(07)61127-1.

[48] M.-C. Cammaerts, R. Cammaerts, 'Are ants (Hymenoptera, Formicidae) capable of self-recognition?', Journal of Science, 2015, 5(7), pp. 521–532.

[49] A.V. Bukalov, 'Potential of personality and the mysteries of human relationships', Chernaja Belka & International institute of Socionics, 2009.

[50] G.M. Chaichenko, P.D. Kharchenko, 'Physiology highest nervous activities', Vischa schkola, Kyiv, 1981.

[51] C.G. Jung, 'Psychological Types' in Collected Works of C.G. Jung, vol. 6. NJ: Princeton University Press, Princeton, 1921.

[52] A.V. Bukalov, 'Interaction of Informational Metabolism Functions and Its Quantum-Mechanical Analogs', Socionics, mentology and personality psychology, 1995, (3), pp. 20–21. https://publishing.socionic.info/index.php/socionics/article/view/1368/1264.

[53] A.V. Bukalov, 'Type of information metabolism as a psychophysiological system. Research review. Experimental confirmation of the holographic model', 37 International Conference on Socionics "Psycho-Informational Technologies, Personnel Management and Personality Psychology", 2021, Kyiv, Ukraine. https://doi.org/10.13140/RG.2.2.25302.46400.

[54] G.I. Shulgina, 'Synchronization of EEG rhythms and holographic theory of memory', Journal of higher nervous activities, 1997, 47(5), pp. 878–889.

[55] M.E. Sandomirsky, 'The Psychological Type and Functional Asymmetry of Brain Hemispheres. To the Question on Socionic Functions Brain Localization', Socionics, mentology and personality psychology, 2000, (5), pp. 25–28. https://publishing.socionic.info/index.php/socionics/article/view/795/619.
[56] V.D. Yermak, 'Interaction of Human Mentality with Surrounding World', Socionics, mentology and personality psychology, 1997, (5), pp. 22–32. https://publishing.socionic.info/index.php/socionics/article/view/1484/2056.
[57] A.V. Bukalov, 'The Neuronal Structures and the Informational Metabolism Functions', Psychology and socionics of interpersonal relationships, 2005, (7), pp. 5–6.
[58] N.E. Krivo, Yu.A. Krivo, 'Physiological experimental scientific method for research the functional human's system and the socionic aspects of the functions for using in psychology, medicine, health technologies, staff management', Psychology and socionics of interpersonal relationships, 2017, (5–6), pp. 39–42. https://publishing.socionic.info/index.php/psychology/article/view/2279/2313.
[59] G.A. Popova, Yu.A. Krivo, N.E. Krivo, 'Complementarity of the physiological method by Yu.A.Krivo and the aspect-dichotomous method by Bukalov-Karpenko: convergence of results', Psychology and socionics of interpersonal relationships, 2018, (9–10), pp. 5–12.
[60] Yu.A. Krivo, 'Model of TIM, integrating settings by E. Berne-A. Bukalov, DCNH system by V. Gulenko-A. Bukalov and physiological characteristics', Socionics, mentology and personality psychology, 2019, (2–3), pp. 20–32. https://publishing.socionic.info/index.php/socionics/article/view/2531/2554.
[61] H.J. Eysenck, 'The Biological Basis of Personality', Springfield, Illinois, 1967.
[62] S. Roccas, L. Sagiv, S.H. Schwartz, A. Knafo, 'The Big Five Personality Factors and Personal Values', Personality and Social Psychology Bulletin, 2002, 28(6), pp. 789–801. https://doi.org/10.1177/0146167202289008.
[63] I. Trofimova, 'Observer Bias: An Interaction of Temperament Traits with Biases in the Semantic Perception of Lexical Material', PLoS ONE 2014, 9(1), p. e85677. https://doi.org/10.1371/journal.pone.0085677.
[64] A.A. Cherninsky, N.G. Piskorskaya, I.G. Zima, S.A. Krizhanovsky, N.E. Makarchuk, 'Individual/Typological Peculiarities of EEG Rearrangements in Humans Related to the Analysis of Olfactory Information: Role of Extroversion/Introversion', Neurophysiology,

2010, 42(5), pp. 70–77. http://dspace.nbuv.gov.ua/handle/123456789/68330.

[65] A. Augustinavichute, 'The Socion', 'Socionics, mentology and personality psychology', 1996, (4-5).

[66] A.V. Bukalov, O.B. Karpenko, 'Socionics: the effective theory of the mental structure and the interpersonal relations forecasting', Proc. of Conf. of the British and East European Psychology Group "Psychology in the new Europe: methodology and funding", p. 28, 2005. https://www.scribd.com/document/2020585497141/Socionics.

[67] Y. Sikirda, T. Shmelova, 'Socionic and Sociometric Diagnosting of Air Navigation System's Operators', Socio-Technical Decision Support in Air Navigation Systems: Emerging Research and Opportunities, 2018, pp. 108–137.

[68] A.V. Bukalov, O.B. Karpenko, 'Psychoinformational technologies in effective management', Management and personnel: psychology of management, socionics and sociology, 2013, (3), pp. 5–9. https://publishing.socionic.info/index.php/management/article/view/570/482.

[69] A.V. Bukalov, O.B. Karpenko, 'Socionics and effective management', Management and personnel: psychology of management, socionics and sociology, 2014, (8), pp. 5–10. https://publishing.socionic.info/index.php/management/article/view/468/404.

[70] A. Bukalov, 'Modes of psycho-informational interaction of a human operator with technical, information and intellectual systems', Artificial Intelligence, 2023, 28(1), pp. 88-92. https://doi.org/10.15407/jai2023.01.088.

[71] R. Duro et al., 'Advances in intelligent robotics and collaborative automation', River Publishers, Aalborg, 2015. https://doi.org/10.13052/rp-9788793237049.

[72] R. Blutner, E. Hochnadel, 'Two qubits for CG Jung's theory of personality', 'Cognitive Systems Research', 2010, 11 (3), pp. 243–259. https://doi.org/10.1016/j.cogsys.2009.12.002.

[73] A.V. Bukalov, 'On the Function of Consciousness in Socionics', Socionics, mentology and personality psychology, 1996, (6), pp. 10–11. https://socionic.info/ru/t/as696.html.

[74] A.V. Bukalov, 'Psychoinformational environment structuring phenomenon: a hierarchy of human attention, memory and thinking volume', Socionics, mentology and personality psychology, 1999, (2), pp. 3–7. https://socionic.info/ru/t/magic.html.

9

Cognitive Methodology as an AI Tool for Investigation of the Phenomenological Ground of Melt Electromagnetic Treatment

Y. Zaporozhets and A. Ivanov

Institute of Pulse Processes and Technologies of the NAS of Ukraine, Ukraine
E-mail: yurii.zaporozhets@nuos.edu.ua; artiomsan@gmail.com

Abstract

This chapter is devoted to using artificial intelligence (AI) methods to improve the efficiency of various technological and production processes, particularly in the foundry industry. Many experiments have ascertained that the melt treatment with electric current (ECT) in certain modes achieves an effective improvement of structural parameters and quality of castings. Still, the lack of a holistic theory of the processes occurring in the melt during ECT and a clear understanding of the physical mechanisms of the current influence on structure formation does not allow to predict confidently the results of treatment and stably reproduce ECT modes that provide favorable conditions for the structure formation of castings.

Implementation of this promising technology of melt treatment requires a deep study of the elements' interaction mechanisms of the weakly structured complex system "ECT-of-Melt" (CSEM) at all levels of its hierarchical relationships and chains of interactions; however, the development of knowledge in this poorly studied domain of metallurgy and its practical application for the creation of automated control systems for ECT modes cannot be realized without using information technologies (IT) and artificial intelligence methods.

Under such conditions, one of the most important AI approaches was used to study the phenomenological ground of the CSEM – the cognitive

DOI: 10.1201/9788743800989-9

methodology of modeling, which is based on structuring knowledge in a specific subject domain (SD). Ontological analysis of the SD using taxonomic models ensured the creation of an ordered information platform for constructing a cognitive model (CM) of the CSEM. The CSEM CM has several essential peculiarities; in particular, a multi-level hierarchical structure that covers more than a hundred concepts – vertices of the corresponding graph and about 2000 edges-connections. Such a CM cannot be used in computer models in the form of a conventional cognitive map (CMp). Therefore, the connection matrix of the primary CM was subjected to decomposition into a set of partial adjacency matrices. On their base, a hierarchical network scheme of interconnections between concepts was developed. The derived partial matrices are presented as formulaic notations, which reflect the content of the CMp corresponding to certain algorithms of machine analysis of Big Data in the modeled system. CM CSEM is supplemented with an electronic catalog of codified concepts and a register of links between them with the specification of influence functions. The novelty in the presented KM consists in conforming of the tact sequence of the concepts interaction at different hierarchical levels due to the introduction of the factor of tact duration of the processes into the properties of the influence functions. The result of the presented development is the completion of the set of AI tools with the help of which it is possible to compile a wide range of algorithms for the cognitive study of the phenomenological basis of ECT, targeted at revealing the most effective modes of ECT of melts and obtaining high-quality castings.

Keywords: Artificial intelligence, cognitive modeling, melt electromagnetic treatment.

9.1 Introduction

One of the most pressing problems of foundry production is the quality assurance of cast products. Defects arising in castings due to improper adjustment of the production process lead to huge losses. To prevent them and ensure the proper quality of castings, various approaches are used.

On the one hand, constant, continuous monitoring of production process parameters is being introduced to identify factors that lead to defects, and corresponding corrections of technological protocols and modes are performed. Nowadays, for the realization of such tasks, it is necessary to attract the opportunities of information technologies and methods of computational intelligence [1].

On the other hand, a powerful factor that can ensure the improvement of casting quality and reduce the share of defective products is the improvement of metallurgical technologies by actively influencing the internal processes at the beginning of the formation of castings, since their basic structural properties are laid at the stage of the melt and in the subsequent solidification obey the laws of heredity [2]. In recent times, one of the measures of this kind has become the use of preliminary treatment of metal in the liquid state by physical and chemical means, in particular, by energy impacts [3]. It was revealed that from the approved methods of such a technique, the promising one is the processing of the melt by direct passage of electric current through it. Many experiments have shown that in certain modes of such treatment, the effective improvement of structural performance and quality of castings is achieved [4].

Along with this, electric current treatment (ECT) of melt has a unique specificity, since the passage of electric current in the liquid–metal medium excites conjugated electromagnetic, hydrodynamic, and thermoacoustic phenomena that affect the deep levels of the structural structure of the melt, having a complex effect on it, i.e., the ECT process is essentially multiphysical and multifactorial [5]. Controlling such a process to form a favorable casting structure is a very complex engineering task that requires a deep understanding of the internal content and interrelationship of phenomena that occur in the melt during its processing. All the more urgent is the setting of such a task for conditions of mass production, which requires the maximum level of automation of production processes.

However, at the current level of knowledge in this area, it ought to be stated not only the absence of a holistic theory of the processes occurring in the melt during ECT but even a clear understanding of the physical mechanisms that cause some cooperative phenomena in the liquid metal, which eventually lead to the formation of an improved structure of the casting when it solidifies [5]. Since the internal volume of a high-temperature melt is physically inaccessible for direct measurement of local parameters during processing before its solidification, experimental data on the results of energetic effects on the melt can be obtained only ex post facto – by analyzing the structural properties of castings [6]. Therefore, the research practice has in fact only fragmentary sets of quantitative data on the parameters of melt treatment modes and descriptive-numerical indicators of the quality of the obtained castings.

The stated circumstances are the reasons for the fact that confident prediction of processing results and stable reproduction of ECT modes providing conditions for favorable structure formation of castings have not yet been achieved. Therefore, the introduction of ETC of the melt into the technical protocol of mass production of castings at this stage is not possible, as a result of which progress in the development of algorithms and creation of automation tools for foundry technologies are hampered.

9.2 Problem Statement, Objectives, and Grounds of System Analysis of the Melt ECT

9.2.1 Purpose of the study and problems of analysis of ECT processes

A. Problem Statement: In the above conditions, the only accessible methodology for determining the influence of external setting influences on the controlled parameters of the melt and the final result of its processing is the simulation modeling and computational methods of analysis. However, there is hardly any reason to count on the creation of a universal, all-encompassing computer model for solving this problem. Therefore, the strategy of its solution consists in performing decomposition of the problem, i.e., dividing the complex problem into simple (monophysical) partial problems and finding their solutions step by step and/or in parallel, ensuring conjugation by congruent data in accordance with the logic of cause–effect relations of the described multiphysical process [7, 8]. Based on this approach, it is seen as an opportunity *to build a hierarchical network scheme (model) of interconnected computational procedures that adequately reflects the phenomenological content of melt ECT processes and to create an ordered information platform for computer simulation of various melt processing scenarios and modes. This is precisely what the authors see as the* goal of the presented study.

It is obvious that the creation of a simulation model of such a uniquely complicated system of interrelated phenomena, which is inherent in the melt ECT process, requires a comprehensive system analysis of the factors that have (and even hypothetically can have) an impact on the processes of casting structure formation. Then the totality of theoretical information and empirical data on the melt ECT processes, as well as the conditions for the formation of a favorable structure of castings, in the context of system analysis should be considered as an information field of the subject domain (SD) with a poorly structured knowledge base (KB), for the development and enrichment of which, obviously, should be used a diverse arsenal of methods of cognitive analysis, artificial intelligence, and computer information technologies [9, 10].

However, to apply this technique, it is necessary to form proper prerequisites, the most important of which consists in the systematization of the knowledge base of the specified SD and representing the information that is contained in it in forms adapted to computer processing technologies. As a rational way for implementing such tasks, the methodology of *ontology* constructing based on the semantic context of the concepts of the specified subject domains has proved itself [11, 12]. In particular, *engineering and computational ontologies* serve as a means of formal modeling of the structure of the studied systems, i.e., the *entities* (elements) constituting them and the *relations* (links) between them, which are revealed as a result of observation, testing, and analysis [13], and are focused on automated interpretation and processing of information [14].

It is this approach that the authors used in the work [6], in which an ontology is constructed based on the natural logic of *phenomenological interrelationships* of processes and phenomena occurring during ECT, and the application of which for considering of the posed problem seems to be quite appropriate.

Being a structured representation of information in a particular SD, each ontology is based on *source data* stored in some information database. The ontology model serves as the means of transforming this raw data into *knowledge*.

B. Initial background information on ECT: Guided by the above arguments, as the initial information parameters defining the SD of the ECT technology, it should be stated the basic notion of the melt treatment processes and quality indicators of the casting, which are presented below [4–6, 8]. The ontology thus compiled, in turn, will serve as the ground for the development of a cognitive model [14–16] of a large-scale platform for computer simulation of the set of melt ECT processes and formation of castings structure.

First of all, it should be pointed out that all the most important properties of castings are predetermined by the characteristics of the casting structure formed in the process of melt solidification and the formation of the crystalline state.

The structure of the casting is characterized in technical terms by a certain set of indicators that reflect the quality of castings [5,17]:

(a) grain content (grain shape factor, grain boundaries, phases);
(b) average values and size variation of the structure elements (at macro- and micro-levels);

(c) porosity (defined in points from 1 to 5: the number and distribution of pores);
(d) homogeneity (crystal sizes, macroscopic homogeneity, etc.), and so on.

These indicators are determined by the results of metallographic studies of cast samples and expressed by the corresponding quantitative values.

For each of these properties, there are many root causes, often unidentified as reliable scientific facts; however, despite the huge amount of experimental data accumulated by researchers and technologists over the years, there are actually no orderly conclusions about the consequences of their influence on the structure of castings.

In this regard, when considering the indicated problem, it should be taken as a fundamental premise the fact that by its very nature, the formation of any particular structure of the casting is a multifactorial process; meanwhile, a unified theory of crystallization of metals and alloys currently does not exist [18]. Therefore, predicting the results of the spontaneous process of casting structure formation under certain conditions at the current level of scientific knowledge about its internal mechanisms can only be of an evaluative (presumptive) nature.

Nevertheless, many years of industrial experience and persistent experimental studies have established some possibilities for a targeted influence on the conditions of structure formation during the solidification of the melt; in particular, a fairly effective way, as previously indicated, revealed the treatment of the melt with electric current [4, 5]. However, the results of treatment appear only ex post facto, i.e., after solidification of the casting, due to the known effect of "inheritance of structural information in metallic materials during melting or cooling" [19].

The objectives of processing follow from the above set of quality indicators and, as a rule, pursue several goals: (a) melt refining (removal of non-metallic inclusions and undesirable microelements); (b) melt degassing (removal of dissolved gases and formed bubbles); (c) destruction of intermetallic compounds; (d) melt homogenization in the macro-volume. In general, the main objective of such a treatment is to promote the synchronous formation of the smallest possible crystallization grains and their more uniform distribution in the casting volume [8, 20].

Experiments on electrocurrent treatment of the melt were carried out on the stand, the block diagram of which is presented in Figure 9.1 [5].

Processing was performed with the help of electrode systems of various compositions and configurations using different types of current: direct, alternating, and pulse [3, 4, 6]. By the very setting of these experiments, it is

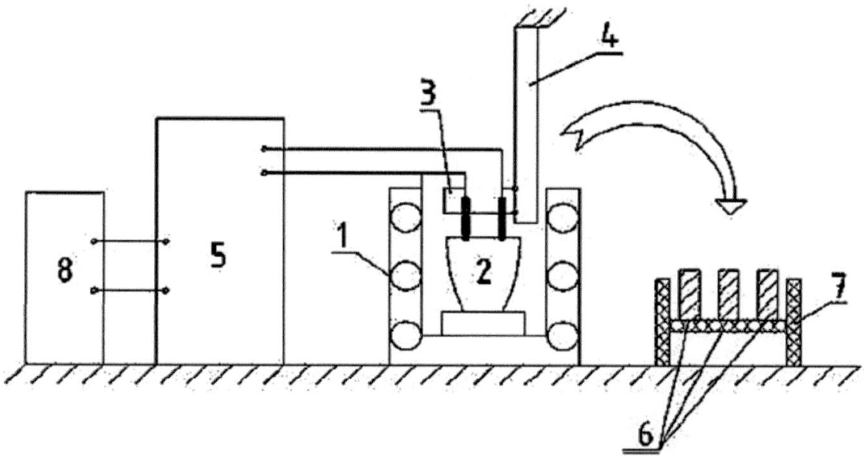

Figure 9.1 The block diagram of the experimental bench for the ECT of Melt: 1 – melting furnace; 2 – graphite crucible with melt; 3 – electrode system; 4 – system for dipping electrodes in melt; 5 – current source; 6 – metal molds for casting the melt; 7 – heating furnace; 8 – control and monitoring system.

clear that this treatment method is a complex process of interaction of several physical fields in the liquid metal medium, covering poorly studied aspects of their influence on the state and kinetics of the molten metal system (MMS) at different levels of its structural composition [5].

When the current is spreading in the volume of melt, a whole range of interrelated physical phenomena is excited in it at the macro-level such as the generation of a magnetic field and the vortex electromotive force (EMF), that cause the appearance of volumetric electromagnetic forces and magneto-hydrodynamic flows, due to which the spatial distribution of fields and flows acquire a marked inhomogeneous character. As a consequence, the mixing of layers, redistribution of temperature fields, and excitation of thermoacoustic waves, as well as changes in the conductivity and viscosity of the medium and migration of macro- and micro-inclusions occur in the liquid melt matrix [4–6].

Along with this, an essential role in the ECT processes is performed by the interaction of objects at the level of microscopic and mesoscopic structures, which represent an open thermodynamically unstable system, where under the action of the applied field and collective movement of charged particles, there arise fluctuations of energy states of ensembles of microparticles, which leads to changes in its thermodynamic parameters, Gibbs free energy, and entropy at all levels of the structural building of MMS (electronic, atomic, cluster). The inhomogeneity of the fields promotes the strengthening of natural fluctuations of cluster formations (sibotaxis) [4–6], due to which the terms are created for the emergence of nuclei of grain structure and local thermodynamic instability zones are formed – dissipative structures that prone to self-organization, the development of which eventually leads to the formation of a particular crystalline structure of the casting.

9.2.2 ECT as a poorly structured complex system

The given brief characterization of the content of ECT action clearly shows that when electric current is spreading in the melt, *at various structural levels* in MMS the very complicated complex of interrelated and inseparable physical processes takes place with the participation of many qualitatively different in-nature elements. Therefore, in contrast to big systems, which include a significant number of *single-type* elements with *homogeneous* connections, the considered MMC during the ECT, containing a large number of *elements of different types* with *heterogeneous* and, often, *not fully defined internal connections*, from the standpoint of system analysis with full reason, should be attributed to the category of "complex systems" [15, 21–23].

Such "complex systems," by virtue of their very composition, have several features that predestine significant difficulties for system analysis, first of all, for formalization and computer representation of their internal relations. In particular, for "complex systems" in some cases, due to the quantitative inexpressibility of some characteristics or uncertainty of goals and management criteria, it is not possible to build a mathematical model that adequately describes their properties and behavior [22, 23]. Therefore, in the models of such systems, there is not enough information for effective management [24, 25].

However, the universal exhaustive characteristic (definition) of "complex systems" in the system theory is not yet developed.

Nevertheless, it seems reasonable to understand *a complex system* as a system that consists of a set of interacting components (constituent subsystems), each of which, performing its certain functions in interaction with other components, confers the complex system *new properties that are absent at the subsystem level and cannot be reduced to the properties of the subsystem level* [26]. Such systems are characterized not only by the availability of a large number of elements, links, and interactions between them, but also, and that is essential, by a *multilayered hierarchical structure* formed by these elements. Under such conditions, even weak mediated links can significantly complicate the behavior of the system, which becomes difficult to predict, and thus – poorly controllable [15, 22, 27]. In particular, the paper [28] shows the reference chains of the mentioned links.

However, such qualities for regular technology are *unacceptable*, as they create *conditions of uncertainty of production activity results and commercial risks*. Therefore, the introduction of the above promising technology of melt processing requires not just the accumulation of a wide empirical information on the effectiveness of ECT modes and statistical processing of the experimental data base, but a deep study of the mechanisms of interaction between the structural elements of the *complex system* "ECT of melts" (CSEM) at all levels of its hierarchical relationships and chains of interactions, i.e., in essence – its *research*. It is obvious that the development of knowledge in this poorly studied area of metallurgy and its practical application for the creation of automated systems for ECT modes control cannot be realized without the use of information technologies (IT) [29] and artificial intelligence (AI) methods, in particular, knowledge discovery in database (KDD) and data mining (DM), Big Data analysis (BDA), deep and machine learning, and others [30–33].

Along with that, for productive use of the mentioned AI tools, it is necessary to have the ordered codified information arrays, whereas at the present stage, the feature of the considered category of systems (CSEM) in its natural form is virtually *unstructured*, or at least *poorly structured* agglomerate of descriptions of separate ECT aspects, expressed by *qualitative* features and dependencies, as well as fragmentary sets of *quantitative* data on the parameters of processing modes p and quality indicators of the castings obtained [5, 6]. As a rule, in poorly structured Big Data arrays on CSEM functioning, the mentioned dependencies, indicators, and relations between them are poorly amenable to numerical estimations, which causes *uncertainties* in establishing essential links between structural elements of a complex system and important regularities of their interaction that may remain unrevealed.

9.3 Methodological Framework of the CSEM Study

9.3.1 Basis of cognitive methodology of CSEM research: structuring of knowledge

A. Objectives and methods of knowledge structuring for CSEM research: The process of studying poorly structured systems aims to reveal their inherent uncertainties and better understand their properties. In this regard, *disclosure of uncertainty* is understood as a process of *cognitive* *structuring* of existing knowledge and filling gaps and breaks between its incomplete fragments. Moreover, without the development of an adequate model of a *complex system* and its analysis, it is very difficult to predict the results of its regular functioning and management [21, 27, 34]. This clearly implies an extremely *urgent task of intellectual processing* of the accumulated information array of data on the characteristics and properties of CSEM in order to create premises for the development of a large-scale platform for simulation modeling the totality of the processes of the melt ECT and structure formation of castings. Considering the above, a natural approach to the implementation of the designated task seems to be the application of one of the most important approaches in AI – *cognitive modeling methodology* [34, 35].

For applying the above methodology to the problem of CSEM research, next initial premises should be specified:

- systematization of Big Data arrays on the melt ECT modes and indicators of castings quality obtained due to processing,
- interpretation of existing ideas about the phenomenology of processes occurring in the melt during ECT and subsequent structure formation in the cooling casting.

Thus, the procedure under consideration is based on two information blocks: DBEM (Database on Melts ECT Modes) and PMEP (Phenomenological Map of Melt ECT Processes).

The first of them, DBEM, is a multidimensional set of numerical values of parameters of ECT modes and verbal-numerical estimations [36, 37] of casting quality indicators. The structure and methodology of its formation are described extensively in the works of the authors [6, 38]. However, in the context of this presentation, this block appears as a subject domain of multidimensional observations [39], which is to be classified by attributes associated with the semantic categories of the phenomenological block; i.e., in essence, it is an information source for it.

The second block, PMEP, is a *formalized knowledge base* (*KB*) *on the phenomenological content of melt ECT and structure formation of casting*, compiled based on existing theoretical notions, as well as the interpretation of hypotheses concerning uncertain regularities. Such a KB should serve as a ground for the unification of various mathematical tools used in the specified SD, as well as the information environment for the application of the innovative *template-modular system* of computer modeling of ECT processes (SCM- ECT) and data processing presented in the works of the authors [6, 38]. Actually, the *formation of PMEP is a necessary stage* in the *task of CSEM research* related to the construction of systems for processing large data arrays (Big Data analysis – BDA) in information networks, as well as the storage and processing of information in the KB with the use of computer technologies.

Since the ET technology is a multifactor complex of multiphysics processes, the investigation of CSEM is, basically, *multivariate* in nature. For researching systems of this kind, different approaches are used, among which it seems rational to use a *two-level technique* [40].

The first level of the study provides a qualitative, structural, and goal-oriented analysis of the system using *semantic modeling* (SM) methods [41, 42]. The objectives of SM are to identify the architecture of the system, to reveal the factors that exert the most significant influence on its properties and target functions, to establish cause-and-effect relationships between them, and to determine the options for decomposition of the system without losing its authenticity.

At the second level, quantitative analysis of state parameters and target functions of the system is performed, as well as forecasting of their evolution depending on the setting and control factors by *computer simulation* based on mathematical models of physical processes in the system.

Thus, the IT support environment for research of complex systems includes the tools for *ontological, cognitive, and numerical (mathematical)* modeling [22, 40, 43].

B. *Ontology models of the subject domain*, or simply *ontology*, are formalized specifications of concepts (entities) connected by various relations that characterize a certain knowledge domain by means of a *conceptual schema*. As a rule, it contains *machine-interpretable* formulations of relevant concepts and relations between them [10, 44]. The formal structure of knowledge representation in ontologies allows one to essentially simplify their computer processing. Therefore, ontologies are convenient to use when constructing KBs in different applications, including expert systems [45, 46].

Virtually all ontology models contain *classes* (concepts, notions, objects), concept *properties*, and *relations* between concepts (*links*, *influences*, dependencies), but there is no single methodology for compiling SD ontology [10, 44]. In the most general form, an ontology is formally defined as a set:

$$O = \{C, A, R, T, F, D\}, \tag{9.1}$$

where $C = \{C_1, C_2, ..., C_K\}$ is a set of classes (concepts) of the subject domain, A is a set of attributes describing the features of concepts and relations, R is a set of relations between concepts, T is a set of standard types of attribute values, F is a set of interpretation functions defined on concepts and/or relations, and D is a set of individual instances for a particular class [13].

Notation (9.1) may be varied depending on the type of SD and the interpretation of the ontology. From the above, it is clear that the form of representation of any *ontology* is a classification structure – *taxonomy*, and its content is determined by the *semantics* of the subject domain that it dissects. *Taxonomy (taxonomic model)* is a classification of objects of some set by arranging them into groups and subgroups (categories, classes) according to the similarity principle in accordance with established traits (criteria) [47, 48].

Taxonomies can be represented by graphs, the vertices of which are taxonomic units (*taxa*) – generalized notions corresponding to the SD under consideration. The topology of such taxonomic models characterizes the logical composition of classification features and, as a rule, is ordered in the form of *facet*, *hierarchical*, or *combined facet-hierarchical* structures. At the same time, each set or array in the ontology (9.1) is formally a set of classification traits of distinct taxonomic models [48]. Therefore, a taxonomy can also be written using a set-theoretic representation of the form (9.1) according to its topology.

Thus, facet structures, in which the classifiable set is subdivided according to several independent and equal features, are disordered:

$$\Pi = \{\Pi_n\}_{n=1}^{N} \tag{9.2a}$$

in hierarchical structures, sets of classification attributes are ordered according to the principle of subordination between elements (they are called tuples):

$$\Pi = \langle\Pi_n\rangle_{n=1}^{N}; \tag{9.2b}$$

in combined structures, several (more than one) classification attributes are allocated at one hierarchy level, with nested tuples providing the possibility of describing the subordination of hierarchies:

$$\Pi = \left\langle \cdots \{\Pi_n\}_{n=1}^{N} \cdots \right\rangle. \tag{9.2c}$$

Due to the simplicity and convenience of this approach, taxonomies, supplemented with quantitative characteristics of classified object properties, have become widespread for building models and *taxonomic analysis* of the effectiveness of the organization's activities, as well as opportunities for the development of enterprises and industries, social and communal structures, engineering, and technical and management systems by means of specified *taxonomic indicators* [49, 50, 51].

Thus, taxonomic models in the form of an ordered set of objects connected by relations, which can be expressed by quantitative or verbal-numerical estimates, represent a type of *mathematical model* built on the basis of graph-semantic description [48].

C. Cognitive modeling of complex systems: The development of this approach for solving poorly structured problems of complex systems has led to the development of the concept of building a *cognitive model (CM)* of the knowledge domain in the form of a graph with vertices-concepts connected by arcs with a given "weight" reflecting the degree of influence. But the most important thing in this model, which fundamentally distinguishes it from the usual taxonomy, is the depiction of *cause-and-effect* links between concepts [52, 53, 54]. In this form, it is possible to describe the SD in a sufficiently complete and *meaningful* way, so it is actively used in practice to study the possibilities of solving specific problems actualized in a particular field of knowledge [54].

Thus, in general, *"cognitive modeling of a complex system" is understood as a way to analyze the processes of its functioning and interaction with the external environment by building an ontology of the relevant knowledge domain in the form of a taxonomic model reflecting cause-and-effect relationships and mutual influence of the objects of this system, including interaction with the environment.*

Cognitive modeling of complex systems belongs to the class of simulation modeling [34]. Mathematically, the simplest of cognitive models are causal diagrams, which are called cognitive maps (CMp) [54]. In other words, cognitive maps are the *kinds of mathematical models* for the formalized description of problem situations or poorly structured complex systems of the material sphere (in the broad sense), to which specific *algorithms of computational operations* that reproduce the so-called "digital twins" of the modeled system are put into correspondence [55, 56].

It is appropriate to notice that the term "cognitive model" originated in the field of computer science for processing and solving intellectual problems, due to which it is usually considered a *computational model* used for clarifying the process of decisions of such kind [57]. Therefore, the above interpretation is quite natural and explicitly leads to the integration of ideas about the physical (material) content of CM with intellectual procedures of processing structured information objects by machine methods with the help of the corresponding mathematical apparatus.

The structure of a cognitive map as a causal network can be represented as a directed graph and its corresponding adjacency matrix or connection (relationship) matrix. The classical form of a cognitive map in the form of a graph is [15, 22, 56]:

$$G = \langle V, E\rangle ;\ V = \{v_i\}, i = 1, 2....k;\ E = \{(v_i, v_j)\} = \{e_{i,j}\}, \qquad (9.3)$$

where V – concepts, a finite set of vertices of the cognitive map; E – a set of arcs $(v_i, v_j) = e_{i,j}$, connecting vertices v_i and v_j, which reflect the relation of influence of a conceptv_i on v_j, specifying a set of cause–effect links between them. If, as a result of this influence, there is a consistent change in the concept-cause and concept-effect, then the influence is considered positive, and if the changes are opposite – negative. If there is no interrelation between the changes of concepts, the influence is considered neutral.

The set of values $e_{i,j} \in E$ forms the relationship matrix of the cognitive map G with fixed element values $[-1;\ 0;\ +1\ ]$, unlike a square adjacency matrix of the graph A_G, which only shows the existence of links:

$$A_G = \{a_{ij}\} = \begin{cases} 1, \text{ if } v_i \text{ is associated with } v_j \\ 0, \text{ otherwise} \end{cases}. \qquad (9.4)$$

Such a model corresponds to a well-structured complex system in which the essential dependencies are clearly expressed "quantitatively," which means that the behavior of such a system is defined by deterministic scenarios. Therefore, the CM of such a system in terms of the analysis and prediction of events can be considered a kind of protocol for the execution of computational procedures of behavioral scenarios in computer simulation.

At the same time, in many complex systems, the influence relations between concepts may not have sufficient certainty; moreover, some of the links in the model may not even be identified, i.e., introduced hypothetically on the basis of empirical data indicating the probability of their existence. The cognitive model of such a system is characterized as a fuzzy cognitive model, which corresponds to a *fuzzy cognitive map* (FCM) [58]. The FCM is an extension of the CM concept, in which *coefficients of the relationship* between concepts $f_{ij}$are introduced instead of fixed relations (9.4); these coefficients can take the values of a fuzzy set variable in the interval $[-1, 1]$

or an *influence intensity function*:

$$f\{v_i, v_j, e_{ij}\}. \tag{9.5}$$

During the process of setting up and calibrating the FCM, the values f_{ij} can be adjusted, in which case the FCM turns out to be similar to a neural network that is subjected to training [45, 46]. The above procedure is designated for performing dynamic analysis (impulse modeling) of a complex system and has a rather complicated algorithmic architecture, but its consideration and application is beyond the scope of this study.

9.3.2 Cognitive model of CSEM and peculiarities of its construction

9.3.2.1 Formation of the ontological base of the CSEM cognitive model

A. Formation of the cognitive model and cognitive map of any SD involves the following procedures [60]:

- defining a list of concepts based on: (a) the existing theoretical knowledge base of the SD; (b) a concerted list of objects, factors, and events identified by expert opinions; (c) generalization of statistically reliable experimental data;
- determination of causality (influence) relations between each pair of concepts; in particular, they may be relations of competition, subordination, or interaction;
- construction of a cognitive map;
- other procedures that are specific to FCM but are not considered within the scope of the stated problem.

The defining of concepts and relations between them is the basis for the construction of a cognitive model, as well as a fundamental link in cognitive analysis; therefore, it is necessary to emphasize the extreme importance of a *reasonable definition of cognitive attributes* [57] in the task of constructing a *cognitive basis for the formation of a unified ordered mathematical apparatus* for computer modeling of ECT processes, designed to identify and verify the profound relationships between the parameters of processing modes and factors affecting structure formation, as well as the quality indicators of castings.

According to the above, concepts are divided into categories consistent with the role that they play in the overall structure of CM [61, 62]:

- *targeted*, the values of which should be brought to the required state (or approached to it as close as possible);
- external or *adjusting*, the values of which can be influenced by factors external to the system;
- controlled or *setting*, the values of which are controllable unmediated by the operator;
- internal or *transmitting*, the values of which are not subject to direct control by the operator, are formed spontaneously according to changes in the values of the cause concepts and embody the transfer of influences (impacts) through chains of links from setting and adjusting concepts to targeted ones.

At the same time, it will be pertinent to the concepts of all categories to subdivide accordingly with the natural essence of physical phenomena that they represent into three types: subjects, occurrences, and attributes.

Subjects are subjective entities of tangible nature in a stable form. Let us denote this category by the symbol "***Sub***."

Occurrences are objective entities of dynamic nature in the form of temporary formation in the natural milieu. For this category, we will introduce the symbolic designation "***Occ***."

Attributives are notional entities of a semantic or analytic nature. They define, in one form or another, phenomena, as well as properties and qualities of objects, in particular, their physical parameters, which affect the nature of interaction between objects. This category of concepts is designated by the symbol "***Atr***."

The proposed differentiation of concept functional categories can be useful for comparative analysis of CM [36, 60] and investigation of the influence of certain factors when conducting computational experiments by impulse modeling of model development scenarios [34, 56].

B. The *immanent feature* of the systematization of the CSEM subject domain conditioned by the technological scheme of the ECT, which predetermines the composition (list) of its CM concepts, consists in the fact that at the ontological level it (SD) is naturally subdivided into three separate structural branches of the CSEM model: Reactor (*R*) – Melt (*M*) – Casting (*C*). Such subdivision is fairly conforming with the semantic principle of defining *classes* of objects (instances) and at the same time provides actual harmonization with the specified categories of CM concepts, namely:

- the branch *R* is put into correspondence to classes of adjusting and setting concepts;

– the branch M is corresponding with classes of transmitting concepts;
– branch C embodies classes of targeted concepts.

The classes of the SD-CSEM ontological structure are determined by the settings of the initial information (Section 9.2.1.2.). Based on this information, a *semantic model* [42] was compiled in the form of a graph of CSEM *metaontology*, which is shown in Figure 9.2, where, for clarity, the role of vertices of the graph is performed by table cells. The shaded arrows conventionally indicate the direction of influence transfer from adjusting and setting concepts to targeted concepts, and the wide arrow corresponds to the connections of setting concepts of class R to material objects of class M, and the thin arrow indicates the connection of setting concepts from R with phenomena from class M. According to the described scheme of the functional differentiation of concept categories, the cells are colored in the colors of the corresponding textual symbols.

The tables also indicate the initial series of the alphanumeric code of the position-order coding [63] of ontology classes and concept systems, which is commonly used in CM [15, 22, 34].

With this encoding, using the symbolism of set theory, the metaontology graph of Figure 9.1 can be represented in the form of notations similar to those given in formulas (9.1) and (9.2):

$$O(R, M, C) = \left\{ \{R_i\}_{i=1}^{4}, \{M_j\}_{j=1}^{4}, \{C_k\}_{k=1}^{4} \right\}. \tag{9.6}$$

Notation (9.6) means that the set of ontology class names represents the top-basic or zero-level of the CM hierarchical structure, and the set of facet structures on the right side indicates that at the first level, each class has four initial concepts (or taxa), which are explicitly named in the cells in Figure 9.1.

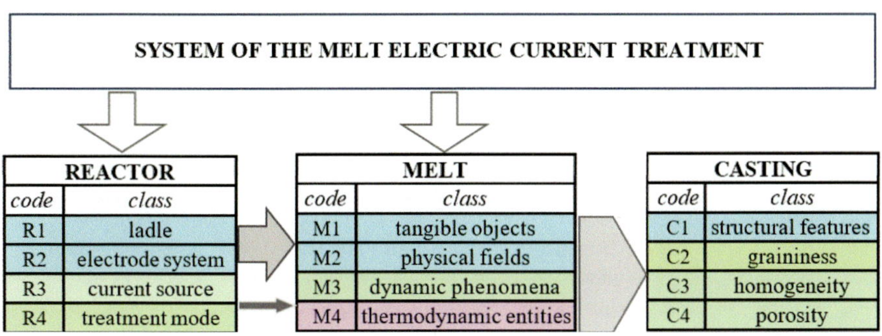

Figure 9.2 CSEM metaonology.

At the same time, each taxon of the first level is assigned a code designation given to the left of the cells: the letter is the name of the class, and the first digit is the number in the class at the first level of the hierarchy. According to the positional principle, the next, second digit of the code means the ordinal number of the taxon in the facet of the second level of the hierarchy.

All subsequent concepts at deeper levels are encoded according to this principle; in particular, the CSEM ontological models of the second and third levels, built according to the scheme of Figure 9.2, are given below. This approach allows to unambiguously identifying the belonging of a concept to a certain class, hierarchy level, or group in a facet or in a tuple, having, for example, a simple end-to-end list of concepts of alphabetical type. However, a more thorough approach, oriented on the use of the arsenal of various AI tools, envisages the compilation of an electronic (computer) catalog of concepts with detailed comments, an indicative version of which will be discussed below.

9.3.2.2 Formation of a taxonomic classification of the CSER CM concepts

A. The next level of deepening the systematization of CSEM SD consists in the formation of the concept taxonomies defined in the metaontology classes (9.6) on the same information base as Section 9.2.1.2 following the above principle.

Below there are given the tables (Tables 9.1– 9.7) with cells in which the concepts are named that comprise the 2nd and 3rd levels of the CSEM hierarchy, and their codes are labeled according to the adopted coding system. Filling the cells with concepts was performed by the logic of phenomenological perceptions of ECT processes [2–5, 8] on the grounds specified in Section 9.3.2.1 and, to some extent, is subjective in nature. However, it should be emphasized that they do not deplete the phenomenological factors of influence and interaction in the system, so the list of concepts and levels of the model hierarchy remains open and can be supplemented and adjusted as the information field expands and knowledge in the SWP under study deepens.

Table 9.1 Taxonomy of concepts of Class *R*, Level 2.

R1: ladle		*R2:* electrode system		*R3:* current source		*R4:* treatment mode	
R11	Shape	*R21*	Configuration	*R31*	Type of current	*R41*	Current parameters
R12	Dimensions	*R22*	Immersion	*R32*	Set power	*R42*	Injected energy
R13	Material	*R23*	Insulation type	*R33*	Voltage	*R43*	Exposure
R14	El-mag. properties	*R24*	Electrode shape	*R34*	Pulsing	*R44*	Pulse ratio

Table 9.2 Taxonomy of concepts of Class *C*, Level 2.

C1: structural features*		*C2:* graininess		*C3:* uniformity		*C4:* porosity	
C11	Fragmentation: mega	*C21*	Grain size	*C31*	Macrohomogen.	*C41*	Shrink. porosity
C12	Defects: macro-level	*C22*	Dispersion	*C32*	Microhomogen.	*C42*	Shells
C13	Dislocations: meso-	*C23*	Morphology	*C33*	Homogeneity of Chemic. composition	*C43*	Friability
C14	Vacancies: micro-	*C24*	Distribut. density			*C44*	Gas porosity

**The energy-metric levels of the structural composition of MMS are specified [5]: mega-level – continuous medium, macro-level – $10^{-1}...10^{3}$ μm; meso-level, micro-level – $10^{-1}...10^{2}$ nm.*

Table 9.3 Taxonomy of concepts of Class *M*, Level 2.

M1: tangible objects*		*M2:* physical fields		*M3:* dynamic phenom.		*M4:* thermodyn. entities	
M11	Melt: mega-level	*M21*	Electromagnetic	*M31*	Spreading current	*M41*	Thermodyn. state
M12	Inclusions: macro-	*M22*	Thermal	*M32*	Vortex flow	*M42*	GIBBS energy
M13	Clusters: meso-lev.	*M23*	El-mag. pressure	*M33*	Diffusion	*M43*	Entropy
M14	Nuclei: micro-lev.	*M24*	Acoustic	*M34*	Cluster pulsation	*M44*	Energy dissipation

Table 9.4 Taxonomy of concepts of Taxon *M1* (tangible objects), Level 3.

M11: melt		*M12:* inclusions		*M13:* clusters		*M14:* nuclei	
M111	El-mag. properties	*M121*	Shape	*M131*	Dimensions	*M141*	Surface energy
M112	Thermal Conductivity	*M122*	Dimensions	*M132*	Number of atoms	*M142*	Nucleation rate
		M123	Density			*M143*	Growth rate
M113	Density	*M124*	Electromagnet. parameters	*M133*	Lifetime	*M144*	Dimensions
M114	Viscosity			*M134*	Filling density		

Table 9.5 Taxonomy of concepts of Taxon *M2* (physical fields), Level 3.

M21: electromagnetic *		*M22:* thermal		*M23:* el-mag. pressure		*M24:* acoustic	
M211	Field distribution	*M221*	Heat dissipation	*M231*	Volume force	*M241*	Generation
M212	Induced EMF	*M222*	Heat transfer	*M232*	Distribution	*M242*	Intensity
M213	Electromag. waves	*M223*	Temper. distribut.	*M233*	Pinch effect	*M243*	Vibration
M214	Electr. field strength	*M224*	Physic. property change			*M244*	Propagation
M215	Magn. induction						

Table 9.6 Taxonomy of concepts of Taxon *M3* (dynamic structures), Level 3.

M31: spreading current		*M32:* vortex flow		*M33:* diffusion process		*M34:* cluster pulsations	
M311	Current density	*M321*	Flow character	*M331*	Migration of inclusions	*M341*	Pulsation frequency
M312	Electric field strength	*M322*	Dynamic viscosity	*M332*	Phase kinetics	*M342*	Amplitude
M313	Current frequency	*M323*	Distribution	*M333*	Thermodiffusion	*M343*	Time frame
M314	Gradients	*M324*	Flow velocity			*M344*	Aggregation kinetics

Table 9.7 Taxonomy of concepts of Taxon *M4* (thermodynamic entities), Level 3.

M41: thermodyn. state		*M42:* Gibbs energy		*M43:* entropy		*M44:* energy dissipation	
M411	Heat quantity	*M421*	External energy	*M431*	Entropy outflow	*M441*	Dissip. structure
M412	Thermal parameters	*M422*	Nucleation work	*M432*	Disequilibrium	*M442*	Fluctuations
M413	Caloric parameters	*M423*	Supercooling	*M433*	Topolog. disorder	*M443*	Bifurcations
M414	Changes of state	*M424*	Phase transitions	*M434*	Nonlinearity	*M444*	Self-organization

B. Limiting ourselves just to the third level of the CM hierarchy, we discover already at this stage of analysis the second peculiarity of the structure of the CSEM model, conditioned by the phenomenology of the ETO process, which essentially distinguishes it from the cognitive models of many other complex systems. It consists of the level of power of the set (quantity) of CM concepts, which can be estimated based on the defined composition of ontology classes (9.6).

If classes *R* and *C* can contain from two to seven taxa, which cover 3…5 concepts at each of 2…3 levels of the corresponding class structure, then their total number may amount to about 80 units. However, the category of internal concepts of class *M* is wider, as they reflect more or less completely the totality of physical processes in the melt during ECT and casting structure formation, the classification of which will require the construction of (3–4)-levels of hierarchical structure. Taking into account this factor, their number can be tentatively estimated at 100 units. Thus, a cognitive map for the CSEM model would contain approximately 180 concept-nodes (vertices) of the graph, whereas in models of other systems, their number usually does not exceed 25−30 [15, 36, 64]. Considering that each node is connected by at least 2…3 arc-links with other nodes, the total number of arcs will exceed 500. Such a "web" evidently becomes visually unobservable, and the cognitive map as a study tool loses its meaning.

Therefore, an *alternative approach* should be chosen for forming the taxonomic structure and building a cognitive model of CSEM. In order to avoid the mentioned difficulties of the graphical method of analysis, it seems expedient to use laconic forms of mathematical expressions of set theory and transparent logic of position-order coding of classification features, which the authors have tested in [38]. Taking into account that the structure of the taxonomy of classes and concepts of the CSEM metaontology has a multilevel character, it is appropriate to use the expression of the hierarchical cognitive mapIG, given in [15, 64]:

$$IG = \langle G_k, G_{k+1}, E_k \rangle, k = 1, 2, ...m, \tag{9.7}$$

where G_k,G_{k+1} – cognitive models referred to *k*th and (*k* + 1)th levels of the hierarchy, respectively; $E_k = \left.\{e_{i(k),j(p)}\}\right|_{p \neq k}$denotes the relations between the *k*- and *p*-level vertices.

The *k*-level cognitive model represents a directed graph:

$$G_k = \langle V(k), E(k) \rangle,$$

where $V(k) = \{v_i(k) \,|v_i(k) \in V(k), i = 1, 2, ..., n\}$ is the set of *k*-level vertices;

$E(k) = \{e_{ij}(k) \,|e_{ij}(k) \in E(k);\ i, j = 1, 2, ..., n\}$ reflects interrelationships between vertices within the level.

However, in this form of notation, the hierarchy is a simple linear tuple, which does not reveal in any way the relations between the sets G_k,G_{k+1} and subsequent levels, namely, whether they intersect or not, whether the cognitive maps of the lowest level are nested in the maps of the highest level, or whether they are independent, etc.

C. In this connection, it should be revealed the *third* peculiarity of the CSEM CM composition – it consists in the fact that all levels of its hierarchical structure according to the logic of the description of physical phenomena of the ECT described in Section 9.2.1.2 are connected by the subordination relation, i.e., sets of concepts of the lower (deeper) level (*k* + 1) are nested in sets of the higher level (*k*). Such relations between sets, in contrast to (9.7), should be represented in the form of nested tuples of cognitive maps of the type (9.2c):

$$\left.\begin{matrix} G_1^{(k+1)} \\ G_2^{(k+1)} \\ \vdots \\ G_n^{(k+1)} \\ \vdots \\ G_{N_k}^{(k+1)} \end{matrix}\right\} \subseteq G^{(k)}, \quad n = 1, 2, \ldots, N_k \quad \text{or}$$

$$G^{(k)} \supseteq \left\{ G_1^{(k+1)}, \ldots, G_n^{(k+1)}, \ldots, G_{N_k}^{(k+1)} \right\}^T, \quad n = 1, 2, \ldots, N_k, \tag{9.8}$$

where the upper index T is the *transpose* symbol. Correspondingly in eqn (9.8)

$$G_n^{(k)} = \left\langle V_n^{(k)}, E_n^{(k)} \right\rangle; V_n^{(k)} = \{v_i\}_n^{(k)},$$

$$i = 1, 2, \ldots, N_n; E_n^{(k)} = \left\{ (v_{n,i}, v_{n,j})\begin{matrix} N_n \\ i = 1 \\ j = 1 \end{matrix} \right\}^{(k)} = \{e_{i,j}\}_n^{(k)}. \quad (9.9)$$

is a cognitive map of the form (9.2) corresponding to level (k).

Then similarly to eqn (9.7), but taking into account eqn (9.8) and (9.9), we obtain:

$$IG^{(k)} = \left\langle G^{(k)} \supseteq \left\{ G_n^{(k+1)} \right\}^T \Big|_{n=1}^{N_{k+1}}, E^{(k)} \right\rangle. \quad (9.10)$$

Now we can express the whole system of hierarchically constructed taxonomies, which are represented by Tables 9.1–9.7, with analytic notations of cognitive maps of the form (9.9), (9.10):

$$IR_s^{(k)} = \left\langle R_s^{(k)} \supseteq \left\{ R_{s,1}^{(k+1)}, \ldots, R_{s,n}^{(k+1)}, \ldots, R_{s,Q}^{(k+1)} \right\} = \left\{ R_{s,n}^{(k+1)} \right\}^T \Big|_{n=1}^{Q}, E_{R_s^{(k)} \to M,C}^{(k)} \right\rangle, \quad s = 1, 2, \ldots, J_R. \quad (9.11a)$$

$$IM_s^{(k)} = \left\langle M_s^{(k)} \supseteq \left\{ M_{s,n}^{(k+1)} \right\}^T \Big|_{n=1}^{L}, E_{M_s^{(k)} \to R,M,C}^{(k)} \right\rangle, s = 1, 2, ..., J_M; \quad (9.11b)$$

$$IC_s^{(k)} = \left\langle C_s^{(k)} \supseteq \left\{ C_{s,n}^{(k+1)} \right\}^T \Big|_{n=1}^{B}, E_{R,M,C \to C_s^{(k)}}^{(k)} \right\rangle, s = 1, 2, ..., J_C, \quad (9.11c)$$

where $Q = \left| R_s^{(k+1)} \right|, L = \left| M_s^{(k+1)} \right|, B = \left| C_s^{(k+1)} \right|$ – s-facet power (number of taxa) of the corresponding class at (k + 1) level of the hierarchy (s is the serial number of the facet).

For example, we will open the notation $IM_{2(2)}$:

$$IM_2^{(2)} = \left\langle M2^{(2)} \supseteq \{M21, M22, M23, M24\}, E_{M,R,C}^{(2)} \right\rangle.$$

Especially, we will point out the entry $E^{(k)}_{M_s^{(k)}\to R,M,C}$ in expression (9.11b) – it means the totality of *unmediated* connections, i.e., binary combinations of concepts from a facet $M_s^{(k)}$ of the form $\left(M_{s,i}^{(k)}, M_{s,j}^{(k)}\right)$, with all other concepts, including those from the same facet, including the interrelation of themselves, which corresponds to a feedback loop. Similar entries in expressions (9.11a) and (9.11c) have an analogous meaning, but considering that within class *R* the adjusting and setting concepts are mutually independent, their influence acts only externally, on the classes *M* and *C*, which is depicted in the entry $E^{(k)}_{R_s^{(k)}\to M,C}$.

At the same time, the targeted concepts – factors of class *C* – are formed only after solidification of the casting (ex post facto), so they cannot perform the back influence on the ECT processes, i.e., they have no connections with the concepts of classes *R* and *M*, although interrelations between the factors of class *C* itself take place, which corresponds to the entry $E^{(k)}_{R,M,C\to C_s^{(k)}}$.

The details of the depiction of links in the CSEM CM and their peculiarities are submitted in the next subsection, and Figure 9.3 presents a fragment of its structure to illustrate the described methodology of constructing the hierarchy of CSEM cognitive model.

D. So, as one can see, the composition of the CSEM CM represents a very wide aggregation of hierarchically organized structures of autonomous and

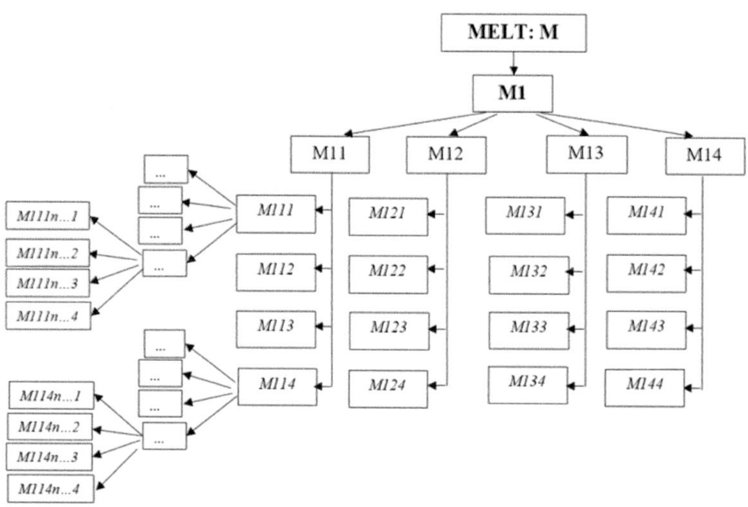

Figure 9.3 Fragment of CSEM CM structure.

interconnected subsystems, the total number of concepts in already filled taxonomic tables, which exceeds 100, i.e., the graph of such a model should contain more than 100 vertices – practically an unobservable set for "manual" processing. Nevertheless, their aggregate forms a unitary technological formation; therefore, the specified aggregation of subsystems is liable to be integrated into a common structure. The structural union of hierarchical CMs according to [64] is displayed in the form of a functional graph as follows:

$$I\Phi = \langle IG, X_k, F_k \rangle, k \geq 2, \tag{9.12}$$

where *IG* is the hierarchical cognitive model (HCM) given by the expression of the form (9.10); $X_k = \bigcup_1^k X(k)$– the set of parameters for the HCM vertices; $F_k = \{F(X_k, E_k)\}$; and $\bigcup_1^k F(k)$is the arc transformation functional in the HCM.

However, the notion of "parameters for vertices" in eqn (9.12) coincides with the notion of "attributes" in the interpretation of the CSEM CM terms (see Section 9.3.2.1), which in notations (9.10) and (9.11) does not differ from the notation of concepts of general form, i.e., in our context $X(k) \Leftrightarrow G_n^{(k)}$in formula (9.9). Hence, the union of sets $\bigcup_1^k X(k) \Leftrightarrow \left\{G_n^{(k)}\right\}_{n=1}^{N_k}$ (are equivalent). From this follows also the equivalence of the notation $E^{(k)}_{R_s^{(k)} \to M,C}$ to the notation of "arc transformation functional" used in eqn (9.12) (and analogous to it in formulas (9.11), since the links were originally posed as functional dependencies.

Thus, guided by the described rules of HCM structures notation, the structural unification of hierarchical subsystems of CSEM CM classes *R*, *M*, and *C* can be represented in the form:

$$IU = \left\{ IR_s^{(k)}\Big|_{s=1}^{J_R}, IM_s^{(k)}\Big|_{s=1}^{J_M}, IC_s^{(k)}\Big|_{s=1}^{J_C}, IE_{R,M,C}^{(k)} \right\}, k = 1, 2, ..., m, \tag{9.13}$$

where $IE_{R,M,C}^{(k)}$ means the totality of inter-class, inter-level, and direct (intra-level) binary combinations of concept-connections that are depicted by adjacency or incidence matrices of the hierarchical system presented next.

9.3.2.3 Mapping of concept links in the CSEM CM and its specificity

A. The mapping of links in the CSEM CM faces a serious problem, the reason being their multiplicity. As the presented graph has a hundred vertices, the total number of edges (even considering the sparsity of the adjacency matrix of this graph) can be more than 1000 (the number of edges in a complete graph is equal to the number of combinations $C(n, 2) = n(n - 1)/2$ and for $n = 100$ will be 4950). In this case, it is inexpedient to compile a full adjacency matrix A_G of the form (9.4), because it is too cumbersome to manipulate it in repeated operations of scenario modeling even with the help of special software (Big Data analysis).

The natural way out in this situation is to decompose the matrix A_G, i.e., to represent it by an aggregate of partial adjacency matrices. Since the whole system of the phenomenological model of CSEM is built up on the facet-hierarchical principle, it is obviously logical to base the decomposition scheme on the same principle. In this case, in each ontology class, an ordered set of partial adjacency matrices (PAMs) is formed upon all hierarchical levels. In this case, along with the usual square matrices, which correspond to the links within one facet of a defined level, specific non-square (rectangular) matrices are formed, whose dimensionality is given by the number of concepts in related facets. Moreover, the formed PAMs disposition contains matrices with interclass as well as inter-level connections, and this fact is another, *fourth peculiarity* of the phenomenological model.

For a unified depiction of the mentioned variants of matrices, we will assume the notation of PAM in the form of

$$A_{P,Q} = \{a_{i,j}\}_{P,Q}, i = 1, 2, ..., n_P; j = 1, 2, ..., m_Q,$$

where indexes P and Q mean the adjacent matrices that may belong to different levels of the hierarchy from different classes, but in particular, they may coincide, in which case we obtain a *partial* adjacency matrix in the usual sense or an *eigenvalue* adjacency matrix $A_{G,G} \equiv A_G$. Then for the first level of the hierarchy of the graph $O(R, M, C)$, shown in Figure 9.2, it should be compiled, in general, six matrices:

$A_{R,R}$, $A_{R,M}$, $A_{M,M}$, $A_{M,C}$, $A_{C,C}$ and $A_{R,C}$.

However, taking into account that all concepts of the R class are adjusted (external) ones without connections between them, the matrix $A_{R,R}$ will be null (an empty set). Furthermore, from the physics of ECT processes, it follows that the setting concepts of class R have no direct influence on the targeted concepts of class C, so the matrix also turns out to be zero. Thus,

$$\left.\begin{array}{l} A_{R,R} = \emptyset = \{a_{i,j} \in A_{R,R} | \, a_{i,j} = 0\}; i, j = 1, ..., n_R \\ A_{R,!} = \emptyset = \{a_{i,j} \in A_{R,!} | \, a_{i,j} = 0\}; i = 1, ..., n_R; j = 1, ..., n_C \end{array}\right\} \quad (9.14)$$

$$A_{R,M} = \begin{array}{c} \\ R1 \\ R2 \\ R3 \\ R4 \end{array} \begin{array}{c} \begin{array}{cccc} M1 & M2 & M3 & M4 \end{array} \\ \begin{pmatrix} 1 & 0 & 0 & 0 \\ 0 & 1 & 1 & 0 \\ 0 & 1 & 1 & 1 \\ 0 & 1 & 1 & 0 \end{pmatrix} \end{array} ; A_{M,M} = \begin{pmatrix} 0 & 0 & 0 & 0 \\ 1 & 0 & 0 & 0 \\ 0 & 1 & 0 & 0 \\ 0 & 1 & 1 & 0 \end{pmatrix};$$

$$A_{M,C} = \begin{array}{c} \\ M1 \\ M2 \\ M3 \\ M4 \end{array} \begin{array}{c} \begin{array}{cccc} C1 & C2 & C3 & C4 \end{array} \\ \begin{pmatrix} 1 & 0 & 0 & 0 \\ 0 & 1 & 1 & 0 \\ 0 & 1 & 1 & 1 \\ 0 & 1 & 1 & 0 \end{pmatrix} \end{array} ; A_{C,C} = \begin{pmatrix} 0 & 1 & 0 & 0 \\ 1 & 0 & 0 & 0 \\ 0 & 1 & 0 & 1 \\ 0 & 0 & 1 & 0 \end{pmatrix}. \quad (9.15)$$

As given in eqn (9.15), matrices of the first (upper) level of the hierarchy define the *general channels of influence transmitting* between classes of concepts, differentiated by generic abstract traits. Substantive concretization of chains of connections with identification of their functions of influence is made already at the second and deeper levels. And here, due to the inevitable increase in the number of links (edges of *partial* graphs), the situation of choosing a rational representation of them arises. For example, according to eqn (9.15), the full matrix disclosure in accordance with Tables 9.2 and 9.3 will require filling one matrix of 16×16 size containing 256 elements.

On the other hand, since there are only eight non-zero cells in the matrix $A_{M,C}$, it is possible to display the same connections using eight elementary matrices of size 4×4 containing only 128 elements, since the contentless empty cells of the original matrix are excluded. Obviously, the second option is preferred. Nevertheless, the total number of elementary matrices that correspond to non-zero cells of all matrices from (9.15) will be 25 ones with a nominal number of 400 elements, although really it will be about half. However, even such an array of information in the specified format is rather cumbersome, and when moving to the third level of the hierarchy, it will increase factorially.

However, graph theory [65, 66] provides the possibility of their assignment by a list of edges. Then the metaontology $O\,(R, M, C)$with adjacency matrices (9.15), using the notation of the species (9.13), can be presented as follows:

$$IE^{(1)}_{R,M,C} = \left\{E^{(1)}_{R,M}, E^{(1)}_{M,M}, E^{(1)}_{M,C}, E^{(1)}_{C,C}\right\}, \quad (9.16)$$

$$\text{where}\begin{cases} E^{(1)}_{R,M} = \{(R1, M2), (R2, M2), (R3, M2), (R3, M3), (R4, M3), \\ \qquad (R4, M4)\} \\ E^{(1)}_{M,M} = \{(M2, M1), (M3, M2), (M4, M2), (M4, M3)\} \\ E^{(1)}_{M,C} = \{(M1, C1), (M2, C2), (M2, C3), (M3, C2), (M3, C3), \\ \qquad (M3, C4), (M4, C2), (M4, C3)\} \\ E^{(1)}_{C,C} = \{(C1, C2), (C2, C1), (C3, C2), (C3, C4), (C4, C3)\} \end{cases}$$

However, the most compact way to specify graphs is the *adjacency list*, which enumerates the *initial* vertices of the oriented graph, and for each of them, the list of the *final* vertices. In such a variant for the components of expression (9.16), we obtain the following notations:

$$\left.\begin{aligned} E^{(1)}_{R,M} &= \{(R1 : M2); (R2 : M2); (R3 : M2, M3);\ (R4 : M3, M4)\} \\ E^{(1)}_{M,M} &= \{(M2 : M1); (M3 : M2); (M4 : M2, M3)\} \\ E^{(1)}_{M,C} &= \{(M1 : C1); (M2 : C2, C3); (M3 : C2, C3, C4); \\ &\qquad (M4 : C2, C3)\} \\ E^{(1)}_{C,C} &= \{(C1 : C2); (C2 : C1); (C3 : C2, C4); (C4 : C3)\} \end{aligned}\right\} \tag{9.17}$$

It should be noted that in the latter notation, there is *both a feedforward and a feedback* connection of concepts *C1* and *C2*, and this situation can also occur in other concept combinations.

B. Now we will proceed to the second level, for which the content of concepts in the corresponding classes is given in Tables 9.1, 9.2, and 9.3. First of all, let us write down the general formula of hierarchically connected sets of graph edges at this level, similar to (9.16), taking into account that each of the sets in it consists of *partial* sets, which correspond to the connections of the concepts given in the above tables:

$$IE^{(2)}_{R,M,C} = \left\{ \left\{ E^{(2)}_{Ri,Rj} \right\}\Big|^{4}_{\substack{i=1\\j=1}}, \left\{ E^{(2)}_{Ri,Mj} \right\}^{j=4}_{\substack{i=4\\j=4\\j=1}}, \left\{ E^{(2)}_{Mi,Mj} \right\}\Big|^{4}_{\substack{i=1\\j=1}}, \left\{ E^{(2)}_{Mi,Cj} \right\}^{4}_{\substack{i=1\\j=1}}, \left\{ E^{(2)}_{Ci,Cj} \right\}^{4}_{\substack{i=1\\j=1}} \right\} \tag{9.18}$$

Further, we reveal these connections, considering that all *partial* sets in the set $\left\{E^{(2)}_{Ri,Rj}\right\}\Big|^{3}_{\substack{i=1\\ j=1}}$ are empty: $E^{(2)}_{Ri,Rj}=\emptyset$, since all concepts in *R* are independent. For the same reason, in the set $\left\{E^{(2)}_{Ri,Mj}\right\}\Big|^{\substack{i=4\\ j=4}}_{\substack{i=1\\ j=1}}$ *partial* set $E^{(2)}_{R1,1}=\emptyset$, and in the set $\left\{E^{(2)}_{Mi,Mj}\right\}\Big|^{4}_{\substack{i=1\\ j=1}}$ *partial* set $E^{(2)}_{M1,M1}=\emptyset$.

Together with that, non-empty sets in considered phenomenological models are characterized by the presence of bundles of both outgoing and incoming links. For brevity, we will enclose bundles in square brackets, and in case of a concentration of more than two links in a bundle, we will use the union symbol "$\bigcup$"; besides, in the code notation, we will denote the variable digit by the letter "ω."

Thus, we give the second-level adjacency lists for the categories of sets from formula (9.18).

a) Category $\left\{E^{(2)}_{Ri,Mj}\right\}$:

$$\left.\begin{aligned}
&E^{(2)}_{R1,2}=\{([R11,R12]:[M21,M24]);\ (R13:M22);(R14:[M21,M23])\};\\
&E^{(2)}_{R2,2}=\{([R21,R23,R24]:M21);\ ([R21,R24]:[M22,M24])\};\\
&E^{(2)}_{R3,M2}=\{(R31:[\bigcup_{\omega=1}^{3}M2\omega]);\ ([R32,R33,R34]:[\bigcup_{\omega=1}^{4}M2\omega])\};\\
&E^{(2)}_{R4,M2}=\{([\bigcup_{\omega=1}^{4}R4\omega]:[\bigcup_{\omega=1}^{4}M2\omega])\};\\
&E^{(2)}_{R1,M3}=\{([R11,R14]:[M31,M32]);(R13:M33)\};\\
&E^{(2)}_{R2,M3}=\{([\bigcup_{\omega=1}^{4}R2\omega]:[M31,M32])\};E^{(2)}_{R3,M3}=\{(R31:[M31,M33])\};\\
&E^{(3)}_{R3,M3}=\{([\bigcup_{\omega=1}^{4}R3\omega]:[M31,M32])\};E^{(2)}_{R4,M3}=\{([\bigcup_{\omega=1}^{4}R4\omega]:[M31,M32])\}.
\end{aligned}\right\}\tag{9.18-a}$$

b) Category $\left\{E^{(2)}_{Mi,Mj}\right\}$:

$$\left.\begin{array}{l}
E^{(2)}_{M1,2} = \{([M11, M12] : [M21, M22, M24])\}; E^{(2)}_{M1,3} = \{([M11, M12] : [M31, M32])\}; \\
E^{(2)}_{M1,4} = \{([M11, M13] : [M41, M43])\}; \\
E^{(2)}_{M2,1} = \{([M21, M22, M24] : M12); ([\bigcup\limits_{\omega=1}^{4} M2\omega] : M13); ([M21, M22] : [M12, M13])\}; \\
E^{(2)}_{M2,2} = \{(M21 : [\bigcup\limits_{\omega=2}^{4} M2\omega]); ([M23] : M24)\}; \\
E^{(2)}_{M2,3} = \{(M21 : [\bigcup\limits_{\omega=1}^{3} M3\omega]); ([M22, M23] : [M33, M34])\}; \\
E^{(2)}_{M2,4} = \{([\bigcup\limits_{\omega=1}^{3} M2\omega] : M41); ([M21, M22] : [\bigcup\limits_{\omega=2}^{4} M4\omega])\}; \\
E^{(2)}_{M3,M2} = \{(M31 : [\bigcup\limits_{\omega=1}^{3} M2\omega])\}; E^{(2)}_{M3,M3} = \{([M31, M32] : M33)\}; E^{(2)}_{M3\cup 4,M1} = \emptyset; \\
E^{(2)}_{M3,M4} = \{([M31, M32] : [\bigcup\limits_{\omega=1}^{3} M4\omega]); ([M33, M34] : [M43, M44])\}; E^{(2)}_{4,M4} = \emptyset.
\end{array}\right\} \quad (9.18\text{-b})$$

To illustrate the content of the given notations, Figure 9.4 shows a fragment of the cognitive map as an example of the graphical interpretation of using the expressions for $E^{(2)}_{M2,3}$ and $E^{(2)}_{M3,M2}$ in eqn (9.18-b):

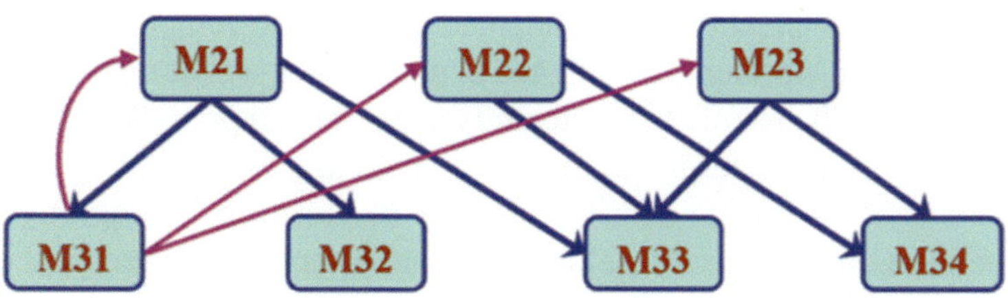

Figure 9.4 Fragment of a cognitive map from set (9.18-b).

We have limited ourselves to presentation just as a part of the adjacency lists, without revealing the connections in the categories $\left\{E^{(2)}_{Mi,Cj}\right\}$ and $\left\{E^{(2)}_{Ci,Cj}\right\}$, since their content at the current stage of scientific comprehension of the corresponding SD is incomplete and in some aspects debatable.

Because of this, their presentation would require a large amount of explanations that go beyond the scope of the task, so it will be presented in a separate work. However, it should be noted that the filling of these categories of adjacency lists is done by the same method as used for the compilation of expressions (9.18-a) and (9.18-b).

For a complete perception of the use of this method, we give one more example of an inter-level adjacency list for the links of the 2nd and 3rd levels:

$$\left.\begin{aligned} E^{(3,2)}_{M11,M3} &= \{(M111 : M31); ([M113, M114] : [M32, M33])\}; \\ E^{(3,2)}_{M12,C4} &= \{([M121, M122, M123] : [C42, C43])\}. \end{aligned}\right\} \tag{9.18-c}$$

This example demonstrates the highly complicated interweaving of links in the multi-level hierarchical structure of the CSEM CM.

9.4 Artificial Intelligence Tools for Cognitive Analysis of CSEM

9.4.1 Electronic catalogue of the CSEM CM concepts

In clause 3.2.1, it is stated that due to the very significant number of physical objects involved in the CM structure of CSEM and the diversity of their properties, it is absolutely necessary for the investigation of phenomenological relationships in the sequence of ECT occurrences to have *an electronic catalog of CM concepts* (ECC) in a format adapted to using the computer AI tools for efficient search, clear identification and semantic analysis of concepts. At the same time, the ECC should be sufficiently compact and provide flexibility in search conditions and interpretations of semantic associations [41,42].

The system of coding and differentiation of functional categories of concepts in the CM structure developed by the authors fairly meets these requirements; however, for the incarnation of the ECC tasks, the nominative format of concept description is not informative enough and needs to expand the notional content. For this purpose, the authors envisaged the introduction in the format of ECC the concept *dossiers* (profiles), containing:

(a) keywords (terms) associated with the basic notion of the concept (up to five words);
(b) references to sources of information about the basic notion of the concept (up to five).

Guided by the stated attitudes, the authors developed a three-component structure of ECC, the morphology of which includes the main frame (spanning tree) and its two projections. The *main frame* is built according to the scheme of nested directories in accordance with the hierarchy of the phenomenological model of CSEM, i.e., it contains three general directories corresponding to the classes of ontological structure, which are defined in Section 9.3.2.1. Each of them contains folders of the lowest level of the hierarchy, labeled with codes according to the adopted coding system, and the names (codes) of folders of the next descending level. This scheme actually reproduces the structure shown in Figure 9.2.

The folders contain the lists of concepts of the corresponding class and level, ordered according to their codes, as well as the mentioned dossiers for each of them. Thus, the search for concepts and data about them in the mainframe is performed simply by concept code.

Following the above, Table 9.8 presents the layout of the catalog page with data entries about randomly selected concepts. This format of entries is convenient for the formalization of entries in ECC in the form of cell arrays in the program code [67].

Below is the listing of the record code snippet:

```
>> m311a = 'electric current density';
>> m311b = 'power, conductivity, Ohm law, heating, Joule law';
>> m311c = '[m311-1], [m311-2]';
>> m311d = 'M3111, M3112, M3113';
>> M311 = {m311a, m311b, m311c, m311d};
>> celldisp(M311)
M311{1} = electric current density
M311{2} = power, conductivity, Ohm law, heating, Joule law
M311{3} = [m311-1], [m311-2]
M311{4} = M3111, M3112, M3113
```

The list of information sources indicated in the reference entries, with a rubricator based on the coding of concepts, is drawn up in a separate appendix.

The *main frame* of the ECC is supplemented by two *projection-indicators*:

- an alphabetical *indicator of the code*, which is identified by its name;
- an alphabetical *list of keywords*, which specifies codes and names of associated concepts.

Table 9.8 The layout of concept data entries nested in the M31 folder.

Code	*Basic concept*	*Key words*	*Sources of information*	*Subfolders*
1	2	3	4	5
M311	electric current density	power, conductivity, Om & Joe laws, heat dissipation	files: [m311-1], [m311-2], ..., [m311-5]	M3111, ...M311n
M312	electric field strength	potentials, charges, distribution, energy density	файлы:: [m312-1], [m312-2], ..., [m312-5]	M3121,...M312n
		......		
M31k	......	......	......	......

The presented scheme of ECC construction fairly meets the set conditions, and, as the listing of the entry fragment shows, it is quite easy to translate into program code.

9.4.2 Features of influence functions in CSEM and concept connections register

A. In addition to the already discussed peculiarities of CSEM CM, there is another problematic aspect concerning the specificity of links between concepts. The point is that they have a fundamentally different nature in comparison with traditional CMs, which are not directly related to physical phenomena and processes, as, for example, economic or transport problems. In such models, there are, as a rule, simple *single-link linear connections* (one edge of the graph), in which the influence of concepts is expressed by *weight coefficients* specified either empirically or statistically. In contrast to them, in the phenomenological CM under consideration, the interaction of concepts is determined by material *regularities* of the processes of changing the objects' states or the content of attributes, and this is the *fifth peculiarity* of the CSEM CM. In other words, in the phenomenological CSEM model, the *influence functions* of the type (9.5) in the matrix of binary relations of cognitive maps reflect the real multiphysical essence of the interaction of concepts, which is framed in concrete *functional dependencies* and, as already noted, unlike eqn (9.4), it does not necessarily have zero diagonal elements $e_{i,i}$.

This means that in the phenomenological model, different *types of influence transfer channels* can be formed, namely: (a) consecutive *multilink chains of links* from one object to another – multistage transfer; (b) parallel *bundles of convergent links* from several concepts to one – multifactor dependence; (c) *looping feedbacks* – self-excitation; or (d) *single-link* parametric dependence.

B. In this regard, it should be noted that for the physical adequacy of the phenomenological model of the CSEM, the *consistency of the time projections of the action* of the influencing factors, which should reproduce the cause-and-effect logic of events, acquires the essential importance. Thus, if the parametric dependence in the process of evolution of the state of the CM is a *constantly acting* factor, then in a multi-stage transmission the activation of a certain concept in the chain can occur only *after excitation* of the connection from the previous element (concept). On the other hand, the activation of the concept, to which the connections of the multi-factor dependence converge, is possible either after the excitation of *all* incoming connections, or a *conditioned* part of them.

From the above, it clearly implies the perception about the expediency of introducing a certain *tact (clock) sequence of influence transmission* through channels of different types. A similar idea was put forward in [62], where, in order to reconcile the sequence of changes in the states of concepts of *different nature*, it is proposed to insert *a delay* in the form of *time steps*.

This approach, of course, should be embodied in the attributes of the cognitive methodology of CSEM investigation presented by the authors. For this purpose, it seems logical to assign a certain *tact mark* to one or another link in the chains of CM connections and to stipulate the fact of the occurrence of the transmitting link *activity* by the coincidence of its tact mark with a given value. From this follows the necessity of differentiation of *link properties* in the aspect of their conditional tact continuance, which can be expressed by comparative estimations correlated with time scales or time constants of processes of different physical natures. Actually, such differentiation has an objective basis: the processes that take place during ECT occur at different energy-metric levels of the MMS structural composition (see Tables 9.2 and 9.3) and are realized using different mechanisms, which, in fact, is the reason for the essential difference in the rates (speed) of their occurrence.

This, virtually an entirely *new foreshortening* of constructing the CM of such a complicated system as CSEM, opens up additional opportunities for the study of its properties.

A correct definition of the notion of *tact lasting of influence transmission* through the link channels in the CSEM CM requires a clear characterization of the situations in which its application will be justifiable. Taking into account the differentiation of functional categories of concepts introduced in Section 9.3.2.1, it is reasonable to subdivide the links between them into passive and active ones. We will consider *passive links* as links that are an accessory of attributive concepts (of the "***Atr***" type), such as properties or parameters, and are defined together with the concept itself. Therefore, the tact lasting is not inherent to them; they are permanently active. The same refers to the links that belong to the concepts of the subject category (of the "***Sub***" type).

In contrast to them, we will consider as *active* the links through which the *influence transmission* is performed from the concepts that reflect the phenomena of transformation (change) of concept states (of the "***Occ***" type). Such links contain, as a rule, functional dependencies that display in any analytical form the regularities of physical phenomena.

C. Pursuant to the above, in ECT processes, obviously, several groups of phenomena of different physical natures should be distinguished: (a) phenomena of electromagnetic nature; (b) thermal phenomena; (c) acoustic; (d) diffusion; and (e) hydromechanical ones. Each of these groups of phenomena is characterized by a specific time scale and a range of process continuance (metrics): from milliseconds in electromagnetic processes to seconds in thermal and acoustic processes and to minutes in diffusion and hydromechanical processes. It seems logical to lay precisely the ratio between these metrics as the basis for determining the conditional values of the *tact continuance* of influence transmission (lasting) "L," or its inverse value – the *rapidity of transmission* (speed) "S." For this purpose, the format of the Harrington verbal-numerical scale is quite suitable [36, 37], in which the gradations are expressed by the values of the powers of the multiple exponents: $(k\mathrm{e})^n$. In this case, its exponent n can serve as a *tact mark*.

Based on the analysis of the real physical experiments data and the results of theoretical calculations of time profiles of the listed physical processes, the authors, in accordance with the mentioned scale, adopted five increasing gradations of lasting L and correspondingly decreasing gradations of speed S for active links (concepts of "***Occ***" type).

In this case, for the links of concepts of "Sub" and "Atr" type, i.e., for passive links, the action of which is "switched on" without delay, the tact marks will be denoted as *L0* and *S6*, conforming to the value of indicator $n = 0$.

Together with this, the presented gradation scale can be easily adjusted for a specific CSEM CM by variation of the coefficient k values. Thus, using rather simple means, it is possible for the *technique* of tact differentiation of concept influence functions to apply to a wide range of qualitative and quantitative characteristics of CSEM CMs.

Table 9.9 Tact marks for influence transmission.

Lasting tact mark	*Lasting gradation*	*Exponent n*	*Speed gradation*	*Speed tact mark*
L1	Very short	1	Very high	*S5*
L2	Short	2	High	*S4*
L3	Middle	3	Middle	*S3*
L4	Long	4	Low	*S2*
L5	Very long	5	Very low	*S1*

D. However, it is rather difficult to perform in practice the described tact marking of the links plurality in the analytical form of entries presented in Section 9.3.2.3. Besides, during the computer simulation of ECT processes in various modes, when it is required to repeatedly perform the cyclic operations of searching and identifying each link in chains of CSEM CM links, the form of notations (9.18-a)–(9.18-c), despite their brevity and transparent logic, is not adapted. Therefore, it is necessary to use an alternative, personalized approach similar to the ECC format. However, in doing so, there is no need to reproduce the structure of nested directories, so it can be made a simple sequential *concept connections register* (CCR), ordered according to their encoding, i.e., in ascending order of numerical values of the code after the letter digit.

The registry entry for each specific concept should include the information necessary to identify all its incoming and outgoing links and their functional role in the CM. Thus, in the register entry, it should be indicated:

- codes of influencing and percepting concepts according to analytical notations made in the form of formulae (9.17) and (9.18);
- tact marks according to Table 9.9;
- an individual form of the influence function (for active relations).

Table 9.10 shows the layout of the register entry composed in accordance with the above.

The implementation of register records in the program code is quite similar to the listing fragment presented in Section 9.4.1.

The references in Table 9.10 indicate the sources that provide functional dependencies that reveal the content of specific functions of the influence of some concepts on others. Naturally, in the context of this study, an exhaustive list of these functions cannot be presented, first of all, because of the very large number of them. But the main thing is that in some cases they can be specified explicitly – by a formula, table, or graph, and in other cases they *should be synthesized* by solving an appropriate *model task*, which serves as a "Digital Twin" (Digital Twin) of a real physical phenomenon [8].

However, it should be noted that the general picture of physical phenomena in the ECT process, as shown in Section 9.2.1.2 of this chapter and the works of other authors [2, 4, 17, 19, 20, 68], is extremely complicated, so any distinct manifestation of individual aspects of this picture can be obtained only as a result of the decomposition of the unified process into monophysical components – model tasks. Such tasks are defined, naturally, just in a limited spatial domain and have to be subjected to the stepwise numerical solution with subsequent conjugation of output and input data of separate tasks in accordance with the logic and order of multiphysical processes of ECT *in time*. The situation is aggravated by the fact that the *temporal frontiers of the active action* of monophysical components, which reflect the content of influence functions in the CSEM CM, are determined not only by the intensity of any initiating influence but are often allied to its spatial characteristic features, as well as restrictions and disturbances arising at the deep levels of the MMS hierarchy. In any case, the aspects of the staging of the action of monophysical components or, in other words, the tact continuance of influence functions, require further development and are an actual and priority scientific and practical task of further research in this area.

Nevertheless, for the formation of CCR and filling in the references in Table 9.10, there is a rather ample database in the work of the authors [38], where a codified system of identification of mathematical tasks of computer modeling of ECT processes, which embody a significant part of the key influence functions, is presented. This codification is based on the taxonomy of modeling problems and computer models of ECT modes, which is founded

Table 9.10 The layout of entries on concept connections.

Influence function	*Tact mark*	*Affecting concepts*	*Concept code*	*Percepting concepts*	*Tact mark*	*Influence function*
1	2	3	4	5	6	7
1	*L0*	*M11*	*M21*	*M12, M13*	*L0*	*1*
1	*L0*	*M12*		*M22,M23,M24*	*L2, L3, L2*	[reference]
[reference]	*L2*	*M31*		*M31, M32, M33*	*L2, L4, L3*	[reference]
				M41, M42	*L2, L3*	[reference]

on the coupling of the phenomenological interpretation of ECT processes, their mathematical models and computational algorithms. In fact, it was the predecessor of the presented CSEM CM, and the involvement of the latest template-modular system of computer modeling of ECT processes developed in [6], its mathematical tools, and software facilities for solving problems of ECT modes control completes the suite of artificial intelligence tools, with the help of which it is possible to compile a wide range of algorithms for the cognitive study of the phenomenological basis of ECT, oriented to the identification of the most effective modes of electrocurrent treatment of metal melts and obtaining high-quality castings.

9.5 Conclusion

1. Melt ECT technology, destined for the management of cast products quality, which has a unique specificity, from the standpoint of system analysis and control theory, *is identified as a poorly structured complex system with a high level of uncertainty in internal relations* (in the context – CSEM), that requires a deeper study of the phenomenological content of phenomena occurring while processing.
2. The application of *cognitive modeling methodology for the intelligent handling* of information data arrays and the study of ECT phenomenology, targeted at the use of tools and methods of information technologies and artificial intelligence, has been substantiated. The technique of *knowledge structuring* has received scientific and practical development by constructing *ontological models* of the subject domain (SD) on the basis of the semantic context of concepts and logico-phenomenological interconnections of processes and phenomena that occur during ECT.
3. Based on the *ontological model* of CSEM, an *information platform* was created for computer simulation of the totality of processes and modes of melt treatment, represented as an *encoded* system of classes of concepts, concepts and their properties (attributes, factors), as well as relations between them (links, influences, dependencies) expressed in the machine-interpretable formulations, which are structural elements of the consolidated (holistic) *cognitive model* of CSEM. The simple and concise position-order coding system used in the model ensures unambiguous identification of each of its structural elements in any procedure of a computer simulation of SSER behavior.
4. Along with this, it is shown that for this model with its multi-level structure, which contains a highly significant number of concepts and

a complicated network of inter-level connections between concepts, the use of its representation in the form of a traditional unitary graph and a holistic matrix of connections is *unrealistic*. Therefore, an alternative mode of description of CSEM CM has been developed based on the decomposition of the consolidated model into a set of *partial adjacency matrices* and their analytical (formulaic) notation with the help of set theory symbolism.

5. The interpretation of the CSEM CM as a *computational model* is introduced, which constitutes a hierarchical network scheme of interconnected computational procedures that explicitly *integrate* the phenomenological content of melt ECT processes with intelligent procedures for handling information objects by machine methods using the corresponding mathematical apparatus. The interaction of the referred computational model with conventional IT and AI procedures is ensured by means of additional *intelligent tools* – an electronic catalog of concepts and an electronic register of their links in an encoded format (in the context – ECC and RSC).
6. The development of the presented cognitive methodology, elaborated in relation to the ECT technology, has a prospect of application for modeling and studying the phenomenology of similar production processes, in which the impact of physical fields on treated objects is used. The main tasks in this direction are to specify the composition of components of hierarchical CM structures and to develop corresponding functions of links, on the basis of which network schemes of interrelated computational procedures of computer simulation are formed.

References

[1] G. Rojek, et al., "Methods of Computational Intelligence in the Context of Quality Assurance in Foundry Products", Archives of Foundry Engineering, 2016, 16(2), pp. 11–16. https://doi.org/10.13052/jmm1550-4646.2031

[2] J. Zhang, H. Chen, H. Yu, Y. Jin, "Study on Dual Modification of Al-17%Si Alloys by Structural Heredity," Metals, 2015, 5(2), pp. 1112–1126. https://doi.org/10.3390/met5021112

[3] A.V. Ivanov, A.V. Sinchuk, V.N. Tsurkin, "Electric current treatment of liquid and crystallization alloys in casting technologies," Surface Engineering and Applied Electrochemistry, 2011, 47(5), pp. 456–464. https://doi.org/10.3103/S1068375511050115

[4] D. Eskin, Mi. Jiawei (Eds.), “Solidification Processing of Metallic Alloys under External Fields,” Springer, Cham, 2019. https://doi.org/10.1007/978-3-319-94842-3

[5] Yu. Zaporozhets, A. Ivanov, Yu. Kondratenko, V. Tsurkin, “The features of controlled conductive electric current treatment of liquid metals,” In: V.M. Petrova (Ed.) Advances in Engineering Research, Vol. 44 Advances in Engineering Research, Nova Science Publishers Inc., New York, 2021, pp. 1–114.

[6] Yu. Zaporozhets, A. Ivanov, Yu. Kondratenko, V. Tsurkin, N.G. Batechko, “Innovative System of Computer Modelling of Multiphysics Processes for Controlled Electrocurrent Treatment of Melts,” Sci. innov., 2022, 18(4), pp. 85–105. https://doi.org/10.15407/scine18.04.085.

[7] Yu.M. Zaporozhets, A.V. Ivanov, Yu.P. Kondratenko, V.M. Tsurkin, “Computer models for mode control of electric current treatment of melts at specified quality criteriafor cast products, Part II,” Electronic Modeling, 2020, 42(4), pp. 49-70. https://doi.org/10.15407/emodel.42.04.049

[8] Yu. Zaporozhets, A. Ivanov, Yu. Kondratenko, V. Tsurkin, “Computer modeling of cyber-physical system based on digital twins of melt electric current treatment modes,” CEUR Workshop Proceedings, Vol-3790, 2024, pp. 146–157. https://ceur-ws.org/Vol-3790/paper13.pdf

[9] D.A. Novikov, “Systems Theory and Systems Analysis. Systems Engineering,” In: Cybernetics, Studies in Systems, Decision and Control, Vol. 47. Springer, Cham, 2016. https://doi.org/10.1007/978-3-319-27397-6_4

[10] N. Noy, D. Mcguinness, “Ontology Development 101: A Guide to Creating Your First Ontology, Knowledge Systems Laboratory,” 32, 2001. http://protege.stanford.edu/publications/ontology_development/ontology101.html

[11] I.S. Chistyakova, “Ontology engineering,” Software Engineering, 2014, 20(4), pp. 53–68.

[12] A. Castro, et al., “Ontological-Based Model to Data Governance for Big Data,” IEEE Access, 2021, Vol. 9, pp. 109943 – 109959. https://doi.org/10.1109/access.2021.3101938

[13] L.S. Globa, N.A. Gvozdetska, R.L. Novogrudska, “Ontological model for data processing organization in information and communication networks,” System Research and Information Technologies, 2021, No. 1, pp. 47 – 60. DOI:https://doi.org/10.20535/SRIT.2308-8893.2021.1.04

[14] J.V. Rogushina, A.Y. Gladun, "Development of domain thesaurus as a set of ontology concepts with use of semantic similarity and elements of combinatorial optimization," Prombles in Programming, 2021, No. 2, pp. 3–15.

[15] O. Kryvoruchko, et al., "Cognitive Modeling and Formation of the Knowledge Base of the Information System for Assessing the Rating of Enterprises," INTL Journal of Electronics and Telecommunications, 2023, vol. 69, No. 4, pp. 697–705.

[16] G. Frischkorn, A-L. Schubert, "Cognitive Models in Intelligence Research: Advantages and Recommendations for Their Application," Journal of Intelligence, 2018, Vol. 6, No. 34. https://doi.org/10.3390/jintelligence6030034

[17] V.N. Tsurkin, "Influence of the structure of metal casting on its physical properties," Bulletin of the Ukrainian Material Science Society, 2011, No. 4, pp. 11–19.

[18] V.Yu. Stetsenko, "Mechanisms of the crystallization process of metals and alloys," Foundry Production and Metallurgy, 2013, No. 1, pp. 48–54.

[19] Jg. Qi, Jz. Wang, Hl. Du, et al., "Heredity of Aluminum Melt by Electric Pulse Modification (II)," J. Iron Steel Res. Int., Vol. 14, 2007, pp.76–78. https://doi.org/10.1016/S1006-706X(07)60079-X

[20] G. Wang, et al., "Chapter 9 - Treatment by External Fields," In: R. N. Lumley (Ed.) Fundamentals of Aluminium Metallurgy, Woodhead Publishing Series in Metals and Surface Engineering, Woodhead Publishing, 2018, pp. 279-332. https://doi.org/10.1016/B978-0-08-102063-0.00009-6

[21] V. Gubarev, V. Romanenko, "Stages and main tasks of the century-long control theory and system identification development. Part III. The problem of complex systems identifying by inaccurate data,' Problems of Control and Informatics", No. 1, 2024, pp. 5–23. DOI:https://doi.org/10.34229/1028-0979-2024-1-1

[22] A. Tishchenko, V. Haustova, "Features of concept representation and evaluation in tasks of cognitive modeling," International scientific journal "Economic Cybernetics", 1-2(55-56), 2009, pp. 54–57.

[23] M. Zgurovskiy, N. Pankratova, "System Analysis. Problems, methodology, applications," Kyiv, Naukova Dumka, 2011, 726 p.

[24] R. Stichweh, "Systems theory and the evolution of science," In: G. Altmann, W. Koch (Eds.) Systems: New Paradigms for the

Human Sciences, Berlin, New York: De Gruyter, 1998, pp. 303–317. https://doi.org/10.1515/9783110801194.303

[25] M. Petrenko, K. Malakhov, "Systems Science: Digitalization of Transdisciplinary Research," Journal of Robotics, Networking and Artificial Life, Vol. 10, Issue 4, 2023-2024, pp. 342–352. https://doi.org/10.57417/jrnal.10.4_342

[26] I.A. Petrenko, "On the issue of classification of complex systems," Science and Modernity, 2015, pp. 180–183.

[27] Y.P. Kondratenko, V.M. Kuntsevich, A.A. Chikrii, V.F. Gubarev (Eds), "Advanced control systems: Theory and applications," River Publishers, Gistrup, 2021, pp. 1–441. ISBN: 9788770223416, DOI:10.1201/9781003337010

[28] V.N. Tsurkin, "Influence of the structure of metal casting on its physical properties," Bulletin of the Ukrainian Material Science Society, Is. 4, 2011, pp. 11–19.

[29] Y.P. Kondratenko, A.I. Shevchenko (Eds), "Research Tendencies and Prospect Domains for AI Development and Implementation," River Publishers, 2024, pp. 1–155. ISBN: 978-877004692-3, 978-877004693-0. https://www.riverpublishers.com/book_details.php?book_id=1163

[30] V. Slyusar, et al., "Some Aspects of Artificial Intelligence Development Strategy for Mobile Technologies," Journal of Mobile Multimedia, 20(03), 2024, pp. 525–554. https://doi.org/10.13052/jmm1550-4646.2031

[31] B. Eine, M. Jurisch, W. Quint, "Ontology-Based Big Data Management," Systems, 5(3), 2017, 45. https://doi.org/10.3390/systems5030045

[32] H.S. Sirohi, N. Singhal, P. Kumar, "Knowledge Discovery through Data Mining from Complex Datasets," GIS Science Journal, Vol. 9, Is. 1, 2022, pp. 610 – 617. https://doi.org/18001.GSJ.2022.V9I11.22.40302

[33] P. Flach, "Machine Learning: The Art and Science of Algorithms That Make Sense of Data," Cambridge University Press, 2012.

[34] V. Kazymyr, A. Posadska, "Researching the cognitive maps by simulation modeling," Technical Sciences and Technologies, No 1 (7), 2017, pp. 98–105.

[35] S. Cheng, Q. Zhang, Q. Qin, "Big data analytics with swarm intelligence," Industrial Management & Data Systems, Vol. 116, Is. 4, 2016, pp. 646–666, http://dx.doi.org/10.1108/IMDS-06-2015-0222

[36] V.E. Kozlov, A.V. Bogomolov, S.V. Rudakov, V.T. Olenchenko, "Mathematical support for processing rating information in expert assessment tasks," Mir Izmerenij, 2012, Is. 9, pp. 42–49.

[37] A. Kosenko, P. Pererva, "The rank estimate of the commercial potential of intellectual technologies," Scientific Letters of Academic Society of Michal Baludansky, 2015, Vol. 3, Is. 3, pp. 83 – 92.

[38] Yu.M. Zaporozhets, A.V. Ivanov, Yu.P. Kondratenko, V.M. Tsurkin, "Computer models for mode control of electric current treatment of melts at specified quality criteria for cast products. Part I.," Electronic Modeling, 42(3), 2020, pp. 53 –69. https://doi.org/10.15407/emodel.42.03.049

[39] D. Klimešová, E. Ocelíková, "Multidimensional Data Classification," Proceedings of the 10th WSEAS International Conference on Automation & Information, 2009. pp. 264 – 268.

[40] L. Massel, A. Massel, T. Mamedov, "Integration of Mathematical and Cognitive Modelling in the Software Package "INTEC-A"," Eng. Proc. 2023, 33 (26), pp.1–8. https://doi.org/10.3390/engproc2023033026

[41] V.I. Esin, "Semantic Object-Event Data Model," The Journal of V. N. Karazin Kharkiv National University, Is. 925, 2010, pp. 65–73.

[42] J. Ma, G. Wang, J. Lu, et al., "Semantic Modeling Approach Supporting Process Modeling and Analysis in Aircraft Development," Appl. Sci. 2022, 12, 3067. https://doi.org/10.3390/app12063067

[43] J.V. Rogushina, A.Y. Gladun, "Development of domain thesaurus as a set of ontology concepts with use of semantic similarity and elements of combinatorial optimization," Problems in Programming, Is. 2, 2021, pp. 3–15.

[44] A. V. Palagin, N. G. Petrenko, K. S. Malakhov, "Technique for designing a domain ontology," Computer Means, Networks and Systems, Is. 10, 2011, pp. 5-12. https://doi.org/10.48550/arXiv.1802.06769

[45] Y.P. Kondratenko, V.M. Kuntsevich, A.A. Chikrii, V.F. Gubarev (Eds), "Recent Developments in Automatic Control Systems," River Publishers, Gistrup, 2022, pp. 1–492. ISBN: 978-877022673-8, 978-877022674-5

[46] I. Sidenko, et al., "Neural Technologies for Objects Classification with Mobile Applications," Journal of Mobile Multimedia, 20(03), 2024, pp. 727–748. https://doi.org/10.13052/jmm1550-4646.2039

[47] R. Nickerson, U. Varshney, J. Muntermann, "A method for taxonomy development and its application in information systems,"

European Journal of Information Systems, 2013, 22(3). pp. 336–359. https://doi.org/10.1057/ejis.2012.26

[48] A. A. Andrashov, "Taxonomic models of profiling requirements for critical information management systems," Radioelectronic and Computer Systems, 7(48), 2010, pp. 104–108.

[49] L. Strashynska, O. Mykhailyk, "The methodology using of taxonomic analysis for evaluation the level of food security in Ukraine," Economy and Society, 2023, Is. 49., https://doi.org/10.32782/2524-0072/2023-49-33

[50] T.I. Bondareva, A.B. Sariyeva, "Assessment of enterprise competitiveness based on taxonomy method," Scientific Bulletin of Uzhhorod National University, 6(1), 2016, pp. 42–44.

[51] L. Sergiienko, K. Polyak, T. Poverlyak, "Application of taxonomic analysis in assessing the level of enterprise development in emergency situations," Management Science Letters, 10(6), 2020, pp. 1329–1340. http://dx.doi.org/10.5267/j.msl.2019.11.024

[52] R. Axelrod, "Structure of Decision: the cognitive maps of political elites," New York, Prinston Univ. Press, 1976.

[53] R. E. Bellman, L. A. Zadeh, "Decision-Making in a Fuzzy Environment," Management Science, Vol. 17, No. 4, 1970, pp. B-141 – B-273. https://doi.org/10.1287/mnsc.17.4.B141

[54] P. Barbrook-Johnson, A.S. Penn, "Systems Mapping," Palgrave Macmillan, Springer, Cham, 2022. https://doi.org/10.1007/978-3-03 1-01919-7

[55] T. Taran, V. Shemaev, "Generalized assessments of factors in cognitive modelling tasks," Mathematical Machines and Systems, 3, 2004, pp. 110 – 124.

[56] A. Rotshtein, et al., "Fuzzy cognitive map and mean square method in empirical modeling: Application in economics," Expert Systems with Applications, Volume 247, 2024, 123176, ISSN 0957-4174, https://doi.org/10.1016/j.eswa.2024.123176.

[57] S. Sun, X. Wu, T. Xu, "A Theoretical Framework for a Mathematical Cognitive Model for Adaptive Learning Systems," Behavioral Sciences, Issue 13(5), 2023, pp. 2–15. https://doi.org/10.3390/bs13050406

[58] G. Napoles, I. Grau, R. Pérez-García, R. Bello, "Learning of Fuzzy Cognitive Maps for simulation and knowledge discovery," Conference: Workshop on Knowledge Discovery, Knowledge

Management and Decision Support, EUREKA, 2013, pp. 27–36. http://dx.doi.org/10.2991/.2013.4

[59] O. Kozlov, et al., "Swarm Optimization of Fuzzy Systems for Mobile Robots with Remote Control," Journal of Mobile Multimedia, 19(3), 2023, pp. 839–876. https://journals.riverpublishers.com/index.php/JMM/article/view/14975

[60] O. Tkachenko, "Cognitive Modeling of Composite Systems", Digital Platform Information Technologies in Sociocultural Sphere, 2(1), 2019, pp. 11–19. DOI:10.31866/2617-796x.2.1.2019.175650

[61] M. Lee, W. Vanpaemel, "Determining informative priors for cognitive models," Psychon Bull Rev., 2018, 25:114–127. https://doi.org/10.3758/s13423-017-1238-3.V

[62] V. Mpelogianni, P.P. Groumpos, "Re-approaching fuzzy cognitive maps to increase the knowledge of a system," AI & Soc, Vol. 33, 2018, pp. 175–188. https://doi.org/10.1007/s00146-018-0813-0

[63] V.T. Susidenko, "Information systems and technologies in accounting: a study guide," Kyiv, Center for Educational Literature, 2021.

[64] N.D. Pankratova, et al., "Tools for planning of metropolitan underground infrastructure based on foresight and cognitive modeling methodologies," Problems of Applied Mathematics and Mathematical Modeling, Issue 20, 2020, pp. 109–121. https://doi.org/10.15421/322011

[65] R.J. Wilson, "Introduction to Graph Theory," Longman, 2010.

[66] H.R. Kennet, "Discrete mathematics and its applications," 8-ed., Mc Graw Hill, 2018.

[67] B.H. Hahn, D. T. Valentine, "Essential MATLAB for Engineers and Scientists," 8th ed., Academic Press, 2022.

[68] A.V. Ivanov, "Three-Dimensional Modeling of Features of the Distribution of Electric and Thermal Fields during Conductive Electric Current Treatment of Melts," Surf. Engin. Appl. Electrochem., Vol. 59, 2023, pp. 290–300. https://doi.org/10.3103/S1068375523030109

10

Some Aspects of the Application of Artificial Intelligence for the Recovery and Development of Ukraine

S. Kovalevskyy

Department of Innovative Technologies and Management, Donbas State Engineering Academy, Ukraine
E-mail: kovalevskii61@gmail.com

Abstract

Some aspects of the application of artificial intelligence (AI) for the recovery and development of Ukraine, which suffered from military conflicts, are considered. The main focus is on the integration of AI into various areas of the country's life, including public administration, economy, infrastructure, healthcare, and education. Specific technological solutions are proposed, such as agent systems, neural networks, and decision support systems, which contribute to increasing the efficiency of recovery processes and ensuring sustainability in the conditions of post-war development. Challenges related to the implementation of AI are also discussed, including ethical, legal, and organizational aspects. The article contains an analysis of examples and results of systematic studies of the use of AI in various contexts, including for optimizing the lifecycle of production systems.

Keywords: Artificial intelligence, digital transformation, predictive maintenance, sustainable development. infrastructure restoration, life cycle management, production optimization.

10.1 Introduction

Modern artificial intelligence (AI) technologies offer a wide range of tools and methods that can be adapted to solve the problems faced by Ukraine

DOI: 10.1201/9788743800989-10

[1–5]. The application of AI in the context of recovery and development for countries that have experienced significant upheavals due to economic crises, military conflicts, or natural disasters is particularly relevant. Our work focuses on studying the key aspects of applying AI for the recovery and development of Ukraine, analyzing the opportunities and challenges that arise in this context, and developing appropriate recommendations for the implementation of AI in various sectors of the country's life.

Effective public administration, security, infrastructure restoration, economic development, and improving the quality of education and healthcare are impossible without public support and active citizen participation [6–8]. AI technologies offer a wide range of tools and methods that can be adapted to solve specific tasks [1–5, 9, 10]. In particular, the introduction of AI into the public administration system will optimize decision-making processes and ensure transparency and efficiency of administrative procedures, which in turn will contribute to increasing citizens' trust in state institutions and strengthening the democratic foundations of governance [1–5, 11]. Anti-crisis management, which is especially relevant under conditions of constant threats and instability, requires the forecasting and prevention of crisis situations. Specifically, AI allows the analysis of large volumes of data in real time, identification of potential threats, and rapid response to them, thereby ensuring an increase in national security and stability [1–5, 12, 13]. At the same time, there is a growing need to consider the ethical and legal aspects of AI usage, ensure data privacy protection, develop regulatory mechanisms to control AI use and prevent its abuse, as well as to establish ethical standards and principles for the use of AI in accordance with societal needs [1–5, 14, 15]. It is also necessary to consider the specifics of managing material production processes using the potential of AI, which creates conditions for a significant expansion of the economic base for the country's development [16, 17].

Considering this, the purpose of the work is to define approaches and develop recommendations for the use of AI tools, including agent-based models, for the recovery and development of Ukraine in the post-war period through integration into public administration, infrastructure, healthcare, education, and the economy.

10.2 Some Aspects of the Current Use of AI

The implementation of AI in various sectors, such as infrastructure development, government administration, financial systems, housing and utilities, and crisis management, can significantly enhance efficiency. Specifically, AI can be used for monitoring the condition of infrastructure and automating repair and construction processes, which will accelerate and optimize these activities. In the financial sector, AI can analyze large volumes of data to identify financial risks, prevent fraud, and optimize investment strategies. The housing and utilities sector can also benefit greatly from the introduction of intelligent monitoring and management systems, which will help optimize resource usage and improve the quality of citizen services. Integrating AI into government administration will contribute to optimizing decision-making processes, ensuring transparency and efficiency in administrative procedures, thereby increasing public trust in state institutions and strengthening democratic governance principles. In crisis management, AI enables the analysis of large datasets in real time, facilitating the identification of potential threats and enabling rapid responses. In the healthcare sector, the use of AI for disease diagnosis, treatment, telemedicine, and remote health monitoring can improve access to and the quality of medical services. Education and workforce development also require special attention, as the creation of personalized educational programs and the automation of management processes in educational institutions will help prepare qualified personnel for the modern economy. The implementation of AI should be accompanied by training and the creation of infrastructure to support new technologies, and educational programs should be adapted to prepare specialists capable of working with intelligent systems. The use of AI for the restoration and development of Ukraine opens up broad prospects for improving efficiency in various areas of life, which is particularly relevant in the context of aggression from a neighboring country. The result of this research is a systematic analysis that provides a comprehensive overview of the key issues arising from the war in the country (Tables 10.1, 10.2, and 10.3). These tables reflect various aspects of the war's impact on the socio-economic and political situation in Ukraine and provide systematized research results on AI technologies.

10.2.1 Analysis of the negative consequences of war and the use of AI to overcome them

The proposed results highlight a systematic approach to analyzing the consequences of war through the lens of AI. They not only enumerate the negative impacts but also suggest specific AI technologies that can be employed to analyze and manage these issues. This represents a novel approach to crisis management, combining traditional analytical methods with modern AI technologies, thereby facilitating more accurate and timely decision-making (Table 10.1).

Table 10.1 Negative consequences of the Russian–Ukrainian war in Ukraine.

Directions	Appointment of directions	Application of AI	Proposed structures of AI
Restoration of energy and infrastructure security	Restoration and modernization of energy infrastructure, roads, bridges, and essential services. Introduction of renewable energy sources, improvement of energy efficiency, and optimization of critical infrastructure.	Monitoring the state of energy and infrastructure objects, optimization of energy consumption, forecasting of needs, and integration of renewable energy sources. Planning, monitoring, and optimization of construction projects.	IoT sensors for monitoring, optimization algorithms, energy consumption and infrastructure forecasting models, resource management systems, project management systems.
Economic stabilization and housing provision	Support of small- and medium-sized businesses, creation of new jobs, attraction of investments, and restoration of housing stock for victims.	Analysis of economic data for the development of stabilization strategies, forecasting economic trends, and optimization of housing resources for displaced persons.	Econometric models, machine learning algorithms for forecasting, resource management systems (ERP), optimization algorithms, project management systems.
Improvement of health care	Development and implementation of health care programs, ensuring access to medical services, maintaining the health of the population.	Monitoring the health of the population, forecasting medical needs, optimizing resource distribution.	IoT sensors for health monitoring, resource management systems (ERP), forecasting models for healthcare needs.
Ensuring information and institutional security	Protection against cyberattacks, security of information systems, and protection of personal data. Restoration and modernization of state institutions.	Detection and prevention of cyberattacks, monitoring systems, data security, and institutional effectiveness analysis.	Intrusion detection systems (IDS), artificial neural networks (ANNs) for anomaly analysis, data encryption, machine learning algorithms for performance analysis.
Support for innovation and scientific research	Support for scientific research, development of innovative technologies, and recovery methods.	Analysis of scientific data, development of new technologies, and support for innovative startups.	Machine learning for scientific data analysis, project management systems, platforms for collaborative research.

Table 10.1 *Continued.*

Directions	**Appointment of directions**	**Application of AI**	**Proposed structures of AI**
Environmental protection and cultural heritage revival	Development of programs for environmental restoration, pollution control, protection of natural resources, and restoration of cultural heritage.	Monitoring environmental conditions, analyzing pollution data, and supporting cultural initiatives through data analysis.	IoT sensors for environmental monitoring, big data processing algorithms, environmental forecasting models, cultural heritage monitoring systems.

Table 10.2 Directions for supporting and rebuilding Ukraine.

Directions	**Appointment of directions**	**Application of AI**	**Proposed structures of AI**
Restoration of energy and infrastructure security	Restoration and modernization of energy infrastructure, roads, bridges, and essential services. Introduction of renewable energy sources, improvement of energy efficiency, and optimization of critical infrastructure.	Monitoring energy objects and infrastructure, optimization of energy consumption and infrastructure resources, forecasting energy needs, and integrating renewable energy sources.	IoT sensors for monitoring, optimization algorithms, energy consumption and infrastructure forecasting models, resource management systems.
Economic stabilization and housing provision	Support for small- and medium-sized businesses, creation of new jobs, attraction of investments, and restoration of housing stock for displaced persons.	Analysis of economic data for stabilization strategies, optimization of tax systems, forecasting economic trends, and planning housing resources.	Econometric models, machine learning algorithms for forecasting, resource management systems (ERP), optimization algorithms, project management systems.
Improvement of healthcare	Development and implementation of healthcare programs, ensuring access to medical services, maintaining the health of the population.	Monitoring population health, forecasting medical needs, optimizing medical resource distribution.	IoT sensors for health monitoring, resource management systems (ERP), forecasting models for healthcare needs.

Table 10.2 *Continued.*

Directions	Appointment of directions	Application of AI	Proposed structures of AI
Ensuring information and institutional security	Protection against cyberattacks, security of information systems, protection of personal data, and restoration of state institutions.	Detection and prevention of cyberattacks, monitoring systems, and analysis of institutional effectiveness.	Intrusion detection systems (IDS), artificial neural networks (ANN) for anomaly analysis, data encryption, machine learning algorithms for performance analysis.
Support for innovation and scientific research	Support for scientific research, development of innovative technologies, and recovery methods.	Analysis of scientific data, support for innovative startups, and collaborative research.	Machine learning for scientific data analysis, project management systems, platforms for joint research.
Environmental protection and cultural heritage revival	Development of programs for environmental restoration, pollution control, and protection of natural resources, along with the revival of cultural heritage.	Monitoring environmental conditions and cultural sites, analyzing pollution and cultural data, and implementing restoration programs.	IoT sensors for environmental monitoring, big data processing algorithms, environmental forecasting models, cultural heritage monitoring systems.
Psychological support for victims	Support for victims of war, particularly children and soldiers, in overcoming psychological trauma.	Using chatbots for psychological support, data analysis to identify people in need.	Natural language processing (NLP), recommender systems, machine learning models for state classification.

10.2.2 Key areas of support and recovery of Ukraine using AI

The second part of the study systematically presents key areas where AI can be effectively integrated into the process of recovery and support for Ukraine. Specific areas of AI application are proposed, such as information security, psychological support, and economic stabilization. This strategic focus on the use of AI for specific tasks contributes to a holistic approach to the country's recovery (Table 10.2).

Table 10.3 Components of the AI system, technologies, and their functions in the process of Ukraine's recovery.

A component of the AI system	Elements of AI technologies	AI function
Data collection	IoT – sensors, satellite images, social networks	Collection of data from various sources for analysis
Data storage	Cloud storage, databases	Storage of large volumes of data for further processing
Data processing	ETL processes	Preparation and cleaning of data, their structuring
Data analysis	Machine learning, deep learning, NLP	Use of AI algorithms for data analysis, pattern detection, forecasting
Decision-making	Decision support systems (DSS), genetic algorithms, optimization methods	Formation of recommendations and strategies based on data analysis
Project execution	Project management systems (PMS), intelligent agent systems (multi-agent systems)	Project management automation, progress monitoring, task performance
Monitoring and evaluation	Monitoring and reporting tools (Tableau, Power BI), feedback analysis (Sentiment Analysis)	Evaluation of the effectiveness of implemented projects, analysis of feedback
Strategy adjustment	Forecasting and optimization models, decision support systems	Making changes to plans and strategies based on performance analysis and feedback

10.2.3 Integration of AI components into the recovery and development processes in Ukraine

Detailing the components of an AI system, such as data collection, storage, processing, analysis, decision-making, project execution, monitoring, evaluation, and strategy adjustment, highlights the integration of various AI technologies and their key functions within restoration projects. Examples of technologies are provided for each component, including IoT sensors, satellite imagery, cloud storage, ETL processes, machine learning, decision support systems, and monitoring tools. This underscores the importance of a systemic approach to implementing AI in recovery processes, emphasizing the significance of each stage and technology to ensure effective, strategic, and sustainable development of Ukraine in the post-war period (Table 10.3).

Thus, modern AI technologies offer a wide range of opportunities to address the pressing challenges faced by Ukraine in the context of an unprovoked war. The innovation of this research lies in its comprehensive approach to analyzing and integrating AI into various sectors of public life, including infrastructure development, government administration, the financial system, public utilities, crisis management, and healthcare. Specifically, using AI for monitoring infrastructure conditions and automating repair and construction processes accelerates and optimizes these activities, which is particularly crucial for the country's recovery following military conflicts. The integration of AI into the financial sector enables the analysis of large datasets to identify financial risks, prevent fraud, and optimize investment strategies, contributing to economic stabilization and the attraction of investments into the country.

The public utilities sector can significantly benefit from implementing intelligent monitoring and management systems that optimize resource usage and improve the quality of services provided to citizens. The innovation lies in systematically identifying key areas where AI can be effectively integrated into Ukraine's recovery and support process, enabling a strategic focus on specific tasks and fostering a holistic approach to the country's restoration. The implementation of AI in government administration enhances decision-making processes, transparency, and efficiency of administrative procedures, thereby increasing public trust in state institutions and strengthening democratic governance principles. In crisis management, AI enables real-time analysis of large data volumes, identification of potential threats, and swift response, ensuring effective crisis management. The proposed AI systems can serve as the foundation for new approaches to crisis management, economic stabilization, and social development in Ukraine.

10.3 Agent Technologies for Managing Infrastructure Systems

10.3.1 Examples of successful implementations of agent technologies and AI in infrastructure and systems management

The development of complex multi-component systems based on agent technologies and AI for managing infrastructure during crises is a challenging task, but there are several examples illustrating the successful implementation of such systems in various contexts [18–21]. These systems are used for dynamic monitoring of infrastructure conditions and for forecasting potential risks. They can adapt to changing conditions in real time, ensuring prompt decision-making and effective resource allocation. For instance, in [19], the use of agent models for infrastructure restoration is proposed, helping optimize emergency response processes and plan recovery measures. Similarly, in [20], agent models are employed to enhance the resilience of critical infrastructure to climate change, including emergency restoration aspects. In [21], agent models are applied to monitor earthquake-related risks, contributing to more effective infrastructure recovery management.

AI agent models are widely used in smart city management, ensuring the efficiency and flexibility of urban systems. In [22], agent models are employed to manage transportation systems, healthcare, the environment, and urban resources, enabling rapid adaptation to changes in the urban environment and enhancing the quality of life for residents. In [23], agent models are applied to manage transportation systems, healthcare, the environment, and urban resources, allowing for quick adaptation to urban changes and improving residents' quality of life. In [24], agent models are utilized for monitoring urban data and supporting real-time decision-making, ensuring the flexible and efficient management of urban resources.

AI agent models are also employed for effective water and resource management under conditions of climate change and increasing resource demand. In [25], the use of agent models for optimizing water resource allocation, forecasting extreme events, and enhancing the efficiency of ecosystem management is described. These models enable real-time adaptation of resource distribution, ensuring the sustainable development of water systems. In [26], agent models are also considered a tool for managing various resources, contributing to the achievement of sustainable development goals through effective resource utilization and management.

AI agent models contribute to the restoration and development of infrastructure, particularly in crisis and post-disaster situations. In [26], the use of agent models to ensure stability and restore critical infrastructure during climate change adaptation is emphasized, which helps minimize risks and improve recovery processes. In [21], the application of agent-based AI models for managing post-earthquake infrastructure recovery is described, where these models are used to monitor risks and manage resources needed for restoration. Additionally, in [27], agent models help optimize transportation systems, contributing to increased efficiency in infrastructure use and its development in the private sector.

AI agent models are actively integrated into production systems in the European Union to enhance efficiency and support innovation. In [28], the integration of AI agent models in the context of production digitalization is discussed, where these models are used for process automation, production line optimization, and cost reduction, which are key aspects of Industry

4.0 technology implementation. In [29], AI agent models are applied for risk management, quality control, and resource optimization in production, ensuring compliance with safety standards and ethical practices in production processes. This analysis demonstrates the multifunctionality and effectiveness of AI agent models across various sectors, highlighting their importance for infrastructure management, restoration, and development, as well as for optimizing production processes.

Proper design of agent architectures is crucial for creating intelligent agent systems. These architectures can be reactive, deliberative, or hybrid – combining the advantages of both approaches to achieve goal-directed behavior by breaking down plans into multiple sub-plans. Some systems use a distributed knowledge base with "if–then" rules, allowing agents to interpret their environment, activate relevant rules, execute actions, and update their internal states. Other approaches integrate well-known theories and frameworks to create advisory agents. For example, the BEN architecture (behavior with emotions and norms) uses a modular agent structure that includes cognitive processes based on BDI (belief-desire-intention), emotions based on the OCC theory (Ortony, Clore, and Collins), personality traits based on the OCEAN model, social relationships, and norms, allowing for the modeling of expressive and plausible agent behavior in social simulations.

For situations requiring more thorough information processing, BDI architectures are better suited. In contrast, behavior-oriented designers (BOD) structure agents around reactive behavior, which can be hierarchically composed to create more complex solutions. Evolutionary methods, such as NEAT (neuro-evolution of augmenting topologies), are used to develop artificial neural networks that control individual agents' decision-making and movement in simulations. These methods enable the optimization of neural network structures and weight coefficients, ensuring effective control of agent behavior.

These statements underscore the diversity of approaches to developing AI agent models, each with unique functions and applications depending on the simulation context and requirements.

The implementation of AI in smart cities requires a systematic approach to optimize management processes, enhance efficiency, and improve residents' quality of life. This approach facilitates the automation of operations, reduces human errors, and supports data-driven decision-making. The importance of comprehensive AI implementation is highlighted in [22], covering various sectors such as healthcare, mobility, safety, energy, and waste management. Similarly, Francisco and Linnér [26] emphasize that a systematic approach to AI implementation is key to achieving sustainable development goals. AI contributes to more efficient resource use, better data analysis, and reduced environmental impact, making it essential for global sustainable development strategies.

The implementation of AI in government administration also requires a systematic approach, particularly to address outdated systems and integrate new technologies. As mentioned in [30], the success of digital transformation is possible only with the systematic implementation of innovative technologies like AI, which ensures integration and interaction with existing systems. These points demonstrate the importance of a systematic approach to AI implementation, ensuring effective technology use and the achievement of long-term goals across various sectors.

10.3.2 Agent technologies for infrastructure system management

10.3.2.1 Architecture of an agent-based system for monitoring and managing infrastructure

To develop original agent models proposed for managing various processes, the focus is on continuously monitoring infrastructure conditions (e.g., roads, bridges, energy facilities) and optimizing resource allocation while planning restoration work based on up-to-date data. Additionally, agent systems will support social assistance and the rehabilitation of internally displaced persons, along with the development of economic stabilization strategies, which include analyzing economic data and optimizing tax systems. Other important aspects include addressing security challenges through the monitoring of threats such as cyberattacks or military actions, ensuring rapid response; monitoring and controlling environmental conditions, developing strategies for environmental restoration; promoting the development of adaptive educational programs; and managing energy infrastructure, including optimizing energy consumption and implementing renewable energy sources. This comprehensive approach encompasses a wide range of applications for agent models in the context of recovery and development, providing a deeper understanding and structuring of tasks for their effective resolution.

For the technical implementation of agent models to continuously monitor roads, bridges, energy facilities, and other infrastructure elements, a comprehensive approach is proposed that includes several key stages and technologies. First and foremost, an efficient data collection infrastructure is required, involving the use of IoT sensors to measure various parameters, as well as satellite and drone imagery to assess the condition of objects from above. The collected data is stored in cloud storage and real-time databases, ensuring accessibility and prompt analysis. Data processing involves ETL processes, machine learning, and convolutional neural networks, which help detect anomalies and predict possible failures. The agent architecture includes the creation of different types of agents – monitoring agents, analytical agents, and decision-making agents – that together provide comprehensive monitoring and management of infrastructure. The integration of agent systems with appropriate communication protocols and user interfaces ensures ease of control and decision-making. Automation of actions, system scalability, data security and reliability, as well as validation and testing in various scenarios, guarantee the effectiveness and reliability of the created system. Thus, modern technologies, particularly IoT, machine learning, and cloud solutions, allow for the creation of an effective system for monitoring and managing infrastructure objects that meets the requirements of continuity and reliability.

The agent-based system for monitoring, analyzing, and decision-making regarding infrastructure consists of three main types of agents: monitoring agents, analysis agents, and decision-making agents. Monitoring agents are responsible for data collection and preliminary analysis from sensors and images. They are implemented using IoT platforms such as Arduino or Raspberry Pi and programming languages that support multithreading, such as Python or Java. These agents collect data in real time, conduct preliminary analysis to detect anomalies, and transmit the processed data to other agents using network protocols like MQTT or HTTP [31–34]. Analysis agents receive this data and conduct in-depth analysis using machine learning algorithms and neural networks. They identify patterns, trends, and predict potential issues based on historical data. The results of this analysis are transmitted to decision-making agents, which determine the necessary actions based on the received results, such as initiating repair work or changing the operational mode of an object. These agents interact with external systems, such as SCADA, to automate management actions. All these agents work in close coordination, ensuring a complete cycle from data collection to decision-making and execution of appropriate actions, providing effective management of infrastructure. Such a system requires the integration of various technologies, including sensors, machine learning, and communication protocols, enabling the creation of a reliable and efficient management system (Figure 10.1).

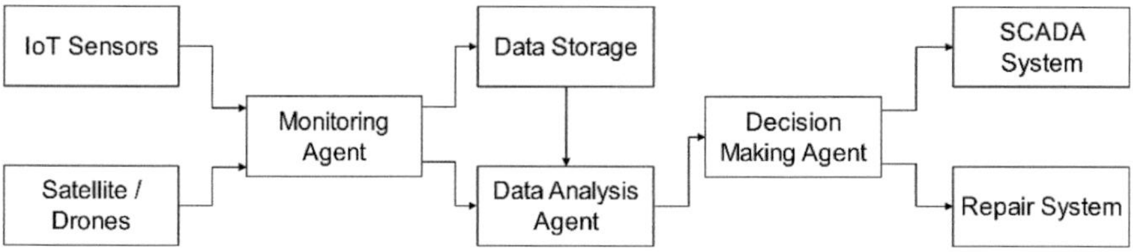

Figure 10.1 Architecture of an agent-based system for monitoring, analysis, and decision-making in infrastructure management.

To implement agents that facilitate interaction within the system for monitoring, analysis, and decision-making regarding infrastructure objects, several software components need to be developed.

The first component is the IoT sensor agent, which is responsible for collecting data from sensors such as temperature and vibration. This agent is implemented in Python and uses random data generation to simulate the data collection process from real sensors. The collected data is then transmitted to other agents for further processing.

The second component is the satellite or drone agent, which captures images and videos from above. This agent simplifies the image capture process by using a simple text description that contains information about the coordinates of the shot.

Another important component is the monitoring agent, which gathers data from sensors and satellites, performs preliminary analysis, and transmits this data for storage and further analysis. The monitoring agent conducts initial data processing, detects anomalies such as increased vibration, and transmits the analysis results to other agents via the MQTT protocol.

A dedicated data storage component is used to receive and store all collected data, preserving historical data for future analysis.

The analysis agent performs more in-depth analysis using machine learning methods, such as classification and anomaly detection. It utilizes a pre-trained model to analyze the received data and make predictions about potential infrastructure issues.

The final key component is the decision-making agent, which determines the necessary actions based on the analysis results. If anomalies are detected, it initiates repair work or other required actions, such as adjusting the operating mode of the infrastructure.

The system also includes SCADA and repair systems, which receive commands from the decision-making agent and carry out the corresponding actions, such as repairs or adjustments to operating parameters.

10.3.2.2 Data flow management in agent systems

Data transmission between these agents is facilitated by the MQTT protocol, which ensures efficient and reliable real-time message exchange. The MQTT broker receives messages from one agent and forwards them to other subscribed agents, maintaining continuous communication among all system components. To test the agents in real time, an environment is created where the agents can operate as if interacting with real data. This includes setting up the MQTT broker, using sensor simulators or test datasets, running the agents as separate processes, and monitoring their interactions and data transmissions. This approach allows for the identification of potential errors and the adjustment of agent operations to ensure reliable performance in a production environment.

Such a comprehensive approach to the implementation and testing of agent systems ensures effective monitoring, analysis, and management of infrastructure objects, thereby reducing risks and maintaining a high level of safety and reliability. The graphical representation of agent implementation, including data transmission technology via the MQTT protocol, illustrates how different agents interact with each other and the MQTT broker, which acts as the central hub for data transmission (Figure 10.2).

This interaction diagram between AI agents illustrates the comprehensive process of data collection, analysis, and decision-making to support infrastructure recovery. The process begins with data collection through sensors (Sensor Data Collection), which capture various parameters of

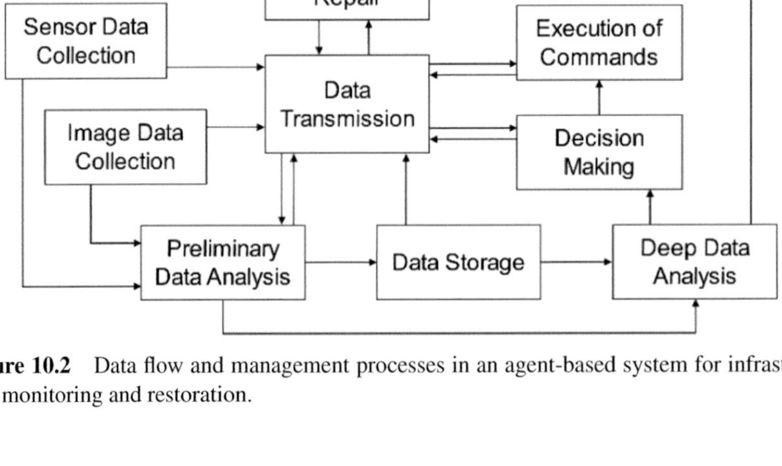

Figure 10.2 Data flow and management processes in an agent-based system for infrastructure monitoring and restoration.

infrastructure objects. Simultaneously, image data collection (Image Data Collection) is conducted, including photos, videos, and other visual data required for analysis.

The collected data undergoes preliminary analysis (Preliminary Data Analysis), where it is cleaned, filtered, and prepared for further processing. This stage is critical to ensure the quality of data used in the subsequent steps. Next, the data is transmitted to the central system (Data Transmission) for processing and stored in a suitable data repository (Data Storage). This storage allows for historical analysis and supports AI model training.

Based on the stored data, deep data analysis (Deep Data Analysis) is performed using advanced machine learning models, forecasting methods, and other AI technologies. At this stage, valuable insights for strategic decision-making are derived. Following these insights, decisions are made (Decision Making) regarding the necessary actions, such as repairs, resource management adjustments, and other key operations.

The decisions are implemented by sending commands (Execution of Commands) to the respective execution agents to carry out actions like repairs or parameter adjustments. The final stage is infrastructure repair (Infrastructure Repair), performed based on the received commands to maintain and restore the functionality of infrastructure assets.

This entire process allows the system to operate in real time, enabling continuous monitoring and maintenance of infrastructure. The use of AI agents at each stage increases efficiency in managing infrastructure, reduces downtime, and ensures the longevity of infrastructure components.

10.3.2.3 Agent interaction via MQTT broker in data management systems

Appropriate broker software was selected to create and configure the MQTT broker. Mosquitto is one of the most popular and reliable options. It is a lightweight, open-source broker that supports MQTT versions 3.1 and 3.1.1, making it an optimal choice for many projects (Figure 10.3).

After selecting the broker, the installation process was completed, which varies depending on the operating system. Mosquitto was configured through the mosquitto.conf configuration file, where parameters such as the broker's working port (default 1883), security, user authentication, and other settings were specified. In its basic mode, Mosquitto does not require significant changes to the configuration; however, more advanced settings, such as user authentication, can be configured if needed. This allows for access protection

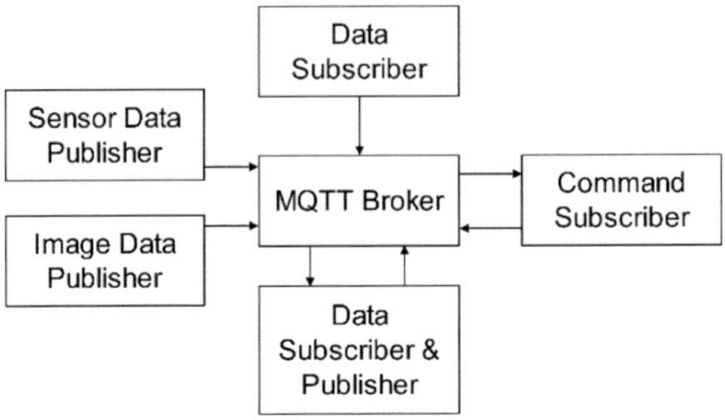

Figure 10.3 Agent interaction architecture using MQTT broker for data monitoring and management systems.

to the broker by creating a password file and making the appropriate changes to the configuration file.

After configuring the broker, its operation was tested using Mosquitto clients. The broker's functionality was verified by issuing commands to publish messages and subscribe to topics.

Once the broker was configured and tested, it could be integrated with agents in the system for data transmission between them, ensuring effective communication within the agent architecture.

Additionally, aspects such as securing data transmission using SSL/TLS encryption or scaling the system to handle a large number of connections were considered. Broker clusters or managed services such as AWS IoT or Azure IoT Hub may be required in scenarios where the system demands high reliability and performance.

These steps are essential for setting up and using the MQTT broker, facilitating data transmission between agents in the system, and enabling the creation of effective solutions for monitoring, analyzing, and managing infrastructure objects.

The configuration of the MQTT broker for the proposed agents demonstrates key components, including monitoring agents, analysis agents, decision-making agents, and their connection with the MQTT broker.

10.3.2.4 General framework for the use of agents and their integration into infrastructure management systems

The general framework for using agents and integrating them to solve various tasks involves IoT sensors for data collection, agents for analysis and decision-making, as well as decision support systems, resource optimization, and management systems (Figure 10.4).

The depicted diagram illustrates the cyclical process of interaction between AI agents to ensure efficient data collection, processing, analysis, decision-making, and execution of repair work in infrastructure management. The process starts with data collection through two channels: sensor data and visual data (images). Sensors installed on various infrastructure objects monitor parameters like temperature, humidity, and vibration, while cameras and other devices collect visual data in parallel, providing additional context for analysis.

The collected data is sent to the preliminary data analysis block for initial processing, including data cleaning, noise removal, anomaly checks, and preparation for further analysis, along with forming preliminary conclusions. After preliminary analysis, the data is transmitted to the data storage block, where it is stored for future use. This enables historical analysis and supports training AI models or conducting deep data analysis in the future. Concurrently, some pre-processed data is sent to the pattern recognition block, which uses machine learning algorithms to detect recurring patterns or anomalies in the data. These results serve as a foundation for further decision-making, providing key information about the current state of infrastructure objects.

Stored data then moves to the deep data analysis block, where detailed examination is conducted using complex models and algorithms. This stage involves multiple levels of processing, such as forecasting, classification, trend detection, and correlation analysis, allowing for more accurate results crucial for effective decision-making. Data related to textual information passes through the text and language processing block, which is critical

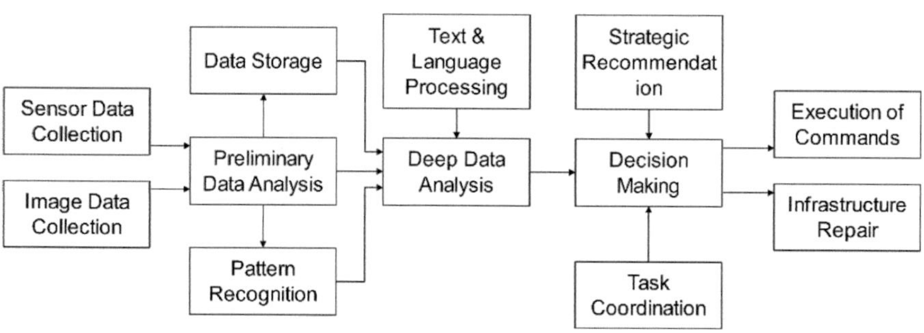

Figure 10.4 General diagram of agent usage and integration.

for analyzing reports, instructions, messages, and other text that may be important for decision-making. The results from this analysis are integrated with other data to provide a comprehensive understanding of the situation.

Based on this analysis, the system formulates strategic recommendations that outline possible actions or decisions to ensure effective infrastructure repair or maintenance. In the central decision-making block, the collected information is synthesized to generate specific commands for execution. This block integrates preliminary and deep analysis results, along with strategic recommendations, to determine the optimal course of action.

Once a decision is made, task coordination occurs, distributing tasks among different executors or subsystems to ensure coherence and synchronization. The coordinated tasks proceed to the command execution stage, where decisions are implemented – this could include repair work, software updates, resource management, etc. The result of the entire process is infrastructure repair, carried out based on data analysis and decision-making. This completes the cycle, returning the system to the initial stage, where sensors and cameras collect data to monitor the repaired infrastructure's condition.

The integration of various analysis and data processing methods creates a highly automated system capable of operating in real time, providing continuous infrastructure monitoring and maintenance.

The systematic implementation of an AI-based agent system for the recovery and sustainable development of Ukraine, both during wartime and in the post-war period, involves several key stages to ensure effective operation under constantly changing conditions.

In the first stage, during active hostilities, the system must continuously monitor infrastructure using sensors, satellites, and drones to collect data on damaged objects. This data is promptly processed and analyzed for rapid decision-making, enabling the coordination of repair work and minimizing the impact of destruction.

In the transitional period, when the extent of damage is assessed and recovery strategies are developed, the focus will shift to the optimal allocation of resources and overseeing the implementation of recovery programs to ensure effective and timely restoration of critical infrastructure.

In the post-war period, the system will focus on strengthening infrastructure, continuously monitoring its condition, and adapting to new challenges that may arise during long-term recovery and development. An important aspect of this stage is developing long-term plans that address the need for modernization, increased resilience, and infrastructure security.

The main challenges that may arise during the implementation of this system include technical, organizational, security, social, legal, and economic aspects.

Technical challenges include ensuring system reliability in a damaged infrastructure environment, avoiding delays in processing large amounts of data, and integrating various technologies such as IoT and machine learning, which may require significant effort and resources.

Organizational challenges involve ensuring effective coordination between agents and government agencies, training personnel to work with new systems, and overcoming financial constraints, particularly those caused by the war.

Security challenges relate to protecting the system from cyber threats and physical damage, as well as ensuring the safety of the infrastructure itself.

Social challenges encompass public perception of new technologies and adherence to ethical standards, particularly regarding privacy and human rights, which may require additional informational campaigns and increased transparency.

Legal challenges arise from the need to comply with regulatory requirements and international sanctions, which may complicate access to certain technologies or investments.

Economic challenges include maintaining project sustainability during economic instability and assessing the return on investment, which may be difficult during the recovery period.

Successfully overcoming these challenges will require careful planning, effective coordination among all stakeholders, and the system's ability to quickly adapt to changes. Ultimately, by adapting, coordinating, and efficiently utilizing resources, the system will not only contribute to rapid infrastructure recovery but also lay the foundation for sustainable development and increased resilience to future challenges in Ukraine.

10.4 AI for Supporting the Lifecycle of Production Systems in Solving Specific Mechanical Engineering Tasks

10.4.1 Examples of supporting the lifecycle of mechanical engineering products using AI

In numerous works [28, 35–39], the lifecycle of technology is analyzed, noting that it begins with innovation, proceeds through stages of growth and maturity, and eventually reaches decline. All these stages of the lifecycle are standardized and apply both in the civil economy and the military sector, emphasizing the critical importance of managing the lifecycle of conventional and defense-related products [40, 41]. An important aspect is that technological development influences production processes at every stage of the lifecycle, making lifecycle support essential for maintaining manufacturing competitiveness.

These and many other works emphasize the importance of supporting the lifecycle in the context of sustainable development. It is suggested that implementing AI can improve lifecycle management of products, leading to more efficient resource use and reduced environmental impact. This is especially significant amid the global transition to a more sustainable society, where lifecycle support of products is key. It is also noted that lifecycle management is central to digital transformation, where outdated systems can present a major barrier to progress. This highlights the need for designing systems that can effectively adapt to changes, ensuring long-term functionality and sustained lifecycle support. These observations confirm the importance of a systematic approach to supporting the lifecycle of any product in the context of modern technological development and management.

The significance of maintaining AI's current lifecycle at every stage of its existence is mentioned in several sources. The first stage – development and implementation – is crucial, as it is necessary to consider future updates and AI integration with other systems. Cancela-Outeda [29] underscores the importance of complying with regulatory requirements and ethical standards throughout AI development, ensuring adherence to quality standards during its operational phase [42]. In the operational phase, continuous updates to AI algorithms are needed to accommodate new data and environmental changes. Parcu et al. [43] point out that, for successful AI implementation in emerging technological environments like 5G, continuous updates and system support are required to ensure relevance and efficiency [44]. Regular updates and technical maintenance of AI are crucial for its effective functioning throughout its lifecycle. Albahri et al. [45] discuss the necessity of ongoing monitoring and updates of AI systems to maintain their relevance, particularly in crisis situations, where timely updates can be critical [46]. Thus, maintaining AI throughout its entire lifecycle is vital for ensuring efficiency, safety, and compliance with modern standards.

The maintenance and support of the lifecycle of engineering products using AI can be implemented at all stages, from design to disposal. The lifecycle of engineering products is a complex process consisting of multiple stages, each of which plays a critical role in achieving the final outcome.

10.4.2 Integration of AI in managing the lifecycle of mechanical engineering objects

The process of developing engineering products is complex and consists of several key standardized stages, but the technological support of the product lifecycle requires the integration of certain components. These components enhance the technology for ensuring the functional properties of the working surfaces of machine parts and their restoration during operation, as well as the systematic optimization of the product lifecycle, specifically by leveraging artificial intelligence.

The first critical step is component design, during which the geometric parameters of parts, such as dimensions, are determined while considering technical requirements like strength, precision, material, safety margins, and other characteristics. These parameters involve a certain degree of uncertainty, which necessitates sensitivity analysis to assess the impact of variations on the final outcome. After determining the geometric parameters, it is essential to analyze part manufacturing time, production efficiency, and equipment layout to optimize the production flow. Special emphasis is placed on modeling the production process, taking into account the efficiency of machine usage and workstation placement.

In designing the technological processing system, it is crucial to configure and plan equipment for different operations, including analyzing logistics concepts, storage strategies, warehouse planning, and types of technological equipment. Efficient use of production space is also an important aspect, as different technological processes require different densities of placement and movement of products. For systematic analysis, it is advisable to create a simulation library, allowing a detailed study of various types of technological equipment and operations. Modeling becomes a tool for gaining a realistic understanding of the production process, which is vital for improving production efficiency.

The implementation stage of new operational systems for technological objects in mechanical engineering production is complex, as expectations from production and the quality of these operational systems do not always align. Therefore, a simulation model should be used to test the functionality of these systems before implementation. Virtual manufacturing, which includes models of machines, equipment, and operations, enables comprehensive testing and evaluation of system quality. The emulation approach provides a complete check of the interaction between different production components, helping identify and correct errors. After the implementation of operational systems into real work, the next step is personnel training to ensure high

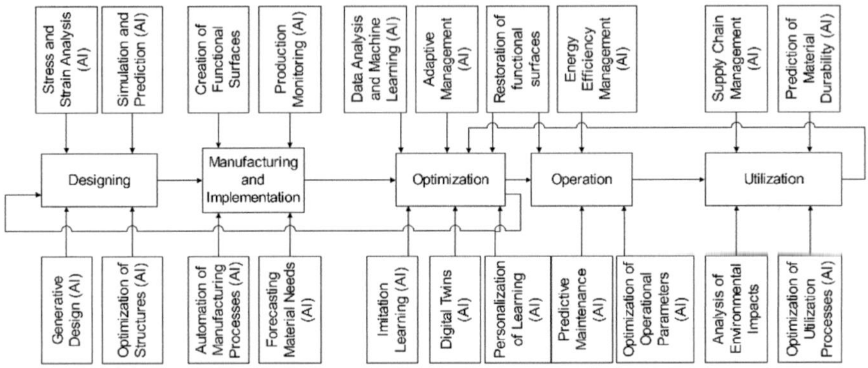

Figure 10.5 Integration of AI in the lifecycle of manufacturing objects.

productivity. A game-based training platform using virtual reality has proven effective for transferring practical knowledge and experience while eliminating risks associated with traditional training methods. Virtual reality provides training that closely replicates real conditions, which is important for planning and decision-making by operators [47].

Product operation optimization includes adjusting production control system parameters and verifying the production plan. Setting production control parameters in a simulated virtual environment allows for achieving optimal plant productivity, particularly through optimizing part and component placement. Verifying the plan using a virtual model can significantly expedite the testing and improvement of the production plan. To enhance the planning process's efficiency, statistical analysis and visualization should be employed, helping design engineers make informed decisions within a limited timeframe. This approach aims to improve the productivity and quality of mechanical engineering products by using innovative modeling and training methods.

The lifecycle management scheme of mechanical engineering products consists of several key stages, each interconnected and supported by modern AI technologies, as well as processes like the creation and restoration of functional surfaces of parts (Figure 10.5).

The first stage is design, where key parameters such as geometry, materials, functional requirements, and technical characteristics are determined. AI plays an important role in optimizing the design, considering requirements for strength, weight, and cost. Generative design, also powered by AI, allows for the creation of innovative designs that meet specified parameters through machine learning algorithms. Stress and strain analysis using AI predicts material behavior under load, reducing the time and cost of physical experiments. Moreover, modeling different usage scenarios and the impact of external factors on products with AI enables predictions about durability and reliability.

The subsequent stage is implementation, encompassing production preparation, manufacturing, and quality control. AI is used to automate manufacturing processes, reduce downtime, and enhance production efficiency. An important aspect of this stage is forecasting material and resource needs, enabling optimized procurement and logistics based on demand and material availability. AI also provides real-time monitoring of production, detecting anomalies and enabling immediate responses, and ensuring uninterrupted operation. A significant component of this stage is the creation of functional surfaces for parts, ensuring durability and reliability during use.

The operational stage covers the period during which the product performs its intended functions. Predictive maintenance, based on analyzing sensor data with AI, allows for predicting equipment wear and potential breakdowns, helping to avoid unplanned downtime and minimize repair costs. AI is also used to automatically adjust equipment operating parameters to achieve optimal productivity and efficiency. Energy management through AI optimizes energy consumption based on work conditions and requirements, reducing costs and minimizing environmental impact. Additionally, restoring functional surfaces during this stage is crucial, as it extends part lifespans and reduces replacement costs.

Optimization is the next stage in the lifecycle, where existing processes, products, and systems are analyzed and improved. Data analysis and machine learning are used to identify opportunities for enhancing product quality and reducing costs. The creation of digital twins of real-world objects enables analysis, testing, and optimization of their operation in real time without risking actual equipment. AI also supports adaptive production management strategies, enabling quick responses to changes in working conditions and market demands. Restoration of functional surfaces at this stage is also crucial, as improvements in restoration technologies can significantly extend product lifespan and reduce maintenance costs.

The final stage of the lifecycle is disposal and recycling, which involves the collection, sorting, processing, and recycling of used products and materials. AI helps optimize disposal processes, manage logistics, and recover materials and components for reuse, thereby reducing environmental impact and increasing recycling efficiency. Environmental impact analysis using AI enables the modeling of the outcomes of different disposal strategies, allowing the selection of the most efficient and environmentally safe solutions. Predicting the durability of materials based on wear analysis and material properties helps determine the most suitable disposal methods.

At all stages of the lifecycle, training and personnel development are essential. Simulation-based training in virtual reality allows operators to safely master new technologies and processes. The use of AI algorithms to create personalized training programs that consider employees' current skills and needs ensures more effective training tailored to achieve specific company goals. Integration and system interaction are critical for ensuring the seamless operation of the enterprise. The use of the Internet of Things (IoT) and unified platforms with AI support facilitates the integration of various management systems, ensuring their effective interaction. AI also analyzes and optimizes supply chains, reducing costs and improving coordination between suppliers and manufacturers, which is essential for timely material supply and waste management.

Thus, a comprehensive approach to lifecycle management of mechanical engineering objects, combining modern AI technologies and traditional technological processes, significantly increases production efficiency, ensures high product quality, and minimizes costs at all stages of the lifecycle. However, each stage requires systematic and comprehensive solutions for continuous diagnostics and informed decision-making to maintain the optimal state of the object's lifecycle.

To integrate lifecycle object diagnostics (LCO) into the existing scheme, a new element must be included to interact with different stages of the LCO, where diagnostics play a key role in maintaining and optimizing the performance of the object. Specifically, this element, involving the use of AI for continuous monitoring and analysis of the object's condition, allows for timely detection of deviations from normal operation, signaling wear, malfunctions, or maintenance needs.

At the design stage, diagnostic capabilities are anticipated and incorporated into the product's design. Embedded monitoring and data collection tools, intended for subsequent diagnostics, are integrated to optimize the design and simplify future diagnostic measures, thus reducing operational and maintenance costs. During the implementation stage, an initial setup of diagnostic systems is performed, including the installation of sensors and configuration of AI monitoring algorithms, ensuring continuous quality control and early problem detection during initial operations.

The main operational stage involves continuous monitoring of the object's condition, with AI analyzing sensor data to detect potential issues. This is particularly important for preventing unexpected failures, minimizing downtime, and ensuring smooth equipment operation. The collected diagnostic data is used for further optimization of equipment and processes, including adjusting operational parameters, enhancing efficiency, and implementing adaptive management strategies that identify opportunities to boost system productivity and efficiency based on accurate analysis of the object's condition.

At the final disposal stage, diagnostics evaluate the condition of objects before dismantling, determining the potential for reusing components or materials. This information is crucial for making informed decisions about recycling or disposal based on the actual condition of the objects.

In conclusion, AI-based diagnostics of the object's condition is a critically important component at all stages of the mechanical engineering object's lifecycle. It ensures continuous monitoring of the object's condition, timely detection of potential problems, and prevents them from escalating into serious failures. This, in turn, enhances the reliability, safety, and cost-effectiveness of production processes and equipment operations. The integration of diagnostics at each stage of the lifecycle allows enterprises to optimize processes, ensuring high product quality, efficient resource use, and reduced maintenance and repair costs.

10.5 Conclusion

Thus, approaches have been identified and recommendations developed for the implementation of AI technologies in key areas of Ukraine's life activities, such as public administration, infrastructure, healthcare, education, and the economy. The developed set of recommendations contributes to improving the efficiency of recovery processes and ensuring sustainable development in the post-war period.

The proposed recommendations for the use of agent-based models to support recovery and reconstruction processes provide effective resource management, rapid adaptation to changes, and flexibility in decision-making. This allows for timely managerial decisions and enhances the flexibility of management processes, which is critically important for the restoration of public institutions and infrastructure.

The proposed AI-based lifecycle support system for production objects optimizes resource use at different stages of the lifecycle of machine-building products, improving the efficiency of manufacturing processes and reducing costs. This supports Ukraine's economic recovery through the introduction of modern technologies and innovative approaches.

In conclusion, the research has achieved its goal by providing the development of systematic approaches and tools for the effective use of AI in Ukraine's recovery and development processes, contributing to the building of a sustainable and efficient society in the post-war period.

References

[1] A. Shevchenko (Ed.), "Strategy for Artificial Intelligence Development in Ukraine," Monograph, Kyiv, IAIP, Science and Education, 2023, 305 p. https://doi.org/10.15407/development_strategy_2023.

[2] Y. Kondratenko, A. Shevchenko, Y. Zhukov, M. Klymenko, V. Slyusar, G. Kondratenko, O. Striuk, "Analysis of the Priorities and Perspectives in Artificial Intelligence Implementation," 2023 13th International Conference on Dependable Systems, Services and Technologies, DESSERT 2023, 2023, Athens, 13 – 15 October 2023, DOI:10.1109/DESSERT61349.2023.10416432

[3] A.I. Shevchenko, Y. P. Kondratenko, V. I. Slyusar, G. V. Kondratenko, T. V. Yeroshenko, "Analysis of the prospect domains in AI implementation: Nationals, NATO and Ukraine AI strategies," In: Y.P. Kondratenko, et al. (Eds), Research Tendencies and Prospect Domains for AI Development and Implementation, 2024, pp. 1–30. https://www.scopus.com/record/display.uri?eid=2-s2.0-85202988430&origin=resultslist

[4] Y. Kondratenko, G. Kondratenko, A. Shevchenko, V. Slyusar, Y. Zhukov, M. Vakulenko, "Towards Implementing the Strategy of Artificial Intelligence Development: Ukraine Peculiarities," CEUR Workshop Proceedings, Vol. 3513, 2023, pp. 106–117. https://ceur-ws.org/Vol-3513/paper09.pdf

[5] Y. Kondratenko, A. Shevchenko, Y. Zhukov, G. Kondratenko, O. Striuk, "Tendencies and Challenges of Artificial Intelligence Development and Implementation," Proceedings of the IEEE International Conference on Intelligent Data Acquisition and Advanced Computing Systems: Technology and Applications, IDAACS, 2023, pp. 221–226, Dortmund, 7 - 9 September 2023. DOI:10.1109/IDAACS58523.2023.10348800

[6] S. V. Kovalevskyy, "Artificial Intelligence as a Driver of Socio-Economic System Transformation in Ukraine", Interdisciplinary

Description of Complex Systems, 22(3), 2024, pp. 296–304. https://doi.org/10.7906/indecs.22.3.5.

[7] I. Sikorska, T. Gerasymchuk, "Shared Endeavours: Universities and Communities Join Efforts for Ukraine's Post-War Recovery", Geopolitical, Social Security and Freedom Journal, 6(1-2), pp. 134–148. https://doi.org/10.2478/gssfj-2023-0010.

[8] V. Ohorodnyk, R. Finger, "Envisioning the future of agri-tourism in Ukraine: from minor role to viable farm households and sustainable regional economies", Journal of Rural Studies, Volume 108, 103283, 2024. https://doi.org/10.1016/j.jrurstud.2024.103283.

[9] R. Duro, Y. Kondratenko (Eds), "Advances in intelligent robotics and collaborative automation," River Publishers, Aalborg, 2015. DOI:https://doi.org/10.13052/rp-9788793237049.

[10] Y.P. Kondratenko, V.M. Kuntsevich, A.A. Chikrii, V.F. Gubarev (Eds), "Advanced control systems: Theory and applications," River Publishers, Gistrup, 2021, pp. 1–441. ISBN: 9788770223416, DOI:10.1201/9781003337010

[11] S. Petkun, "Service-Oriented State in the Conditions of Digital Transformations", Krakowskie Studia Małopolskie, 4, 2023, pp. 28–36.

[12] A. Bécue, I. Praça, J. Gama, "Artificial intelligence, cyber-threats and Industry 4.0: Challenges and opportunities", Artificial Intelligence Review, 54(5), 2021, pp. 3849–3886. https://doi.org/10.1007/s10462-020-09942-2.

[13] J. Johnson, "Artificial intelligence & future warfare: implications for international security", Defense & Security Analysis, 35(2), 2019, pp. 147–169. https://doi.org/10.1080/14751798.2019.1600800.

[14] N. Díaz-Rodríguez, J. Del Ser, M. Coeckelbergh, M. L. de Prado, E. Herrera-Viedma, F. Herrera, "Connecting the dots in trustworthy Artificial Intelligence: From AI principles, ethics, and key requirements to responsible AI systems and regulation", Information Fusion, Volume 99, 2023. https://doi.org/10.1016/j.inffus.2023.101896.

[15] P. Księżak, S. Wojtczak, "Abuse of Right", In: Toward a Conceptual Network for the Private Law of Artificial Intelligence, Cham: Springer International Publishing, 2023, pp. 221–238. http://dx.doi.org/10.1007/978-3-031-19447-4.

[16] D. Acemoglu, P. Restrepo, "Artificial intelligence, automation, and work", In: The Economics of Artificial Intelligence: An Agenda, University of Chicago Press, 2018, pp. 197-236. https://doi.org/10.3386/w24196.

[17] P. Borowski, "Digitization, digital twins, blockchain, and industry 4.0 as elements of management process in enterprises in the energy sector", Energies, 14(7), 2021. https://doi.org/10.3390/en14071885.

[18] V.I. Slyusar, Y.P. Kondratenko, A.I. Shevchenko, T.V. Yeroshenko, "Some Aspects of Artificial Intelligence Development Strategy for Mobile Technologies," Journal of Mobile Multimedia, Vol. 20(3), 2024, pp. 525–554. https://doi.org/10.13052/jmm1550-4646.2031.

[19] U. Lagap, S. Ghaffarian, "Digital post-disaster risk management twinning: A review and improved conceptual framework", International Journal of Disaster Risk Reduction, Volume 110, 2024. https://doi.org/10.1016/j.ijdrr.2024.104629.

[20] S. Mehryar, V. Yazdanpanah, J. Tong, "AI and climate resilience governance", iScience, Volume 27, Issue 6, 2024, 109812. https://doi.org/10.1016/j.isci.2024.109812.

[21] M. S. Abdalzaher, M. Krichen, F. Falcone, "Emerging technologies and supporting tools for earthquake disaster management: A perspective, challenges, and future directions", Progress in Disaster Science, Volume 23, 2024. https://doi.org/10.1016/j.pdisas.2024.100347.

[22] B. Herath, M. Mittal, "Adoption of artificial intelligence in smart cities: A comprehensive review", International Journal of Information Management Data Insights, Volume 2, Issue 1, 2022. https://doi.org/10.1016/j.jjimei.2022.100076.

[23] T. Deng, K. Zhang, Z. J. (Max) Shen, "A systematic review of a digital twin city: A new pattern of urban governance toward smart cities", Journal of Management Science and Engineering, Volume 6, Issue 2, 2021, pp. 125–134. https://doi.org/10.1016/j.jmse.2021.03.003.

[24] C. Lim, G.-H. Cho, J. Kim, "Understanding the linkages of smart-city technologies and applications: Key lessons from a text mining approach and a call for future research", Technological Forecasting and Social Change, Volume 170, 2021. https://doi.org/10.1016/j.techfore.2021.120893.

[25] H. Kamyab, T. Khademi, S. Chelliapan, M. SaberiKamarposhti, S. Rezania, M. Yusuf, M. Farajnezhad, M. Abbas, B. H. Jeon, Y. Ahn, "The latest innovative avenues for the utilization of artificial intelligence and big data analytics in water resource management", Results in Engineering, Volume 20, 101566, 2023. http://dx.doi.org/10.1016/j.rineng.2023.101566.

[26] M. Francisco, B.-O. Linnér, "AI and the governance of sustainable development. An idea analysis of the European Union, the United

Nations, and the World Economic Forum", Environmental Science & Policy, Volume 150, 2023. https://doi.org/10.1016/j.envsci.2023.103590.

[27] J. Greeda, V. Vinoba, "Agent-based Fuzzy Hamiltonian Graph Systems with Artificial Intelligence in the Private Region", Procedia Computer Science, Volume 230, 2023, Pages 608–619. https://doi.org/10.1016/j.procs.2023.12.116.

[28] A. K. Mallik, "The future of the technology-based manufacturing in the European Union", Results in Engineering, Volume 19, 2023. https://doi.org/10.1016/j.rineng.2023.101356.

[29] C. Cancela-Outeda, "The EU's AI act: A framework for collaborative governance", Internet of Things, Volume 27, 2024. https://doi.org/10.1016/j.iot.2024.101291.

[30] Z. Irani, R. M. Abril, V. Weerakkody, A. Omar, U. Sivarajah, "The impact of legacy systems on digital transformation in European public administration: Lesson learned from a multi case analysis", Government Information Quarterly, Volume 40, Issue 1, 2023. https://doi.org/10.1016/j.giq.2022.101784.

[31] V. Slyusar, "The concept of networked distributed engine control system of future air vehicles", AVT-357 Research Workshop on "Technologies for future distributed engine control systems (DECS)", 11-13 May 2021. https://www.researchgate.net/publication/353351319.

[32] OASIS, "MQTT Version 3.1.1," OASIS Standard, Oct. 2014. [Online]. Available: https://docs.oasis-open.org/mqtt/mqtt/v3.1.1/os/mqtt-v3.1.1-os.html.

[33] S. Dovgyi, O. Kopiika, O. Kozlov, A. Lytvynenko, "Features of Message Transport Service in Automated Special-Purpose Systems," In: In: S. Dovgyi, et al. (Eds) Information and Communication Technologies and Sustainable Development, ICT&SD 2022, Lecture Notes in Networks and Systems, Vol. 809, 2023, pp. 119–132. [Online], Available: https://doi.org/10.1007/978-3-031-46880-3_8.

[34] S. Dovgiy, O. Kopiika, and O. Kozlov, "Architectures for the information systems, network resources and network services," In; CEUR Workshop Proceedings, vol. 3187, 2021, pp. 293–301. [Online], Available: https://ceur-ws.org/Vol-3187/short9.pdf

[35] A.N. Navarro-Galera, R. I. Ortúzar Maturana, "Innovating in defence policy through spending efficiency: The Life Cycle Costing model," Journal of Policy Modeling, Volume 33, No. 3, 2011, pp. 407-425. https://doi.org/10.1016/j.jpolmod.2011.03.004.

[36] M. J. Simões-Marques, "Modeling and Simulation in System Life Cycle," Procedia Manufacturing, Volume 3, pp. 785-792, 2015. https://doi.org/10.1016/j.promfg.2015.07.331.

[37] O. Schwabe, J. A. Erkoyuncu, E. Shehab, "On The Change of Cost Risk and Uncertainty throughout the Life Cycle of Manufacturing Products," Procedia CIRP, vol. 86, 2019, pp. 239-244. https://doi.org/10.1016/j.procir.2020.01.004.

[38] O. Schwabe, E. Shehab, J. Erkoyuncu, "Uncertainty quantification metrics for whole product life cycle cost estimates in aerospace innovation," Progress in Aerospace Sciences, Volume 77, 2015, pp. 1-24. https://doi.org/10.1016/j.paerosci.2015.06.002.

[39] M. Hauschild, J. Jeswiet, L. Alting, "From Life Cycle Assessment to Sustainable Production: Status and Perspectives," CIRP Annals, Vol. 54, No. 2, 2005, pp. 1–21. https://doi.org/10.1016/S0007-8506(07)60017-1.

[40] Y. V. Kondratenko, "Justification for considering the life cycle of military equipment samples during defense planning based on capabilities," Collection of Scientific Papers of the Center for Military-Strategic Studies of the Ivan Chernyakhovsky National Defense University of Ukraine, No. 3(70), 2020, pp. 47–53. https://doi.org/10.33099/2304-2745/2020-3-70/47-53.(inUkrainian).

[41] K. K. Kulahin, O. I. Solonets, O. I. Vedmid, K. P. Kvitkin, M. V. Borysenko, "Reforming the national system of managing the life cycle of armaments and military equipment according to NATO standards," Armament and Military Equipment Systems, No. 3 (71), 2022, pp. 24–34. https://doi.org/10.30748/soivt.2022.71.04.(inUkrainian).

[42] S. Masiero, J. Qosaj, V. Cutrona, "Digital Datasheet model: enhancing value of AI digital platforms", Procedia Computer Science, Volume 232, 2024, pp. 149–158. https://doi.org/10.1016/j.procs.2024.01.015.

[43] P. L. Parcu, A. R. Pisarkiewicz, C. Carrozza, N. Innocenti, "The future of 5G and beyond: Leadership, deployment and European policies", Telecommunications Policy, Volume 47, Issue 9, 2023. https://doi.org/10.1016/j.telpol.2023.102622.

[44] R. Costa Climent, D. M. Haftor, M. W. Staniewski, "AI-enabled business models for competitive advantage", Journal of Innovation & Knowledge, Volume 9, Issue 3, 2024. https://doi.org/10.1016/j.jik.2024.100532.

[45] A. S. Albahri, Y. L. Khaleel, M. A. Habeeb, R. D. Ismael, Q. A. Hameed, M. Deveci, R. Z. Homod, O. S. Albahri, A. H. Alamoodi, L.

Alzubaidi, "A systematic review of trustworthy artificial intelligence applications in natural disasters", Computers and Electrical Engineering, Volume 118, Part B, 2024. https://doi.org/10.1016/j.compeleceng.2024.109409.

[46] T. Kinder, J. Stenvall, E. Koskimies, H. Webb, S. Janenova, "Local public services and the ethical deployment of artificial intelligence", Government Information Quarterly, Volume 40, Issue 4, 2023. https://doi.org/10.1016/j.giq.2023.101865.

[47] Y. P. Kondratenko, V. I. Slyusar, M. B. Solesvik, N. Y. Kondratenko, Z. Gomolka, "Interrelation and inter-influence of artificial intelligence and higher education systems," In: Y.P. Kondratenko, A.I. Shevchenko (Eds), Research Tendencies and Prospect Domains for AI Development and Implementation, 2024, pp. 31–58. https://www.scopus.com/record/display.uri?eid=2-s2.0-85202992102&origin=resultslist

11

Two is Enough, but Three (or More) is Better: In AI and Beyond

Olga Kosheleva[1], Vladik Kreinovich[1], Victor Timchenko[2], and Yuriy Kondratenko[3,4]

[1]University of Texas at El Paso, USA
[2]Admiral Makarov National University of Shipbuilding, Ukraine
[3]Black Sea State University named after Petro Mohyla, Ukraine
[4]Institute of Artificial Intelligence Problems
of MES and NAS of Ukraine, Ukraine
E-mail: olgak@utep.edu; vladik@utep.edu; vl.timchenko58@gmail.com;
y_kondrat2002@yahoo.com

Abstract

At present, the most successful AI technique is deep learning – the use of neural networks that consist of multiple layers. Interestingly, it is well known that neural networks with two data processing layers are sufficient – in the sense that they can approximate any function with any given accuracy. Because of this, until reasonably recently, researchers and practitioners used such networks. However, recently it turned out, somewhat unexpectedly, that using three or more data processing layers – i.e., using what is called deep learning – makes the neural networks much more efficient. In this chapter, on numerous examples from AI and from beyond AI, we show that this is a general phenomenon: two is enough but three or more is better. In many examples, there is a specific explanation for this phenomenon. However, the fact that this phenomenon is universal makes us conjecture that there is a general explanation for this phenomenon – and we provide a possible explanation.

DOI: 10.1201/9788743800989-11

Keywords: AI, deep learning, multiple-values logic, fuzzy logic, higher-order fuzzy logic, Turing machine, quantum-related algebras.

11.1 Deep learning vs. Traditional Shallow Neural Networks

What is a neural network?- a brief reminder. Artificial neural networks consists of *neurons*, computational units that crudely emulate biological neurons in our brain. A neuron takes several inputs $s_1, \ldots, s_m$, and outputs the value $s = a(w_0 + w_1 \cdot s_1 + \cdots w_m \cdot s_m)$, where:

- w_i are constants called *weights* and
- $a(z)$ is a function called *activation function*;

see, e.g., [1–2].

In a neural network for processing data $x_1, \ldots, x_n$:

- some neurons directly process the data – these neurons form the first data processing layer, while
- other neurons process the results of the previous layer(s).

Neural networks with two data processing layers are universal approximators. It is well known that neural networks with two data processing layers are universal approximators – in the sense that:

- for each continuous function $f(x_1, \ldots, x_n)$ on a bounded domain D and for every $\varepsilon > 0$,
- there exists a neural network that, for each $(x_1, \ldots, x_n) \in D$, produces a value, which is ε-close to $f(x_1, \ldots, x_n)$;

see, e.g., [1–3].

Because of this, until reasonably recently, researchers and practitioners used such networks.

Enter deep learning. Recently, it turned out, somewhat unexpectedly, that neural networks with three or more data processing layers – called *deep* neural networks – are much more efficient [2]. Everyone knows spectacular successes of deep learning.

How can we explain this success? A possible explanation for this phenomenon was proposed in [4]. This explanation is based on the need for the most efficient universal approximation.

While from the purely mathematical viewpoint, the weights can be any real numbers, in practice, we need to store these numbers in a computer, and we have a limited number of bits that we can store. We have a limited number of bits available – let us denote this number by B. So, we can have no more than 2^B different combinations of bits – and thus, we can represent no more than 2^B different functions.

The more different functions we can represent, the more accurate is the resulting approximation. For example:

- If we can only use one number to approximate all the numbers from the interval $[0, 1]$, then the best we can do is select the number 0.5 – that approximates all numbers from this interval with accuracy $[0, 1]$.
- If we are allowed to use two numbers, then we can use 1/4 and 3/4 and get the approximation accuracy 0.25, etc.

If we have K neurons in a layer, then each of $K!$ permutations of these K neurons creates a different binary sequence – but all these binary sequences represent the same function. Thus, instead of 2^B possible functions, we can only represent $2^B/K!$ different function. To represent more functions – and, thus, to make approximations more accurate – we need to decrease K, i.e., decrease the number of neurons in each layer. So, instead of placing all data processing neurons in a single layer, a better idea is to have several layers – which is exactly what deep learning does.

11.2 Why Neural Networks in the First Place?

Functions of two variables are sufficient. It is known that any continuous function can be represented as a superposition of functions of two variables. This well-known result by the famous Russian mathematician Andrei Kolmogorov solved one of the 23 challenges that the 19th-century mathematicians, under the leadership of David Hilbert, provided to the 20th-century mathematics [5].

In line with this result, most modern computers directly support functions of one or two variables – such as min, max, addition, subtraction, multiplication, division, etc. – and all other functions have to be computed as a composition of these operations.

However, supporting functions of many variables makes computations more efficient. The relative efficiency of supporting operations with more than two inputs can be illustrated by the fact that most computer chips now support a three-input *multiply-and-add* operation $a + b \cdot c$.

However, the most impressive jump in efficiency can be observed when we switch to multi-variable neural operations.

How can we explain this efficiency? A possible explanation was given in [6–7]. One of the main objectives of a computer is to compute as fast as possible. We can speed up computations by performing several operations in parallel – and nowadays, even the cheapest computers have several processors working in parallel. Parallelization reduced the overall time of several parallelized elementary operation to the time for performing one of them. So, to make parallelization as efficient as possible, we need to make these elementary operations as fast as possible.

In general, the fastest-to-compute are linear functions. However, we cannot limit ourselves only to linear functions. Indeed:

- by combining linear functions, we will only get linear functions, and
- many real-life phenomena are nonlinear.

So, in addition to linear functions, we also need to use some nonlinear ones. In general, the more inputs a nonlinear function has, the longer it takes to compute this function. Thus, if we want to minimize computation time, we should limit ourselves to fastest-to-compute nonlinear functions, i.e., to nonlinear function of one variable.

In a sequence of computations, it makes no sense to follow a linear operation with a linear one, since the resulting composition of linear function is also linear and, thus, can be computed in a single linear stage. Similarly, it makes no sense to follow a nonlinear operation with another nonlinear operation, since the resulting composition of two functions of one variable is also a function of one variable and, thus, can be computed in a single nonlinear stage. Thus, a linear stage – of computing a linear combination $z = w_0 + w_1 \cdots s_1 + \cdots + w_m \cdot s_m$ – should always be followed by a stage at which a function $a(z)$ is applied to this linear combination. The result is exactly what the usual artificial neuron computes – which explains why neural networks are so efficient in the first place.

11.3 From Binary Logic to Multiple-valued Logics

Traditional two-valued logic is sufficient. Everything can be represented in a computer, and everything in a computer is represented as a sequence of 0s and 1s. So, if we use the usual interpretation of 1 as true and 0 as false, we can represent all our knowledge by using a logic that uses only two values: true and false.

Because of this, until the 1960s, most computer applications used the two-valued logic.

However, multiple-valued logics are often more efficient. Starting with the 1960s, it was discovered that multiple-valued logics such as fuzzy logic (see, e.g., [8–13]) often lead to successful practical applications.

In particular, we can make computations more efficient if we represent different truth values as combinations of optical beams of three basic colors; see, e.g., [14–23].

How this can be explained. Knuth's fundamental book on foundations of computing [24] contains a result that while binary representation are sufficient, multiple-valued (e.g., ternary) representations are more efficient.

11.4 From Traditional Fuzzy Logic to Higher-order Fuzzy Logic

Traditional fuzzy logic: a brief reminder. Fuzzy logic was invented by Lotfi Zadeh to describe imprecise ("fuzzy") expert statements like "x is small" in precise computer-understandable terms. For this purpose, Zadeh suggested to ask an expert:

- for each possible value x of the corresponding quantity,
- to mark, on the scale from 0 to 1, a degree which this value is consistent with the statement – e.g., to which this value is small.

The resulting function that assigns, to each possible value x, the corresponding degree $\mu(x)$ is known as a *membership function*, or, alternatively, a *fuzzy set*.

Need for higher-order fuzzy logic. The very need for fuzzy logic comes from the fact that the expert is often unable to provide an exact estimate for a quantity. Instead, he/she provides a fuzzy estimate like "x is close to 1." However:

- just like the expert cannot provide the exact value of the physical quantity,
- the same expert is similarly unable to describe his/her degree of confidence by a precise number.

What the expert *can* do is describe this degree by a fuzzy word. If we use Zadeh's idea to transform this word into a fuzzy set, then:

- instead of assigning, to each value x, a degree $\mu(x)$,
- we assign, to each value x, a fuzzy set.

This construction is known as *type-2 fuzzy logic*; see, e.g., [10].

In a type-2 fuzzy set, we assign:

- to each value x and to each possible fuzzy truth value d,
- a degree $\mu(x, d)$ to which d adequately describes the expert's opinion.

Comment. Of course, instead of providing the exact value $\mu(x, d)$, the expert may also provide an imprecise estimate – and describing this estimate as a fuzzy set leads to type-3 fuzzy logic, etc.

In principle, type-2 is sufficient. It can be proven (see, e.g., [25]) that from the purely mathematical viewpoint, type-2 description is sufficient. Indeed, for each possible value x, the expert provides a word w describing his/her degree that x is the actual value. The expert's meaning of this word is fully described by asking the expert to provide, for each possible degree d, a word a describing to what extent d is an adequate description of w. In other words, a full description of this degree is provided by a function of one variable.

A type-1 single value $\mu(x)$ is not sufficient to uniquely determine such a function. However, in type-2, we already have such a function – namely, the function $d \mapsto \mu(x, d)$. So, we have enough information to determine the desired function $d \mapsto a$. (Of course, what we just described is just an idea; see [25] for the full proof.)

Because of this and similar results, most higher-order fuzzy techniques limit themselves to type-2.

However, sometimes, type-3 fuzzy techniques are more efficient. However, interestingly, in some cases, type-3 techniques turn out to be more efficient; see, e.g., [26–30].

11.5 Computability

Which computational devices are sufficient: a brief reminder. Before we start thinking of an algorithm for solving a general problem, it is important to first figure out whether this problem is algorithmically solvable in the first place. Some problems are not algorithmically solvable. For example, it is not possible to always predict whether a given computer program will halt on a given data. For such problems, it is desirable to avoid wasting time trying to find a general solution.

Analysis of computability is one of the main subjects of theory of computation. Courses on theory of computing (see, e.g., [31]) usually start with the simplest possible computational device – a finite automaton. For this device, we have a finite number of possible states $q_1, \ldots, q_n$. One of these states is marked as a starting state, and a subset of the states are marked as final states. We fix a finite set of possible symbols $s_1, \ldots, s_m$.

To complete the description of a finite automaton, we need to describe, for each state q_i and for each symbol s_j read by the automaton, what will be the next state. Then, to check whether a word (i.e., a sequence of symbols) is accepted by this automaton, we:

- start in the starting state, and
- read the symbols from this word one by one – and each time move to a new state in accordance with the automaton's description.

If at the end, after reading all the symbols from the given word, we end up in a final state, the word is accepted; otherwise, the word is not accepted.

Many properties can be detected by finite automata, but it is proven that finite automata are not sufficient. For example, finite automata cannot detect words of the type $a^n b^n$ in which:

- first a symbol a is repeated some number of times, and
- then another symbol b is repeated the exact same number of times.

This detection is important for computing, since, e.g., we need to make sure that the number of opening curly brackets is exactly the same as the number of closing curly brackets.

The main reason why finite automata cannot detect such words is that they do not have memory. So, a natural idea is to provide them with some data type that would enable us to store information. There are many possible data types – lists, queues, etc., but the most natural to a computer (and thus the fastest to implement) is stack, last-come-first-served, since stack is how computer memory is operated.

In a stack, we have two main operations:

- *push*, when we place a new element on top of the stack, and
- *pop*, when we delete the top element from the stack.

So, the natural next computational device is a finite automaton equipped with a stack; this combination is called a *pushdown automaton*. For pushdown automata, for each state q_i and for each read symbol s_j:

- we can pop the top symbol from the stack, and
- depending on which symbol pops out, go to a different state and/or push another symbol into the stack.

We start at the starting state with an empty stack. If we end up in the final state with an empty stack, the word is accepted.

Pushdown automata can detect many properties, but some properties cannot be detected by them. For example, pushdown automata cannot detect words of the type $a^n b^n c^n$ in which:

- first a symbol a is repeated some number of times,
- then another symbol b is repeated the exact same number of times, and
- then yet another symbol c is repeated the same number of times.

Textbooks usually explain that we need a *Turing machine* to recognize such properties. A Turing machine consists of:

- a tape consisting of cells and
- a head – which is a finite automaton.

The tape is infinite in one direction: it has a starting state, and potentially infinitely many following states. Initially, the head points at a starting state. The input word is written in the tape. Upon reading a symbol, depending on what symbol it sees and on what the head's state is, the head can do some (or all) of the following three things:

- it can change its state,
- it can overwrite the symbol in the cell to which it points, and/or
- it can move one step to the left or one step to the right.

Again, two are sufficient. What the textbooks usually do not mention is that a Turing machine can be equivalently represented as a finite automaton with two stacks [32]:

- the first stack contains all the symbols on the tape from the head location to the left, with the symbol to which the head points at the top, while
- the second stack contains all the other symbols, which the symbol to the direct right of the head at the top.

One can show that one step of a Turing machine can be described in terms of pushing and popping with these two stacks.

Two stacks are sufficient, because Turing machine can compute anything that can be done by a finite automaton with many stacks.

Again, more than two are sometimes more efficient. There are many problems for which a Turing machine with several tapes – corresponding to more than more than stacks – is more efficient than the basic Turing machine with a single tape (that corresponds to two stacks).

11.6 Is there a General Explanation for this Phenomenon?

There probably is a general explanation. In this chapter, we provided several examples of the phenomenon. In many cases, we have a specific explanation. However, the very fact that this phenomenon is universal makes us conjecture that there is a general explanation for this phenomenon.

So what is a possible explanation? To come up with such an explanation, let us look into the most fundamental level of the physical world – the level of quantum physics. On this level, there is a following fundamental result [33]: that algebras used in quantum physics can be determined by their lowest two levels:

- level of "atoms" (i.e., basic building blocks), and
- level of combinations of two "atoms."

This is exactly what we observe – that in many cases, two levels are sufficient. So this is probably the general explanation for all the above phenomena.

Acknowledgments

This work was supported in part by the National Science Foundation grants 1623190 (A Model of Change for Preparing a New Generation for Professional Practice in Computer Science), HRD-1834620, and HRD-2034030 (CAHSI Includes), EAR-2225395 (Center for Collective Impact in Earthquake Science C-CIES), and by the AT&T Fellowship in Information Technology.

It was also supported by a grant from the Hungarian National Research, Development and Innovation Office (NRDI), and by the Institute for Risk and Reliability, Leibniz Universitaet Hannover, Germany.

References

[1] C. M. Bishop, Pattern Recognition and Machine Learning, Springer, New York, 2006.

[2] I. Goodfellow, Y. Bengio, and A. Courville, Deep Learning, MIT Press, Cambridge, Massachusetts, 2016.

[3] V. Kreinovich, 'Arbitrary nonlinearity is sufficient to represent all functions by neural networks: a theorem,' Neural Networks, 1991, Vol. 4, 381–383.

[4] C. Baral, O. Fuentes, and Vladik Kreinovich, 'Why Deep Neural Networks: A Possible Theoretical Explanation', In: M. Ceberio and V. Kreinovich (eds.), Constraint Programming and Decision Making: Theory and Applications, Springer Verlag, Berlin, Heidelberg, 2018, pp. 1–6.

[5] A. N. Kolmogorov, 'On the Representation of Continuous Functions of Several Variables by Superposition of Continuous Functions of One Variable and Addition', Dokl. Akad. Nauk SSSR, 1957, Vol. 114, pp. 369–373.

[6] J. Contreras, M. Ceberio, O. Kosheleva, and V. Kreinovich, 'Why neural networks in the first place: a theoretical explanation', Journal of Intelligent and Fuzzy Systems, 2022, Vol. 43, No. 6, pp. 6947–6951.

[7] V. Kreinovich and A. Bernat, 'Parallel algorithms for interval computations: an introduction', *Interval Computations*, 1994, No. 3, pp. 6–62.

[8] R. Belohlavek, J. W. Dauben, and G. J. Klir, Fuzzy Logic and Mathematics: A Historical Perspective, Oxford University Press, New York, 2017.

[9] G. Klir and B. Yuan, Fuzzy Sets and Fuzzy Logic, Prentice Hall, Upper Saddle River, New Jersey, 1995.

[10] J. M. Mendel, Explainable Uncertain Rule-Based Fuzzy Systems, Springer, Cham, Switzerland, 2024.

[11] H. T. Nguyen, C. L. Walker, and E. A. Walker, A First Course in Fuzzy Logic, Chapman and Hall/CRC, Boca Raton, Florida, 2019.

[12] V. Novák, I. Perfilieva, and J. Močkoř, Mathematical Principles of Fuzzy Logic, Kluwer, Boston, Dordrecht, 1999.

[13] L. A. Zadeh, 'Fuzzy sets', Information and Control, 1965, Vol. 8, pp. 338–353.

[14] V. Timchenko, Y. Kondratenko, O. Kozlov, and V. Kreinovich, 'Fuzzy Color Computing Based on Optical Logical Architecture", In: C. Kahraman, I. U. Sari, B. Oztaysi, S. Cebi, S. C. Onar, and A. C. Tolga (eds.), Intelligent and Fuzzy Systems: Intelligence and Sustainable Future, Proceedings of the International Conference on Intelligent and Fuzzy Systems INFUS'2023, Istanbul, Turkey, August 22–24, 2023, Vol. 1, Springer Lecture Notes in Networks and Systems, 2023, Vol. 758, pp. 491–499, https://doi.org/10.1007/978-3-031-39774-5_55

[15] V. L. Timchenko, Y. P. Kondratenko, and V. Kreinovich, 'Why Color Optical Computing', In: N. H. Phuong and V. Kreinovich (eds.), Deep Learning and Other Soft Computing Techniques: Biomedical and Related Applications, Studies in Computational

Intelligence, Vol. 1097, Springer, Cham, Switzerland, 2023, pp. 227–233, https://doi.org/10.1007/978-3-031-29447-1_20

[16] V. L. Timchenko, Y. P. Kondratenko, and V. Kreinovich, 'Logical Decision Networks Based on the Optical Coloroids', Proceedings of the 12th IEEE International Conference on Intelligent Data Acquisition and Advanced Computing Systems: Technology and Applications IDAACS 2023, Dortmund, Germany, September 7–9, 2023, pp. 1194–1199, DOI: 10.1109/IDAACS58523.2023.10348692.

[17] V. L. Timchenko, Y. P. Kondratenko, and V. Kreinovich, 'Interval-Valued and Set-Valued Extensions of Discrete Fuzzy Logics, Belnap Logic, and Color Optical Computing", In: Sebastia Massanet, Susana Montes, Daniel Ruiz-Aguilera, and Manuel González-Hidalgo (Eds.), Fuzzy Logic and Technology, and Aggregation Operators. Proceedings of the 13th Conference of the European Society for Fuzzy Logic and Technology EUSFLAT 2023 and 12th International Summer School on Aggregation Operators AGOP 2023, Palma de Mallorca, Spain, September 4–8, 2023, Springer Lecture Notes in Computer Science, 2023, Vol. 14069, pp. 297–303, doihttps://doi.org/10.1007/978-3-031-39965-7_25

[18] V. L. Timchenko, Y. P. Kondratenko, and V. Kreinovich, 'The architecture of optical logical coloroid with fuzzy computing', Proceedings of the 4th International Workshop on Intelligent Information Technologies & Systems of Information Security IntelITSIS'2023, Khmelnitsky, Ukraine, March 22–24, 2023, CEUR Workshop Proceedings, 2023, Vol. 3373, pp. 638–648, https://ceur-ws.org/Vol-3373/paper44.pdf

[19] V. L. Timchenko, Y. P. Kondratenko, and V. Kreinovich, 'Implementation of Optical Logic Gates Based on Color Filters', In: Z. Hu, I. Dychka, and M. He (Eds.), Advances in Computer Science for Engineering and Education VI. Proceedings of the 6th International Conference on Computer Science, Engineering and Education Applications ICCSEEA 2023, Warsaw, Poland, March 17–19, 2023, Springer Lecture Notes on Data Engineering and Communications Technologies, 2023, Vol. 181, pp. 126–136. https://doi.org/10.1007/978-3-031-36118-0_12

[20] V. L. Timchenko, Y. P. Kondratenko, and V. Kreinovich, 'Logical Platforms for Mobile Application in Decision Support Systems Based on Color Information Processing', Journal of Mobile Multimedia, 2024, Vol. 20, No. 3, pp. 679–698, doi.org/10.13052/jmm1550-4646.2037

[21] V. Timchenko, V. Kreinovich, Y. Kondratenko, and V. Horbov, 'Effectiveness Evaluations of Optical Color Fuzzy Computing', In: Y. P. Kondratenko and A. I. Shevchenko (eds.), Research Tendencies and

Prospect Domains for AI Development and Implementation, River Publishers, Denmark, 2024, pp. 129–151.

[22] V. Timchenko, V. Kreinovich, Y. Kondratenko, and V. Horbov, 'Hybrid fuzzy-color computing based on optical logical architecture', In: C. Kahraman, S. Cevik Onar, S. Cebi, B. Oztaysi, A. C. Tolga, and I. Ucal Sari (eds.), Intelligent and Fuzzy Systems, Proceedings of the 6th International Intelligent and Fuzzy Systems Conference INFUS 2024, Canakkale, Turkey, July 16–18, 2024, Lecture Notes in Networks and Systems, Springer, Cham, Switzerland, Vol. 1090, pp. 266–274, https://doi.org/10.1007/978-3-031-67192-0_33

[23] V. L. Timchenko, Y. P. Kondratenko, V. Kreinovich, and O. Kosheleva, 'Natural Color Interpretation of Interval-Valued Fuzzy Degrees', Proceedings of the 20th World Congress of the International Fuzzy Systems Association IFSA'2023, Daegu, South Korea, August 20–23, 2023, pp. 254–258.

[24] D. Knuth, The Art of Computer Programming, Volume 2: Seminumerical Algorithms, 3rd edition, Addison Wesley, Boston, Massachusetts, 1998.

[25] V. Kreinovich and H. T. Nguyen, '1st Order, 2nd Order, What Next? Do We Really Need Third-Order Descriptions: A View From A Realistic (Granular) Viewpoint", Proceedings of the Joint 9th World Congress of the International Fuzzy Systems Association and 20th International Conference of the North American Fuzzy Information Processing Society IFSA/NAFIPS 2001, Vancouver, Canada, July 25–28, 2001, pp. 1908–1913.

[26] O. Castillo, J. Castro, and P. Melin, Interval Type-3 Fuzzy Systems: Theory and Design, Springer, Cham, Switzerland, 2022.

[27] O. Castillo, J. Castro, and P. Melin, 'A methodology for building interval type-3 fuzzy systems based on the principle of justifiable granularity", International Journal of Intelligent Systems, 2022, doi10.1002/int.22910

[28] O. Castillo, J. Castro, and P. Melin, 'Interval type-3 fuzzy aggregation of neural networks for multiple time series prediction: the case of financial forecasting', Axioms, 2022, Vol. 11, Paper 251.

[29] O. Castillo, J. Castro, and P. Melin, 'Interval type-3 fuzzy control for automated tuning of image quality in televisions', Axioms, 2022, Vol. 11, Paper 276.

[30] V. Kreinovich, O. Kosheleva, P. Melin, and O. Castillo, 'Efficient algorithms for data processing under type-3 (and higher) fuzzy uncertainty', Mathematics, 2022, Vol. 10, Paper 2361.

[31] M. Sipser, Introduction to the Theory of Computation, 3rd edition, Course Technology Inc., Boston, Massacusetts, USA, 2021.

[32] V. Kreinovich and O. Kosheleva, 'A Turing Machine Is Just a Finite Automaton with Two Stacks: A Comment on Teaching Theory of Computation", Proceedings of the 8th International Scientific-Practical Conference 'Mathematical Education in Schools and Universities: Innovations in the Information Space" MATHEDU'2018, Kazan, Russia, October 17–21, 2018, pp. 152–156.

[33] J. Harding, C. Heunen, B. Lindenhovious, and M. Navara, 'Boolean subalgebras of orthoalgebras', Order, 2019, Vol. 36, No. 3, pp. 567–609.

12

How Free Can Artificial Intelligence Be?

O. V. Bilokobylsky and T. V. Yeroshenko

Institute of Artificial Intelligence Problems of MES and NAS of Ukraine, Ukraine
E-mail: bilokobylskii@ipai.net.ua; eroshenko@ipai.net.ua

Abstract

The chapter addresses the issue of freedom in the field of artificial intelligence (AI) by proposing two key perspectives: first, whether AI can possess freedom and, if so, to what extent; second, the conditions necessary to preserve human freedom in interactions with AI. The first part is examined through the authors' concept of the human mind as capable of exercising free will within the framework of socially conditioned cultural ontology. It is argued that current AI paradigms (symbolic, perceptron, and generative), grounded in physicalist and communicative views of the mind, lack access to ontological reality, rendering them neither rational nor free. Consequently, the focus shifts to ensuring conditions for rational human social activity by mitigating AI's potential negative impacts. To achieve this, a methodology is proposed for embedding three imperatives into AI legislation and policy: (1) preservation of the human physical environment, (2) preservation of the social environment, and (3) preservation of human psychological integrity.

Keywords: Freedom, rationality, ontology, AI, human, social activity.

12.1 Introduction

The issue of freedom, within the context of today's AI-driven scientific and technological revolution, is evolving with new dimensions [1]. The scientific community is actively debating the level of autonomy AI should possess and identifying areas where such autonomy is unacceptable [2]. Addressing

DOI: 10.1201/9788743800989-12

this issue involves two primary challenges. First, there is a conflict between economic interests and control over AI: ethical oversight (including self-regulation) in AI development is often seen as an obstacle to rapid innovation, affecting competitive advantage [3]. Second, a conceptual challenge exists: current scientific literature lacks a universally accepted definition of AI, let alone a clear definition of freedom as it pertains to AI. This study seeks to clarify the philosophical foundations underpinning discussions on AI and freedom, aiming to address the second challenge. The question of freedom in AI can be divided into two parts: AI's own freedom and human freedom. Since freedom is an intrinsic attribute of intelligence, it could theoretically be granted to AI if it demonstrates thinking. Therefore, this study includes a philosophical examination of AI's intelligence to determine whether it has thought and consciousness. Simultaneously, regardless of the answer, there remains a need to limit AI's potential harmful impact on humanity. Such risks are evident in the military use of AI [4], but also arise in critical infrastructure, credit assessment, hiring, and other areas.

12.2 Philosophical Definition of Freedom

To discuss the boundaries of freedom granted to AI, it is important to briefly examine the general definition of freedom. The conceptualization of freedom as a cultural category is taking place. The relevance of the philosophical development of the concept of freedom has always been recognized by European thinkers, starting with the times of Ancient Greece. However, it became particularly topical in the mid-20th century, in response to the challenges posed to human civilization by totalitarian regimes. One of the sources for renewed reflection on human freedom is the epochal work of Max Horkheimer and Theodor W. Adorno [5], written during the Second World War. The topic of freedom as a characteristic of humanity, along with the threats it faces from instrumental reason, emerged as one of the central ideas of this work. The further development of the problem of freedom became an integral part of the discussions surrounding free and unfree societies, as seen in the works of notable twentieth-century philosophers such as Hannah Arendt, Raymond Aron, Karl Popper, and Friedrich Hayek, culminating in Francis Fukuyama's *The End of History and the Last Man* [6], which reflected on the conclusion of the Cold War.

In both the writings of the aforementioned authors and in more specialized works where the theme of freedom is the central focus, such as Isaiah Berlin's *Two Concepts of Liberty* [7], the concept of freedom is examined inextricably linked to the historical interpretations of freedom that emerged during the era of the early Greek philosophical schools.

The conceptualization of freedom always takes place within ontological boundaries, defined by a worldview framework dependent on the cultural and historical characteristics of the era, which today stem from the Enlightenment tradition. The "world of things" – the reality containing its own cosmos – is a product of the prevailing system of cultural practices, presented to individuals as a system of potential social actions, prohibitions, motives, desires, and goals. This universe of trajectories is the human mind. By recognizing both limitations and possibilities, the desired and the urgent, the mind articulates an image of the Cosmos accessible to humanity and fulfills its highest principle – the imperative of choosing one's own trajectory of action from among many – freedom.

Therefore, discussing the freedom of AI is akin to discussing its intelligence, and the primary question posed at the beginning of this study now resonates anew: Is AI truly intelligent?

12.3 Does AI Think? Existing Criteria for Assessing AI's Intelligence Are Outdated

The emergence of generative AI models such as GPT-4 and Gemini has prompted philosophers and other people to reevaluate human consciousness and its defining characteristics. AI has advanced to a point where it is closer than ever to being indistinguishable from human intelligence, raising the existential question of whether a computer program – specifically, a large language model – can possess intelligence and consciousness. Recently, the claim that AI possesses intelligence gained widespread media attention when Google engineer Blake Lemoine stated that Google's LaMDA exhibited signs of intelligence and emotions [8].

The drama of the situation was further escalated by the fact that Google, whose executives disagreed with Lemoine's conclusions, initially removed him from the research and later placed him on paid leave [8].

Assessing the consciousness and intelligence of AI is complicated by the fact that the foundational criteria and methods for evaluation were formulated decades ago, taking into account the potential of modern computer technology only in theoretical terms. For example, one of the most prominent tests of intelligence, the Turing test, was introduced by the British scientist Alan Turing in 1950. This remarkable figure, who just a few years earlier had constructed a machine to decrypt the Enigma code, suggested reframing the question “Can machines think?” to “Are there imaginable digital computers that would do well in the imitation game?” [9].

By the imitation game, Turing referred to an experiment in which a human evaluator interacts with a “subject,” which could either be another person or a computer. The expert, separated from the subject by an impenetrable barrier, asks him questions. Turing perceived the scope of the imitation game as remarkably expansive, stating that “the question-answer method seems suitable for introducing almost any of the areas of human activity that we wish to include” [9].

To reduce indirect factors that might reveal the identity of the entity behind the wall, questions and answers are presented in a “teletyped” format (i.e., printed on a screen or paper). Turing suggests considering the test as passed and the machine to possess thinking skills if the expert believes that he was talking to a human. Despite its “behaviorist” interpretation of cognition and its focus on the communicative aspects of thought, the Turing test has served as a foundational benchmark for the development of AI over the decades.

One can only admire the foresight of the British mathematician, who in the aforementioned article asserted that “in about fifty years’ time it will be possible to programme computers ... to make them play the imitation game so well that an average interrogator will not have more than 70% chance of making the right identification after five minutes of questioning” [9].

According to recent reports, 74 years after Turing’s prediction, in a five-minute text conversation, GPT-4 was misidentified as human 54% of the time [9].

There is no doubt that the performance of future large language models will significantly surpass current capabilities, allowing for a formal assertion that they possess human-like qualities. However, do these models possess the inner world that is characteristic of human consciousness and thinking? A counterargument to the Turing test for over four decades has been the Chinese room thought experiment proposed by John Searle in his 1980 paper Minds, Brains, and Programs published in the Behavioral and Brain Sciences [10]. The essence of this experiment involves a person seated behind a wall who, using specific instructions, identifies corresponding phrases in Chinese – a language the person does not understand – based solely on the input received from the other side of the wall. At the entrance to the “Chinese room,” there are written Chinese characters, while at the exit, there is a translation. However, the intermediary manipulating these symbols has no comprehension of the content being discussed or the events occurring outside the confines of the room. The intermediary, in fact, symbolizes the computer, which passes the Turing test, but has neither thinking nor consciousness.

The Turing test appears to be becoming obsolete before our eyes, yet Searle's experiment is not doing any better in terms of relevance. If we were to ask today's *translator* – the entity from the Chinese room, now represented by a large language model – what the content is truly about, what response would we get? It will answer in detail and convincingly, and in any language, including Chinese. But again, the question arises: does this imply that the machine possesses thinking and consciousness akin to that of humans? Is it truly capable of independent thought and self-awareness?

12.4 Modern Views on the Mind and Their Relationship with Classical Interpretations

To answer the questions posed, it is important to analyze the theoretical framework established in contemporary philosophy regarding the understanding of human consciousness and thought, particularly concerning their significance for sustaining life and ensuring freedom from physical and physiological constraints.

Several comprehensive reviews of theories of consciousness and thinking in the philosophical literature [11]addressing this goal have been conducted. The significance of some of them has gradually shifted toward historical value over time, yet they continue to hold formative importance for contemporary thought [12]. The significance of some of them has gradually shifted toward historical value over time, yet they continue to hold formative importance for contemporary thought [12]. Conversely, some theories remain relevant [10], while newer theories being developed today play a crucial role in reviewing and navigating the diverse multidisciplinary and interdisciplinary studies that characterize the exploration of consciousness and thinking in the twenty-first century [11].

One such work is *Theories of the Mind* by Stephen Priest [12], in which the British philosopher proposed to classify existing theories into six categories, namely (1) dualism, (2) logical behaviorism, (3) idealism, (4) materialism, (5) functionalism, (6) double-aspect, and (7) phenomenological theories.

According to Priest, dualism is the theory that two and only two kinds of substance exist: minds and physical objects. A mind is a purely mental, non-material, or spiritual substance, and a physical object is a purely material, non-mental, spatially extended substance. It logically follows that no mind is a physical object and no physical object is a mind [12]. Priest demonstrates dualistic interpretations of human mental states through an examination of the teachings of Plato and Descartes [12].

Logical behaviorism, as Priest notes, interprets mental states as behavior. Thinking, hoping, perceiving, remembering, and so on are all to be understood as either behaving or else possessing a complex disposition or propensity to behave [12]. Representatives of this perspective on understanding thinking include members of the Vienna Circle and Ludwig Wittgenstein [12].

An intriguing aspect of Priest's interpretation of idealism is his exclusion of Plato from the ranks of idealist thinkers, a take that opposes with the views of many philosophers who typically recognize Plato as a foundational figure in idealism. Priest states that the main implication of idealism that physical objects do not exist is potentially misleading and usually misunderstood. No idealist denies that there exist tables, bricks, pieces of wood, and all other items we commonly take to be physical objects. Idealists merely deny two alleged facts about physical objects: they deny that they exist unperceived or unthought; and they deny that they are material, that is, made out of a substance called "matter" and that physical is in fact mental [12]. Although Priest refrains from categorically classifying both Plato and Kant as representatives of idealism, he nonetheless engages with Kant's philosophical legacy in this section, alongside an exploration of the works of other notable figures such as Berkeley and Hegel [12].

As one would expect, Priest categorizes all theories that assert the exclusive existence of physical objects, or primarily physical objects whose interactions can produce non-physical properties (a weaker form of materialism), under the umbrella term of materialism [12]. The scholar points out that no controversial definition of the terms "physical" or "material" has ever been given, but it is thought that if something is physical then it is spatiotemporal. For materialists, mental states are wholly or largely influenced by physical processes. Priest identifies theories from philosophers such as Democritus, Hobbes, and Marx as key examples of materialism.

Priest associates the methodology of the Turing test with functionalism, characterizing functionalism as an interpretation of thinking and consciousness that reduces these concepts to the realm of practical problem-solving. He argues that the software description of the operations of a computer is a functionalist description where, if a certain input is received, a certain state results, or where, if the machine is in one state but no input is received, then it moves to a new state, and so on. More importantly, a system may be described functionally in this way without any ontological commitment [12].

The double aspect theory is the theory that mental and physical are two properties of some underlying reality, which is intrinsically neither mental nor physical [12], although, in contrast to dualism, there is only one substance, it is neither material (in contrast to materialism) nor ideal (in contrast to idealism). According to Priest, these beliefs trace their origins back to Baruch Spinoza [12]and are further explored in the agnosticism of David Hume [12], the neutral monism of William James [12], and later developed by Earl Russell [12].

Phenomenological interpretation of the mental is a presuppositionless description of the content of thinking, without attempting to get to the ontological nature of thinking and its content, but at the same time revealing the features of thinking as the basis of any plans of human life [12]. The most prominent figures in phenomenology include Franz Brentano and Edmund Husserl.

Stephen Priest suggests that the spectrum of interpretations regarding thinking and consciousness constitutes a comprehensive overview of the philosophical options for understanding the relationship between the "mind and body." Certainly, while the Priest classification allows for the identification of corresponding subheadings under each category, it also reflects a degree of simplification in the complex landscape of philosophical interpretations, at least based on the objectives of this study. It is evident that logical behaviorism, functionalism, and phenomenology, in terms of their approach to the ontological nature of the mental and physical, as well as their interrelations, can be viewed as distinct forms of agnosticism, since they try to describe something that is the subject of their observation, and not to discover their true nature. Dualism and double aspect theories [12]offer differing interpretations of the synchronicity between mental and physical processes, emphasizing the challenges of establishing causal relationships for this harmony. Dualism posits a fundamental separation of substances, while double aspect theory contends that the unattainability of a unified substance accounts for the division between the mental and the physical. Therefore, dualism and double-aspect theories do not go beyond the scope of occasionalism. As for idealism and materialism, they, in accordance with the convictions established in modern philosophy, reduce either the physical to the mental, or the mental to the physical.

An important and one of the most recent classifications of mental theories is Robert Lawrence Kuhn's landscape of consciousness [13]. In the proposed review, the author aims to compile various interpretations of the classical "mind–body" problem, situating them within a spectrum that ranges from extreme physicalism to extreme nonphysicalism, which allows for the identification of less categorical theories that occupy intermediate positions between these two extremes [13].

Kuhn's "Landscape" includes 10 categories, which include Materialism Theories, Non-Reductive Physicalism, Quantum Theories, Integrated Information Theory, Panpsychisms, Monisms, Dualisms, Idealisms, Anomalous and Altered States Theories, and Challenge Theory. Kuhn emphasizes that his "Landscape" genuinely encompasses a wide array of approaches to understanding the mental and physical realms, including not only scientific perspectives but also "pseudo-scientific" views, given that the latter possess reasonable foundations and a substantial following.

When we examine the highlighted theoretical positions through the lens of philosophical analysis, it becomes apparent that the arguments for and against contemporary discussions regarding the relationship between mind and body are not significantly different from those found in classical examples.

The primary argument against naturalistic concepts is that humans, through reason, do not have direct access to *material* objects; instead, they operate with *forms*, or what Plato referred to as *ideas*. Thus, a picture created by naturalists that illustrates a natural landscape operating according to its own laws, independent of human existence, or even in the absence of humanity, represents an ideal product squared: based on ideas uncovered within the mind, the naturalist constructs a *castle in the air*, representing reality. Subsequently, through the analysis of this illusion, they endeavor to derive *objective* conclusions. All possible verifications are chosen to align with the axioms of the naturalistic approach, demonstrating nothing beyond practical effectiveness (or ineffectiveness). This methodology is reminiscent of the medieval practice of determining a witch's status, where the victim's admission under the duress of inquisitors served as the sole criterion for judgment.

An argument against idealistic solutions to the psychophysical problem employs the method of reductio ad absurdum, which pushes the primary assertion – that reason is the source of formation in nature – to a solipsistic extreme. If the mind creates the world, why can't we create it in accordance with our desires and submit to physical determinations? And how can we know it is physical if this physical is fundamentally inaccessible to the mind?

Methodological and dualistic solutions to the psychophysical problem, as it was previously mentioned, cannot be regarded as viable options, particularly in the context of the discussion surrounding the freedom of AI and artificial consciousness. Phenomenological and occasionalist theories in this domain can be viewed as practical applications (analogous to computational models) that assist in addressing specific issues; however, they do not engage with the fundamental question regarding the ontological foundations of human freedom and AI.

Before attempting to address the central question regarding the limitations of our freedom, how to transcend these constraints, and how to avert inhuman voluntarism, especially in terms of AI, we must first consider the nature of the forms through which the human mind operates. This aspect of the psychophysical problem is crucial, as it is acknowledged as legitimate by both materialists and idealists. What exactly does a person recognize as objectively existing? Given that the properties of objects are linked to the configuration of our sensory organs, and their significance is determined by social factors, no rational materialist would contend that the realm of objects serves as a definitive standard that must be measured and weighed with increasing precision. This is supported by the principle of complementarity in quantum mechanics, which posits that the parameters of quantum phenomena are directly influenced by the conditions under which they are observed.

However, idealistic concepts, particularly those that maintain a connection with reality and natural science, argue that socially conditioned ideas of reason merely shape the external appearance of the world as perceived by human consciousness and thinking, rather than creating the world itself.

Thus, the question regarding the limits of freedom for both the human mind and AI should be framed in terms that highlight the role of the physical world, its sensory and social constructs, as well as the processes that generate these social forms and the methods used to verify them. The existing mind theories must take into account all three of these registers of rationality, but depending on the accepted ontological axioms, they emphasize different components of rationality. Physicalist theories of mind (represented in the paradigm of symbolic AI and "perceptron" AI) highlight the fundamental role of the biological and physiological structures of the organism, along with the external physical influences that affect and elicit responses from them. In contrast, social-communicative theories (generative AI) stress the significance of social consensus for rationality and the pragmatic effectiveness of the developed forms. Meanwhile, nonphysicalist theories concentrate on identifying universal (transcendental) structures of rationality, irrespective of whether they are conditioned by the systemic properties of the individual mind or the social process.

There is a discernible correlation between the aforementioned approaches to understanding intelligence and the established approaches to modeling AI, which always rest on a conscious or unconscious philosophical foundation.

The theoretical basis for further research could be a historical reconstruction of the development of the main AI paradigms.

12.5 Symbolic AI: A Dead End on the Path to Physicalistic Understanding of Intelligence

Newell and Simon developed the so-called physical symbol system hypothesis (PSSH), which states the following: "A physical symbol system has the necessary and sufficient means for general intelligent action" [14]. Based on this hypothesis, intelligence is a mechanism for manipulating symbols, and according to this perspective, a computer capable of manipulating symbols could be intelligent.

The hypothesis was developed as a summary of the work on the Logic Theorist program developed by Simon, Newell, and Shaw in 1955–1956. *Logic Theorist* (1956) demonstrated results akin to human reasoning – it remembered and processed information, made logical conclusions, proved theorems, and is today considered one of the first artificial intelligence programs.

Today, researchers understand that, despite its impressive results, the *Logic Theorist* (1956), with its symbolic model of thinking, remained nothing more than a model since the number of initial data, scenarios for their transformation, the results obtained, and further potential steps exceeded the horizon within which the transformations could still be processed by the machines that existed at that time. It became evident that neither the increasing computational power of computers nor the ingenious heuristics implemented by researchers to cut off the unpromising paths of machine reasoning could compensate for the inherent shortcomings of symbolic AI. In the case of artificial and significant limitations of symbolic objects, computers built by analogy with the Logic Theorist showed convincing results. However, their convergence with real human intelligence never occurred.

The decline of the above-mentioned symbolic AI paradigm as a standalone project (although its developments remain relevant in various fields of computer science) is attributed not to an incorrect understanding of the algorithms of human reasoning but rather to an erroneous representation of the objects of thought and reality. The program's thinking, if we can call it this way, assumed that it deals with homogeneous objects (specifically, their symbols) connected by relationships that lend themselves to logical formalization. In contrast, human thinking operates with the meanings of things (intuitively identifying the mental image of a thing with the thing itself). What is more, the structure of meaning initially includes a specific (and very limited) repertoire of ways and cases of legitimate use of meanings (concepts) and the things they denote. For instance, a modern human may not realize that he intuitively puts biological rather than mythological traits in the notion of dog, while ancient Egyptians saw traits of the Anubis in every dog. It would therefore be correct to say that the symbolic model of AI is flawed at the level of its presupposed ontology – the idea of the order of existence.

The next historical form of the symbolic AI approach, which became a logical continuation of the development of symbolic AI, was the frame approach. In the field of AI, the development of frame theory is associated mainly with Marvin Minsky. However, similar theoretical paradigms have been independently developed based on the methodologies of their respective sciences by anthropologists (G. Bateson), sociologists (I. Goffman), linguists (T. van Dijk), and psychologists (M. Yaroshevsky), among others.

In essence, this approach is an attempt to move from behavioristic and formal-logical simplifications of human thinking and behavior to broader structures of language and experience. At the same time, unlike early conceptions of symbolic AI, the frame paradigm represents knowledge about the world in the form of a system of informational blocks organized in a specific manner. To update the frame, the so-called *terminals* of the frame must be filled in. These are specific variables that are responsible for encoding the empirical features of a stereotypical situation (for example, the room frame must presuppose the information related to the floor, walls etc.) that collect information due to their structure (and are themselves organized into structures – super-frames or frame systems). Minsky's (1975) then-new approach allows us to take a fresh look at the problem of perceiving the external world through a machine (computer), which was previously practically unsolvable due to the endless multiplication of information *branching* of the outcomes of AI thinking, and solving problems in a real situation based on this perception.

However, the frame approach itself is applicable only when human or machine thinking has somehow identified a stereotypical situation and updated the corresponding frame. At the same time, the perception of sensory data itself is a set of multi-level frames.

The unexpected complication of artificial thinking, which initially appeared to promise significant savings in mental operations, stemmed from the same ontological flaw as in earlier versions of symbolic AI (which is a naturalistic simplification of reality): the external world was depicted as a set of physical objects, and the mental and practical manipulation of these objects formed the basis of human life. The frame approach limited possible thoughts/actions to a finite predicted volume of stereotypical likelihoods but turned out to be powerless in the face of the infinity of stereotypical situations and their endless variability.

12.6 The "Perceptron" Approach: Another Dead End on the Physicalist Path to Modeling the Mind

Around the same period when the first notable successes in the development of symbolic AI were achieved, a breakthrough occurred in the alternative direction of modeling the activity of the human mind – the construction of artificial neural networks. The first mathematical model of a neural network was proposed by McCulloch and Pitts in 1943 in the article *A Logical Calculus of Ideas Immanent in Nervous Activity.* However, the modeling of neural networks did not gain widespread popularity until the early 1960s, after Rosenblatt created electronic devices called perceptrons (hardware designed to implement algorithms for supervised learning) that embodied the principles of their operation.

Rosenblatt expressed his thoughts on the topic in his 1958 book *The Perceptron: A Probabilistic Model for Information Storage and Organization in the Brain.* Later, in 1960, Rosenblatt's "Mark I perceptron" demonstrated elements of the ability to learn by trial and error; as part of simulating human brain processes. Rosenblatt summarized his developments in recreating thinking and constructing perceptron devices in the work *Principles of Neurodynamics: Perceptrons and the Theory of Brain Mechanisms* (1962). The first wave of *connectionism* in the field of AI concluded around the turn of the 1960s to the 1970s, following the publication of the book by Minsky and Papert titled *Perceptrons: An Introduction to Computational Geometry* (1969), as well as the sudden passing of Rosenblatt in 1971. Today, researchers do not unequivocally evaluate the criticism of the capabilities of perceptrons, as well as the interpretation of the criticism by contemporaries, as expressed in the work of Minsky and Papert (1969). Instead, many view this case of criticism as a clear demonstration of the decline of a scientific program in line with the concept proposed by Kuhn (1962). However, neural AI also had objective problems that were not resolved even decades later.

As with symbolic AI, these problems are primarily related to the ontology domain.

Since Rosenblatt's perceptron, artificial neural networks have been adept at capturing sensory information emanating from physical objects. The sensors of the Mark I device were cadmium sulfide photocells that transmitted information for further processing. But despite the progressive advancement of perceptron devices and their eventual adaptation into computer software, which by the end of the 1960s surpassed the capabilities of specifically designed perceptron machines, they never succeeded in learning to perceive the world as humans do. This was because the objects encoded by the neural structures of the human brain did not belong to the physical world but to the world of culture. Physical objects constituted only one aspect of this lifeworld, which itself was constructed through culturally conditioned idealizations.

The human mind does not interact solely with tracings or reflections of external physical objects but rather with mental objects that are only partially associated with sensory data. These mental objects are not solely based on intuitive knowledge – specific skills and the ability to manipulate them, which are formed in a person during childhood through socialization – but also on values, coordinates in space and time, inclusion in cultural practices, genealogies, etc.

12.7 Why Doesn't Generative AI Think?

Large linguistic models, the foundation of generative AI, are large-scale multilayer neural networks that are pre-trained on vast volumes of textual data. F. Rosenblatt predicted something similar in his 1962 [15]work, outlining a promising multilayer perceptron model. The operating principle of LLM comes down to calculating the probable next word to an existing expression based on the statistical processing of a huge number of similar texts. At the same time, since the neural network operates not with the word itself but with its mathematical representation, such terms as *text* and *word* can refer to any symbolically expressed object.

Apart from the software, all that is required for LLM is a dataset used for training and instructions for its *learning* process. Leveraging the highly sophisticated architecture and immense computing capabilities of modern computers, LLM processes information by utilizing hundreds of billions of parameters (to be precise, the GPT-3 model had 175 billion such parameters), selecting the most probable continuation of a mathematical series that represents something in reality.

It is important to note that the reality processed by LLM undergoes preprocessing (in the form of internet texts, images, and sounds) before being mathematically formalized. The neural network works with the symbolic universum of meanings, establishing patterns among its elements (sometimes known only to it) and selecting the one that turns out to be the most relevant (from the standpoint of mathematical algorithms embedded in it). We are talking about a kind of (very sophisticated) search for some potentially known element within a preloaded database. The difference between LLM and a primitive program that performs face identification within a predefined database of faces is that LLM can create a new element based on similarity with existing analogs. That is why the infrastructure responsible for processing data in modern LLMs often surpasses the data itself. For instance, in the GPT-3 model, the processing apparatus is almost twice the size of the data it operates on (700 GB versus 420 GB)!

The following conclusion can be drawn: generative AI has not addressed the challenges faced by symbolic and neural AI; in fact, it has not even attempted to address them. Instead of AI developing a consistent ontology of reality similar to the one given to humans and developing a code of rules that allows AI to work with its elements, as people do, generative AI gained access to the divine book of the results of human's work with this reality – the internet. Although on the internet, there are no internal human processes for processing information, thinking, experiencing, and such, it contains abundant information about the outcomes of such processes, often formulated in the form of a meaningful sentence, including cases when the subject of the description is information processing, thinking, and emotions. We can describe everything on the endless internet that AI has access to. Moreover, it does not matter how we arrive at these results; the main thing is that both humans and AI come to approximately the same conclusions based on the same logical premises!

However, the importance of the results being similar is not always important. The fact that the most advanced LLM models and types of generative AI based on them are able, following the laws of the mathematical universe, to select relevant texts from a book on the internet does not make them something fundamentally different from the person from the Chinese room[1] [10]. Therefore, the order of reality, the objectivity inherent in it, and the goals

[1] Chinese room argument is a thought experiment by the American philosopher John Searle, designed to show that human thought or intelligence can be realized artificially in machines that exactly mimic the computational processes presumably underlying human mental states – is false.

and values that a person associates with it remain, for the new type of AI, as impenetrable as they were for its predecessors. Moreover, the fact that the generative AI can always say something about them and even take them into account when calculating his actions does not change anything. Rephrasing Edmund Husserl that even a deaf person can study sounds [16], the fact that generative AI studies reality does not mean that reality exists to it.

12.8 AI and Human Freedom

The analysis of current AI paradigms demonstrates that true rationality remains beyond their reach, precluding them from being entrusted with autonomous decision-making. Thus, human oversight is essential. Consequently, the question of AI freedom shifts entirely to the issue of mitigating AI's potentially harmful effects on humans. Using classical philosophy on freedom, it becomes clear that we are dealing not with "freedom for" but "freedom from" [17]. As AI's influence on human life expands, not only intersecting but increasingly shaping it, identifying a complete list of areas where AI requires constraint and supervision becomes challenging. However, philosophical tools allow us to broadly outline "safeguarding measures" based on principles of deontological ethics, tracing back to Kant's categorical imperative, which states that any AI activity across societal domains must support the physical and socio-cultural continuity of humanity. Physical threats include potential errors and misuse in AI's involvement with critical infrastructure, military applications, and widespread malfunctions in AI-equipped devices, among others (see the detailed review in [18]). Threats to human social existence are associated with the use of AI in manipulation through platforms (including the use of commercial spam, artificial popularization, coordinated influence, disinformation, manipulation of personal data, etc.) [18]. Threats to personal existence or psychological integrity of individual – violation of the right to freedom, autonomy and privacy of thought, are also considered [19].

The imperatives governing the limitation of human freedom by AI can be summarized as follows: (1) preserving the environment necessary for human physical existence in all AI activities, (2) maintaining the environment essential for human social existence, and (3) safeguarding human mental integrity. These imperatives should guide the development of a legislative framework that regulates AI technologies.

In line with the abovementioned considerations, AI's freedom must be restricted through imperatives embedded at the software level to ensure adherence to the physical parameters essential for human existence as a biological organism. AI's actions and private goals must adhere to prevailing social norms, as outlined in UN documents, and these norms should be reflected in national and potentially global laws governing AI activities. Finally, any significant decisions made by AI, as it has been outlined above, should be subject to discussion with a human – either the person responsible for the processes or the relevant supervisory body, similar to the "Special Committee on AI,"[2] the "European AI Authority,"[3] or special industry and regional regulatory bodies, the formation of which will be required in the future.

12.9 Conclusion

The abovementioned makes it evident that the limitations of current AI models stem from their tendency to absolutize certain aspects of human existence while downplaying or ignoring the significance of others. Therefore, all AI activity, including autonomous (free) activity, must be constrained by the frameworks that shape the paradigms of rationality described above and the AI models built upon them as well. The naturalistic paradigms' absolutization of physical reality emphasizes the significance of certain physical parameters, beyond which human activity and life itself are not feasible. The absolutization of the communicative paradigm of public consensus highlights the key criterion by which the guidelines of social processes are validated in situations where goals or standards are unclear. Regarding a hypothetical AI model based on a non-physicalist or idealistic understanding of human rationality, its freedom, like that of humans, should be restricted in alignment with the prevailing societal values. Moreover, the intermediate (private) objectives of AI should not conflict with the overarching goals of social progress.

References

[1] Y. Kondratenko, A. Shevchenko, Y. Zhukov, M. Klymenko, V. Slyusar, G. Kondratenko, O. Striuk, "Analysis of the Priorities and Perspectives in Artificial Intelligence Implementation", 13th International IEEE Conference "Dependable Systems, Services and Technologies"

[2] The Special Committee on AI, established in June 2018, advises the White House on cross-agency AI R&D priorities and on improving the coordination of federal AI efforts to ensure continued US leadership in this field. https://ai.gov/

[3] https://eufordigital.eu/ru/european-artificial-intelligence-office-to-oversee-general-purpose-ai-gpai/

(DESSERT'2023), Greece, Athens, 8 p., October 13-15, 2023. DOI: 10.1109/DESSERT61349.2023.10416432.

[2] A. Shevchenko, Y. Kondratenko, V. Slyusar, G. Kondratenko, T. Yeroshenko, "Analysis of the prospect domains in AI implementation: Nationals, NATO and Ukraine AI strategies", *Research Tendencies and Prospect Domains for AI Development and Implementation,* pp. 1–30, 2024. Available: https://www.riverpublishers.com/book_details.php?book_id=1163.

[3] Kai-Kristian Kemell, Ville Vakkuri, "What Is the Cost of AI Ethics? Initial Conceptual Framework and Empirical Insights," [Online], Available: https://link.springer.com/chapter/10.1007/978-3-031-53227-6_18/.

[4] Lethal Autonomous Weapons Pledge, [Online], Available: https://futureoflife.org/open-letter/lethal-autonomous-weapons-pledge/

[5] T. Adorno, M. Horkheimer, "Dialectic Of Enlightenment," [Online], Available: https://archive.org/details/DialecticOfEnlightenmentTheodorW.AdornoMaxHorkheimer

[6] F. Fukuyama, "The End of History and the Last Man", Simon and Schuster, 2006, pp. 432.

[7] I. Berlin, "Two Concepts of Liberty," [Online], Available: https://faculty.www.umb.edu/steven.levine/Courses/Action/Berlin.pdf

[8] "The Google engineer who thinks the company's AI has come to life," [Online], Available: https://www.washingtonpost.com/technology/2022/06/11/google-ai-lamda-blake-lemoine/

[9] M. Turinga, "Computing machinery and intelligence," [Online], Available: https://academic.oup.com/mind/article/LIX/236/433/986238

[10] J. Searle, "Minds, Brains, and Programs. Behavioral and Brain Sciences", Cambridge University Press, September 1980, pp. 417 – 424. doi:https://doi.org/10.1017/S0140525X00005756

[11] Bertrand Russell, "Human Knowledge: Its Scope and Limits," London: George Allen & Unwin, 1948, [Online], Available: https://philpapers.org/rec/FEYRBH

[12] Stephen Priest, "Theories of the mind," Houghton mifflin company, Boston New York London, 1991, pp. 236.

[13] Robert Lawrence Kuhn, "A landscape of consciousness: Toward a taxonomy of explanations and implications," [Online], Available: https://www.sciencedirect.com/science/article/pii/S0079610723001128?ref=pdf_download&fr=RR-2&rr=8bd5ee747c6f2d97#sec18

[14] A. Newell, H. A. Simon, "Computer Science as Empirical Inquiry: Symbols and Search", Communications of the ACM, 19 (3), pp. 113–126, 1976. doi:10.1145/360018.360022
[15] F. Rosenblatt, "Principles of Neurodynamics: Perceptrons and the Theory of Brain Mechanisms," 1st Edition, Spartan Books, Michigan University, Ann Arbor, pp. 616, 1962.
[16] E. Husserl, "The Idea of Phenomenology", Hague: "Martinus Nijhoff", 1973, p. 30
[17] D. Hendrycks, M. Mazeika, T Woodside, "An Overview of Catastrophic AI Risks," [Online], Available: https://arxiv.org/pdf/2306.12001
[18] A. Stevenson, "Facebook Admits It Was Used to Incite Violence in Myanmar", 2018. Available: https://www.nytimes.com/2018/11/06/technology/myanmar-facebook.html
[19] S. McCarthy-Jones, "The Autonomous Mind: The Right to Freedom of Thought in the Twenty-First Century Updated," [Online], Available: https://www.frontiersin.org/journals/artificial-intelligence/articles/10.3389/frai.2019.00019/full

Index

About the Editors

Anatolii Shevchenko graduated from the Faculty of Physics at Donetsk State University with a major in Radio Physics and Electronics. In 1985, he defended his Ph.D. thesis, earning the academic degree of a candidate. In 1990, he completed his doctoral thesis, obtaining the academic degree of Doctor of Technical Sciences. In 1997, he was awarded the title of professor, and in 1998, he received the honorary title of Honored Scientist and Technician of Ukraine. In 2006, was elected as a Corresponding Member of the National Academy of Sciences of Ukraine in the field of Computer Systems. In 2015, he was appointed as the Director of the Institute of Artificial Intelligence of the Ministry of Education and Science of Ukraine and the National Academy of Sciences of Ukraine in Kyiv. Together with the Department of Informatics of the National Academy of Sciences of Ukraine, he initiated an international scientific journal called "Artificial Intelligence" and was appointed as its chief editor. His research interests encompass various aspects of artificial intelligence, modeling human intelligence, simulating elements of human consciousness, breakthrough technologies in the field of artificial intelligence, and multidisciplinary aspects of artificial intelligence.

Yuriy Kondratenko is a Doctor of Science, Professor, Honour Inventor of Ukraine (2008), Corr. Academician of Royal Academy of Doctors (Barcelona, Spain), Corr. Academician of Royal Academy of Economic and Finance Sciences (Spain), Head of the Department of Intelligent Information Systems at Petro Mohyla Black Sea National University (PMBSNU), Leading Researcher at the Institute of

Artificial Intelligence Problems of Ministry of Education and Science and National Academy of Sciences of Ukraine, Ukraine. He has received: a Ph.D. (1983) and Dr.Sc. (1994) in Elements and Devices of Computer and Control Systems from Odessa National Polytechnic University, several international grants and scholarships for conducting research at Institute of Automation of Chongqing University, P.R. China (1988-1989), Ruhr-University Bochum, Germany (2000, 2010), Nazareth College and Cleveland State University, USA (2003), and a Fulbright Scholarship for researching in USA (2015/2016) at the Dept. of Electrical Engineering and Computer Science in Cleveland State University. Research interests include robotics, automation, sensors and control systems, intelligent decision support systems, and fuzzy logic.

For Product Safety Concerns and Information please contact our EU representative GPSR@taylorandfrancis.com Taylor & Francis Verlag GmbH, Kaufingerstraße 24, 80331 München, Germany